AMERICAN IDENTITIES

D0336010

AMERICAN IDENTITIES

An Introductory Textbook

Edited by
Lois P. Rudnick, Judith E. Smith, and Rachel Lee Rubin

Blackwell
Publishing

Editorial material and organization © 2006 by Blackwell Publishing Ltd

BLACKWELL PUBLISHING
350 Main Street, Malden, MA 02148-5020, USA
9600 Garsington Road, Oxford OX4 2DQ, UK
550 Swanston Street, Carlton, Victoria 3053, Australia

First published 2006 by Blackwell Publishing Ltd

1   2006

Library of Congress Cataloging-in-Publication Data

American identities : an introductory textbook / edited by Lois P. Rudnick, Judith E. Smith,
and Rachel Lee Rubin
p. cm
Includes bibliographical references and index.
ISBN-13: 978-0-631-23431-9 (hard cover : alk. paper)
ISBN-10: 0-631-23431-4 (hard cover : alk. paper)
ISBN-13: 978-0-631-23432-6 (pbk. : alk. paper)
ISBN-10: 0-631-23432-2 (pbk. : alk. paper)   1. United States—History—1945– 2.
United States—History—1945—Sources. 3. United States—Social conditions—1945–4.
United States—Social conditions—1945—Sources. I. Rudnick, Lois Palken, 1944–II.
Smith, Judith E., 1948– III. Rubin, Rachel, 1964–
E742.A66 2006
973.92—dc22

2005014105

A catalogue record for this title is available from the British Library.

Set in 10½/13pt Dante
by SPI Publisher Services, Pondicherry, India
Printed and bound in the United Kingdom
by TJ International Ltd, Padstow, Cornwall

For further information on
Blackwell Publishing, visit our website:
www.blackwellpublishing.com

Table of Contents

The United States as Borderlands

Alternative Table of Contents:
Organized by Genre and Discipline

Preface:
How to Use This Book

American Identities is designed as an introduction to the field of American Studies for high school and first-year college students. It addresses the often-asked question of what (and who) Americans are by focusing on the many different ways "American" has been defined from World War II to the present. Through the abridged works of scholars in the fields of history, sociology, economics, and cultural studies, and the first-person accounts of political activists, journalists, poets, songwriters, fiction writers, and memoirists, students can explore the powerful individual and social dynamics that shape family, ethnic, class, gender, sexual, and racial experiences and that form national and transnational identities.

The organizing principles of *American Identities* are chronological and topical: from World War II and the era of the Cold War (1940–1960), to the generation that came of age during the Civil Rights Movement and the Vietnam War (1960–1975), and conclude with the impact of globalization and various "border crossings" on American society and culture (1975–2000). Each section of the book offers a comparative thematic focus on family/community life and work, and internal and international migrations and wars, as they are intersected by race, class, and gender.

The study questions that follow each text in this textbook are designed to stimulate active learning, engage students with the key thematic issues of the text, and help them to see patterns and make linkages across cultures, places, and times. The accompanying Instructor's Guide contains sample syllabi; family history guidelines for student family history projects; excerpts from student family histories; suggested timelines for each chronological section of the textbook that highlight important political, social, and cultural events, movements, and productions; viewing and listening guides for multimedia presentations; recommended US history textbooks to accompany the textbook; recommended history texts for international/immigrant students whose family histories begin outside of the USA; and short bibliographies and videographies of sources that enhance the themes of the course.

Acknowledgments

This book was a labor of love that could not have been completed without the inspiration and collaboration of the hundreds of students at the University of Massachusetts Boston who have taken our *American Identities* course. They continue to motivate us to find better ways to support their becoming engaged historians and active citizens of the US and the global community of which they are a part. We are indebted to our wonderful colleagues who have shared the teaching of various versions of this course, Shirley Tang, Patricia Raub, and Phil Chassler at UMass Boston; Carol Siriani and Annie Brown at Cambridge Rindge and Latin High School; and Eric Goodson at The Dana Hall School. We owe many thanks to our terrific editorial assistant, Ellen Kuhl, for her research for the headnotes, fact checking, and illustrations. We are also grateful to our outstanding administrative assistant, Shauna Manning, whose efficient running of our office makes it possible for us to do this kind of work. And last, but by no means least, is our gratitude to our editor, Jayne Fargnoli, whose continuing encouragement and enthusiasm for this book is what finally made it happen, and to the staff we have worked with at Blackwell Publishing for their very helpful support of this project.

Introduction

About American Identities

American Identities addresses the often-asked question of what (and who) Americans are by focusing on the many different ways "American" has been defined in the era from World War II to the present. Through the abridged works of scholars in the fields of history, sociology, economics, and cultural studies, and the first-person accounts of political activists, journalists, poets, songwriters, fiction writers, and memoirists, students can explore the powerful individual and social dynamics that shape family, ethnic, class, gender, sexual, and racial experiences and that form national and transnational identities. Our instructor's guide offers practical advice for researching and writing family histories that are linked to the time period of the textbook, and for helping students analyze the multimedia texts and contexts that reflect how Americans have been represented from the second half of the twentieth century through the first decade of the twenty-first.

Who is This Book For?

American Identities is designed as an introduction to the field of American Studies for high school and first-year college students, providing the methods and texts necessary for students to read US society and culture from an interdisciplinary perspective. Our book has grown out of several years of practice at the University of Massachusetts Boston. UMass Boston's 12,000 students are mostly self-supporting, and work part or full time. About 39 percent of undergraduates are nonwhite, and a substantial number are the first in their families to attend college. Because "American Identities" serves a highly diverse student body as both an introduction to the major, a general distribution course, and a freshman seminar in the General Education program, it has multiple agendas, perhaps the most important of which is acculturating students to college-level academic work.

American Identities has also been taught successfully at two area high schools, Cambridge Rindge and Latin, a large public secondary school, and the Dana Hall School, a small private academy. At Cambridge Rindge and Latin, the course has carried college credit for students who complete our requirements and has served as a vehicle for introducing students who are not college-bound to university-level work. This textbook reflects the collaborative nature of our project and our commitment to cross the boundaries between secondary and university education in order to provide our students with the requisite critical thinking and writing skills.

What Do We Mean by "American Identities"?

We have constructed our textbook to highlight the ways in which American identities are made and remade over time, shaped by impetus from *the inside* (creating a public persona, choosing affiliations, and allying with communities) and from *the outside* (the class, race, gender positions we are born into, the social authority/public legitimacy associated with presumptions about our visible characteristics and occupational positions). Our reading selections play off one another in order to highlight how identities are constructed in the encounter with difference, as well as how identities change over time and in response to historical events: Japanese-American citizens are more racialized and seen as more alien as a result of the World War II internment order; African-American civil rights activism offered models for other racial and ethnic groups as they came to be articulated in the late 1960s and 1970s.

Asking students to consider and analyze the creation of American identities challenges any assumptions of overarching commonality or static categories. But we are also invested in a "both...and" strategy of teaching diversity. Ronald Takaki has criticized the growth of multiculturalism because of its "tendency to fragmentize the study of society and thus deny opportunities for different groups to learn about one another...intergroup relationships remain invisible, and the big picture is missing" (Takaki 1994: 10). Thus we have organized our textbook to enable students "to connect the differences," to see the ways in which individual and group experiences are part of a larger national (and increasingly transnational) narrative. We have tried to balance readings that give attention to historically shaped common reference points with readings that demonstrate how even common experiences become multiple as they are filtered through unequal access to resources, social respect, and authority.

How is the Book Organized?

American Identities raises the question of multiple and conflicting identities within the context of historically situated social and economic processes. Our organizing principles are chronological and topical. We begin with World War II and the era of the

Cold War (1940–60), move on to the generation that came of age during the Civil Rights Movement and the Vietnam War (1960–75), and conclude with the impact of globalization and various "border crossings" on American society and culture (1975–2000). Each section of the textbook provides a comparative thematic focus on family/community life and work, and internal and international migrations and wars, as they are intersected by race, class, and gender.

The book begins with a section on "Identity, Family, and Memory," which introduces students to the ways in which we come to know who we are as individuals and groups, the ways that political and social forces shape our idea of the family, and the ways in which different age cohorts construct different community memories. In every part of the textbook, students have the opportunity to discover the various methods and kinds of knowledge used and generated by men and women working in different disciplines and writing from different social locations and political agendas. Thus Kesaya Noda's autobiographical essay, "Growing Up Asian in America", personalizes the theories about the formulation of individual, family, and community that are presented by the scholarly authors of the first three readings. At the same time, it asks students to confront the issue of "What does it mean to be an American?"

American Identities and the Family History Project

Noda's essay serves another purpose that has been important in the creation of this textbook: providing a model for how to write a richly historical family history. Although there are myriad ways the textbook can be used by secondary school and college teachers, our central project has involved students in creating a three-generation family history and timeline in which they link their families' stories to relevant political, social, economic, and cultural events and movements they study during the course.

We prepare students for this semester-length project in a variety of ways: nightly homework assignments; in-class study groups on selected texts; family history workshops; and student oral reports that place social and political movements, cultural productions, and historical actors in their sociohistorical contexts. We have developed study guides for reading, viewing, and listening to all of the assigned texts, which are geared to help high school and beginning college students learn how to analyze history texts, fiction, music, television, and documentary film.

Pedagogical Resources for the Instructor

The study questions that accompany each text in our textbook are designed to stimulate active learning, engage students with the key thematic issues of the text, and help them to see patterns and make linkages across cultures, places, and times. Our instructor's guide contains syllabi for the four versions of the course we teach;

family history guidelines for the student family history project; excerpts from our students' family histories; suggested timelines for each chronological section of the textbook that highlight important political, social, and cultural events, movements, and productions; viewing and listening guides for our multimedia presentations; recommended US history textbooks to accompany the textbook; recommended history texts for international/immigrant students whose family histories begin outside of the United States; and short bibliographies and videographies of sources we use in our course or that enhance the themes of the course.

Our Goals for the Reader

In designing this textbook and the accompanying family history guidelines and assignments, one of our greatest concerns as teachers has been to break down the substantial gulf that exists between our students' lives and the academic discourses they are expected to assimilate. We are also concerned with the deep alienation that many of our students feel toward the study of the past, and with their belief that they are "outside" history and historical forces. Thus one of our most important goals is to prepare them to become cultural and historical analysts of their own texts, through experiencing the agency of locating themselves and their families within historical frameworks.

We have had enough success over the past eight years to believe that other teachers can use these materials, in a variety of ways, to help students become historians of their own past, as it is linked to larger national and international arenas. When students are able to make these linkages between their family stories and the outside forces that provided for or withheld the social and cultural capital necessary for "success," they develop the means to more fully assess and shape their own dearly held American dreams.

Reference

Takaki, Ronald (1994). "Teaching American History Through a Different Mirror," *Perspectives* 32 (7): 1, 9–14.

PART I

Identity, Family, and Memory

W hat makes you who you are? What does it mean to be an "American"?
The first four essays in this book introduce you to the variety of ways
that your identity is constructed, and to the forces *within* and *outside* of
yourself that define your multiple and sometimes conflicting identities. These identities are individual, sexual, familial, racial, communal, national, and international, to
name a few. They are determined by personal choice as well as by the historical
"moment" or generation in which you have grown up. We hope you will find the
challenge of figuring out your identity as an individual, and our collective identity as a
nation, a fascinating puzzle, one that each of you will solve in your own way.

From the earliest days of American history, immigrants and travelers to the United
States have been asking questions about what it means to be an American. They have
come up with an array of definitions, many of them associated with the promises
expressed in *The Declaration of Independence*, which asserts the American dream that
all of us are "created equal" and have a basic right to "life, liberty, and the pursuit of
happiness." While that promise originally excluded the majority of those living in the
US in 1776, it has become a rallying cry for every group that has fought for equality
since then, including Native Americans, slaves, women, and workers.

The first essay in this section, "Identities and Social Locations," will help you begin
to figure out how to make sense of the social and cultural factors that influence your
personal development and identity. The three essays that follow explore the ways in
which different generations understood, experienced, and acted on the promises of
American life as they grew up at different historic moments during the second half of
the twentieth century. Whether your family has lived in the US for generations or are
recent arrivals, we think you will find these essays useful for thinking about how your
family's past has shaped its present, and for discovering how your family has
contributed to shaping the nation (or nations) in which they have lived and worked.

CHAPTER 1

Identities and Social Locations:
Who Am I? Who Are My People?

Gwyn Kirk and Margo Okazawa-Rey

Born and educated in Great Britain, Gwyn Kirk (1945–) is a political sociologist, peace activist, and multimedia producer. Margo Okazawa-Rey (1949–) is a Japanese-born educator and social worker active in numerous public policy organizations and grassroots educational efforts. Both women work in the United States as writers, lecturers, lobbyists, and teachers. The following essay, excerpted from a chapter of their textbook, Women's Lives: Multicultural Perspectives *(2004), provides a perceptive analysis of the complex factors that shape our identities.*

Our identity is a specific marker of how we define ourselves at any particular moment in life. Discovering and claiming our unique identity is a process of growth, change, and renewal throughout our lifetime. As a specific marker, identity may seem tangible and fixed at any given point. Over the life span, however, identity is more fluid. For example, an able-bodied woman who suddenly finds herself confined to a wheelchair after an automobile accident, an assimilated Jewish woman who begins the journey of recovering her Jewish heritage, an immigrant woman from a traditional Guatemalan family "coming out" as a lesbian in the United States, or a young, middle-class college student, away from her sheltered home environment for the first time and becoming politicized by an environmental justice organization on campus, will probably find herself redefining who she is, what she values, and what "home" and "community" are. [. . .]

Identity formation is the result of a complex interplay among a range of factors: individual decisions and choices, particular life events, community recognition and expectations, societal categorization, classification and socialization, and key national or international events. It is an ongoing process that involves several key questions:

Who am I? Who do I want to be?
Who do others think I am and want me to be?
Who and what do societal and community institutions, such as schools, religious
  institutions, the media, and the law, say I am?
Where/what/who are my "home" and "community"?
Which social group(s) do I want to affiliate with?
Who decides the answers to these questions, and on what basis?

Answers to these questions form the core of our existence. In this chapter, we examine the complex issue of identity and its importance in women's lives.

The *American Heritage Dictionary* (1993) defines *identity* as

> the collective aspect of the set of characteristics by which a thing is definitely known or recognizable;
> a set of behavioral or personal characteristics by which an individual is recognizable as a member of a group;
> the distinct personality of an individual regarded as a persisting entity; individuality.

The same dictionary defines *to identify* as "to associate or affiliate (oneself) closely with a person or group; to establish an identification with another or others."

These definitions point to the connections between us as individuals and how we are perceived by other people and classified by societal institutions. They also involve a sense of individual agency and choice regarding affiliations with others. Gender, race, ethnicity, class, nationality, sexual orientation, age, religion, disability, and language are all significant social categories by which people are recognized by others. Indeed, on the basis of these categories alone, others often think they know who we are and how we should behave. Personal decisions about our affiliations and loyalties to specific groups are also shaped by these categories. For example, in many communities of color, women struggle over the question of race versus gender. Is race a more important factor than gender in shaping their lives? If a Latina speaks out publicly about sexism within the Latino community, is she betraying her people? This separation of categories, mirrored by our segregated social lives, tends to set up false dichotomies in which people often feel that they have to choose one aspect of their identity over another. It also presents difficulties for mixed-race or bisexual people, who do not fit neatly into such narrow categories.

In order to understand the complexity and richness of women's experiences, we must examine them from the micro, meso, macro, and global levels of social relations. [...]

Critically analyzing the issue of identity at all of these levels of analysis will allow us to see that identity is much more than an individual decision or choice about who we are in the world. Rather, it is a set of complex and often contradictory and conflicting psychological, physical, geographical, political, cultural, historical, and spiritual factors, as shown in the readings that follow.

Being Myself: The Micro Level

At the micro level, individuals usually feel the most comfortable as themselves. Here one can say, for example, "I am a woman, heterosexual, middle class, with a movement disability; but I am also much more than those categories." At this level we define ourselves and structure our daily activities according to our own preferences. At the micro level we can best feel and experience the process of identity formation, which includes naming specific forces and events that shape our identities. At this level we also seem to have more control of the process, although there are always interconnections between events and experiences at this level and the other levels.

Critical life events, such as entering kindergarten, losing a parent through death, separation, or divorce, or the onset of puberty, may all serve as catalysts for a shift in how we think about ourselves. A five-year-old Vietnamese American child from a traditional home and community may experience the first challenge to her sense of identity when her kindergarten teacher admonishes her to speak only in English. A White, middle-class professional woman who thinks of herself as "a person" and a "competent attorney" may begin to see the significance of gender and "the glass ceiling" for women when she witnesses younger, less experienced male colleagues in her law office passing her by for promotions. A woman who has been raped who attends her first meeting of a campus group organizing against date rape feels the power of connection with other rape survivors and their allies. An eighty-year-old woman, whose partner of fifty years has just died, must face the reality of having lost her life-time companion, friend, and lover. Such experiences shape each person's ongoing formulation of self, whether or not the process is conscious, deliberate, reflective, or even voluntary.

Identity formation is a lifelong endeavor that includes discovery of the new; recovery of the old, forgotten, or appropriated; and synthesis of the new and old [...]. At especially important junctures during the process, individuals mark an identity change in tangible ways. An African American woman may change her name from the anglicized Susan to Aisha, with roots in African culture. A Chinese Vietnamese immigrant woman, on the other hand, may adopt an anglicized name, exchanging Nu Lu for Yvonne Lu as part of becoming a US citizen. Another way of marking and effecting a shift in identity is by altering your physical appearance: changing your wardrobe or makeup; cutting your hair very short, wearing it natural rather than permed or pressed, dyeing it purple, or letting the gray show after years of using hair coloring. More permanent changes might include having a tattoo, having your body pierced, having a face lift or tummy tuck, or, for Asian American women, having eye surgery to "Europeanize" their eyes. Transsexuals – female to male and male to female – have surgery to make their physical appearance congruent with their internal sense of self. Other markers of a change in identity include redecorating your home, setting up home for the first time, or physically relocating to another neighborhood, another city, or another part of the country in search of a new home.

For many people, home is where we grow up until we become independent, by going to college, for example, or getting married; where our parents, siblings, and maybe grandparents are; where our needs for safety, security, and material comfort are met. In reality, what we think of as home is often a complicated and contradictory place where some things we need are present and others are not. Some people's homes are comfortable and secure in a material sense but are also places of emotional or physical violence and cruelty. Some children grow up in homes that provide emotional comfort and a sense of belonging, but as they grow older and their values diverge from those of their parents, home becomes a source of discomfort and alienation.

Regardless of such experiences – perhaps because of them – most people continue to seek places of comfort and solace and others with whom they feel they belong and with whom they share common values and interests. Home may be a geographic, social, emotional, and spiritual space where we hope to find safety, security, familiarity, continuity, acceptance, and understanding, and where we can feel and be our best, whole selves. Home may be in several places at once or in different places at different times of our lives. Some women may have a difficult time finding a home, a place that feels comfortable and familiar, even if they know what it is. Finally, this search may involve not only searching outside ourselves but also piecing together in some coherent way the scattered parts of our identities – an inward as well as an outward journey.

Community Recognition, Expectations, and Interactions: The Meso Level

It is at the meso level – at school, in the workplace, or on the street – that people most frequently ask "Who are you?" or "Where are you from?" in an attempt to categorize us and determine their relationship to us. Moreover, it is here that people experience the complexities, conflicts, and contradictions of multiple identities, which we consider later.

The single most visible signifier of identity is physical appearance. How we look to others affects their perceptions, judgments, and treatment of us. Questions such as "Where do you come from?" and questioning behaviors, such as feeling the texture of your hair or asking if you speak a particular language, are commonly used to interrogate people whose physical appearances especially, but also behaviors, do not match the characteristics designated as belonging to established categories. At root, we are being asked, "Are you one of us or not?" These questioners usually expect singular and simplistic answers, assuming that everyone will fit existing social categories, which are conceived of as undifferentiated and unambiguous. Among people with disabilities, for example, people wanting to identify each other may expect to hear details of another's disability rather than the fact that the person being questioned also identifies equally strongly as, say, a woman who is White, working class, and bisexual.

Community, like home, may be geographic and emotional, or both, and provides a way for people to express group affiliations. "Where are you from?" is a common-place question in the United States among strangers, a way to break the ice and start a conversation, expecting answers like "I'm from Tallahassee, Florida," or "I'm from the Bronx." Community might also be an organized group like Alcoholics Anonymous, a religious group, or a political organization like the African American civil rights organization, the National Association for the Advancement of Colored People (NAACP). Community may be something much more abstract, as in "the women's community" or "the queer community," where there is presumed to be an identifiable group. In these examples there is an assumption of shared values, interests, culture, or language sometimes thought of as essential qualities that define group membership and belonging. This can lead to essentialism, where complex identities get reduced to specific qualities deemed to be essential for membership of a particular group: being Jewish or gay, for example.

At the community level, individual identities and needs meet group standards, expectations, obligations, responsibilities, and demands. You compare yourself with others and are subtly compared. Others size up your clothing, accent, personal style, and knowledge of the group's history and culture. You may be challenged directly, "You say you're Latina. How come you don't speak Spanish?" "You say you're working class. What are you doing in a professional job?" These experiences may both affirm our identities and create or highlight inconsistencies, incongruities, and contradictions in who we believe we are, how we are viewed by others, our role and status in the community, and our sense of belonging.

Some individuals experience marginality if they can move in two or more worlds and, in part, be accepted as insiders (Stonequist 1961). Examples include bisexuals, mixed-race people, and immigrants, who all live in at least two cultures. Margaret, a White, working-class woman, for instance, leaves her friends behind after high school graduation as she goes off to an elite university. Though excited and eager to be in a new setting, she often feels alienated at college because her culture, upbringing, and level of economic security differ from those of the many upper-middle-class and upper-class students. During the winter break she returns to her hometown, where she discovers a gulf between herself and her old friends who remained at home and took full-time jobs. She notices that she is now speaking a slightly different language from them and that her interests and preoccupations are different from theirs. Margaret has a foot in both worlds. She has become sufficiently acculturated at college to begin to know that community as an insider, and she has retained her old community of friends, but she is not entirely at ease or wholly accepted by either community. Her identity is complex, composed of several parts. [. . .]

Social Categories, Classifications, and Structural Inequality: Macro and Global Levels

Classifying and labeling human beings, often according to real or assumed physical, biological, or genetic differences, is a way to distinguish who is included and who is excluded from a group, to ascribe particular characteristics, to prescribe social roles, and to assign status, power, and privilege. People are to know their places. Thus social categories such as gender, race, and class are used to establish and maintain a particular kind of social order. The classifications and their specific features, meanings, and significance are socially constructed through history, politics, and culture. The specific meanings and significance were often imputed to justify the conquest, colonization, domination, and exploitation of entire groups of people, and although the specifics may have changed over time, this system of categorizing and classifying remains intact. For example, Native American people were described as brutal, uncivilized, and ungovernable savages in the writings of early colonizers on this continent. This justified the near-genocide of Native Americans by White settlers and the US military and public officials, as well as the breaking of treaties between the US government and Native American tribes (Zinn 1995). Today, Native Americans are no longer called savages but are often thought of as a vanishing species, or a nonexistent people, already wiped out, thereby rationalizing their neglect by the dominant culture and erasing their long-standing and continuing resistance. [. . .]

Colonization, Immigration, and the US Landscape of Race and Class

Global-level factors affecting people's identities include colonization and immigration. Popular folklore would have us believe that the United States has welcomed "the tired, huddled masses yearning to breathe free" (Young et al. 1997). This ideology that the United States is "a land of immigrants" obscures several important issues excluded from much mainstream debate about immigration. Not all Americans came to this country voluntarily. Native American peoples and Mexicans were already here on this continent, but the former experienced near-genocide and the latter were made foreigners in their own land. African peoples were captured, enslaved, and forcibly imported to this country to be laborers. All were brutally exploited and violated – physically, psychologically, culturally, and spiritually – to serve the interests of those in power. The relationships between these groups and this nation and their experiences in the United States are fundamentally different from the experiences of those who chose to immigrate here, though this is not to negate the hardships the latter may have faced. These differences profoundly shaped the social, cultural, political, and economic realities faced by these groups throughout history and continue to do so today.

Robert Blauner (1972) makes a useful analytical distinction between colonized minorities, whose original presence in this nation was involuntary, and all of whom are people of color, and immigrant minorities, whose presence was voluntary.

According to Blauner, colonized minorities faced insurmountable structural inequalities, based primarily on race, that have prevented their full participation in social, economic, political, and cultural arenas of US life. Early in the history of this country, for example, the Naturalization Law of 1790 (which was repealed as recently as 1952) prohibited peoples of color from becoming US citizens, and the Slave Codes restricted every aspect of life for enslaved African peoples. These laws made race into an indelible line that separated "insiders" from "outsiders." White people were designated insiders and granted many privileges while all others were confined to systematic disadvantage. [. . .]

Studies of US immigration "reveal discrimination and unequal positioning of different ethnic groups" (Yans-McLaughlin 1990, p. 6), challenging the myth of equal opportunity for all. According to political scientist Lawrence Fuchs (1990), "Freedom and opportunity for poor immigrant Whites in the seventeenth and eighteenth centuries were connected fundamentally with the spread of slavery" (p. 294). It was then that European immigrants, such as Irish, Polish, and Italian people began to learn to be White (Roediger 1991). Thus the common belief among descendants of European immigrants that the successful assimilation of their foremothers and forefathers against great odds is evidence that everyone can pull themselves up by the bootstraps if they work hard enough does not take into account the racialization of immigration that favored White people.

On coming to the United States, immigrants are drawn into the racial landscape of this country. In media debates and official statistics, this is still dominated by a Black/White polarization in which everyone is assumed to fit into one of these two groups. Demographically, the situation is much more complex and diverse, but people of color, who comprise the more inclusive group, are still set off against White people, the dominant group. Immigrants identify themselves according to nationality – for example, as Cambodian or Guatemalan. Once in the United States they learn the significance of racial divisions in this country and may adopt the term *people of color* as an aspect of their identity here. [. . .]

This emphasis on race tends to mask differences based on class, another important distinction among immigrant groups. For example, the Chinese and Japanese people who came in the nineteenth century and early twentieth century to work on plantations in Hawai'i, as loggers in Oregon, or building roads and railroads in several western states were poor and from rural areas of China and Japan. The 1965 immigration law made way for "the second wave" of Asian immigration (Takaki 1987). It set preferences for professionals, highly skilled workers, and members of the middle and upper-middle classes, making this group "the most highly skilled of any immigrant group our country has ever had" (quoted in Takaki 1987, p. 420). The first wave of Vietnamese refugees who immigrated between the mid-1970s and 1980 were from the middle and upper classes, and many were professionals; by contrast, the second wave of immigrants from Vietnam was composed of poor and rural people. The class backgrounds of immigrants affect not only their sense of themselves and their expectations but also how they can succeed as strangers in a foreign land. For example, a poor woman who arrives with no literacy skills in her own language will have a more difficult time learning to become literate in English than one who has formal schooling in her country of origin that may have included basic English.

Multiple Identities, Social Location, and Contradictions

The social features of one's identity incorporate individual, community, societal, and global factors [. . .]. Social location is a way of expressing the core of a person's existence in the social and political world. It places us in particular relationships to others, to the dominant culture of the United States, and to the rest of the world. It determines the kinds of power and privilege we have access to and can exercise, as well as situations in which we have less power and privilege.

Because social location is where all the aspects of one's identity meet, our experience of our own complex identities is sometimes contradictory, conflictual, and paradoxical. We live with multiple identities that can be both enriching and contradictory and that push us to confront questions of loyalty to individuals and groups. [. . .]

It is also through the complexity of social location that we are forced to differentiate our inclinations, behaviors, self-definition, and politics from how we are classified by larger societal institutions. An inclination toward bisexuality, for example, does not mean that one will necessarily act on that inclination. Defining oneself as working class does not necessarily lead to activity in progressive politics based on a class consciousness.

Social location is also where we meet others socially and politically. Who are we in relation to people who are both like us and different from us? How do we negotiate the inequalities in power and privilege? How do we both accept and appreciate who we and others are, and grow and change to meet the challenges of a multicultural world? [. . .]

Study Questions

1   What do Kirk and Okazawa-Rey claim are the most important factors that shape our identities?

2   Explain the macro, meso, and micro levels of social relations. Which of Kirk's and Okazawa-Rey's examples are most helpful to you in understanding these concepts? Which of these levels have had the most impact on the formation of your identity? Why?

3   Do you agree with Kirk and Okazawa-Rey that we all live with multiple identities? Using yourself as an example, explain your agreement/disagreement.

4   Explain "social location" in your own words. Is "social location" a useful concept for analysis in thinking about your own identity formation? Why or why not?

References

Blauner, R. *Racial Oppression in America*. New York: Harper & Row, 1972.

Fuchs, L. "The Reaction of Black Americans to Immigration," *Immigration Reconsidered*. Ed. V. Yans-McLaughlin. New York: Oxford University Press, 1990.

Roediger, D. R. *The Wages of Whiteness: Race and the Making of the American Working Class*. New York: Verso, 1991.

Stonequist, E. V. *The Marginal Man: A Study in Personality and Cultural Conflict*. New York: Scribner & Sons, 1961.

Takaki, R. *Strangers from a Different Shore: Perspectives on Race and Ethnicity*. New York: Oxford University Press, 1987.

Yans-McLaughlin, V. Ed. *Immigration Reconsidered*. New York: Oxford University Press, 1990.

Young, M. E., M. A. Nosek, C. A. Howland, G. Chanpong, and D. H. Rintala. "Prevalence of Abuse in Women with Disabilities." *Archives of Physical Medicine and Rehabilitation* 78: S34–S38 (1997).

Zinn, H. *People's History of the United States: 1492– Present*. Rev. and updated ed. New York: HarperPerennial, 1995.

CHAPTER 2

What We Really Miss About the 1950s

Stephanie Coontz

Stephanie Coontz (1944–) is a professor of history and family studies, and a social commentator. Her books include The Way We Never Were: American Families and the Nostalgia Trap *(1992), and* The Social Origins of Private Life: A History of American Families *(1988). She has also published articles in numerous media outlets, such as* The New York Times, Newsweek, *and* Vogue, *and appeared as a guest on television talk shows. In this essay, excerpted from her 1997 book,* The Way We Really Are: Coming to Terms With America's Changing Families, *Coontz identifies and examines an enduring myth of the American family.*

In a 1996 poll by the Knight-Ridder news agency, more Americans chose the 1950s than any other single decade as the best time for children to grow up.[1] And despite the research I've done on the underside of 1950s families, I don't think it's crazy for people to feel nostalgic about the period. For one thing, it's easy to see why people might look back fondly to a decade when real wages grew more in any single year than in the entire ten years of the 1980s combined, a time when the average 30-year-old man could buy a median-priced home on only 15–18 percent of his salary.[2]

But it's more than just a financial issue. When I talk with modern parents, even ones who grew up in unhappy families, they associate the 1950s with a yearning they feel for a time when there were fewer complicated choices for kids or parents to grapple with, when there was more predictability in how people formed and maintained families, and when there was a coherent "moral order" in their community to serve as a reference point for family norms. Even people who found that moral order grossly unfair or repressive often say that its presence provided them with something concrete to push against. [. . .]

Nostalgia for the 1950s is real and deserves to be taken seriously, but it usually shouldn't be taken literally. Even people who *do* pick the 1950s as the best decade generally end up saying, once they start discussing their feelings in depth, that it's not the family arrangements in and of themselves that they want to revive. They don't miss the way women used to be treated, they sure wouldn't want to live with most of the fathers they knew in their neighborhoods, and "come to think of it" – I don't know how many times I've recorded these exact words – "I communicate with my kids *much* better than my parents or grandparents did." When Judith Wallerstein recently interviewed 100 spouses in "happy" marriages, she found that only five "wanted a marriage like their parents'." The husbands "consciously rejected the role models provided by their fathers. The women said they could never be happy living as their mothers did."[3]

People today understandably feel that their lives are out of balance, but they yearn for something totally *new* – a more equal distribution of work, family, and community time for both men and women, children and adults. If the 1990s are lopsided in one direction, the 1950s were equally lopsided in the opposite direction.

What most people really feel nostalgic about has little to do with the internal structure of 1950s families. It is the belief that the 1950s provided a more family-friendly economic and social environment, an easier climate in which to keep kids on the straight and narrow, and above all, a greater feeling of hope for a family's long-term future, especially for its young. The contrast between the perceived hopefulness of the fifties and our own misgivings about the future is key to contemporary nostalgia for the period. Greater optimism *did* exist then, even among many individuals and groups who were in terrible circumstances. But if we are to take people's sense of loss seriously, rather than merely to capitalize on it for a hidden political agenda, we need to develop a historical perspective on where that hope came from.

Part of it came from families comparing their prospects in the 1950s to their unstable, often grindingly uncomfortable pasts, especially the two horrible decades just before. In the 1920s, after two centuries of child labor and income insecurity, and for the first time in American history, a bare majority of children had come to live in a family with a male breadwinner, a female homemaker, and a chance at a high school education. Yet no sooner did the ideals associated with such a family begin to blossom than they were buried by the stock market crash of 1929 and the Great Depression of the 1930s. During the 1930s domestic violence soared; divorce rates fell, but informal separations jumped; fertility plummeted. Murder rates were higher in 1933 than they were in the 1980s. Families were uprooted or torn apart. Thousands of young people left home to seek work, often riding the rails across the country.[4]

World War II brought the beginning of economic recovery, and people's renewed interest in forming families resulted in a marriage and child-bearing boom, but stability was still beyond most people's grasp. Postwar communities were rocked by racial tensions, labor strife; and a right-wing backlash against the radical union movement of the 1930s. Many women resented being fired from wartime jobs they had grown to enjoy. Veterans often came home to find that they had to elbow their way back into their families, with wives and children resisting their attempts to reassert domestic authority. In one recent study of fathers who returned from the war, four times as many reported painful, even traumatic, reunions as remembered happy ones.[5]

By 1946 one in every three marriages was ending in divorce. Even couples who stayed together went through rough times, as an acute housing shortage forced families to double up with relatives or friends. Tempers frayed and generational relations grew strained. "No home is big enough to house two families, particularly two of different generations, with opposite theories on child training," warned a 1948 film on the problems of modern marriage.[6]

So after the widespread domestic strife, family disruptions, and violence of the 1930s and the instability of the World War II period, people were ready to try something new. The postwar economic boom gave them the chance. The 1950s was the first time that a majority of Americans could even *dream* of creating a secure oasis in their immediate nuclear families.

There they could focus their emotional and financial investments, reduce obligations to others that might keep them from seizing their own chance at a new start, and escape the interference of an older generation of neighbors or relatives who tried to tell them how to run their lives and raise their kids. Oral histories of the postwar period resound with the theme of escaping from in-laws, maiden aunts, older parents, even needy siblings.

The private family also provided a refuge from the anxieties of the new nuclear age and the cold war, as well as a place to get away from the political witch-hunts led by Senator Joe McCarthy and his allies. When having the wrong friends at the wrong time or belonging to any "suspicious" organization could ruin your career and reputation, it was safer to pull out of groups you might have joined earlier and to focus on your family. On a more positive note, the nuclear family was where people could try to satisfy their long-pent-up desires for a more stable marriage, a decent home, and the chance to really enjoy their children.

The 1950s Family Experiment

The key to understanding the successes, failures, and comparatively short life of 1950s family forms and values is to understand the period as one of *experimentation* with the possibilities of a new kind of family, not as the expression of some longstanding tradition. At the end of the 1940s, the divorce rate, which had been rising steadily since the 1890s, dropped sharply; the age of marriage fell to a 100-year low; and the birth rate soared. Women who had worked during the depression or World War II quit their jobs as soon as they became pregnant, which meant quite a few women were specializing in child raising; fewer women remained childless during the 1950s than in any decade since the late nineteenth century. The timing and spacing of childbearing became far more compressed, so that young mothers were likely to have two or more children in diapers at once, with no older sibling to help in their care. At the same time, again for the first time in 100 years, the educational gap between young middle-class women and men increased, while job segregation for working men and women seems to have peaked. These demographic changes increased the dependence of women on marriage, in contrast to gradual trends in the opposite direction since the early twentieth century.[7]

The result was that family life and gender roles became much more predictable, orderly, and settled in the 1950s than they were either twenty years earlier or would be twenty years later. Only slightly more than one in four marriages ended in divorce during the 1950s. Very few young people spent any extended period of time in a nonfamily setting: They moved from their parents' family into their own family, after just a brief experience with independent living, and they started having children soon after marriage. Whereas two-thirds of women aged 20 to 24 were not yet married in 1990, only 28 percent of women this age were still single in 1960.[8]

Ninety percent of all the households in the country were families in the 1950s, in comparison with only 71 percent by 1990. Eighty-six percent of all children lived in two-parent homes in 1950, as opposed to just 72 percent in 1990. And the percentage living with both biological parents – rather than, say, a parent and stepparent – was dramatically higher than it had been at the turn of the century or is today: 70 percent in 1950, compared with only 50 percent in 1990. Nearly 60 percent of kids – an all-time high – were born into male breadwinner–female homemaker families; only a minority of the rest had mothers who worked in the paid labor force.[9]

If the organization and uniformity of family life in the 1950s were new, so were the values, especially the emphasis on putting all one's emotional and financial eggs in the small basket of the immediate nuclear family. Right up through the 1940s, ties of work, friendship, neighborhood, ethnicity, extended kin, and voluntary organizations were as important a source of identity for most Americans, and sometimes a *more* important source of obligation, than marriage and the nuclear family. All this changed in the postwar era. The spread of suburbs and automobiles, combined with the destruction of older ethnic neighborhoods in many cities, led to the decline of the neighborhood social club. Young couples moved away from parents and kin, cutting ties with traditional extrafamilial networks that might compete for their attention. A critical factor in this trend was the emergence of a group of family sociologists and marriage counselors who followed Talcott Parsons in claiming that the nuclear family, built on a sharp division of labor between husband and wife, was the cornerstone of modern society. [. . .]

The call for young couples to break from their parents and youthful friends was a consistent theme in 1950s popular culture. In *Marty,* one of the most highly praised TV plays and movies of the 1950s, the hero almost loses his chance at love by listening to the carping of his mother and aunt and letting himself be influenced by old friends who resent the time he spends with his new girlfriend. In the end, he turns his back on mother, aunt, and friends to get his new marriage and a little business of his own off to a good start. Other movies, novels, and popular psychology tracts portrayed the dreadful things that happened when women became more interested in careers than marriage or men resisted domestic conformity.

Yet many people felt guilty about moving away from older parents and relatives; "modern mothers" worried that fostering independence in their kids could lead to defiance or even juvenile delinquency (the recurring nightmare of the age); there was considerable confusion about how men and women could maintain clear breadwinner–homemaker distinctions in a period of expanding education, job openings, and consumer aspirations. People clamored for advice. They got it from the new family education specialists and marriage counselors, from columns in women's magazines, from government pamphlets, and above all from television. While 1950s TV melodramas warned against letting anything dilute the commitment to getting married and having kids, the new family sitcoms gave people nightly lessons on how to make their marriage or rapidly expanding family work – or, in the case of *I Love Lucy*, probably the most popular show of the era, how *not* to make their marriage and family work. Lucy and Ricky gave weekly comic reminders of how much trouble a woman could get into by wanting a career or hatching some hare-brained scheme behind her husband's back.

At the time, everyone knew that shows such as *Donna Reed*, *Ozzie and Harriet*, *Leave It to Beaver*, and *Father Knows Best* were not the way families really were. People didn't watch those shows to see their own lives reflected back at them. They watched them to see how families were *supposed* to live – and also to get a little reassurance that they were headed in the right direction. The sitcoms were simultaneously advertisements, etiquette manuals, and how-to lessons for a new way of organizing marriage and child raising. I have studied the scripts of these shows for years, since I often use them in my classes on family history, but it wasn't until I became a parent that I felt their extraordinary pull. The secret of their appeal, I suddenly realized, was that they offered 1950s viewers, wracked with the same feelings of parental inadequacy as was I, the promise that there were easy answers and surefire techniques for raising kids. [. . .]

Similarly, the 1950s sitcoms were aimed at young couples who had married in haste, women who had tasted new freedoms during World War II and given up their jobs with regret, veterans whose children resented their attempts to reassert paternal authority, and individuals disturbed by the changing racial and ethnic mix of postwar America. The message was clear: Buy these ranch houses, Hotpoint appliances, and child-raising ideals; relate to your spouse like this; get a new car to wash with your kids on Sunday afternoons; organize your dinners like that – and you too can escape from the conflicts of race, class, and political witch-hunts into harmonious families where father knows best, mothers are never bored or irritated, and teenagers rush to the dinner table each night, eager to get their latest dose of parental wisdom.

Many families found it possible to put together a good imitation of this way of living during the 1950s and 1960s. Couples were often able to construct marriages that were much more harmonious than those in which they had grown up, and to devote far more time to their children. Even when marriages were deeply unhappy, as many were, the new stability, economic security, and educational advantages parents were able to offer their kids counted for a lot in people's assessment of their life satisfaction. And in some matters, ignorance could be bliss: The lack of media coverage of problems such as abuse or incest was terribly hard on the casualties, but it protected more fortunate families from knowledge and fear of many social ills.[10]

There was tremendous hostility to people who could be defined as "others": Jews, African Americans, Puerto Ricans, the poor, gays or lesbians, and "the red menace." Yet on a day-to-day basis, the civility that prevailed in homogeneous neighborhoods allowed people to ignore larger patterns of racial and political repression. Racial clashes were ever-present in the 1950s, sometimes escalating into full-scale antiblack riots, but individual homicide rates fell to almost half the levels of the 1930s. As nuclear families moved into the suburbs, they retreated from social activism but entered voluntary relationships with people who had children the same age; they became involved in PTAs together, joined bridge clubs, went bowling. There does seem to have been a stronger sense of neighborly commonalities than many of us feel today. Even though this local community was often the product of exclusion or repression, it sometimes looks attractive to modern Americans whose commutes are getting longer and whose family or work patterns give them little in common with their neighbors.[11]

The optimism that allowed many families to rise above their internal difficulties and to put limits on their individualistic values during the 1950s came from the sense that America was on a dramatically different trajectory than it had been in the past, an upward and expansionary path that had already taken people to better places than they had ever seen before and would certainly take their children even further. This confidence that almost everyone could look forward to a better future stands in sharp contrast to how most contemporary Americans feel, and it explains why a period in which many people were much worse off than today sometimes still looks like a better period for families than our own.

Throughout the 1950s, poverty was higher than it is today, but it was less concentrated in pockets of blight existing side-by-side with extremes of wealth, and, unlike today, it was falling rather than rising. At the end of the 1930s, almost two-thirds of the population had incomes below the poverty standards of the day, while only one in eight had a middle-class income (defined as two to five times the poverty line). By 1960, a majority of the population had climbed into the middle-income range.[12]

Unmarried people were hardly sexually abstinent in the 1950s, but the age of first intercourse was somewhat higher than it is now, and despite a tripling of nonmarital birth rates between 1940 and 1958, more then 70 percent of nonmarital pregnancies led to weddings before the child was born. Teenage birth rates were almost twice as high in 1957 as in the 1990s, but most teen births were to married couples, and the effect of teen pregnancy in reducing further schooling for young people did not hurt their life prospects the way it does today. High school graduation rates were lower in the 1950s than they are today, and minority students had far worse test scores, but there were jobs for people who dropped out of high school or graduated without good reading skills – jobs that actually had a future. People entering the job market in the 1950s had no way of knowing that they would be the last generation to have a good shot at reaching middle-class status without the benefit of postsecondary schooling.

Millions of men from impoverished, rural, unemployed, or poorly educated family backgrounds found steady jobs in the steel, auto, appliance, construction, and shipping industries. Lower middle-class men went further on in college during the 1950s than they would have been able to expect in earlier decades, enabling them to make the transition to secure white-collar work. The experience of shared sacrifices in the depression and war, reinforced by a New-Deal inspired belief in the ability of government to make life better, gave people a sense of hope for the future. Confidence in government, business, education, and other institutions was on the rise. This general optimism affected people's experience and assessment of family life. It is no wonder modern Americans yearn for a similar sense of hope.

But before we sign on to any attempts to turn the family clock back to the 1950s we should note that the family successes and community solidarities of the 1950s rested on a totally different set of political and economic conditions than we have today. Contrary to widespread belief, the 1950s was not an age of laissez-faire government and free market competition. A major cause of the social mobility of young families in the 1950s was that federal assistance programs were much more generous and widespread than they are today.

In the most ambitious and successful affirmative action program ever adopted in America, 40 percent of young men were eligible for veterans' benefits, and these benefits were far more extensive than those available to Vietnam-era vets. Financed in part by a federal income tax on the rich that went up to 87 percent and a corporate tax rate of 52 percent, such benefits provided quite a jump start for a generation of young families. The GI bill paid most tuition costs for vets who attended college, doubling the percentage of college students from prewar levels. At the other end of the life span, Social Security began to build up a significant safety net for the elderly, formerly the poorest segment of the population. Starting in 1950, the federal government regularly mandated raises in the minimum wage to keep pace with inflation. The minimum wage may have been only $1.40 as late as 1968, but a person who worked for that amount full-time, year-round, earned 118 percent of the poverty figure for a family of three. By 1995, a full-time minimum-wage worker could earn only 72 percent of the poverty level.[13]

An important source of the economic expansion of the 1950s was that public works spending at all levels of government comprised nearly 20 percent of total expenditures in 1950, as compared to less than 7 percent in 1984. Between 1950 and 1960, nonmilitary, nonresidential public construction rose by 58 percent. Construction expenditures for new schools (in dollar amounts adjusted for inflation) rose by 72 percent; funding on sewers and waterworks rose by 46 percent. Government paid 90 percent of the costs of building the new Interstate Highway System. These programs opened up suburbia to growing numbers of middle-class Americans and created secure, well-paying jobs for blue-collar workers.[14]

Government also reorganized home financing, underwriting low down payments and long-term mortgages that had been rejected as bad business by private industry. To do this, government put public assets behind housing lending programs, created two new national financial institutions to facilitate home loans, allowed veterans to put down payments as low as a dollar on a house, and offered tax breaks to people who bought homes. The National Defense Education Act funded the socioeconomic mobility of thousands of young men who trained themselves for well-paying jobs in such fields as engineering.[15]

Unlike contemporary welfare programs, government investment in 1950s families was not just for immediate subsistence but encouraged long-term asset development, rewarding people for increasing their investment in homes and education. Thus it was far less likely that such families or individuals would ever fall back to where they started, even after a string of bad luck. Subsidies for higher education were greater the longer people stayed in school and the more expensive the school they selected. Mortgage deductions got bigger as people traded up to better houses.[16]

These social and political support systems magnified the impact of the postwar economic boom. "In the years between 1947 and 1973," reports economist Robert Kuttner, "the median paycheck more than doubled, and the bottom 20 percent enjoyed the greatest gains." High rates of unionization meant that blue-collar workers were making much more financial progress than most of their counterparts today. In 1952, when eager home buyers flocked to the opening of Levittown, Pennsylvania, the largest planned community yet constructed, "it took a factory worker one day to earn enough money to pay the closing costs on a new Levittown house, then selling for $10,000." By 1991, such a home was selling for $100,000 or more, and it took a factory worker *eighteen weeks* to earn enough money for just the closing costs.[17]

The legacy of the union struggle of the 1930s and 1940s, combined with government support for raising people's living standards, set limits on corporations that have disappeared in recent decades. Corporations paid 23 percent of federal income taxes in the 1950s, as compared to just 9.2 percent in 1991. Big companies earned higher profit margins than smaller firms, partly due to their dominance of the market, partly to America's postwar economic advantage. They chose (or were forced) to share these extra earnings, which economists call "rents," with employees. Economists at the Brookings Institution and Harvard University estimate that 70 percent of such corporate rents were passed on to workers at all levels of the firm, benefiting secretaries and janitors as well as CEOs. Corporations routinely retained workers even in slack periods, as a way of ensuring workplace stability. Although they often received more generous tax breaks from communities than they gave back in investment, at least they kept their plants and employment offices in the same place. AT&T, for example, received much of the technology it used to finance its postwar expansion from publicly funded communications research conducted as part of the war effort, and, as current AT&T Chairman Robert Allen puts it, there "used to be a lifelong commitment on the employee's part and on our part." Today, however, he admits, "the contract doesn't exist anymore."[18]

Television trivia experts still argue over exactly what the fathers in many 1950s sitcoms did for a living. Whatever it was, though, they obviously didn't have to worry about downsizing. If most married people stayed in long-term relationships during the 1950s, so did most corporations, sticking with the communities they grew up in and the employees they originally hired. Corporations were not constantly relocating in search of cheap labor during the 1950s; unlike today, increases in worker productivity usually led to increases in wages. The number of workers covered by corporate pension plans and health benefits increased steadily. So did limits on the work week. There is good reason that people look back to the 1950s as a less hurried age: The average American was working a shorter workday in the 1950s than his or her counterpart today, when a quarter of the work-force puts in 49 or more hours a week.[19]

So politicians are practicing quite a double standard when they tell us to return to the family forms of the 1950s while they do nothing to restore the job programs and family subsidies of that era, the limits on corporate relocation and financial wheeling-dealing, the much higher share of taxes paid by corporations then, the availability of union jobs for noncollege youth, and the subsidies for higher education such as the National Defense Education Act loans. Furthermore, they're not telling the whole story when they claim that the 1950s was the most prosperous time for families and the most secure decade for children. Instead, playing to our understandable nostalgia for a time when things seemed to be getting better, not worse, they engage in a tricky chronological shell game with their figures, diverting our attention from two important points. First, many individuals, families, and groups were excluded from the economic prosperity, family optimism, and social civility of the 1950s. Second, the all-time high point of child well-being and family economic security came not during the 1950s but *at the end of the 1960s.*

We now know that 1950s family culture was not only nontraditional; it was also not idyllic. In important ways, the stability of family and community life during the 1950s rested on pervasive discrimination against women, gays, political dissidents, non-Christians, and racial or ethnic minorities, as well as on a systematic cover-up of the underside of many families. Families that were harmonious and fair of their own free will may have been able to function more easily in the fifties, but few alternatives existed for members of discordant or oppressive families. Victims of child abuse, incest, alcoholism, spousal rape, and wife battering had no recourse, no place to go, until well into the 1960s.[20]

At the end of the 1950s, despite ten years of economic growth, 27.3 percent of the nation's children were poor, including those in white "underclass" communities such as Appalachia. Almost 50 percent of married-couple African-American families were impoverished – a figure far higher than today. It's no wonder African Americans are not likely to pick the 1950s as a golden age, even in comparison with the setbacks they experienced in the 1980s. When blacks moved north to find jobs in the postwar urban manufacturing boom they met vicious harassment and violence, first to prevent them from moving out of the central cities, then to exclude them from public space such as parks or beaches. [...]

The Fifties Experiment Comes to an End

The social stability of the 1950s, then, was a response to the stick of racism, sexism, and repression as well as to the carrot of economic opportunity and government aid. Because social protest mounted in the 1960s and unsettling challenges were posed to the gender roles and sexual mores of the previous decade, many people forget that families continued to make gains throughout the 1960s and into the first few years of the 1970s. By 1969, child poverty was down to 14 percent, its lowest level ever; it hovered just above that marker until 1975, when it began its steady climb up to contemporary figures (22 percent in 1993; 21.2 percent in 1994). The high point of health and nutrition for poor children was reached in the early 1970s.[21]

So commentators are being misleading when they claim that the 1950s was the golden age of American families. They are disregarding the number of people who were excluded during that decade and ignoring the socio-economic gains that continued to be made through the 1960s. But they are quite right to note that the improvements of the 1950s and 1960s came to an end at some point in the 1970s (though not for the elderly, who continued to make progress). [. . .]

Study Questions

1 What is the "myth" of the American family, according to Coontz? Where does this myth come from? What purposes does it serve? Who is left out of the myth?

2 Why did the white, middle-class family become the American ideal during the 1950s? What political, social, and economic factors supported the formation of the ideal family in that period? What historic realities contradicted the myth?

3 How did/does the American media and popular culture support the myth of the ideal family?

4 How do you define what constitutes a family?

Notes

1. Steven Thomma, "Nostalgia for '50s Surfaces," *Philadelphia Inquirer*, Feb. 4, 1996.

2. Frank Levy, *Dollars and Dreams: The Changing American Income Distribution* (New York: Russell Sage, 1987), p. 6; Frank Levy, "Incomes and Income Inequality," in Reynolds Farley, ed., *State of the Union: America in the 1990s*, vol. 1 (New York: Russell Sage, 1995), pp. 1–57; Richard May and Kathryn Porter, "Poverty and Income Trends, 1994," Washington, D.C.: Center on Budget and Policy Priorities, March 1996; Rob Nelson and Jon Cowan, "Buster Power," *USA Weekend*, October 14–16, 1994, p. 10.

3. Judith Wallerstein and Sandra Blakeslee, *The Good Marriage: How and Why Love Lasts* (Boston: Houghton Mifflin, 1995), p. 15.

4. Donald Hernandez, *America's Children: Resources from Family, Government and the Economy* (New York: Russell Sage, 1993), pp. 99, 102; James Morone, "The Corrosive Politics of Virtue," *American Prospect* 26 (May–June 1996), p. 37; "Study Finds U.S. No. 1 in Violence," *Olympian*, November 13, 1992. See also Stephen Mintz and Susan Kellogg, *Domestic Revolutions: A Social History of American Family Life* (New York: The Free Press, 1988).

5. William Tuttle, Jr., *"Daddy's Gone to War": The Second World War in the Lives of America's Children* (New York: Oxford University Press, 1993).

6. "Marriage and Divorce," *March of Time*, film series 14 (1948).

7. Arlene Skolnick and Stacey Rosencrantz, "The New Crusade for the Old Family," *American Prospect*, Summer 1994, p. 65; Hernandez, *America's Children*, pp. 128–132; Andrew Cherlin, "Changing Family and Household: Contemporary Lessons from Historical Research," *Annual Review of Sociology* 9 (1983), pp. 54–58; Sam Roberts, *Who We Are: A Portrait of America Based on the Latest Census* (New York: Times Books, 1995), p. 45.

8. Levy, "Incomes and Income Inequality," p. 20; Arthur Norton and Louisa Miller, *Marriage, Divorce, and Remarriage in the 1990s*, Current Population Reports Series P23–180 (Washington, D.C.: Bureau of the Census, October 1992); Roberts, *Who We Are* (1995 ed.), pp. 50–53.

9. Dennis Hogan and Daniel Lichter, "Children and Youth: Living Arrangements and Welfare," in Farley, ed., *State of the Union*, vol. 2, p. 99; Richard Gelles, *Contemporary Families: A Sociological View* (Thousand Oaks, Calif.: Sage, 1995), p. 115; Hernandez, *America's Children*, p. 102. The fact that only a small percentage of children had mothers in the paid labor force, though a full 40 percent did not live in male breadwinner–female homemaker families, was because some children had mothers who worked, unpaid, in farms or family businesses, or fathers who were unemployed, or the children were not living with both parents.

10. For discussion of the discontents, and often searing misery, that were considered normal in a "good- enough" marriage in the 1950s and 1960s, see Lillian Rubin, *Worlds of Pain: Life in the Working-Class Family* (New York: Basic Books, 1976); Mirra Komarovsky, *Blue Collar Marriage* (New Haven, Conn.: Vintage, 1962); Elaine Tyler May, *Homeward Bound: American Families in the Cold War Era* (New York: Basic Books, 1988).

11. See Robert Putnam, "The Strange Disappearance of Civic America," *American Prospect*, Winter 1996. For a glowing if somewhat lopsided picture of 1950s community solidarities, see Alan Ehrenhalt, *The Lost City: Discovering the Forgotten Virtues of Community in the Chicago of the 1950s* (New York: Basic Books, 1995). For a chilling account of communities uniting against perceived outsiders, in the same city, see Arnold Hirsch, *Making the Second Ghetto: Race and Housing in Chicago, 1940–1960* (Cambridge, Mass.: Harvard University Press, 1983). On homicide rates, see "Study Finds United States No. 1 in Violence," *Olympian*, November 13, 1992; *New York Times*, November 13, 1992, p. A9; and Douglas Lee Eckberg, "Estimates of Early Twentieth-Century U.S. Homicide Rates: An Econometric Forecasting Approach," *Demography* 32 (1995), p. 14. On lengthening commutes, see "It's Taking Longer to Get to Work," *Olympian*, December 6, 1995.

12. The figures in this and the following paragraph come from Levy, "Incomes and Income Inequality," pp. 1–57; May and Porter, "Poverty and Income Trends, 1994"; Reynolds Farley, *The New American Reality: Who We Are, How We Got Here, Where We Are Going* (New York: Russell Sage, 1996), pp. 83–85; Gelles, *Contemporary Families*, p. 115; David Grissmer, Sheila Nataraj Kirby, Mark Bender, and Stephanie Williamson, *Student Achievement and the Changing American Family*, Rand Institute on Education and Training (Santa Monica, Calif.: Rand, 1994), p. 106.

13. William Chafe, *The Unfinished Journey: America Since World War II* (New York: Oxford University Press, 1986), pp. 113, 143; Marc Linder, "Eisenhower-Era Marxist-Confiscatory Taxation: Requiem for the Rhetoric of Rate Reduction for the Rich," *Tulane Law Review* 70 (1996), p. 917; Barry Bluestone and Teresa Ghilarducci, "Rewarding Work: Feasible Antipoverty Policy," *American Prospect* 28 (1996), p. 42; Theda Skocpol, "Delivering for Young Families," *American Prospect* 28 (1996), p. 67.

14. Joel Tarr, "The Evolution of the Urban Infrastructure in the Nineteenth and Twentieth Centuries," in Royce Hanson, ed., *Perspectives on Urban Infrastructure* (Washington, D.C.: National Academy Press, 1984); Mark Aldrich, *A History of Public Works Investment in the*

United States, report prepared by the CPNSAD Research Corporation for the U.S. Department of Commerce, April 1980.

15. For more information on this government financing, see Kenneth Jackson, *Crabgrass Frontier: The Suburbanization of the United States* (New York: Oxford University Press, 1985); and S. Coontz, *The Way We Never Were* (New York: Basic Books, 1992), chapter 4.

16. John Cook and Laura Sherman, "Economic Security Among America's Poor: The Impact of State Welfare Waivers on Asset Accumulation," Center on Hunger, Poverty, and Nutrition Policy, Tufts University, May 1996.

17. Robert Kuttner, "The Incredible Shrinking American Paycheck," *Washington Post National Weekly Edition*, November 6–12, 1995, p. 23; Donald Bartlett and James Steele, *America: What Went Wrong?* (Kansas City: Andrews McMeel, 1992), p. 20.

18. Richard Barnet, "Lords of the Global Economy," *Nation*, December 19, 1994, p. 756; Clay Chandler, "U.S. Corporations: Good Citizens or Bad?" *Washington Post National Weekly Edition*, May 20–26, 1996, p. 16; Steven Pearlstein, "No More Mr. Nice Guy: Corporate America Has Done an About-Face in How It Pays and Treats Employees," *Washington Post National Weekly Edition*, December 18–24, 1995, p. 10; Robert Kuttner, "Ducking Class Warfare," *Washington Post National Weekly Edition*, March 11–17, 1996, p. 5; Henry Allen, "Ha! So Much for Loyalty," *Washington Post National Weekly Edition*, March 4–10, 1996, p. 11.

19. Ehrenhalt, *The Lost City*, pp. 11–12; Jeremy Rifken, *The End of Work: The Decline of the Global Labor Force and the Dawn of the Post-Market Era* (New York: G. P. Putnam's Sons, 1995), pp. 169, 170, 231; Juliet Schorr, *The Overworked American: The Unexpected Decline of Leisure* (New York: Basic Books, 1991).

20. For documentation that these problems existed, see chapter 2 of *The Way We Never Were*.

21. *The State of America's Children Yearbook, 1996*, (Washington, DC: Children's Defense Fund, 1996) p. 77; May and Porter, "Poverty and Income Trends: 1994," p. 23; Sara McLanahan et al., *Losing Ground: A Critique*, University of Wisconsin Institute for Research on Poverty, Special Report No. 38, 1985.

CHAPTER 3

Generational Memory in an American Town

John Bodnar

John Bodnar (1944–) is a professor of history who writes on labor, immigration, public and community memory, and the treatment of history in popular culture. He is the author of The Transplanted: A History of Immigrants in Urban America *(1985),* Remaking America: Public Memory, Commemoration, and Patriotism in the Twentieth Century *(1992), and* Blue-Collar Hollywood: Liberalism, Democracy, and Working People in American Film *(2003). The following essay is based upon a series of interviews that Bodnar and his students conducted with individuals who grew up in the same Midwestern town, and whose sense of identity, values, and community were deeply influenced by the generational history of their times.*

T he idea of generational memory is widely invoked by scholars of modern American history. Drawing on the insights of Mannheim, who argued that social and political events encountered in early adulthood can permanently shape outlook, numerous historians have explained conflict and debate in modern America in terms of the disparate memories of respective generations. In the most familiar case, scholars have noted the divergent recollections of people who lived through the cataclysmic decades of the 1930s and 1960s, suggesting that the imprint of those times determined subsequent moral and political viewpoints.[1]

In the scholarly formulation, the "depression generation" apparently concluded that the central institutions and authorities that patterned their lives were responsible for pulling them through hard times and the war experience that followed, and that they would never need to be changed. Thus, they resolutely defended the traditional family, communal ties, religion, corporate capitalism, and the American nation. Terkel's renowned study of remembering the Great Depression argued that the event left "an invisible scar" on those who lived it; and his oral history of World War II revealed how much those who experienced hard times appreciated the jobs that the war produced. Conflict with institutions and authorities existed in the various accounts, but ultimately, people recalled solidarity in families, communities, workplaces, and the nation as a whole. Rieder argued that residents in a section of Brooklyn, New York, in the 1970s resisted racial integration of their neighborhood, modern ideas of sexual liberation, and the critics of their country because, "as children of the Great Depression" and as participants in World War II, they exalted such values as homeownership, traditional families and mores, and patriotism.[2]

The members of the "sixties generation" are generally regarded as mirror images of their parents. They tend to recall traditional authorities as repressive and untrustworthy. A survey of the "baby boomers," born between 1946 and 1964, conducted by *Rolling Stone* magazine in 1988, claimed that they "challenged virtually all the social mores and political values that had come before." The study stressed their commitment to new sexual norms, their flight from marriage, and their experimentation with drugs and new musical forms. "Boomers," themselves, although often idealizing the model of a traditional family, told the magazine's investigators that they placed less emphasis on a "close-knit family" and "respect for authority" than did the generation that preceded them. Indeed, nearly all scholars who have looked at this group have stressed its tendency to rebel against traditional institutions as a hallmark of its collective identity. In one of the most complete investigations of the age group, Roof found that, despite their differences, those in the "sixties generation" were unified by their shared rebellion against traditional institutions, which further explained their involvement in numerous kinds of searches for meaning at midlife; they had already rejected many of the traditional prescriptions for living. A Gallup Poll from 1985 made a similar point: This generation was even less likely to trust social and political institutions and their leaders than people who were born after them.[3]

The manner by which people recall the past and use it to fashion outlooks in the present can be determined from life histories. This study of generational memory is based on a collection of accounts from individuals in Whiting, Indiana, an industrial town near Chicago, in 1991. The limitations are obvious. One town, one class, and one scholar's predispositions do not make for a representative national sample. Whiting is not America. Nonetheless, what was remembered in Whiting was clearly linked to many of the issues that pervaded the nation's political discourse in the past and in the present.

The town manifests a pattern representative of the midwest industrial belt: economic and population expansion early in this century, an interlude of economic contraction in the 1930s, economic stability in the period from the 1940s to the 1960s, and a rapid decline of 30 percent in population from 1970 to 1990 and of 70 percent in employment at the town's major source of jobs – the refinery of Standard Oil of Indiana – from 1960 to 1990. Economic turmoil was accompanied by broad transformations in the politics and culture of postwar America. Traditional religious, corporate, and governmental institutions lost some of their authority and ability to command loyalty, and individual goals came to supersede collective ones. The institutional pillars of Whiting – the Catholic Church, Standard Oil, and the Democratic Party – all suffered losses during this period. Fathers could no longer assure their sons of jobs at the refinery, as their own fathers had been able to do. Young people were more likely to divorce and avoid church attendance than their parents were. Republicans won the majority of the votes for president in 1972 and 1980 in a town that had otherwise voted Democratic since the 1920s. In American culture as a whole, authority became more decentralized, and the idea of personal fulfillment contested the constraints on individualism that flourished under the regime of church, party, family, and corporation.[4]

Psychologists have demonstrated that narratives, along with abstract propositions, are the two fundamental forms of human cognition. Narratives in the form of life histories render complex experience understandable. Like all narratives they are subjective, despite their objective components, "reconstructing" rather than simply "resurrecting" the past in order to justify life choices. They are not only selective and subjective but also defensive and didactic. Their engagement with both the past and the present mitigates explanations of generational memories grounded solely in history but not those that are based in culture.[5]

The attempts of the people from Whiting to display their personal identities in life histories did not produce great variety. In their construction, these life histories resembled autobiographies, verifying Eakin's contention that self-portrayals usually involve "culturally sanctioned models of identity." Three such "models" were found in Whiting. Individuals of an older generation presented themselves as morally upright, selfless, thrifty, hard working, and devoted to the welfare of others in the community and in the nation. They were not imprinted so much by past decades or events as by their long relationship with institutions and ideologies that venerated their preferred ideals: Standard Oil embodied a paternalism that promised jobs for hard toil; the Catholic Church guaranteed salvation for sacrifice and adherence to marital roles; and the nation offered fair treatment in return for patriotism.[6]

A second model of identity was exhibited by residents born in the town after 1940. This group evinced a relationship with authorities and ideologies that sanctioned a greater variety of lifestyles. Their narratives celebrated, rather than censured, self-fulfillment and mounted a stronger attack upon the power of parents and, especially, the corporations that influenced their lives. In a remarkable turn of events, the third model emerged from members of the older generation who had left Whiting and retired to Arizona. That these citizens, who had lived through the Great Depression and World War II, told of making lifestyle changes in the southwest desert implied that the imprint of the years prior to 1950 was not beyond reformulation. [...]

Generational Narratives

The older generation in Whiting, born between 1902 and 1924, revered the ideal of obligation in an era when Americans argued about the pervasiveness of selfishness and the need for cohesion. They recalled lives of mutualism, duty, and care and criticized contemporaries who saw life as a process of self-realization. Their memories valorized their ability to serve their families, their employers, their working-class community, and their nation. Authority was to be accommodated rather than resisted. But their loyalty was not blind. They granted it, as they told it, because they expected and received justice in return. At home, they benefited from familiar support; at church, they participated in a mutual effort at salvation; and at the refinery, they received steady jobs and pensions. Ultimately, their narratives represented a collective belief that they once upheld a common enterprise with other citizens and powerful institutions – the very basis of their loyalty – and that this communal foundation for just treatment was now disintegrating. Their accounts of the past were not only ventures into history and longing, but also demands for the reinstatement of justice in a society dominated by the state, the marketplace, and the media. And yet there was disaffection in their ranks. Although their peers who had retired to Arizona shared many of their memories of a moral community, they had decided in the present to embark upon a more determined quest for personal happiness.

The next generation – born between 1943 and 1962 in this sample, and coming of age after World War II – revealed a different collective memory and identity. This group blended experiences that were unique to the times in which their identities were formed with some of the personal knowledge and values of their elders. They rendered accounts of mutualism in families and neighborhoods, but they affirmed, in much stronger terms, that economic security and occupational stability were best obtained through individual resourcefulness rather than through loyalty to an institution. Their sense of self-reliance was cultivated when relationships with authority throughout American society had become problematic. Conservatives had mounted a widespread attack against individual claims upon the state, and advertisers against constraints on self-fulfillment. Moreover, cultural critics have suggested that the electronic media – especially television – tended to demystify power, fostering a "decline in prestige" of all who held it.[7]

In Whiting, this deterioration was rooted in the more immediate issue of Standard Oil's reduction in the workforce. Sons and daughters could no longer anticipate the lifetime jobs and benefits that accrued to their parents. Released from their parents' attachment to the refinery, they were free to characterize themselves as more self-sufficient than their elders and overtly question their authority. However, their rebellion contained something of a longing for the advantages of an earlier era that were denied them.

The Older Generation

Whiting's older generation were the children of immigrants who came to the town in the first two decades of this century to work at Standard Oil and mills in the area. Their parents were East European Catholics who relied on friends and kin to find them homes and jobs. Their life stories contained extensive accounts of family life that stressed the themes of justice/injustice and concern/indifference. Their narratives resolved these oppositions with the idealization of duty over rebellion and selflessness over egoism. Their values did not emanate simply from events like the Great Depression but from ongoing encounters with familial, religious, corporate, and national authorities whom they considered fair and deserving of allegiance. When they gave loyalty to the community, they gave it to all of the institutions that pervaded that community. However, when they perceived that the institutions that once commanded their allegiance and supported their community were in decline – and no longer able to grant justice and benevolence – they became indignant. The nation no longer appeared to consist of caring and responsible individuals and institutions. Their patriotism had gone unrewarded; their identities were no longer validated.

The life histories of the older generation in Whiting always began with descriptions of their immigrant families. They recalled learning about the need to limit independence and to respect authority, even before the Great Depression. Family members were expected to take care of each other. According to one man born in 1919,

> Every kid had their chores to do. Every fall we'd chop wood and make kindling for storage and pile it in the woodsheds. That was the fall duty. After school, [we] had to bring it on the porch. And we used to help my grandmother out. She lived downstairs. But cleaning the kitchen, doing the dishes, well, that my sister Mary did. Housecleaning was mostly a girl's job. But the guys used to scrub floors. Our home life was like a family deal. Everybody helped each other out. I tried to bring that tradition to my kids. My dad always told us, "you guys stick together, no matter through thick or thin. In the case of an emergency, you guys come out and help." That's how we were brought up.[8]

[. . .] Consideration and esteem were the rewards for loyalty and submission. The older generation shared the memory of a moral community in which individualism was constrained and redefined, but not obliterated. Egoism and domination were tempered by the ideals of reciprocity and benevolence. The collective memory of this generation expressed what the past was like for them, as well as the timeless value of a moral society in the present. Their story emphasized the continued importance of recognizing individual needs and rewarding people for meeting collective exigencies, and it embodied a call for solidarity – "a realization that each person must take responsibility for the other because as consociates all must have an interest in the other."[9]

Persistent anecdotes about justice and solidarity revealed the older generation's fundamental adherence to authority. Workers at the refinery described men who were so loyal to the company that they would alert a foreman when a light bulb burned out so as not to retard the pace of production. Countless reiterations confirmed how much the local population prized rewards for their devotion, such as the pension system at Standard Oil, in which employees could contribute a portion of their income to a stock purchase plan that the company would partially match. In the view of some workers, men who earned such benefits had an easier time attracting marriage partners than those who did not.[10] [. . .]

During World War II, this generation described its participation in the national mobilization as voluntary. The people served the nation as they had their families and employers by joining the armed services, donating blood, buying war bonds, and producing gasoline products at the refinery. One man claimed that he decided to enlist as soon as he heard the news about the bombing of Pearl Harbor. A woman born in 1916 who admitted that everyone feared the war also recalled that "people were working so hard buying bonds and everything to help our country." At St. John's Catholic Church in Whiting, a shrine was built to "Our Lady of Victory" in 1942 "for our boys in the service, for victory, and for peace." Prelates at the church maintained that "God and His Blessed Mother" deserved such reverence and that the shrine was the best possible aid that the congregation could render "to our country and our boys in the armed forces." The pursuit of common interests was reinforced at the refinery, where the company newspaper took pride in the workers' production of vital oil supplies, purchase of bonds, and exhibition of the "discipline and teamwork" that would serve many of them well in the military.[11] [. . .]

The Younger Generation

The life histories and identities of Whiting's younger residents also affirmed the value of a tightly knit community and expressed concern about modern disintegration, although the image of communal decline in their narratives was contested by examples of resourceful individuals free from the constraints of traditional authority and hopeful of economic rejuvenation. Pride of individual achievement and hope for progress stood in place of calls for justice and moral outrage. From the perspective of middle age, these people focused more on the prospects of the future rather than a veneration of the past. Their encounter with economic decline gave them no reason to lionize authorities and institutions that held no promise of fairness or benevolence.

This working-class sample was not so likely to attend college or achieve affluence as many of their peers who are normally associated with the sixties generation. Their encounter with the 1960s and 1970s was not liberating but disappointing. Traditional authorities and paths to economic security had little to offer them. Because it was difficult to find permanent jobs at Standard Oil and other plants in the area after 1970, they resigned themselves to making a living through their own ingenuity.

This generation was no stranger to families of modest means and traditional values; family relationships accounted for most of their memories of mutualism. Unlike the older group's experience with authority, theirs seldom involved benevolence or justice, and, as a result, their memory of authority – even that of their parents – was more critical. One woman recalled with disdain how her father had forced her and her sister to return the pants that a neighbor had made for them because he would not let them wear anything but dresses. A man born in 1952 remembered his Southern Baptist upbringing with bitterness: "We went to church three times a week; that was very important. We prayed before every meal. We read the Bible daily.... It was either [obey] or be thrown out." Still another confessed that the death of his autocratic father did not have too traumatic effect on him.[12]

The younger generation stressed discontinuity more than continuity. In an era of sharp economic and cultural change, this group described their lives mainly as the result of individual decisions, not as the result of following occupational footsteps of their parents. Their emphasis on self-reliance explicitly contested their parents' commemoration of mutualism and justice. Lasch held that a preoccupation with self-sufficiency can emerge, ironically, from feelings of powerlessness in modern life. The economic decline of Whiting and northwest Indiana after 1945 forced members of the postwar cohort into a more difficult job search than that faced by those who routinely entered the refinery during an earlier era, perhaps explaining why baby boomers produced stronger narratives of personal initiative than the preceding generation.[13] [...]

Although both generations recalled the recent past as a time of decline – a deterioration in the formative community in their lives – the older generation saw the problem in moral terms. For those who matured after World War II, however, the demise of Whiting did not end with moral outrage but with a dream of economic revitalization. In the early 1990s, the younger people talk of the return of progress as a way of muting fears of economic decline. They are receptive to messages of individualism and self-fulfillment from contemporary culture, not only because they challenge the moral authoritarianism of their elders, but also because they sense that individualism may be the only viable resource in an economy so much more unpredictable and unjust than the one their parents knew. In their grievance with declining solidarity, they share memories and values with their elders, but in their celebration of individualism, depart from them. [...]

Generational memory is formed in the passage of time, not simply born in pivotal decades and events. Revising the deterministic paradigm of much scholarly thinking, this study – with its subjective, limited perspective openly acknowledged – suggests that generational memory is best understood as the result of long-term encounters with economic forces and powerful authorities. Regardless of the impact of the past, however, generational views are also under constant review and discussion in the present. Whiting's oldest generation revealed, late in life, that their basic narrative was molded from memories of their formative years – the 1920s through the 1950s – and from their reaction to the ideas that emerged later. Undoubtedly, they asserted their critique of social change in American history as elderly people who longed for the past; but they were not just looking backward. [...]

Finally, the concept of generation itself is not without its problems. This study implies not only that the imprint of the past is indeterminate but also that boundaries between generations are imprecise. Generations can agree as well as disagree. For instance, both generations lamented economic decline and tended to be critical of corporate layoffs; and differences in generation did not always eliminate bonds fostered by class, although further investigation is necessary to reveal whether this connection was more pronounced for the working class or the middle class. More-over, despite the obvious influence of life stage in remembering, both the young and the old in Whiting were concerned about the future. The former were more hopeful and the latter more pessimistic, but their respective memories and attitudes were driven, in part, by speculation about what was to come. Both groups tended to manipulate the past. Assumptions to the effect that generational outlooks are defined by pivotal events like the Great Depression or the "sixties" are wrong. Both young and old in Whiting demonstrated an ongoing connection to the process of creating meaning and exchanging information within their community and the larger society. They affirmed their commitment to participate in the continuous project of restating the reality of the past, present, and future in the contested culture of contemporary America.

Study Questions

1　What does Bodnar mean by "generational memory"? How does it affect our understanding of both the past and the present? Give an example of how it affects the historical understanding of each of the generations he interviewed.

2　Why does Bodnar argue that Whiting, Indiana can serve as a model for understanding important generational differences in attitudes toward gov-ernment, authority, religion, and work between the 1930s and the 1990s? What differences did you find most interesting?

3　Give an example of differences in generational memory within your own family.

Notes

1　Karl Mannheim, *Essays on the Sociology of Knowledge* (London, 1952), 292–299, 301. Mann-heim also argued that older groups tend to cling to the views of their youth and transmit them to subsequent generations, and that younger groups were, to a greater extent than their elders, in "fresh contact" with present experience. On the strength and weaknesses of using the concept of generations, see Alan B. Spitzer, "The Historical Problem of Generations," *American Historical Review,* LXXVIII (1973), 1353–1385; Philip Abrams, *Historical Sociology* (Ithaca, 1982), 240–241; Michael X. Delli Caprini, "Age and History: Generations and Sociopolitical Change," in Roberta S. Sigel (ed.), *Political Learning in Adulthood: A Sourcebook of Theory and Research* (Chicago, 1982), 12–14; David Kertzer, "Generation as a Sociological Problem," *American Sociological Review,* IX (1983), 125–149.

2　Studs Terkel, *Hard Times: An Oral History of the Great Depression* (New York, 1986), 3, 89, 131; idem, *"The Good War:" An Oral History of World War Two* (New York, 1984); Jonathan Rieder, *Canarsie: The Jews and Italians of Brooklyn against Liberalism* (Cambridge, 1985), 17–18. The title of Glenn H. Elder's, *Children of the Great Depression: Social Change in Life Experience* (Chicago, 1974) implies that the Great Depression was more decisive in its impact than the book's actual contents do. Elder's book demonstrates that the 1930s reveal a complex relationship between hard times and personal lives. For instance, he found that the Depression did not alter many traditional conceptions of marriage and family, including the centrality of having children. However, it did influence the "timing" of childbirth. Thus, decisions to delay having children in the 1930s contributed to a "baby boom" after 1945 (282–289). The people studied by Elder were examined at later stages of their lives in John A. Clausen, *American Lives: Looking Back at the Children of the Great Depression* (New York, 1993). Clausen further minimizes the impact of the Depression, finding that viewpoints and characteristics acquired in concrete relationships during formative periods of their lives were more influential. See also Todd Gitlin, *The Sixties: Years of Hope, Days of Rage* (Toronto, 1987), 17. A 1985 telephone survey by two sociologists asked American citizens what events seemed most important to them. Those born before 1930 most frequently cited World War II, but those born between 1941 and 1965 cited the conflict in Vietnam. The authors suggested that social and political events could make a "distinctive imprint" on people at a young age. See Howard Schuman and Jacqueline Scott, "Generations and Collective Memories," *American Sociological Review,* LIV (1989), 359–381, which tests Mannheim's assertions that generations receive distinguishing characteristics from social and political events during their youth. Mannheim, *Essays,* 276–320, makes the crucial point that generations are much more loosely bonded together than "concrete groups" like tribes or communities; he called them "cliques." Delli Caprini, "Age and History," 21.

3 David Sheff, "Portrait of a Generation," *Rolling Stone,* 524 (1988), 46–57; Wade Clark Roof, *A Generation of Seekers: The Spiritual Journeys of the Baby Boom Generation* (New York, 1993), 40–41; Paul Light, *Baby Boomers* (New York, 1988), 32, 145–146.

4 Whiting's population of 10,880 in 1930 had dropped to 5,155 by 1990. Nearly all of that decline (80 percent) took place after 1950. The Mexican population rose to 10 percent of the town's total in 1980 and stood at 13 percent a decade later. Although the population of Lake County increased between 1950 and 1970, the western portion of the county that contained Whiting suffered a loss of close to 10 percent. Job losses in refining were also striking in this era – nearly 4,000 in Indiana between 1958 and 1966, and in Lake County, 36 percent between 1960 and 1969. Manufacturing jobs in Lake County, outside Gary and Hammond, also declined by 4.7 percent. See D. Jeanne Patterson, *Indiana Regional Economic Development and Planning* (Bloomington, 1971), II, 27, 81, 93; Indiana Dept. of Commerce, *Indiana: an Economic Perspective* (Indianapolis, 1970), 9; Peter Clecak, *America's Quest for the Ideal Self: Dissent and Fulfillment in the 60's and 70's* (New York, 1983), 1–21; James Davison Hunter, *Culture Wars: The Struggle to Define America* (New York, 1991), 120–126. On the changing nature of authority in modern America, see Morris Janowitz, *The Last Half-Century: Societal Change and Politics in America* (Chicago, 1978), 221–263.

5 Regina Gagnier, *Subjectivities: A History of Self-Representation in Britain, 1832–1920* (New York, 1991), 3–10 (thanks to John Eakin for this reference). Patrick H. Hutton, "Collective Memory and Collective Mentalities," *Historical Reflections,* XV (1980), 311–322; Peter Niedermuller, "From Stories of Life to Life History: Historic Context, Social Processes, and the Biographical Method," in Tamas Hofer and Niedermuller (eds.), *Life History as Cultural Construction* (Budapest, 1988), 451–452; Barbara Myerhoff, *Number Our Days* (New York, 1978), 221. On the public construction of memory see Pierre Nora, "Between Memory and History: Les Lieux de Memorie," *Representations,* XXVI (1989), 7–24; Michael Kammen, *Mystic Chords of Memory: The Transformation of Tradition in American Culture* (New York, 1991); Bodnar, *Remaking America: Public Memory, Commemoration, and Patriotism* (Princeton, 1992).

6 Paul John Eakin, *Touching the World: Reference in Autobiographies* (Princeton, 1992), 72. On the matter of self-representation in oral histories, see Luisa Passerini, *Fascism in Popular Memory* (Cambridge, 1987), 22–23, 60–61. See the insightful discussion about the subjectivity of oral sources in Alessandro Portelli, *The Death of Luigi Trastulli and Other Stories:*

Form and Meaning in Oral History (Albany, 1991), ix, 48–53. On the importance of narratives in human cognition and moral thinking, see Jerome Bruner, *Actual Minds, Possible Worlds* (Cambridge, Mass., 1986).

7 Joshua Meyrowitz, *No Sense of Place: The Impact of Electronic Media on Social Behavior* (New York, 1985), 309.

8 Whiting Project Interview (hereinafter WPI), 91–14. The Whiting Oral History Project consisted of 100 interviews conducted between 1990 and 1992. Most interviews were conducted in Whiting, but sessions were also held with former residents who had moved to other Indiana towns and to Arizona. The respondents were selected at random from a list of names generated by contacting such organizations as churches and labor unions, and from suggestions given by interviewees. Interviewers included the author, Chad Berry, David Dabertin, Lisa Orr, and John Wolford. Transcripts of all interviews are on deposit at the Oral History Research Center at Indiana University, Bloomington.

9 Michael Walzer, *Spheres of Justice: A Defense of Pluralism and Equality* (New York, 1983), 31, 64–94. Due to considerations of space, the discussion of moral outlook in this research note does not go beyond the practice of justice, or fairness, and solidarity, or caring. Some scholars might argue that the former is more characteristic of men and the latter of women. Focusing on the issue of generations inevitably submerges the issue of gender differences, but the Whiting data does not strongly affirm the gendered arguments of such scholars as Carol Gilligan that women's identities are more oriented to relationships and less centered on independence than men's are, and, thus, that their stories include a stronger plea for caring than for justice. In Whiting's older generation, both men and women presented themselves as strong individuals who were also bound to the concerns of the working-class community in which their identities and moral outlook was formed. There was a *tendency* for women to talk more about caregiving but no evidence of a significant gender division on this point. See David L. Norton, *Democracy and Moral Development* (Berkeley, 1991), 28; Gilligan, *In a Different Voice; Psychological Theory and Women's Development* (Cambridge, 1982), 73–75; Jürgen Habermas, "Justice and Solidarity: On the Discussion concerning State 6," in Thomas E. Wren (ed.), *The Moral Domain: Essays in the Ongoing Discussion Between Philosophy and the Social Sciences* (Cambridge, Mass., 1990), 224–251.

10 WPI, 91–23; 91–24; 91–19.

11 *Stanolind Record*, 24 May 1943, 1–10; 26 May 1945, 1–4. *St. John's Parish News* (Whiting, Indiana), 16 Aug. 1942; 1 Nov. 1942.

12 WPI 91–29; 91–32; 91–173.

13 Christopher Lasch, *The Culture of Narcissism* (London, 1980), 84–87; Giddens, *Modernity and Self-Identity* (Stanford, 1991), 173–175, argued that Lasch tended to deny the potential for individual agency in a modern culture free of traditional authorities.

CHAPTER 4

Growing Up Asian in America

Kesaya E. Noda

Born in Palo Alto, California to Japanese-American parents, Kesaya E. Noda (1950–) grew up on a family farm in rural New Hampshire. She studied for two years in Japan after high school, and graduated from Stanford University in 1973. In 1981 she published The Yamato Colony: 1906–1960, Livingston, California, *a history of the Japanese-American farming community where her grandparents settled after migrating from Japan. Since earning her MA from Harvard Divinity School in 1987, Noda has worked in higher education, and as a poet and activist. In the following memoir, originally published in* Making Waves *(1989) an Asian-American Studies women's movement reader, she explores her social location as a middle-class Japanese-American woman whose multiple identities are rooted at the intersection of US and family history.*

Sometimes when I was growing up, my identity seemed to hurtle toward me and paste itself right to my face. I felt that way, encountering the stereotypes of my race perpetuated by non-Japanese people (primarily white) who may or may not have had contact with other Japanese in America. "You don't like cheese, do you?" someone would ask. "I know your people don't like cheese." Sometimes questions came making allusions to history. That was another aspect of the identity. Events that had happened quite apart from the me who stood silent in that moment connected my face with an incomprehensible past. "Your parents were in California? Were they in those camps during the war?" And sometimes there were phrases or nicknames: "Lotus Blossom." I was sometimes addressed or referred to as racially Japanese, sometimes as Japanese American, and sometimes as an Asian woman. Confusions and distortions abounded.

How is one to know and define oneself? From the inside – within a context that is self defined, from a grounding in community and a connection with culture and history that are comfortably accepted? Or from the outside – in terms of messages received from the media and people who are often ignorant? Even as an adult I can still see two sides of my face and past. I can see from the inside out, in freedom. And I can see from the outside in, driven by the old voices of childhood and lost in anger and fear.

I am Racially Japanese

A voice from my childhood says: "You are other. You are less than. You are unalterably alien." This voice has its own history. We have indeed been seen as other and alien since the early years of our arrival in the United States. The very first immigrants were welcomed and sought as laborers to replace the dwindling numbers of Chinese, whose influx had been cut off by the Chinese Exclusion Act of 1882. The Japanese fell natural heir to the same anti-Asian prejudice that had arisen against the Chinese. As soon as they began striking for better wages, they were no longer welcomed.

I can see myself today as a person historically defined by law and custom as being forever alien. Being neither "free white," nor "African," our people in California were deemed "aliens, ineligible for citizenship," no matter how long they intended to stay here. Aliens ineligible for citizenship were prohibited from owning, buying, or leasing land. They did not and could not belong here. The voice in me remembers that I am always a *Japanese* American in the eyes of many. A third-generation German American is an American. A third-generation Japanese American is a Japanese American. Being Japanese means being a danger to the country during the war and knowing how to use chopsticks. I wear this history on my face.

I move to the other side. I see a different light and claim a different context. My race is a line that stretches across ocean and time to link me to the shrine where my grandmother was raised. Two high, white banners lift in the wind at the top of the stone steps leading to the shrine. It is time for the summer festival. Black characters are written against the sky as boldly as the clouds, as lightly as kites, as sharply as the big black crows I used to see above the fields in New Hampshire. At festival time there is liquor and food, ritual, discipline, and abandonment. There is music and drunkenness and invocation. There is hope. Another season has come. Another season has gone.

I am racially Japanese. I have a certain claim to this crazy place where the prayers intoned by a neighboring Shinto priest (standing in for my grandmother's nephew who is sick) are drowned out by the rehearsals for the pop singing contest in which most of the villagers will compete later that night. The village elders, the priest, and I stand respectfully upon the immaculate, shining wooden floor of the outer shrine, bowing our heads before the hidden powers. During the patchy intervals when I can hear him, I notice the priest has a stutter. His voice flutters up to my ears only occasionally because two men and a woman are singing gustily into a microphone in the compound testing the sound system. A prerecorded tape of guitars, samisens, and drums accompanies them. Rock music and Shinto prayers. That night to loud applause and cheers, a young man is given the award for the most *netsuretsu* – passionate, burning – rendition of a song. We roar our approval of the reward.

Never mind that his voice had wandered and slid, now slightly above, now slightly below the given line of the melody. Netsuretsu. Netsuretsu.

In the morning, my grandmother's sister kneels at the foot of the stone stairs to offer her morning prayers. She is too crippled to climb the stairs, so each morning she kneels here upon the path. She shuts her eyes for a few seconds, her motions as matter of fact as when she washes rice. I linger longer than she does, so reluctant to leave, savoring the connection I feel with my grandmother in America, the past, and the power that lives and shines in the morning sun.

Our family has served this shrine for generations. The family's need to protect this claim to identity and place outweighs any individual claim to any individual hope. I am Japanese.

I am a Japanese American

"Weak." I hear the voice from my childhood years. "Passive," I hear. Our parents and grandparents were the ones who were put into those camps. They went without resistance; they offered cooperation as proof of loyalty to America. "Victim," I hear. And, "Silent."

Our parents are painted as hard workers who were socially uncomfortable and had difficulty expressing even the smallest opinion. Clean, quiet, motivated, and determined to match the American way; that is us, and that is the story of our time here.

"Why did you go into those camps," I raged at my parents, frightened by my own inner silence and timidity. "Why didn't you do anything to resist? Why didn't you name it the injustice it was?" Couldn't our parents even think? Couldn't they? Why were we so passive?

I shift my vision and my stance. I am in California. My uncle is in the midst of the sweet potato harvest. He is pressed, trying to get the harvesting crews onto the field as quickly as possible, worried about the flow of equipment and people. His big pickup is pulled off to the side, motor running, door ajar. I see two tractors in the yard in front of an old shed; the flat bed harvesting platform on which the workers will stand has already been brought over from the other field. It's early morning. The workers stand loosely grouped and at ease, but my uncle looks as harried and tense as a police officer trying to unsnarl a New York City traffic jam. Driving toward the shed, I pull my car off the road to make way for an approaching tractor. The front wheels of the car sink luxuriously into the soft, white sand by the roadside and the car slides to a dreamy halt, tail still on the road. I try to move forward. I try to move back. The front bites contentedly into the sand, the back lifts itself at a jaunty angle. My uncle sees me and storms down the road, running. He is shouting before he is even near me.

"What's the matter with you," he screams. "What the hell are you doing?" In his frenzy, he grabs his hat off his head and slashes it through the air across his knee. He is beside himself. "Don't you know how to drive in sand? What's the matter with you? You've blocked the whole roadway. How am I supposed to get my tractors out of here? Can't you use your head? You've cut off the whole roadway, and we've got to get out of here."

I stand on the road before him helplessly thinking, "No, I don't know how to drive in sand. I've never driven in sand."

"I'm sorry, uncle," I say, burying a smile beneath a look of sincere apology. I notice my deep amusement and my affection for him with great curiosity. I am usually devastated by anger. Not this time.

During the several years that follow I learn about the people and the place, and much more about what has happened in this California village where my parents grew up. The issei, our grandparents, made this settlement in the desert. Their first crops were eaten by rabbits and ravaged by insects. The land was so barren that men walking from house to house sometimes got lost. Women came here too. They bore children in 114 degree heat, then carried the babies with them into the fields to nurse when they reached the end of each row of grapes or other truck farm crops.

I had had no idea what it meant to buy this kind of land and make it grow green. Or how, when the war came, there was no space at all for the subtlety of being who we were – Japanese Americans. Either/or was the way. I hadn't understood that people were literally afraid for their lives then, that their money had been frozen in banks; that there was a five-mile travel limit; that when the early evening curfew came and they were inside their houses, some of them watched helplessly as people they knew went into their barns to steal their belongings. The police were patrolling the road, interested only in violators of curfew. There was no help for them in the face of thievery. I had not been able to imagine before what it must have felt like to be an American – to know absolutely that one is an American – and yet to have almost everyone else deny it. Not only deny it, but challenge that identity with machine guns and troops of white American soldiers. In those circumstances it was difficult to say, "I'm a Japanese American." "American" had to do.

But now I can say that I am a Japanese American. It means I have a place here in this country, too. I have a place here on the East Coast, where our neighbor is so much a part of our family that my mother never passes her house at night without glancing at the lights to see if she is home and safe; where my parents have hauled hundreds of pounds of rocks from fields and arduously planted Christmas trees and blueberries, lilacs, asparagus, and crab apples; where my father still dreams of angling a stream to a new bed so that he can dig a pond in the field and fill it with water and fish. "The neighbors already came for their Christmas tree?" he asks in December. "Did they like it? Did they like it?"

I have a place on the West Coast where my relatives still farm, where I heard the stories of feuds and backbiting, and where I saw that people survived and flourished because fundamentally they trusted and relied upon one another. A death in the family is not just a death in a family; it is a death in the community. I saw people help each other with money, materials, labor, attention, and time. I saw men gather once a year, without fail, to clean the grounds of a ninety-year-old woman who had helped the community before, during, and after the war. I saw her remembering them with birthday cards sent to each of their children.

I come from a people with a long memory and a distinctive grace. We live our thanks. And we are Americans. Japanese Americans.

I am a Japanese American Woman

Woman. The last piece of my identity. It has been easier by far for me to know myself in Japan and to see my place in America than it has been to accept my line of connection with my own mother. She was my dark self, a figure in whom I thought I saw all that I feared most in myself. Growing into womanhood and looking for some model of strength, I turned away from her. Of course, I could not find what I sought. I was looking for a black feminist or a white feminist. My mother is neither white nor black.

My mother is a woman who speaks with her life as much as with her tongue. I think of her with her own mother. Grandmother had Parkinson's disease and it had frozen her gait and set her fingers, tongue, and feet jerking and trembling in a terrible dance. My aunts and uncles wanted her to be able to live in her own home. They fed her, bathed her, dressed her, awoke at midnight to take her for one last trip to the bathroom. My aunts (her daughters-in-law) did most of the care, but my mother went from New Hampshire to California each summer to spend a month living with grandmother, because she wanted to and because she wanted to give my aunts at least a small rest. During those hot summer days, mother lay on the couch watching the television or reading, cooking foods that grandmother liked, and speaking little. Grandmother thrived under her care.

The time finally came when it was too dangerous for grandmother to live alone. My relatives kept finding her on the floor beside her bed when they went to wake her in the mornings. My mother flew to California to help clean the house and make arrangements for grandmother to enter a local nursing home. On her last day at home, while grandmother was sitting in her big, overstuffed armchair, hair combed and wearing a green summer dress, my mother went to her and knelt at her feet. "Here, Mamma," she said. "I've polished your shoes." She lifted grandmother's legs and helped her into the shiny black shoes. My grandmother looked down and smiled slightly. She left her house walking, supported by her children, carrying her pocket book, and wearing her polished black shoes. "Look, Mamma," my mom had said, kneeling. "I've polished your shoes."

Just the other day, my mother came to Boston to visit. She had recently lost a lot of weight and was pleased with her new shape and her feeling of good health. "Look at me, Kes," she exclaimed, turning toward me, front and back, as naked as the day she was born. I saw her small breasts and the wide, brown scar, belly button to pubic hair, that marked her because my brother and I were both born by Caesarean section. Her hips were small. I was not a large baby, but there was so little room for me in her that when she was carrying me she could not even begin to bend over toward the floor. She hated it, she said.

"Don't I look good? Don't you think I look good?"

I looked at my mother, smiling and as happy as she, thinking of all the times I have seen her naked. I have seen both my parents naked throughout my life, as they have seen me. From childhood through adulthood we've had our naked moments, sharing baths, idle conversations picked up as we moved between showers and closets, hurried moments at the beginning of days, quiet moments at the end of days.

I know this to be Japanese, this ease with the physical, and it makes me think of an old, Japanese folk song. A young nursemaid, a fifteen-year-old girl, is singing a lullaby to a baby who is strapped to her back. The nursemaid has been sent as a servant to a place far from her own home. "We're the beggars," she says, "and they are the nice people. Nice people wear fine sashes. Nice clothes."

> If I should drop dead,
> bury me by the roadside!
> I'll give a flower
> to everyone who passes.
> What kind of flower?
> The cam-cam-camellia [tsun-tsun-tsubaki]
> watered by Heaven
> alms water.

The nursemaid is the intersection of heaven and earth, the intersection of the human, the natural world, the body, and the soul. In this song, with clear eyes, she looks steadily at life, which is sometimes so very terrible and sad. I think of her while looking at my mother, who is standing on the red and purple carpet before me, laughing, without any clothes.

I am my mother's daughter. And I am myself.

I am a Japanese American woman.

Epilogue

I recently heard a man from West Africa share some memories of his childhood. He was raised Muslim, but when he was a young man, he found himself deeply drawn to Christianity. He struggled against this inner impulse for years, trying to avoid the church yet feeling pushed to return to it again and again. "I would have done *anything* to avoid the change," he said. At last, he became Christian. Afterwards he was afraid to go home, fearing that he would not be accepted. The fear was groundless, he discovered, when at last he returned – he had separated himself, but his family and friends (all Muslim) had not separated themselves from him.

The man, who is now a professor of religion, said that in the Africa he knew as a child and a young man, pluralism was embraced rather than feared. There was "a kind of tolerance that did not deny your particularity," he said. He alluded to zestful, spontaneous debates that would sometimes loudly erupt between Muslims and

Christians in the village's public spaces. His memories of an atheist who harrangued the villagers when he came to visit them once a week moved me deeply. Perhaps the man was an agricultural advisor or inspector. He harrassed the women. He would say:

> "Don't go to the fields! Don't even bother to go to the fields. Let God take care of you. He'll send you the food. If you believe in God, why do you need to work? You don't need to work! Let God put the seeds in the ground. Stay home."

The professor said, "The women laughed, you know? They just laughed. Their attitude was, 'Here is a child of God. When will he come home?'"

The storyteller, the professor of religion, smiled a most fantastic, tender smile as he told this story. "In my country, there is a deep affirmation of the oneness of God," he said. "The atheist and the women were having quite different experiences in their encounter, though the atheist did not know this. He saw himself as quite separate from the women. But the women did not see themselves as being separate from him. 'Here is a child of God,' they said. 'When will he come home?'"

Study Questions

1 How does Noda figure out her identity as a Japanese-American woman? What is her "social location"?
2 Compare Noda's discussion of "outside" influences versus "inside" influences to Kirk's and Okazawa-Rey's concept of the macro, meso, and micro levels of social relationships.
3 How does Noda's sense of personal, community, and national identity change as she comes to understand what Bodner would call her family's "generational memory"?
4 What events of the 1960s and 1970s, the decades when Noda was growing up, influenced the way she wrote about her identity in 1989?

PART II

World War II and the Postwar Era, 1940–1960

World War II brought an end to the Great Depression (1929–40), the worst economic crisis in US history, during which a substantial number of Americans were unemployed. In 1940, the US population was approximately 131,000,000. According to historian Richard Polenberg, the majority of Americans, 60 to 70 percent, were working class or lower middle class, with incomes of $1,200 to $1,600 a year; 15 to 25 percent were poor, earning less than $1,000 a year; and 15 percent belonged to the upper middle classes, with incomes of $2,500 to $5,000 a year. About 25 percent of Americans had graduated from high school, and 5 percent from college. The US was not yet a "middle-class" nation.

World War II was a major turning point in the lives of the majority of Americans of every class, race, and region: 16 million men and women served in the armed forces; 15 million more migrated to take war-related jobs, including 4.5 million women who became 36 percent of the labor force. After Japan attacked Pearl Harbor, there was an enormous effort on the part of the government and mass media to "sell" the war as a people's war for freedom. Wartime mobility disrupted ethnic neighborhoods, and people mixed, met, and worked together from many different backgrounds. This led to the strong sense of national solidarity that united most Americans in support of the war. But it also led to violent conflict and the suppression of civil rights, particularly in the case of Japanese and Japanese Americans whom the government forcibly moved into internment camps. African-American leaders called for a "double 'V' victory," against fascism abroad and racism at home, laying the groundwork for the postwar Civil Rights Movement.

After the war, federal government programs provided hiring preferences and stipends for college tuition to veterans, as well as loan guarantees and low interest mortgages for buying homes, farms, and small businesses, which primarily benefited white working-class and middle-class families. Many Americans also benefited from the millions of miles of highways built with federal taxes, which literally paved the way for the US to become a predominantly suburban (and segregated) nation. Labor unions achieved some of their greatest victories after the end of the war, entering into a partnership with business and the federal government that made it possible for a substantial number of blue-collar workers to invest in homes. You might ask your families if they benefited from any of these government programs.

The 1950s saw the growth of the US economy in many sectors, along with the development of a "Cold War" between the USA and the USSR and China that led to the persecution of Americans who were communists or so-called communist sympathizers. The international Cold War was accompanied on the domestic front by the return of many working women to the home, and the growth of the suburban family ideal, which has had a profound influence on the way that many Americans think about the family and the nation.

CHAPTER 5

War Babies

Maria Fleming Tymoczko

Maria Fleming Tymoczko, a professor of comparative literature, was the first person in her family to go to college. She was born in Providence, Rhode Island, in 1943. When her father shipped off to World War II before she was a year old, she grew up with her mother's Czechoslovakian immigrant mother, sisters, and brothers, in Cleveland. Tymoczko's books include The Irish "Ulysses" *(1994) and* Translation in a Postcolonial Culture *(1999). This essay was originally published in* Born Into a World at War *(2000), a collection of essays written by members of the Harvard and Radcliffe Class of 1965, reflecting on how their lives were shaped by being children born during World War II.*

As infants, most of us in the Class of 1965 were called "war babies." We were regarded as somewhat different, marked out as anomalous – [...] precious life springing from death, little lives created and salvaged out of the peril and rubble that were consuming half the world. There weren't a lot of us and we were cherished accordingly. We were the affirmation of the fecundity and endurance of the species, even in the face of the chaos that wrenched our fathers and mothers apart. We were seen as the epitome of the future for which the fighting was engaged, the hope held in the hearts of all the adults whose lives were being ravaged. We came to awareness of ourselves with the label *war baby* in our ears, with a subliminal sense of the price paid for our lives and our future. That price included sacrifice by those who held us most dear and sometimes the wounding, disabling, or even death of our own relatives. For American war babies those relatives at risk were usually fathers and uncles, though there were some grandfathers involved as well.

World War II brought an early politicization to my life. My family was working-class and none of my grandparents had completed a high school education. My father's parents were both factory workers, my grandfather having come as a child from Scotland. My father's mother was from British Isles stock that had been settled in America a long time, long enough at any rate for her great-grandfather to have starved to death in the Confederate prison at Andersonville. As the oldest child of six, she had a hard life, particularly after her father was killed in an accident working on the railroad. Because of her father's accident, my grandmother dropped out of school at the age of 12 to help support the family. In 1941 the aspirations of my father and his siblings were bounded by the prospects of their own parents' lives – factory work, or bartending, or manual labor of some sort. Or maybe the exotic: in the case of my good-looking Aunt Louise, a stint in the chorus line of the Roxy, the local burlesque house on the national circuit, which she tried for a short time, until her career was cut short by her mother's adamant opposition. Louise retaliated by marrying a minor member of the Mafia, but that's another story.

My mother's family were immigrants from Czechoslovakia, the sort of immigrants who were doing their best to be upwardly mobile. My grandfather was a shoemaker, a small-scale entrepreneur who had dreams of becoming landed gentry in Slovakia by buying land there with profits from his American shops. My maternal grandmother had nowhere to go but up. She was the daughter of peasants who lived in one room in a farm complex owned by a landlord, peasants whose only possessions were household goods and a clutch of geese. Like my father's mother, this grandmother also began to work at the age of 12, when she was sent to the small city nearest her village to be a servant for a rich Hungarian family. It was an experience that made her determined to seek a better life in America, where she aspired to freedom, equality of a rudimentary sort, and flush toilets. [. . .]

My parents met initially in a junior high school in Cleveland, Ohio, and they married in 1942 shortly after Pearl Harbor. My father had graduated from high school but my mother dropped out of tenth grade to marry just after she turned 16. Both were fresh-faced, bright teenagers, with aspirations molded by the Roosevelts and images of stability from the 1930s. My father had led a somewhat wayward and wild youth, which probably was attractive to my mother, who came from a strict and pious Baptist household. She also liked the fact that he was "a real American" – he didn't have the faintest trace of ethnicity.

The 1930s was a very difficult time for people like my parents' families. Survival was the paramount concern and it tightened people's focus on themselves. Both my grandmothers slaved to keep their children alive, one on the assembly lines, the other washing floors. The stories my father told of his youth were not political. They were about living in foster homes so his mother could earn a livelihood, and forays to the library for amusement, and going (with a suitcase of history books) to summer camp for poor children, and hitchhiking cross-country, and minor theft, and local bootleg-ging. My mother told about wanting to be American, and refusing to speak Slovak, and being angry, and stealing green tomatoes from vines, and yearning for a Shirley Temple doll. World War II shattered that emotional isolationism bred of economic impoverishment.

During the war and afterward, the world became the context of our lives. What happened elsewhere mattered in a new way. It had a connection to us and to our daily doings in Cleveland. All the men of my parents' generation were caught up in the war, except my father's brother Bill, who was a quadriplegic, and my mother's brother Johnny, 13 years old when I was born. My father's older brother Jack joined the marines and became leader of his platoon by virtue of being able to beat all the other men in the group in hand-to-hand fighting. He had been decathlon champion of his high school and a semi-pro boxer before he joined up. My mother's brother Paul had been in the Civilian Conservation Corps during high school and he joined the army with a band of buddies just after war was declared. I was born in December 1943 and my 19- year-old father enlisted in the army shortly thereafter. Even the men who stayed at home did so because they were part of the war effort. Uncle Joe worked at a foundry in Cleveland, casting parts for bombers, a valuable part of war work that earned him an exemption month after month.

The world became somewhere family members might be sent and, later, after the war was done, it was somewhere uncles or friends or neighbors had been. We learned that what happened elsewhere mattered. It had connection. You couldn't ignore it, because what happened in the world, in politics, might come home, catch your own life up, and change you forever. Because his eyes were so weak, my own father was never shipped out, but he was terrified that he might be during the big buildup before the Normandy landings. So Normandy was close to us. My father might have been there, part of that desperate scramble through the waves, under fire, to gain a beachhead. The Pacific islands were where Uncle Jack was landing with his marines, and, later, the place where he rescued one of his men hit in a Japanese ambush, and, later still, the place he was machine-gunned himself and pulled to safety by his loyal and grateful men. Australia was the place where one uncle had a brief marriage and a war bride who wouldn't return to America with him. Her dark sepia photograph was in our family album, smiling and beautiful, flat and unchanging, but she herself, soft and warm, who had kissed my uncle, was still there, in Australia.

Even as a primary school child, struggling to learn the geography of the housing project I lived in with my parents, and then, as my circles widened, the geography of the neighborhood and the geography of Cleveland, I can remember my father talking to me about events that were happening in the world. Telling me they mattered. Places that were only words to me as a girl – Nuremberg and Korea and Taiwan and Berlin – were a part of our kitchen conversation, had an entitlement on our lives. The family conversations were reinforced at school by the *Weekly Reader*, which included stories about Egypt, the Suez Canal, Israel, India, and Pakistan, as if those places were our backyard and the politics of those countries a matter which even we children should think about. That sense of our lives being played out across the globe, the whole world, set a context for my response to Vietnam and the US presence in Vietnam decades later, a context shared by many of our generation. [...]

The war radically altered expectations among the working classes of Cleveland, and I grew up – we all grew up – on the other side of a tectonic shift. Even though women have always worked in my family – as women always do in preindustrial cultures, in peasant cultures, in farming cultures, in poor cultures – a middle-class American ideal had seeped into their consciousnesses in the 1930s, the ideal of women being supported by their husbands and staying home like ladies to keep the house and kids. That's what the young women of my family were earnestly heading toward, but during the war they learned the pleasures of paid work, pleasures never abandoned afterward.

It happened because the men were at war. Rosie the Riveter has become a sort of national icon, especially in the women's movement, but we forget people like my mother, Annie the Pharmacist's Helper. One day Grandma came home with news from the clinic where she had been and later was again a charwoman, having given up that job for a better-paid position on the munitions assembly lines during the war. One of the doctors had approached her to say, "I need your eldest daughter to come work for me. My pharmacist has been drafted, they're taking every able-bodied man. I need someone to count out the pills and give the people the medicines they need. She's a smart girl and she doesn't have any children to take care of. We need her." Aunt Mary talked it over with her husband, but they came to the conclusion that she shouldn't go to work – he was man enough to support her, and it would be more patriotic for her to continue volunteer war work than take a paid position that someone else might need. But my 19-year-old mother said, "I want to do it."

So Mother became the acting pharmacist and never looked back. She worked her whole life in the medical profession, finally taking exams to become certified as a physician's assistant in the 1970s (along with a lot of Vietnam War vets), and work became one of the most satisfying parts of her life. Many of us have mothers who during the war took over for men at some sort of work, running their husbands' businesses, or driving buses, or working in factories, or being union stewards, like my father's mother. When we were infants, before our conscious memories, we grew up seeing women in the world, at work, managing civilian life. And those women who did so in our own families entered into a sense of self-possession, a sense of entitlement, that lies there at the threshold of our awareness. This public presence of women at work faded out gradually during our childhoods, especially during the 1950s when there was a campaign to get women back in the kitchen, but I'll never forget how much I liked it when the bus driver was a woman and how much I missed those women drivers as they were gradually replaced by men.

Another tectonic shift also predates my conscious memories or my conscious understanding of the order of things, the class shift that happened after the war to working families such as my own as a result of the GI Bill. Many if not most of the members of the Harvard-Radcliffe Class of 1965 have a long family tradition of higher education, some for generations at Harvard itself. For a few of us, however, the entitlement to higher education can be traced directly to the GI Bill, and women who come from such backgrounds, like myself, may be conscious of being the first women of their families to have a college education.

My family's educational expectations shifted radically because of the war. The men who returned from the war all went to college on the GI Bill. They were the direct beneficiaries of that amazing democratization of education that happened in the United States in the late 1940s, that opened up the lives of people who didn't grow up with privilege, and that shifted their careers and class irrevocably. Uncle Jack, the marine, became a civil engineer. Uncle Paul became a math teacher. My father headed himself toward teaching history. And their influence spread to the younger members of the family as well. My mother's twin siblings, too young to be in the war, were sent to college when the time came, and they too became teachers. College and university educations opened people up in all sorts of other ways as well, and, as a consequence of the war and its aftermath, my cousins and siblings and I inhabit a much larger world than did our parents and grandparents.

I remember my father being in college. His oak desk and typewriter had pride of place in our small public-housing living room. [. . .]

For those of us born in the war, the time during World War II itself gave many of us a rather different psychosexual foundation from those of our older or younger siblings and, indeed, an orientation different from the standard presumed in Western culture and Western psychology. When our fathers went off to war, many of our mothers moved back into their own mothers' homes, bringing their young children along, even giving birth to new children in those homes. As a result, we the children grew up in multigenerational families. In some cases more than one daughter came home, so the family grouping was extended and complex. Sometimes the head of the clan was a grandfather, beloved or tyrannical or both, but often these complex families had female heads of household. This is what happened to me.

My parents were living in Rhode Island when I was born, so I started life in a conventional nuclear family. When I was three months old, my father enlisted in the army and my mother packed up and took me on the train from Providence back to her family in Cleveland. My grandmother had decided this was what should be done and she paid for the train ticket.

My grandmother lived in the central part of Cleveland in a Slovak-Italian ethnic neighborhood on a tiny property that had two houses on it. The "big" house had four small rooms and an unheated attic where the young people slept. Mother and I lived there with Grandma, the young twins Emily and John, and Aunt Bessie, who was just a little older than Mother. There was no central heating, just a kerosene stove in the living room and another stove in the kitchen. The running water in the bathroom was cold, unless you lit the tiny gas heater mounted on the wall. In the little house on the property (three rooms, located four feet behind Grandma's house on the same lot) lived Aunt Mary and Uncle Joe.

Grandma gave up her bedroom so that my mother and I had a place to live. Aunt Emily says she can't remember her mother lying down to sleep for a long time during those years: she'd just rest on the couch. We ate most suppers together, all pell-mell around my grandmother's wooden kitchen table. When I was big enough to graduate from a high chair, I sat squeezed in on the bench behind the table with my teenage Auntie Emily and Uncle Johnny, and sometimes with my mother as well. Everyone was in charge of me, everyone took turns taking care of me, especially while my mother was sick. (She was quite ill with a thyroid problem that kept her bedridden for weeks after we arrived in Cleveland, a problem that ultimately required surgery and then more bed rest). I felt loved by everyone, even my young aunt and uncle who were themselves displaced as the babies of the family by me. We were all crowded together under the rule of my matriarchal grandmother, whom everyone but me called "Mama," living as one household complete with cats and African violets in a space that probably was little bigger than the dining room of my present house.

In many ways it was a very difficult time for us all, with my mother sick and difficulty getting various kinds of food and other commodities, and anxiety about the safety of the young men of the family who were soldiers. From 1942, when Uncle Paul was shipped to the Pacific theater, he was not seen again until after the war, and for nine of those months he was missing in action separated from his battalion, hiding behind enemy lines in the jungles of Luzon. So there was constant worry.

And yet in other ways the war created a wonderful environment for a baby's first two years, in many ways better than the isolated nuclear family environments of the suburbs that babies born in the 1950s grew up in. It was an environment more typical of an earlier era, when extended families lived together in villages or on multi-generational farms. My family lived in a real neighborhood, where people knew each other and visited together, where people from "the old country" gathered together, speaking their native languages, even as the young were becoming American. I became the baby of more than just a family, recognized and indulged by various friends and neighbors as well. Like many others born in the war, because of my nuclear family's displacement, I was raised by a village, so to speak, in our case a village within a city. For my own life, this was infinitely better and more stable than a childhood spent along with two teenage parents. Those years when Mother was 18 to 20 and I grew from infant to two-and-a-half-year-old toddler were critical for us. Many years later my mother acknowledged that, by taking us in during the was, Grandma had "saved both our lives."

I trace many of my personal strengths to that formative period of living with my extended family, full of loving caretakers and multiple role models. My earliest memories took shape with Mother working and me being watched part of most days by someone else – Auntie Mary, or Grandma, or the twins, Johnny and Emily. There was almost always someone to meet my needs willingly, something interesting going on to watch and listen to, and someone to keep me in line. There was a surfeit of love and words – stories, debates, arguments, quarrels, reading aloud, praying, or singing – in at least three languages, the English and Slovak spoken in our house and the Italian I could hear spoken by our noisy, voluble neighbors, the Costellis, just 15 feet away.

It was an anomalous period when our domestic world, almost devoid of men, was utterly ruled by a hierarchy of women: first Grandma, then Aunt Mary as oldest married sister, then Mother as the one with the child, then Aunt Bessie, then Aunt Emily as the dominant twin. Although any of them could lose her temper and shout, and although my grandmother was strict and straitlaced and uncompromising, I don't remember ever being frightened or terrorized in those early years. I was safe in my grandmother's house. And when my father came back from the war and I began to live for the first time in my remembered life with my parents alone, I was desolate. I felt I had been torn from my real family and sent away for fosterage, away from most of my mothers. Over the years I've wondered whether my feminism – and perhaps the feminism of other women my age – is anchored in the experiences of those formative and preconscious years, when our psyches were being shaped in a woman's world, where women's love enveloped us, where women worked and ruled, where women felt good about themselves, where women held power by right, where women's ways and bodies were the norm.

One of the darkest sides of being born in the war was that reunion with the men who straggled back from the fighting in '45 and '46 and '47 to shatter our civilian peace. So many of those young soldiers came home damaged, some physically, but more mentally. They came home strangers to their children, strangers to their wives and parents, and strangers to themselves. This is the insight most striking to my women's political group and to others I've talked with who were born in the war: how aware our generation is that many of our own men were damaged in one way or another by the Vietnam War – either by being soldiers in the war or by not being soldiers in it – and how the damage done to the men of our own generation was preceded by the damage done to our fathers and uncles and family friends during World War II. What is different in the two cases, however, is that our own generation can talk about the trauma of the Vietnam War, setting the personal in the context of a political analysis, admitting doubts about war itself. Perhaps we learned to speak from the silence of our fathers, who so often could talk of nothing about the war, could only hold it in, repress the experiences, as they tried to protect their women and children, and themselves. [. . .]

My father never fulfilled that early promise of being a history teacher. He had a breakdown in his early thirties and was permanently disabled. In 1961 I was one of two students at Radcliffe College on a full scholarship, one of four National Merit Scholars that year to list for father's occupation "unemployed." How the ghosts and skeletons of World War II figured in his breakdown I don't know, but I do know that there was guilt and shame at his own cowardice and fear while he was a soldier, fear strong enough to make him inhale talcum powder so as to damage his lungs, rather than face the possibility of combat duty. Throughout the rest of his 49 short years of life, he never breathed right and he never slept right again.

Looking back, I see our fathers caught in silence. They had won the war. They were heroes. Yet their own experience of themselves was so often one of failure, of having feelings that heroes should not speak about in our culture: terror, cowardice, shirking, disgust, disillusionment, indifference, loathing, nausea, torment. Between the women and the men a terrible gulf grew, the gulf of the unspoken war. I can hear my mother's voice even now, impatient, when my father spoke of the army, spoke of the hardships of being in the army. "It's over, Bob," she seems to repeat in my memory, "the war is done." I can still hear the contempt in her voice when she told me years later how he confessed to her about the talcum powder. Those nightmares of war and the alienation from civilian life that they spawned were in some cases named and acknowledged for the first time when the fiftieth anniversaries of World War II brought the experiences alive again. Even those men who did not serve in the military fared scarcely better than the soldiers. Old enough to serve, but kept at home for industry, they often remained curiously embryonic, failing to realize their man-hood. Although many, perhaps most, of the women of my world came out of World

War II stronger, going from strength to strength later in their lives, the men came out battered, further widening that gulf between the sexes in the 1950s. It's hardly a wonder that those of us born in the war – who as "terrible twos" met and first lived with our alienated fathers at the war's end – were not at all happy to find our own generation called to a battlefield that did not even seem just or worthy of sacrifice.

The changes of the United States in the last 50 years are the changes of my family writ large. It is in part from the evolution of countless lower-class families such as my own that we write the palimpsest of the history of America in the last half century. And it is experiences such as those that formed me that separate our younger siblings, the Baby Boomers, from those of us who were born in the war.

Study Questions

1   How did Tymoczko's family life change as a result of the strategies her mother chose for coping with her father's absence in World War II?
2   How did the war affect the family's class position? How did their educational expectations change as a result of the war?
3   Why did Tymoczko's father have such a difficult time adjusting to peacetime?
4   Compare the ways that Kesaya Noda's and Maria Tymoczko's identities were shaped by their families' wartime experiences.

CHAPTER 6

From *Citizen 13660*

Miné Okubo

American artist Miné Okubo (1912–2001) was born in Riverside, California, to Japanese immigrant parents. She took her undergraduate degree at Riverside College and her MFA at the University of California at Berkeley. She received a fellowship to study painting in Paris, but the United States' entry into World War II forced her to return home. In May 1942, as a result of the federal government's suspicion of Japanese Americans, Okubo and her brother were sent to Tanforan, where they lived for six months before being sent to Utah's Topaz internment camp, where they lived for a year and a half. They were among 110,000 people of Japanese descent, nearly two-thirds of whom were US citizens, who were interned during the war. In 1946, she published Citizen 13660, *her account of camp life, from which the following excerpt is taken. Of the book, Okubo has said, "I am recording what happens so others can see and this may not happen to others." The book was republished in 1984 with the original 200 pen and ink drawings, and won the American Book Award that year.*

From Preface to the 1983 Edition

After the attack on Pearl Harbor, the [...] propaganda against the Japanese spread quickly across the country. President Franklin D. [...] Roosevelt issued Executive Order 9066, ordering the mass evacuation from the West Coast and internment all people of Japanese descent.

In the history of the United States this was the first mass evacuation of its kind, in which civilians were removed simply because of their race. Nothing had been prepared or planned for this rushed and forced evacuation. There were untold hardships, sadness, and misery.

At the time of the evacuation, I had just returned from two years of travel and study in Europe on a University of California/Berkeley Fellowship and was working on the Federal Arts Program doing mosaic and fresco murals commissioned by the

United States Army. Although curfew was from 8:00 PM to 6:00 AM and we were not allowed to go beyond a five-mile radius of our home, I received a special permit to travel from Berkeley to Oakland so that I could finish the murals before being evacuated to Tanforan.

In the camps, first at Tanforan and then at Topaz in Utah, I had the opportunity to study the human race from the cradle to the grave, and to see what happens to people when reduced to one status and condition. Cameras and photographs were not permitted in the camps, so I recorded everything in sketches, drawings, and paintings. *Citizen 13660* began as a special group of drawings made to tell the story of camp life for my many friends who faithfully sent letters and packages to let us know we were not forgotten. The illustrations were intended for exhibition purposes.

I left camp when *Fortune* magazine asked me to come to New York to help illustrate the April 1944 issue on Japan. I then decided to make New York my home. In 1946 *Citizen 13660*, the first personal documentation of the evacuation story, was published by Columbia University Press. [. . .]

The US Commission on Wartime Relocation and Internment of Civilians was established in July 1980, and in 1981 ten public hearings were held in cities in the

United States, including three in Alaska. Oral and written testimony was presented to the Commission by many evacuees and others.

I testified at the hearing in New York City. As *Citizen 13660* had been widely reviewed and was considered an important reference book on the Japanese American evacuation and internment, I presented the Commission with a copy of the book in addition to my oral testimony. In my testimony I stressed the need for young people from grade school through college to be educated about the evacuation. I believe that some form of reparation and an apology are due to all those who were evacuated and interned. [. . .]

I am often asked, why am I not bitter and could this happen again? I am a realist with a creative mind, interested in people, so my thoughts are constructive. I am not bitter. I hope that things can be learned from this tragic episode, for I believe it could happen again.

Citizen 13660

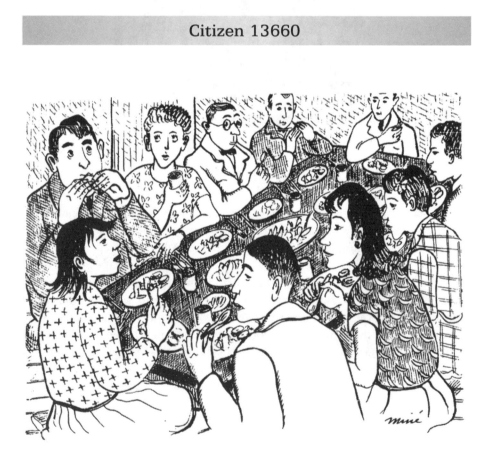

I had a good home and many friends. Everything was going along fine.

Then on December 7, 1941, while my brother and I were having late breakfast I turned on the radio and heard the flash – "Pearl Harbor bombed by the Japanese!" We were shocked. We wondered what this would mean to us and the other people of Japanese descent in the United States.

Our fears came true with the declaration of war against Japan. Radios started blasting, newspapers flaunted scare headlines.

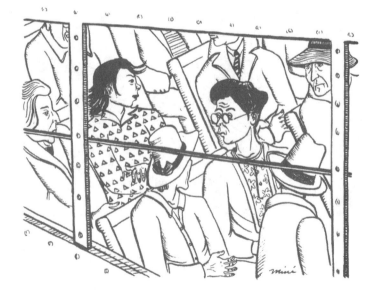

On December 11 the United States declared war on Germany and Italy. On the West Coast there was talk of possible sabotage and invasion by the enemy. It was "Jap" this and "Jap" that. Restricted areas were prescribed and many arrests and detentions of enemy aliens took place. All enemy aliens were required to have certificates of identification. Contraband, such as cameras, binoculars, short-wave radios, and firearms had to be turned over to the local police.

At this time I was working on mosaics for Fort Ord and for the Servicemen's Hospitality House in Oakland, California. I was too busy to bother about the reports of possible evacuation. [. . .]

The people looked at all of us, both citizens and aliens, with suspicion and mistrust.

On February 19, 1942, by executive order of the President, the enemy alien problem was transferred from the Department of Justice to the War Department. Restriction of German and Italian enemy aliens and evacuation of all American citizens and aliens of Japanese ancestry was ordered.

Public Proclamations Nos. 1 and 2 appeared in the newspapers. Three military areas were designated, including practically all of the coastal states of Washington, Oregon, and California, and the inland states of Arizona, Idaho, Montana, Nevada, and Utah. [. . .]

We tagged our baggage with the family number, 13660, and pinned the personal tags on ourselves; we were ready at last.

Our friends came to take us to the Civil Control Station. We took one last look at our happy home.

The first month [in Tanforan] was the hardest because adjustments had to be made to the new mode of life. The naked barracks and whitewashed stalls had to be fixed up into living quarters, and we had to get used to the lack of privacy of camp life.

As we had not brought our carpentry tools with us we had to send for them. While we waited for them to arrive, we searched the scrap-lumber piles for good pieces of wood. As more and more evacuées came into the center, the lumber piles shrank until they disappeared. Some of the people even went so far as to remove lumber from the unused horse stables, while the carpenters at work in the center field were having building materials snatched from under their noses. [...]

All residential blocks looked alike; people were lost all the time.

The clanging of thirty-six makeshift iron bells indicated chowtime in camp [Topaz]. There was the usual line-up and the slow-moving procession to the food counter. Unlike Tanforan, dishes and silverware were provided. The main course was served at the counter and tea was served at the table by the waiters. Side dishes were placed on the tables.

Each mess hall fed from two hundred and fifty to three hundred persons. Food was rationed, as it was for the civilian population on the outside. The allowance for food varied from 31 cents to 45 cents a day per person. Often a meal consisted of rice, bread, and macaroni, or beans, bread, and spaghetti. At one time we were served liver for several weeks, until we went on strike. [. . .]

The Buddhists held an impressive parade and folk dances to celebrate *Hanamatsuri* (a Flower Festival) on the anniversary of the birth of Buddha.

Study Questions

1   What does Okubo suggest about the experience of internment? What are the clues from the visual evidence? What are the clues from the words/text?
2   In 1946, when she wrote this book, how might Okubo have felt vulnerable or endangered as a recent internee? How did she deal with these concerns in the way she chose to present the camps?
3   Take note of Okubo's self-portraits, which appear in most of her pictures. Why do you think she has included these images of herself? How would you characterize the way she looks or what she is doing in the pictures?
4   Compare Okubo's sense of what it means to be Japanese in America with Kesaya Noda's. What historical changes in the times they wrote might account for the differences in their stories?

CHAPTER 7

Containment at Home:
Cold War, Warm Hearth

Elaine Tyler May

Elaine Tyler May (1947–), a professor of US History and American Studies, was born in Los Angeles, the daughter of an endocrinologist father and a mother who helped run his fertility and birth control clinics. May specializes in twentieth-century family history and social history. Her books include Great Expectations: Marriage and Divorce in Post-Victorian America *(1980) and* Barren in the Promised Land: Childless Americans and the Pursuit of Happiness *(1995). This except comes from her 1988 book,* Homeward Bound: American Families in the Cold War Era.

> *I think that this attitude toward women is universal. What we want is to make easier the life of our housewives.*
>
> —VICE PRESIDENT RICHARD NIXON, 1959

In 1959, when the baby boom and the cold war were both at their peak, Vice President Richard M. Nixon traveled to the Soviet Union to engage in what would become one of the most noted verbal sparring matches of the century. In a lengthy and often heated debate with Soviet Premier Nikita Khrushchev at the opening of the American National Exhibition in Moscow, Nixon extolled the virtues of the American way of life, while his opponent promoted the Communist system. What was remarkable about this exchange was its focus. The two leaders did not discuss missiles, bombs, or even modes of government. Rather, they argued over the relative merits of American and Soviet washing machines, televisions, and electric ranges – in what came to be known as the "kitchen debate." [. . .]

For Nixon, American superiority rested on the ideal of the suburban home, complete with modern appliances and distinct gender roles for family members. He proclaimed that the "model" home, with a male breadwinner and a full-time female homemaker, adorned with a wide array of consumer goods, represented the essence of American freedom:

> To us, diversity, the right to choose, . . . is the most important thing. We don't have one decision made at the top by one government official. . . . We have many different manufacturers and many different kinds of washing machines so that the housewives have a choice. . . . Would it not be better to compete in the relative merits of washing machines than in the strength of rockets?[1]

Nixon's focus on household appliances was not accidental. After all, arguments over the strength of rockets would only point out the vulnerability of the United States in the event of a nuclear war between the superpowers; debates over consumer goods would provide a reassuring vision of the good life available in the atomic age. So Nixon insisted that American superiority in the cold war rested not on weapons, but on the secure, abundant family life of modern suburban homes. In these structures, adorned and worshipped by their inhabitants, women would achieve their glory and men would display their success. Consumerism was not an end in itself; it was the means for achieving individuality, leisure, and upward mobility.

The American National Exhibition was a showcase of American consumer goods and leisure-time equipment. But the main attraction, which the two leaders toured, was the full-scale "model" six-room ranch-style house. This model home, filled with labor-saving devices and presumably available to Americans of all classes, was tangible proof, Nixon believed, of the superiority of free enterprise over communism.

In the model kitchen in the model home, Nixon and Khrushchev revealed some basic assumptions of their two systems. Nixon called attention to a built-in panel-controlled washing machine. "In America," he said, "these [washing machines] are designed to make things easier for our women." Khrushchev countered Nixon's boast of comfortable American housewives with pride in productive Soviet female workers: in his country they did not have that "capitalist attitude toward women." Nixon clearly did not understand that the Communist system had no use for full-time housewives, for he replied, "I think that this attitude toward women is universal. What we want is to make easier the life of our housewives." Nixon's knock-out punch in his verbal bout with the Soviet Premier was his articulation of the American postwar domestic dream: successful breadwinners supporting attractive homemakers in affluent suburban homes. [. . .]

With such sentiments about gender and politics widely shared, Nixon's visit was hailed as a major political triumph. Popular journals extolled his diplomatic skills in the face-to-face confrontation with Khrushchev. Many observers credit this trip with establishing Nixon's political future. Clearly, Americans did not find the kitchen debate trivial. The appliance-laden ranch-style home epitomized the expansive, secure lifestyle that postwar Americans wanted. Within the protective walls of the modern home, worrisome developments like sexual liberalism, women's emancipation, and affluence would lead not to decadence but to a wholesome family life. Sex would enhance marriage, emancipated women would professionalize homemaking, and affluence would put an end to material deprivation. Suburbia would serve as a bulwark against communism and class conflict, for according to the widely shared belief articulated by Nixon, it offered a piece of the American dream for everyone. Although Nixon vastly exaggerated the availability of the suburban home, he described a type of domestic life that had become a reality for many Americans – and a viable aspiration for many more. [. . .]

While the home seemed to offer the best hope for freedom, it also appeared to be a fragile institution, subject to forces beyond its control. Economic hardship had torn families asunder, and war had scattered men far from home and drawn women into the public world of work. The postwar years did little to alleviate fears that similar disruptions might occur again. In spite of widespread affluence, many believed that the reconversion to a peacetime economy would lead to another depression. Even peace was problematic, since international tensions were palpable. The explosion of the first atomic bombs over Hiroshima and Nagasaki marked not only the end of World War II but the beginning of the cold war. At any moment, the cold war could turn hot. The policy of containment abroad faced its first major challenge in 1949, with the Chinese revolution. In the same year, the USSR exploded its first atomic bomb. The nation was again jolted out of its sense of fragile security when the Korean War broke out in 1950. Many shared President Truman's belief that World War III was at hand.[2]

Insightful analysts of the nuclear age have explored the psychic impact of the atomic bomb. Paul Boyer's study of the first five years after Hiroshima showed that American responses went through dramatic shifts. Initial reactions juxtaposed the thrill of atomic empowerment with the terror of annihilation. The atomic scientists were among the first to organize against the bomb, calling for international control of atomic energy, and others soon followed suit. By the end of the 1940s, however, opposition had given way to proclamations of faith in the bomb as the protector of American security. As support grew for more and bigger bombs, arguments for international control waned, and the country prepared for the possibility of a nuclear war by instituting new civil defense strategies. Psychologists were strangely silent on the issue of the fear of atomic weapons, and by the early fifties, the nation seemed to be apathetic. Boyer echoed Robert J. Lifton in suggesting that denial and silence may have reflected deep-seated horror rather than complacency; indeed, in 1959, two out of three Americans listed the possibility of nuclear war as the nation's most urgent problem.

Lifton argued that the atomic bomb forced people to question one of their most deeply held beliefs: that scientific discoveries would yield progress. Atomic energy presented a fundamental contradiction: science had developed the potential for total technological mastery as well as for total technological devastation. Lifton attributed "nuclear numbing" to the powerful psychic hold that the fear of nuclear annihilation had on the nation's subconscious. He pointed to unrealistic but reassuring civil defense strategies as the efforts of governmental officials to tame or "domesticate" the fear.[3]

Americans were well poised to embrace domesticity in the midst of the terrors of the atomic age. A home filled with children would create a feeling of warmth and security against the cold forces of disruption and alienation. Children would also be a connection to the future and a means of replenishing a world depleted by war deaths. Although baby-boom parents were not likely to express conscious desires to repopulate the country, the devastation of thousands of deaths could not have been far below the surface of the postwar consciousness. The view of childbearing as a duty was painfully true for Jewish parents, after six million of their kin were snuffed out in Europe. But they were not alone. As one Jewish woman recalled of her decision to bear four children, "After the Holocaust, we felt obligated to have lots of babies. But it was easy because everyone was doing it – non-Jews, too."[4]

In secure postwar homes with plenty of children, American women and men might be able to ward off their nightmares and live out their dreams. The family seemed to be the one place where people could control their destinies and perhaps even shape the future. Of course, nobody actually argued that stable family life could prevent nuclear annihilation. But the home represented a source of meaning and security in a world run amok. Marrying young and having lots of babies were ways for Americans to thumb their noses at doomsday predictions. Commenting on the trend toward young marriages, one observer noted, "Youngsters want to grasp what little security they can in a world gone frighteningly insecure. The youngsters feel they will cultivate the one security that's possible – their own gardens, their own . . . home and families."[5]

Thoughts of the family rooted in time-honored traditions may have allayed fears of vulnerability. Nevertheless, much of what had provided family security in the past became unhinged. For many Americans, the postwar years brought rootlessness. Those who moved from farms to cities lost a familiar way of life that was rooted in the land. Children of immigrants moved from ethnic neighborhoods with extended kin and community ties to homogeneous suburbs, where they formed nuclear families and invested them with high hopes. Suburban homes offered freedom from kinship obligations, along with material comforts that had not been available on the farm or in the ethnic urban ghetto. As Whyte noted about the promoters of the Illinois suburb he studied, "At first they had advertised Park Forest as housing. Now they began advertising happiness." But consumer goods would not replace community, and young mobile nuclear families could easily find themselves adrift. Newcomers devoted themselves to creating communities out of neighborhoods composed largely of transients. As Whyte noted, "In suburbia, organization man is trying, quite consciously, to develop a new kind of roots to replace what he left behind."[6] [. . .]

Postwar America was the era of the expert. Armed with scientific techniques and presumably inhabiting a world that was beyond popular passions, the experts had brought us into the atomic age. Physicists developed the bomb, strategists created the cold war, and scientific managers built the military-industrial complex. It was now up to the experts to make the unmanageable manageable. As the readers of *Look* magazine were assured, there was no reason to worry about radioactivity, for if ever the time arrived when you would need to understand its dangers, "the experts will be ready to tell you." Science and technology seemed to have invaded virtually every aspect of life, from the most public to the most private. Americans were looking to professionals to tell them how to manage their lives. The tremendous popularity of Benjamin Spock's *Baby and Child Care* reflects a reluctance to trust the shared wisdom of kin and community. Norman Vincent Peale's *The Power of Positive Thinking* provided readers with religiously inspired scientific formulas for success. Both these best-selling books stressed the centrality of the family in their prescriptions for a better future.[7] [. . .]

Study Questions

1 Discuss the promises of happiness that were associated with the new domestic ideal for suburban family life in the 1950s.
2 What postwar political and social concerns and problems did this new suburban family life help to alleviate?
3 How did your family fit/not fit the postwar suburban ideal? If your family was living in another country at this time, what was the norm for the "ideal" family?

Notes

1. Quotes from the debate between Vice President Richard Nixon and Soviet Premier Nikita Khrushchev in Moscow are drawn from "The Two Worlds: A Day-Long Debate," *New York Times*, 25 July 1959, pp. 1, 3; "When Nixon Took On Khrushchev," a report of the meeting, and the text of Nixon's address at the opening of the American National Exhibition in Moscow on 24 July 1959, printed in "Setting Russia Straight on Facts about the U.S.," *U.S. News and World Report*, 3 August 1959, pp. 36–39, 70–72; and "Encounter," *Newsweek*, 3 August 1959, pp. 15–19.
2. *See* Martin Sherwin, *A World Destroyed: The Atom Bomb and the Grand Alliance* (New York: Alfred A. Knopf, 1975); John Lewis, *A Critical Appraisal of Postwar National Security Policy* (New York: Oxford University Press, 1982); Truman's belief about World War III is discussed in William Chafe, *The Unfinished Journey: America Since World War II* (New York: Oxford University Press, 1986), pp. 248–51.
3. Paul Boyer, *By the Bomb's Early Light: American Thought and Culture at the Dawn of the Atomic Age* (New York: Pantheon, 1985). On the unrealistic nature of civil defense strategies, *see* the excellent documentary film by The Archives Project, *The Atomic Cafe*, 1982, Thorn Emi Video. Robert J. Lifton, *Broken Connections: On Death and the Continuity of Life* (New York: Simon & Schuster, 1979), p. 338. Data from the poll appear in Boyer, *By the Bomb's Early Light*, p. 335.
4. Conversation with Jewish writer Ruth F. Brin, 11 April 1987, Minneapolis, Minn.
5. Mildred Gilman, "Why They Can't Wait to Wed," *Parents Magazine*, November 1958, p. 46.
6. Judith Smith shows that this process began before 1940 and intensified after the war. *See* Judith Smith, *Family Connections: A History of Italian and Jewish Immigrant Lives in*

Providence, Rhode Island, 1900–1940 (Albany: State University of New York Press, 1985), pp. 107–23. William Whyte, *The Organization Man* (New York: Simon & Schuster, 1956), p. 284. *See also*: Kenneth Jackson, *Crabgrass Frontier: The Suburbanization of the United States* (New York: Oxford University Press, 1985).

7.   Of course, the cult of the professional or expert did not emerge suddenly after World War II, although it was institutionalized in new ways then, especially during the Eisenhower years. *See*, for example, Burton J. Bledstein, *The Culture of Professionalism: The Middle Class and the Development of Higher Education in America* (New York: Norton, 1976); Terrence Ball, "The Politics of Social Science," in Lary May, ed., *Recasting America: Culture and Politics in the Age of Cold War* (Chicago: University of Chicago Press, 1989); Robert Griffith, "Dwight D. Eisenhower and the Corporate Commonwealth," *American Historical Review* 87 (February 1982), pp. 87–122; and Joseph Veroff, Richard A. Kulka, and Elizabeth Douvan, *Mental Health in America: Patterns of Help-seeking from 1957 to 1976* (New York: Basic Books, 1981), pp. 8, 10, 226; Christopher Lasch, *Haven in a Heartless World: The Family Besieged* (New York: Basic Books, 1977). For the professionalization of motherhood through expertise, *see* Nancy Pottishman Weiss, "Mother; the Invention of Necessity: Dr. Benjamin Spock's *Baby and Child Care*," *American Quarterly* 29 (Winter 1977), pp. 519–46. On Peale, *see* Donald Meyer, *The Positive Thinkers: A Study of the American Quest for Health, Wealth, and Personal Power from Mary Baker Eddy to Norman Vincent Peale* (Garden City, N.Y.: Doubleday & Co., 1965). Quote from *Look* magazine is from an undated, unpaginated clipping in the Social Welfare History Archives, University of Minnesota (SWHA).

CHAPTER 8

The Problem That Has No Name

Betty Friedan

Betty Friedan (1921–) was born Bettye Goldstein in Peoria, Illinois, to a jewelry storeowner and a mother who left her job as a newspaper editor to raise her family. Graduating from Smith College in 1942, Goldstein worked as a labor journalist until 1952. She married Carl Friedan in 1947, and became mother to three children. Her critique of postwar ideals for women, which defined them exclusively in terms of their domestic roles, is encapsulated in The Feminine Mystique *(1963). The book sold over 300,000 copies in its first year and had a powerful impact on the burgeoning women's movement of the 1960s. The first chapter is excerpted here. Friedan went on to cofound the National Organization for Women (NOW) in 1966, along with Pauli Murray, serving as its first president.*

The problem lay buried, unspoken, for many years in the minds of American women. It was a strange stirring, a sense of dissatisfaction, a yearning that women suffered in the middle of the twentieth century in the United States. Each suburban wife struggled with it alone. As she made the beds, shopped for groceries, matched slipcover material, ate peanut butter sandwiches with her children, chauffeured Cub Scouts and Brownies, lay beside her husband at night – she was afraid to ask even of herself the silent question – "Is this all?"

For over fifteen years there was no word of this yearning in the millions of words written about women, for women, in all the columns, books and articles by experts telling women their role was to seek fulfillment as wives and mothers. Over and over women heard in voices of tradition and of Freudian sophistication that they could desire no greater destiny than to glory in their own femininity. Experts told them how to catch a man and keep him, how to breastfeed children and handle their toilet training, how to cope with sibling rivalry and adolescent rebellion; how to buy a dishwasher, bake bread, cook gourmet snails, and build a swimming pool with their own hands; how to dress, look, and act more feminine and make marriage more exciting; how to keep their husbands from dying young and their sons from growing into delinquents. They were taught to pity the neurotic, unfeminine, unhappy women who wanted to be poets or physicists or presidents. They learned that truly feminine women do not want careers, higher education, political rights – the independence and the opportunities that the old-fashioned feminists fought for. Some women, in their forties and fifties, still remembered painfully giving up those dreams, but most of the younger women no longer even thought about them. A thousand expert voices applauded their femininity, their adjustment, their new maturity. All they had to do was devote their lives from earliest girlhood to finding a husband and bearing children.

By the end of the nineteen-fifties, the average marriage age of women in America dropped to 20, and was still dropping, into the teens. Fourteen million girls were engaged by 17. The proportion of women attending college in comparison with men dropping from 47 per cent in 1920 to 35 per cent in 1958. A century earlier, women had fought for higher education; now girls went to college to get a husband. By the mid-fifties, 60 per cent dropped out of college to marry, or because they were afraid too much education would be a marriage bar. Colleges built dormitories for "married students," but the students were almost always the husbands. A new degree was instituted for the wives – "Ph.T." (Putting Husband Through).

Then American girls began getting married in high school. And the women's magazines, deploring the unhappy statistics about these young marriages, urged that courses on marriage, and marriage counselors, be installed in the high schools. Girls started going steady at twelve and thirteen, in junior high. Manufacturers put out brassieres with false bosoms of foam rubber for little girls of ten. And an advertisement for a child's dress, sizes 3–6x, in the *New York Times* in the fall of 1960, said: "She Too Can Join the Man-Trap Set."

By the end of the fifties, the United States birthrate was overtaking India's. The birth-control movement, renamed Planned Parenthood, was asked to find a method whereby women who had been advised that a third or fourth baby would be born dead or defective might have it anyhow. Statisticians were especially astounded at the fantastic increase in the number of babies among college women. Where once they had two children, now they had four, five, six. Women who had once wanted careers were now making careers out of having babies. So rejoiced *Life* magazine in a 1956 paean to the movement of American women back to the home. [. . .]

The suburban housewife – she was the dream image of the young American women and the envy, it was said, of women all over the world. The American housewife – freed by science and labor-saving appliances from the drudgery, the dangers of childbirth and the illnesses of her grandmother. She was healthy, beautiful, educated, concerned only about her husband, her children, her home. She had found true feminine fulfillment. As a housewife and mother, she was respected as a full and equal partner to man in his world. She was free to choose automobiles, clothes, appliances, supermarkets; she had everything that women ever dreamed of.

In the fifteen years after World War II, this mystique of feminine fulfillment became the cherished and self-perpetuating core of contemporary American culture. Millions of women lived their lives in the image of those pretty pictures of the American suburban housewife, kissing their husbands goodbye in front of the picture window, depositing their stationwagonsful of children at school, and smiling as they ran the new electric waxer over the spotless kitchen floor. They baked their own bread, sewed their own and their children's clothes, kept their new washing machines and dryers running all day. They changed the sheets on the beds twice a week instead of once, took the rug-hooking class in adult education, and pitied their poor frustrated mothers, who had dreamed of having a career. Their only dream was to be perfect wives and mothers; their highest ambition to have five children and a beautiful house, their only fight to get and keep their husbands. They had no thought for the unfeminine problems of the world outside the home; they wanted the men to make the major decisions. They gloried in their role as women, and wrote proudly on the census blank: "Occupation: housewife." [...]

If a woman had a problem in the 1950's and 1960's, she knew that something must be wrong with her marriage, or with herself. Other women were satisfied with their lives, she thought. What kind of a woman was she if she did not feel this mysterious fulfillment waxing the kitchen floor? She was so ashamed to admit her dissatisfaction that she never knew how many other women shared it. If she tried to tell her husband, he didn't understand what she was talking about. She did not really understand it herself. For over fifteen years women in America found it harder to talk about this problem than about sex. Even the psychoanalysts had no name for it. When a woman went to a psychiatrist for help, as many women did, she would say, "I'm so ashamed," or "I must be hopelessly neurotic." "I don't know what's wrong with women today," a suburban psychiatrist said uneasily. "I only know something is wrong because most of my patients happen to be women. And their problem isn't sexual." Most women with this problem did not go to see a psychoanalyst, however. "There's nothing wrong really," they kept telling themselves. "There isn't any problem."

But on an April morning in 1959, I heard a mother of four, having coffee with four other mothers in a suburban development fifteen miles from New York, say in a tone of quiet desperation, "the problem." And the others knew, without words, that she was not talking about a problem with her husband, or her children, or her home. Suddenly they realized they all shared the same problem, the problem that has no name. They began, hesitantly, to talk about it. Later, after they had picked up their children at nursery school and taken them home to nap, two of the women cried, in sheer relief, just to know they were not alone.

Gradually I came to realize that the problem that has no name was shared by countless women in America. As a magazine writer I often interviewed women about problems with their children, or their marriages, or their houses, or their communities. But after a while I began to recognize the telltale signs of this other problem. I saw the same signs in suburban ranch houses and split-levels on Long Island and in New Jersey and Westchester County; in colonial houses in a small Massachusetts town; on patios in Memphis; in suburban and city apartments; in living rooms in the Midwest. Sometimes I sensed the problem, not as a reporter, but as a suburban housewife, for during this time I was also bringing up my own three children in

Rockland County, New York. I heard echoes of the problem in college dormitories and semi-private maternity wards, at PTA meetings and luncheons of the League of Women Voters, at suburban cocktail parties, in station wagons waiting for trains, and in snatches of conversation overheard at Schrafft's. The groping words I heard from other women, on quiet afternoons when children were at school or on quiet evenings when husbands worked late, I think I understood first as a woman long before I understood their larger social and psychological implications.

Just what was this problem that has no name? What were the words women used when they tried to express it? Sometimes a woman would say "I feel empty some-how ... incomplete." Or she would say, "I feel as if I don't exist." Sometimes she blotted out the feeling with a tranquilizer. Sometimes she thought the problem was with her husband, or her children, or that what she really needed was to redecorate her house, or move to a better neighborhood, or have an affair, or another baby. Sometimes, she went to a doctor with symptoms she could hardly describe: "A tired feeling ... I get so angry with the children it scares me ... I feel like crying without any reason." (A Cleveland doctor called it "the housewife's syndrome.") A number of women told me about great bleeding blisters that break out on their hands and arms. "I call it the housewife's blight," said a family doctor in Pennsylvania. "I see it so often lately in these young women with four, five and six children who bury themselves in their dishpans. But it isn't caused by detergent and it isn't cured by cortisone."

Sometimes a woman would tell me that the feeling gets so strong she runs out of the house and walks through the streets. Or she stays inside her house and cries. Or her children tell her a joke, and she doesn't laugh because she doesn't hear it. I talked to women who had spent years on the analyst's couch, working out their "adjust-ment to the feminine role," their blocks to "fulfillment as a wife and mother." But the desperate tone in these women's voices, and the look in their eyes, was the same as the tone and the look of other women, who were sure they had no problem, even though they did have a strange feeling of desperation. [...]

In 1960, the problem that has no name burst like a boil through the image of the happy American housewife. In the television commercials the pretty housewives still beamed over their foaming dishpans and *Time*'s cover story on "The Suburban Wife, an American Phenomenon" protested: "Having too good a time ... to believe that they should be unhappy." But the actual unhappiness of the American housewife was suddenly being reported – from the *New York Times* and *Newsweek* to *Good House-keeping* and CBS Television ("The Trapped Housewife"), although almost everybody who talked about it found some superficial reason to dismiss it. It was attributed to incompetent appliance repairmen *(New York Times)*, or the distances children must be chauffeured in the suburbs *(Time)*, or too much PTA *(Redbook)*. Some said it was the old problem – education: more and more women had education, which naturally made them unhappy in their role as housewives. "The road from Freud to Frigidaire, from Sophocles to Spock, has turned out to be a bumpy one," reported the *New York Times* (June 28, 1960). "Many young women – certainly not all – whose education plunged them into a world of ideas feel stifled in their homes. They find their routine lives out of joint with their training. Like shut-ins, they feel left out. In the last year, the problem of the educated housewife has provided the meat of dozens of speeches made by troubled presidents of women's colleges who maintain, in the face of complaints, that sixteen years of academic training is realistic preparation for wife-hood and motherhood." [. . .]

The year American women's discontent boiled over, it was also reported *(Look)* that the more than 21,000,000 American women who are single, widowed, or divorced do not cease even after fifty their frenzied, desperate search for a man. And the search begins early – for seventy per cent of all American women now marry before they are twenty-four. A pretty twenty-five-year-old secretary took thirty-five different jobs in six months in the futile hope of finding a husband. Women were moving from one political club to another, taking evening courses in accounting or sailing, learning to play golf or ski, joining a number of churches in succession, going to bars alone, in their ceaseless search for a man.

Of the growing thousands of women currently getting private psychiatric help in the United States, the married ones were reported dissatisfied with their marriages, the unmarried ones suffering from anxiety and, finally, depression. Strangely, a number of psychiatrists stated that, in their experience, unmarried women patients were happier than married ones. So the door of all those pretty suburban houses opened a crack to permit a glimpse of uncounted thousands of American housewives who suffered alone from a problem that suddenly everyone was talking about, and beginning to take for granted, as one of those unreal problems in American life that can never be solved – like the hydrogen bomb. By 1962 the plight of the trapped American housewife had become a national parlor game. Whole issues of magazines, newspaper columns, books learned and frivolous, educational conferences and tele-vision panels were devoted to the problem. [. . .]

It is no longer possible to ignore that voice, to dismiss the desperation of so many American women. This is not what being a woman means, no matter what the experts say. For human suffering there is a reason; perhaps the reason has not been found because the right questions have not been asked, or pressed far enough. I do not accept the answer that there is no problem because American women have luxuries that women in other times and lands never dreamed of; part of the strange newness of the problem is that it cannot be understood in terms of the age-old material problems of man: poverty, sickness, hunger, cold. The women who suffer this problem have a hunger that food cannot fill. It persists in women whose husbands are struggling internes and law clerks, or prosperous doctors and lawyers; in wives of workers and executives who make $5,000 a year or $50,000. It is not caused by lack of material advantages; it may not even be felt by women preoccupied with desperate problems of hunger, poverty or illness. And women who think it will be solved by more money, a bigger house, a second car, moving to a better suburb, often discover it gets worse.

It is no longer possible today to blame the problem on loss of femininity: to say that education and independence and equality with men have made American women unfeminine. I have heard so many women try to deny this dissatisfied voice within themselves because it does not fit the pretty picture of femininity the experts have given them. I think, in fact, that this is the first clue to the mystery: the problem cannot be understood in the generally accepted terms by which scientists have studied women, doctors have treated them, counselors have advised them, and writers have written about them. Women who suffer this problem, in whom this voice is stirring, have lived their whole lives in the pursuit of feminine fulfillment. They are not career women (although career women may have other problems); they are women whose greatest ambition has been marriage and children. For the oldest of these women, these daughters of the American middle class, no other dream was possible. The ones in their forties and fifties who once had other dreams gave them up and threw themselves joyously into life as housewives. For the youngest, the new wives and mothers, this was the only dream. They are the ones who quit high school and college to marry, or marked time in some job in which they had no real interest until they married. These women are very "feminine" in the usual sense, and yet they still suffer the problem. [. . .]

It is easy to see the concrete details that trap the suburban housewife, the continual demands on her time. But the chains that bind her in her trap are chains in her own mind and spirit. They are chains made up of mistaken ideas and misinterpreted facts, of incomplete truths and unreal choices. They are not easily seen and not easily shaken off.

How can any woman see the whole truth within the bounds of her own life? How can she believe that voice inside herself, when it denies the conventional, accepted truths by which she has been living? And yet the women I have talked to, who are finally listening to that inner voice, seem in some incredible way to be groping through to a truth that has defied the experts.

I think the experts in a great many fields have been holding pieces of that truth under their microscopes for a long time without realizing it. I found pieces of it in certain new research and theoretical developments in psychological, social and biological science whose implications for women seem never to have been examined. I found many clues by talking to suburban doctors, gynecologists, obstetricians, child-guidance clinicians, pediatricians, high-school guidance counselors, college professors, marriage counselors, psychiatrists and ministers – questioning them not on their theories, but on their actual experience in treating American women. I became aware of a growing body of evidence, much of which has not been reported publicly because it does not fit current modes of thought about women – evidence which throws into question the standards of feminine normality, feminine adjustment, feminine fulfillment, and feminine maturity by which most women are still trying to live.

I began to see in a strange new light the American return to early marriage and the large families that are causing the population explosion; the recent movement to natural childbirth and breastfeeding; suburban conformity, and the new neuroses, character pathologies and sexual problems being reported by the doctors. I began to see new dimensions to old problems that have long been taken for granted among women: menstrual difficulties, sexual frigidity, promiscuity, pregnancy fears, child-birth depression, the high incidence of emotional breakdown and suicide among women in their twenties and thirties, the menopause crises, the so-called passivity and immaturity of American men, the discrepancy between women's tested intellectual abilities in childhood and their adult achievement, the changing incidence of adult sexual orgasm in American women, and persistent problems in psychotherapy and in women's education.

If I am right, the problem that has no name stirring in the minds of so many American women today is not a matter of loss of femininity or too much education, or the demands of domesticity. It is far more important than anyone recognizes. It is the key to these other new and old problems which have been torturing women and their husbands and children, and puzzling their doctors and educators for years. It may well be the key to our future as a nation and a culture. We can no longer ignore that voice within women that says: "I want something more than my husband and my children and my home."

Study Questions

1 What is "the problem that has no name"?
2 How does Friedan know it is a problem? What is her evidence? What women is she writing about? Who is her intended audience?
3 According to Friedan, what historical, social, and cultural factors helped to create and perpetuate the problem? How does her explanation compare with Stephanie Coontz's or Elaine May's analysis of women's roles and identities in the 1950s?

CHAPTER 9

The Civil Rights Revolution, 1945–1960

William H. Chafe

William H. Chafe, a professor of US history with research specialties in race and gender equality, was born in 1942, and grew up in a working-class neighborhood in Cambridge, Massachusetts. Among his books are Civilities and Civil Rights: Greensboro, North Carolina and the Black Struggle for Freedom *(1980),* The Paradox of Change: American Women in the Twentieth Century *(1991), and his coedited volume,* Remembering Jim Crow: African Americans Tell About Life in the Segregated South *(2003). The following excerpt, taken from an essay written for a collection on US history after World War II, was published in 1982.*

"Do you want to get killed?" he asked me.
"Hell, no!"
"Then, for God's sake, learn how to live in the south! . . . Look, you're black, black, black, see? Can't you understand that?" . . . "You act around white people as if you didn't know that they were white. And they see it."
"Oh, Christ, I can't be a slave," I said hopelessly.
"But you've got to eat. . . . When you're in front of white people think before *you act, think* before *you speak; your way of doing things is alright among* our *people, but not for white people. They won't stand for it." (Richard Wright,* Black Boy*)*

No black person growing up in the American south during the 1930s could avoid the pervasive reality of race. It shaped one's life, dictated one's ambitions, determined where and how one would speak, what kind of job one would hold – sometimes even whether one would survive. White people were in control. They could fire you from your job, evict you from your land, slap you for having the wrong "look" in your eye.

Sometimes their terrorism knew no bounds. In 1934 Claude Raines, a black man in Georgia, was arrested for allegedly molesting a white woman. Seized by a lynch mob, he was carried through town after town in southern Georgia and then across the border into Florida, with leaflets left in each place advertising the lynching that was about to happen. By the time the mob reached its final destination, thousands had gathered to witness the mutilation of Raines's body. No law enforcement agent acted to prevent the murder.[1] In such a context open rebellion was not an option because destruction of life and possessions was the almost certain response.

Yet the absence of mass protest did not signify passive acceptance of the status quo. If whites controlled the outer reality, they could not control the inner spirit. Throughout the years of Jim Crow, when America's laws said that blacks could not vote, share restaurant facilities, or go to school with whites, the black struggle to overcome oppression gathered strength. At times, of necessity, it took the form of playing the role of Uncle Tom in order to secure funds for a new school, a better playground, or a decent college. At other times it consisted of teaching pride in black institutions, churches, and businesses, preparing for the day when those institutions would serve as a base from which to attack the oppressor. And at still other times the struggle meant pushing back the boundaries of control and beginning to challenge segregation itself. During the late 1930s and 1940s, more and more black Americans took this third course.

Ella Baker was born and reared in Warren County, North Carolina, on a farm owned by her family since the 1870s. After graduating from Shaw University, a black school started during Reconstruction, she moved to New York City to work for the YWCA. Then, in the middle 1930s, she accepted the position of field secretary for the NAACP. The South was her territory. Traveling from town to town, she recruited blacks to join the NAACP – an act which at that time represented the equivalent of joining the Black Panthers in the late 1960s. In 1943 she went to Greensboro, North Carolina. There she so impressed Randolph Blackwell, a young high school student, that he organized an NAACP youth chapter. Blackwell subsequently initiated voter registration campaigns in Greensboro, ran for the state legislature, and helped form the Southern Christian Leadership Conference. Ella Baker, Randolph Blackwell, and the NAACP youth group that they formed together, would help reshape history in the 1950s and 1960s.[2]

Two hundred miles to the south and east, in Clarendon County, South Carolina, J. A. DeLaine pastored an A.M.E. church and taught school. ("If you set out to find the place in America . . . where life among black folk had changed least since the end of slavery," Richard Kluger wrote in 1974, "Clarendon County is where you might have come.") With a decent job and an honored position in the community. DeLaine might have been expected to act with caution. But he had a fire within him. As a youngster he had been sentenced to twenty-five lashes for pushing back a white boy who had shoved his sister off the sidewalk. In the church he pastored – as in most black churches – he drew constant parallels between the liberation promised in Scripture and the reality of contemporary life. It was not surprising, then, that when DeLaine heard an NAACP lecturer in the summer of 1947 at a black college in Columbia, South Carolina, he decided to lead the struggle to equalize education in Clarendon County. It was, after all, an area that in 1949 spent $179 per white child in public schools and $43 per black child. Shortly thereafter, DeLaine met Thurgood

Marshall, general counsel of the NAACP and a graduate of Howard University Law School, whose imagination, courage, and sheer energy were now directed toward demolishing the legal fortress of segregation. DeLaine and Marshall, too, would be heard from again.[3]

Throughout the South such acts of assertion were growing. Overt protest was never easy, but the challenge was beginning. Based on the achievements of their forefathers in a segregated world, people like Baker and Blackwell and DeLaine were launching an assault that would eventually undermine segregation itself. At a time when all too often we assume that change comes from above, it is important to remember where the civil rights movement began, who started it, and what price was paid before anyone in authority even noticed.

The new challenge grew out of the changes wrought by World War II. By causing a massive dislocation of population and forcing millions of people into new experiences, the war created a context in which many blacks – and some whites – perceived the possibility of racial activism in a new way. The vicious cycle of social control that had compelled obedience to the status quo as a price for survival was at least partially broken by the massive jolt of full-scale war. Although little was accomplished in the way of permanent progress toward equality, the changes that did occur laid the foundation for subsequent mass protest.

The war generated an accelerated migration of blacks from the South, and within the South from farm to city. Whether lured by a specific job in a munitions plant, ordered by a directive from the selective service, or simply beckoned by the hope of a better life elsewhere, hundreds of thousands of black southerners boarded trains and buses and headed north and west. When they arrived at their destination, they found living situations often less attractive than they had expected. The urban ghetto, with its overcrowded housing, hard-pressed social facilities, and oppressive discrimination, was not much better than what they had left behind. Yet there was also a difference. A northern urban political machine sought votes and offered some political recognition in return. There was more psychological space, more opportunity to talk freely. The community was new, the imminent tyranny of small-town authority was removed, and different ground rules applied. The very act of physical mobility brought independence from the overwhelming social constraints that had been enforced in small southern communities. If the controls existed in different forms, there was at least now the possibility of a different response as well as a heightened sense of what might be done to achieve a better life.

World War II's second major impact came in the area of the economy. Some two million blacks were employed in defense plants during the war, and another two hundred thousand joined the federal civil service. Most of these jobs were at low levels. Indeed, when attempts were made to upgrade black employees, whites frequently rebelled, as when twenty thousand white workers in Mobile walked off their jobs and rioted when efforts were made to hire twelve blacks as welders in a shipyard. A wartime Fair Employment Practices Committee [FEPC], established by President Roosevelt after A. Philip Randolph threatened to bring 50,000 blacks to march on Washington in protest against discrimination in defense industries, offered little in the way of substantive help because it lacked enforcement power. For the most part, blacks continued to be hired as janitors or scrubwomen, not as technicians, secretaries, or skilled craftsmen.

Nevertheless, the war had some positive impact. In 1940 the number of blacks employed in professional, white-collar, and skilled or semiskilled jobs had been less than 20 percent. A decade later the figure had climbed to 33 percent, largely as a result of wartime changes. Black members of labor unions doubled to 1,250,000 during the war years. The end result was thus another contradiction: some upward mobility – enough to spur hope – yet pervasive discrimination as well to remind one constantly of the depths of racism to be overcome.

A third impact came in the armed forces. There, the struggle was in some ways the hardest. When blacks in Tennessee demanded that the governor appoint Negroes to the state's draft board, he responded: "This is a white man's country.... The Negro had nothing to do with the settling of America." The army set a quota for the number of blacks to be inducted, the navy restricted Negroes to the position of mess boys, Red Cross workers segregated blood supplies into "white" and "colored" bottles, and training camps, especially in the South, became infamous for their persecution of blacks. A Negro private at Fort Benning, Georgia, was lynched; military officials refused to act when a black army nurse was brutally beaten for defying Jim Crow seating on a Montgomery, Alabama, bus; and religious services were segregated, the sign at one base proclaiming separate worship for "Catholics, Jews, Protestants, and Negroes." But even in the armed services, some positive changes occurred: more and more blacks were trained for combat positions; some integration took place on an experimental basis; and above all, thousands upon thousands of soldiers experienced some taste of life without prejudice in places like France and Hawaii.[4]

Significantly, each of these changes exhibited a common theme: the interaction of some improvement together with daily reminders of ongoing oppression. The chemistry of the process was crucial. Simultaneous with new exposure to travel, the prospect of better jobs, and higher expectations, came the reality of daily contact with Jim Crow in the armed forces, housing, and on the job. The juxtaposition could not help but spawn anger and frustration. The possibility of some improvement generated the expectations for still more, and when those expectations were dashed, a rising tide of protest resulted.

World War II thus provided the forge within which anger and outrage, long suppressed, were shaped into new expressions of protest. Searing contradictions between the rhetoric of fighting a war against racism abroad while racism continued unabated at home galvanized anger and transformed it into political and social activism. "Our war is not against Hitler and Europe," one black columnist proclaimed, "but against the Hitlers in America." Epitomizing the ideological irony at the heart of America's war effort was the slogan among black draftees: "Here lies a black man killed fighting a yellow man for the glory of a white man."

To fight against such absurdity, blacks rushed to join protest organizations like the NAACP. Local chapters tripled in number while national membership increased 900 percent to over 500,000 people. As black newspapers took up the cry for the "double

V" campaign – victory at home as well as victory abroad – their circulation increased by 40 percent. Negroes had their "own war" at home, declared the Pittsburgh *Courier,* a war "against oppression and exploitation from without and against disorganization and lack of confidence within." As if to illustrate the changes that were occurring, southern black leaders meeting in Durham, North Carolina, in October 1942 demanded complete equality for the Negro in American life "[We are] fundamentally opposed to the principle and practice of compulsory segregation in our American society," the Durham meeting declared. Ten years earlier such a statement would have been inconceivable.[5]

As the war against Hitler drew to a close, this sense of ferment and protest grew. Something had changed. Whether in northern cities or southern towns, black Americans exhibited a powerful determination to build on the energies of the war years, to secure a permanent FEPC, to abolish the poll tax, to achieve the basic right of citizenship involved in voter registration, to outlaw forever the terrorism of lynching. Over a million black soldiers had fought in a war to preserve democracy and eliminate racism. Hundreds of thousands more had achieved a glimmer of hope of what their society might become. They were not about to return quietly to the status quo of racism as usual. It was a moment of possiblity.

[. . .]

Study Questions

1 How did social and economic circumstances set in motion by World War II open up new possibilities for activists to protest racial segregation? Discuss the three main areas of the war's impact identified by Chafe.
2 What do Chafe's sketches of Ella Baker, Randolph Blackwell, and Rev. J. A. DeLaine tell us about the nature of local southern grassroots protest against segregation in the 1940s?
3 How did the postwar activism that Chafe describe set the stage for the Civil Rights Movement of the 1950s and 1960s? What continuities do you find with Martin Luther King's "Letter from Birmingham City Jail"?

Notes

1. For a discussion of lynching during the 1930s, see Robert L. Zangrando, "The NAACP and a Federal Anti-lynching Bill, 1934–1940," *Journal of Negro History* 50 (April, 1955): 106–17; and John B. Kirby, "The Roosevelt Administration and Blacks: An Ambivalent Legacy," in *20th Century America: Recent Interpretations*, ed. Barton Bernstein and Allan Matusow (New York, 1972). On the antilynching movement, see Jacquelyn Dowd Hall, *Revolt against Chivalry* (New York, 1978). Eleanor Roosevelt engaged in extensive correspondence about the Raines case with Walter White, executive secretary of the NAACP. See the Walter White

correspondence file for 1934 in the Eleanor Roosevelt Papers, Franklin D. Roosevelt Library, Hyde Park, New York.

2. Author's interview with Ella Baker, 1977–78; author's interview with Randolph Blackwell, 1973; Eugene Walker's interview with Ella Baker, 1973; Sara Evan's interview with Randolph Blackwell, 1973. For further discussion of Ella Baker, see James Forman, *The Making of a Black Revolutionary* (New York, 1975), and the film on her life directed by Joanne Grant.

3. DeLaine's life is discussed extensively in Richard Kluger, *Simple Justice* (New York, 1975), pp. 3–26.

4. On the black experience during World War II, see Richard Dalfiume, "The Forgotten Negro Revolution," *Journal of American History* 55 (June 1968): 90–106; Harvard Sitkoff, "Racial Militance and Interracial Violence in the Second World War," *Journal of American History* 58 (December 1971): 661–81; and Richard Dalfiume, *Desegregation of the U.S. Armed Forces: Fighting on Two Fronts, 1939–53* (Columbia, S.C., 1969). On the FEPC see Herbert Garfinkel, *When Negroes March* (Glencoe, Ill., 1959); and Jervis Anderson, *A. Philip Randolph* (New York, 1973).

5. See Dalfiume, "The Forgotten Negro Revolution," and Sitkoff, "Racial Militance and Interracial Violence." Despite evidence of considerable change, there was also reason for skepticism. Whatever leverage blacks could mobilize at a time of national vulnerability was dwarfed by the power of white political and economic leaders to define the national agenda and control the government's response. President Roosevelt himself consistently refused to endorse black objectives. Throughout his administration he did virtually nothing to support antilynching legislation, not even permitting his attorney general to invoke the Lindbergh kidnapping statute to prosecute the mob that lynched Claude Raines in 1934. He failed to endorse abolition of the poll tax, refused to have the Justice Department join in the challenge to the white primary, and, after the Supreme Court had invalidated such techniques of disfranchisement, refused to instruct his attorney general to prosecute those who sought to enact new obstacles to voting rights. Even the FEPC represented, in retrospect, a hollow concession, lacking all enforcement power and serving primarily the purposes of exhortation and propaganda. Indeed, were it not for Eleanor Roosevelt's role behind the scenes in advocating antilynching legislation and the FEPC, there would have been virtually no one in the White House concerned about civil rights.

CHAPTER 10

From *Like One of the Family:*
Conversations from a Domestic's Life

Alice Childress

Prize-winning novelist and playwright, Alice Childress (1920–94) was born in Charleston, South Carolina, and raised from the age of five by her maternal grandmother in Harlem. After high school, she worked as an apprentice machinist, a salesperson, an insurance agent, and as a domestic, among other jobs. She studied acting with Harlem's American Negro Theatre beginning in 1940, directing and performing in plays for 11 years. Childress was the first woman to win an OBIE award, for Trouble in Mind *(1955), a play challenging the narrow, stereotypical roles imagined for black actors in theater.* Like One of the Family: Conversations from a Domestic's Life *is a series of fictional conversations between a black domestic worker named Mildred and her friend Marge. They first appeared in Paul Robeson's Harlem newspaper* Freedom, *and the Baltimore Afro-American, before being published as a book in 1956.*

Like One of the Family

Hi Marge! I have had me one hectic day. . . . Well, I had to take out my crystal ball and give Mrs. C . . . a thorough reading. She's the woman that I took over from Naomi after Naomi got married. . . . Well, she's a pretty nice woman as they go and I have never had too much trouble with her, but from time to time she really gripes me with her ways.

When she has company, for example, she'll holler out to me from the living room to the kitchen: "Mildred dear! Be sure and eat *both* of those lamb chops for your lunch!" Now you know she wasn't doing a thing but tryin' to prove to the company how "good" and "kind" she was to the servant, because she had told me *already* to eat those chops.

Today she had a girl friend of hers over to lunch and I was real busy afterwards clearing the things away and she called me over and introduced me to the woman.... Oh no, Marge! I didn't object to that at all. I greeted the lady and then went back to my work....And then it started! I could hear her talkin' just as loud...and she says to her friend, "We *just* love her! She's *like* one of the family and she *just adores* our little Carol! We don't know *what* we'd do without her! We don't think of her as a servant!" And on and on she went...and every time I came in to move a plate off the table both of them would grin at me like chessy cats.

After I couldn't stand it any more, I went in and took the platter off the table and gave 'em both a look that would have frizzled a egg.... Well, you might have heard a pin drop and then they started talkin' about something else.

When the guest leaves, I go in the living room and says, "Mrs. C..., I want to have a talk with you."

"By all means," she says.

I drew up a chair and read her thusly: "Mrs. C..., you are a pretty nice person to work for, but I wish you would please stop talkin' about me like I was a *cocker spaniel* or a *poll parrot* or a *kitten*....Now you just sit there and hear me out.

"In the first place, you do not *love* me; you may be fond of me, but that is all....In the second place, I am *not* just like one of the family at all! The family eats in the dining room and I eat in the kitchen. Your mama borrows your lace table-cloth for her company and your son entertains his friends in your parlor, your daughter takes her afternoon nap on the living room couch and the puppy sleeps on your satin spread...and whenever your husband gets tired of something you are talkin' about he says, 'Oh, for Pete's sake, forget it....' So you can see I am not *just* like one of the family.

"Now for another thing, I do not *just* adore your little Carol. I think she is a likable child, but she is also fresh and sassy. I know you call it 'uninhibited' and that is the way you want your child to be, but *luckily* my mother taught me some inhibitions or else I would smack little Carol once in a while when she's talkin' to you like you're a dog, but as it is I just laugh it off the way you do because she is *your* child and I am *not* like one of the family.

"Now when you say, 'We don't know *what* we'd do without her' this is a polite lie...because I know that if I dropped dead or had a stroke, you would get somebody to replace me.

"You think it is a compliment when you say, 'We don't think of her as a servant....' but after I have worked myself into a sweat cleaning the bathroom and the kitchen...making the beds...cooking the lunch...washing the dishes and ironing Carol's pinafores...I do not feel like no weekend house guest. I feel like a servant, and in the face of that I have been meaning to ask you for a slight raise which will make me feel much better toward everyone here and make me know my work is appreciated.

"Now I hope you will stop talkin' about me in my presence and that we will get along like a good employer and employee should."

Marge! She was almost speechless but she *apologized* and said she'd talk to her husband about the raise.... I knew things were progressing because this evening

Carol came in the kitchen and she did not say, "I want some bread and jam!" but she did say, "*Please*, Mildred, will you fix me a slice of bread and jam."

I'm going upstairs, Marge. Just look...you done messed up that buttonhole!

The Health Card

Well, Marge, I started an extra job today.... Just wait, girl. Don't laugh yet. Just wait till I tell you.... The woman seems real nice.... Well, you know what I mean.... She was pretty nice, anyway. Shows me this and shows me that, but she was real cautious about loadin' on too much work the first morning. And she stopped short when she caught the light in my eye.

Comes the afternoon, I was busy waxin' woodwork when I notice her hoverin' over me kind of timid-like. She passed me once and smiled and then she turned and blushed a little. I put down the wax can and gave her an inquirin' look. The lady takes a deep breath and comes up with, "Do you live in Harlem, Mildred?"

Now you know I expected somethin' more than that after all the hesitatin'. I had already given her my address so I didn't quite get the idea behind the question. "Yes, Mrs. Jones," I answered, "that is where I live."

Well, she backed away and retired to the living room and I could hear her and the husband just a-buzzin'. A little later on I was in the kitchen washin' glasses. I looks up and there she was in the doorway, lookin' kind of strained around the gills. First she stuttered and then she stammered and after beatin' all around the bush she comes out with, "Do you have a health card, Mildred?"

That let the cat out of the bag. I thought real fast. Honey, my brain was runnin' on wheels. "Yes, Mrs. Jones," I says, "I have a health card." Now Marge, this is a lie. I do not have a health card. "I'll bring it tomorrow," I add real sweet-like.

She beams like a chromium platter and all you could see above her taffeta house coat is smile. "Mildred," she said, "I don't mean any offense, but one must be careful, mustn't one?"

Well, all she got from me was solid agreement. "Sure, I said, 'indeed *one* must, and I am glad you are so understandin', 'cause I was just worryin' and studyin' on how I was goin' to ask you for yours, and of course you'll let me see one from your husband and one for each of the three children."

By that time she was the same color as the housecoat, which is green, but I continue on: "Since I have to handle laundry and make beds, you know..." She stops me right there and after excusin' herself she scurries from the room and has another conference with hubby.

Inside fifteen minutes she was back. "Mildred, you don't have to bring a health card. I am sure it will be all right."

I looked up real casual kind-of and said, "On second thought, you folks look real clean, too, so..." And then she smiled and I smiled and then she smiled again ....Oh, stop laughin' so loud, Marge, everybody on this bus is starin'. [...]

Nasty Compliments

Marge, I can see why you say you don't like this butcher shop on the corner even if they do have the best quality of meat.... I know you have had words with the man that owns the place, but I guess I will really avoid goin' in there after today!... Sure, he is sickenin'!... I don't pay him too much mind although I have had to jack him up about callin' me "girlie" and "honeychile," but every once in a while I will find myself wantin' a nice piece of steak and will go in there 'cause it is the closest shop to my house.

When I went in there tonight, he tries to pick a conversation with me by sayin', "There's some *fine* colored people around here, and I can say this: I'd rather know a Negro any day than to know a Jew." All the time he's talkin' he's also grinnin' at me like a chessy-cat! I suppose he thought he was payin' me a compliment!

So, I says, "You mean that if you had to keep some unpleasant company, you would rather it would be mine." He says, "Oh, no, I mean that colored people are better to deal with than Jews. A Jew will always try to take advantage of you and a Jew will..."

I cut him off then. "I'm not interested," I says, "because folks that talk about Jews that way will be very quick to call me 'nigger'!" "Oh, no," he says, "I'd never say anything like that!"

Now, Marge, all this time he is busy cuttin' my round steak and gettin' ready to grind it in the machine. I answered him real snappy, "You're a liar and the truth ain't in you! I have heard you say 'spick' after some Spanish person left the store. I also heard you say 'wop' one day, and I know that if you like nasty words like that you just couldn't resist sayin' 'nigger'."

Well, he looks kind of flustered-like and says, "I'm sorry, sister, all I meant was that I like you people." "I know what you meant," I says, "and I don't wanna hear no talk out of you 'bout how you think I'm better than some folks who you consider to be nothin' 'cause if the truth is to be known, I can't imagine *anybody* bein' interested in makin' *your* acquaintance!" The next thing I did was shake my finger at him and read him some more, "You oughta be tickled pink that anybody buys your old, crummy dogmeat!"

...Now, Marge, I know the meat is good, but I just called it "dogmeat" in order to be mean! "Furthermore," I says, "I'm not gonna buy that round steak, and I'm gonna tell all the people I see not to come in here and buy anything you got. I'll bet if everyone was to stay away from this place for a while you'd be tickled to death whenever you finally did get a customer, any customer!"

I'm tellin' you, those kinda people make me sick!... Sure, I remember the time that woman told you about Puerto Ricans. Ain't that some nerve! She's gonna ask *you* what you think of so many of 'em movin' in her neighborhood! I'm glad you told her that you was plannin' on movin' over there *yourself.* I guess that held her for a while! Folks who rent apartments got a real crust to come talkin' about *their* neighborhood!

Marge, if there is one thing I can't stand it's gettin' one of them back-handed compliments! I remember a man tellin' me once that he liked me 'cause I was "different." I said, "Different from what?" Then he went into a big old wringin' and twistin' 'bout how some colored people was terrible, but I was very nice. I told him, "You can get off of that 'cause I'm just exactly like most of the colored people I know!"

...You are so right! I know a lot of folks swallow that old line when it gets thrown at them!...Don't I see 'em grinnin' and smilin' with that thank-you-so-much look on their faces! But if the fools only knew that as soon as they turned their back another name was pinned on them they'd grin out of the other side of their mouth. No, *nobody* is gonna get in my good graces by tellin' me that some other folk is so distasteful to them that I look nice by comparison! We gotta straighten these name-callers out!

We Need a Union Too

Marge, who likes housework?...I guess there's a few people who do, but when a family starts makin' money what is the first thing that happens?... You are right! They will get themselves a maid to do the housework. I've never heard of no rich folk who just want to go on doin' it out of pure love and affection! Oh, they might mix up a cake once in a while or straighten a doily, but for the most part they're gettin' a kick out of doin' that simply 'cause they don't have to do it. Honey, I mean to tell you that we got a job that almost nobody wants!

That is why we need a union! Why shouldn't we have set hours and set pay just like busdrivers and other folks, why shouldn't we have vacation pay and things like that?...Well, I guess it would be awful hard to get houseworkers together on account of them all workin' off separate-like in different homes, but it would sure be a big help and also keep you out of a lot of nasty arguments!

For example, I'd walk in to work and the woman would say to me, "Mildred, you will wax the floors with paste wax, please." Then I say, "No, that is very heavy work and is against the union regulations." She will say, "If you don't do it, I will have to get me somebody else!" Then I say, "The somebody else will be union, too, so they will not be able to do it, either." "Oh," she will say, "if it's too heavy for you and too heavy for the somebody else then it must be also too heavy for me! How will I get my floors done?" "Easy," I say, "the union will send a *man* over to do things like paste wax, window washin', scrubbin' walls, takin' down venetian blinds and all such."

She will pat her foot then and say, "Well! *That* will cost me extra!"... "Exactly," I will say, "'cause it is extra wear and tear on a man's energy, and wear and tear on energy costs money!"

...Oh, Marge, you would have to put a problem in the thing! All right, suppose she says, "Never mind, I don't want you or anybody else from that union, I will search around and find me somebody who does not belong to it!" Well, then the union calls out all the folks who work in that buildin', and we'll march up and down in front of that apartment house carryin' signs which will read, "Miss So-and-so of Apartment 5B is unfair to organized houseworkers!" . . . The other folks in the buildin' will not like it, and they will also be annoyed 'cause their maids are out there walkin' instead of upstairs doin' the work. Can't you see all the neighbors bangin' on Apartment 5B!

Study Questions

1   What are some of the notions about African-American identity that Mildred challenges? How does Mildred's use of humor affect those challenges? How does Mildred respond to stereotypes of other ethnic and racial groups?

2   Why do you think Childress lets us "overhear" these stories as they are told to Mildred's friend Marge?

3   Why did Childress choose a domestic worker for her heroine? How might Mildred respond to the postwar domestic ideal discussed by Elaine May or by Betty Friedan?

4   What does Mildred have in common with the African-American activists discussed by William Chafe?

CHAPTER 11

Songs of the Chicago Blues

Some 1.6 million African Americans migrated from the rural South to industrial cities of the North and West in the 1940s. Most found overcrowding in homes and schools, poor city services, and job discrimination. From 1945 to 1960, Chicago's South Side was second only to Harlem as a center of black American culture. There in Chicago's bars and honky-tonks southern-born musicians developed the urban Blues – characterized by amplified instruments, rough vocal styles, heavy backbeat, and lyrics about city life. Postwar Chicago Blues shared a number of persistent themes, especially migration, explicit sexuality, and working-class experience.

Bo Diddley (1928–) was born Otha Ellas Bates in Mississippi. He moved with his family to Chicago's South Side in the mid-1930s. During and after high school, he played the Chicago area with the Langley Avenue Jive Cats while supporting himself as a truck driver, a construction worker, and a semiprofessional boxer. "I'm a Man" (1955), the first record he cut, immediately topped the Rhythm and Blues charts. Diddley is considered one of the strongest influences on rock and roll. He is associated with his trademark beat ("bomp bomp bomp – bomp bomp"), which he claims to have borrowed from singing cowboy Gene Autry.

Born McKinley Morganfield in Rolling Fork, Mississippi, Muddy Waters (1915–83) was the son of a sharecropper and the grandson of former slaves. He was raised in Clarksdale, Mississippi, by his grandmother and worked as a farm laborer as a young man. He moved to Chicago in 1943 and made money by laboring in a paper mill and driving trucks while playing in bars and clubs. He learned to play guitar by listening to Robert Johnson recordings. With his electric guitar sound, he revolutionized the sound of the Blues.

Jimmy Reed (1925–76) was one of 10 children in a Dunleith, Mississippi sharecropping family. Reed dropped out of school at the age of 13 with only three years of formal education. Reed moved to Chicago in 1943 before being drafted into the Navy. After the war he worked in a meatpacking plant in Indiana, then moved back to Chicago and recorded his first track in 1953. Reed was the first Chicago Blues artist to have crossover hits. Among the musicians who have covered his songs are Elvis Presley, Aretha Franklin, Lou Rawls, Neil Young, Van Halen, the Grateful Dead, the Rolling Stones, Bruce Springsteen, Jerry Lee Lewis, and the Plimsouls.

Taken together, the following blues songs create a commentary on postwar American life.

Bo Diddley "I'm a Man" (1955)

Now when I was a little boy at the age of five,
I had somethin' in my pocket to keep a lot of folks alive.
Now I'm a man, made 21, you know baby
We can have a lot of fun.
I'm a Man, I spell it M-A-N.
All you pretty women, stand in line.
I can make love to you baby in a hour's time.
I'm a man, spelled M-A-N, Man.
I'm goin' back down to Kansas to
Bring back a second cousin
Little John the Conqueroo.*
I'm a man, spelled M-A-N.
The line I shoot will never miss,
The way I make love, they can't resist.
I'm a man, I spell M-A-N.

*In African-American folk culture, John the Conqueror root is a tuber (related to sweet potato), named after a folk hero, that is carried to bring luck at games of chance or enhance personal sexual power.

Muddy Waters, "Just Make Love to Me" (1954)

I don't want you to be no slave,
I don't want you to work all day,
I don't want you to be true,
I just want to make love to you.
I don't want you to wash my clothes,
I don't want you to keep a home,
I don't want your money too,
I just want to make love to you.
I can tell by the way you switch and walk,
I can see by the way you baby talk,
I can know by the way you treat your man,
I wanna love you baby, it's a crying shame.

I don't want you to cook my bread,
I don't want you to make my bed,
I don't want you because I'm sad and blue,
I just want to make love to you.

Jimmy Reed, "Bright Lights, Big City" (1961)

Bright lights, big city
They've gone to my baby's head.
I tried to tell the woman
But she don't believe a word I said.

All right, pretty baby,
You'll need my help someday.
You gonna wish you'd listened
To some of those things I said.
Go ahead pretty baby,
Honey, knock yourself out.
Go ahead pretty baby,
Honey, knock yourself out.

I still love ya baby but
You don't what it's all about.

Bright lights, big city,
They went to my baby's head.
Hope you remember
Some of those things I said.

Study Questions

1 What does the music tell you about city life in postwar Chicago? Consider both what the *lyrics* say and the *sound* of the music itself.
2 How do these songs define what it means to be a man?
3 Compare male–female relationships as pictured in the blues songs with those relationships as depicted by Betty Friedan in "The Problem That Has No Name."

CHAPTER 12

Halfway to Dick and Jane:
A Puerto Rican Pilgrimage

Jack Agüeros

Jack Agüeros (1934–) was born in East Harlem, and raised as an only child by his father, who was a restaurant worker, and his mother, who was a seamstress. A writer, critic, and community activist, who earned his BA from Brooklyn College, and his MA in Urban Studies from Occidental College, his community projects have included youth outreach and fund raising for antipoverty projects. He has also served as director of El Museo del Barrio, one of the leading Latino cultural institutions in the nation. Agüeros's books include Dominoes & Other Stories from the Puerto Rican *(1993) and* Sonnets from the Puerto Rican *(1996). In the following memoir, published in 1971, Agüeros gives us a vivid portrait of the ways that Puerto Rican and US history and culture shaped his family's history and identity.*

My father arrived in America in 1920, a stowaway on a steamer that shuttled between San Juan and New York. At sixteen, he was through with school and had been since thirteen or fourteen when he left the eighth grade. Between dropout and migrant, the picture is not totally clear, but three themes dominate: baseball, cockfighting, and cars. At sixteen, my father had lived in every town of Puerto Rico, had driven every road there in Ford Models A and T, had played basketball, baseball, studied English and American History, hustled tourists, and had heard the popular and classical music of two cultures.

With a superficial knowledge of America, wholly aware that the streets were not paved in gold, interested specifically in neither employment nor education, my father visited New York in the same spirit in which a family might drive out in the country on a Sunday afternoon. But it was winter 1920, and my father's romantic picture of snow was shattered. His clothes were inadequate for cold weather, and he himself was not prepared either physically or emotionally for cold. The light English patter he had charmed the tourists with was no match for the rapid-fire slurred English of New York's streets. His school English, with its carefully pronounced "water" and "squirrel," seemed like another language compared to "wudder" and "squaral."

It was a three-day winter for my father. In seventy-two hours, he thought he understood New York: the flatness of its geography and humanity, the extreme cold of climate and character, the toe to toe aloneness. On the fourth day, Joaquin Agüeros went back to San Juan.

He came back "north" again in his early twenties, but again there is an unclear time span. There appears to have been a short hitch in the Puerto Rican National Guard, and during this time, there was an upheaval in island and mainland politics. Governors of Puerto Rico were appointed by the White House and had considerable powers over the island's economy and politics. The new governor began a thorough shake-up of the civil service, and as a result, my father left the National Guard and my grandfather, Ramon Agüeros, was relieved of his title and duties of police captain. My father's family, composed of my grandparents, three brothers, a sister, and one or two *hermanos de crianza* (literally, "brothers of upbringing," or children brought up as if brothers), was plunged into total poverty. My grandfather was not and had never been a landowner. His policeman's pay was the only source of income. Joaquin was the oldest son, and unemployed. The family was spared starvation by the Order of the Masons, which delivered trucks full of food once or twice a month (Grandpa was a master).

The tyranny of the new gringo governor was causing serious repercussions on the island. Puerto Rico was an extraordinarily underdeveloped country, very poor and depressed, without a unanimity of affection for America. There was a massacre of civilians at Ponce by the police. This was blamed on the new governor, as were all the island's problems. My father has told me that talk and rumors of assassination were common. Many people expected to hear of the governor's death. Nevertheless, the governor was not assassinated, and there were no more Ponce massacres. Capitan Ramon Agüeros was readmitted to the force but not reinstated in rank. Soon thereafter, his eldest son Joaquin also became a policeman.

In my youth, I loved to look at the pictures of Father and Grandfather in their police uniforms. Of Ramon, bald and clean shaven in his *capitan's* jacket, I remember a large chest, a strong jaw, and tough eyes. Set in a gilded oval frame with an American eagle at the top, it hung under glass in my parents' bedroom. Of my father, I remember a patched-up photo, probably torn up by my mother after a spat. In it a tall, very handsome young man was standing full length with hat and riding boots. Face not stern like Ramon's, but with a look of forced seriousness. Joaquin bore a resemblance to Rudolf Valentino and to Carlos Gardel, the Argentinian singer and film star. [. . .]

I was told that my father left the police force because he had shot and wounded a moonshiner in a raid on a still. (Not very unlikely, for such raids were common: there is a photo, sepiaed by time, Grandpa and Father, guns pointing at a group of desperados with hands held high up against a wall of vats, jugs, and plumbing.) The wounded moonshiner turned out to be a member of high society, and my father was accused of misconduct and promiscuous use of a firearm [. . .]

Joaquin, like many Puerto Ricans, has always been proud to a fault. Standing departmental hearings, he was exonerated of the charges. But the exoneration was meaningless; outraged that his integrity had been questioned at all, he resigned from the force. [...]

That's what I know about my old man's early life – he was a picaresque character from a Spanish novel. It is a collage of information, some of it concrete and verifiable, most of it gathered haphazardly and connected by conjecture. Does it matter what the governor's name is? Does it matter whether any or all of it is fact or fiction? What matters is that I thought my old man enjoyed life, let no grass grow under his feet, and it also matters that he came back to New York.

I was born in Harlem in 1934. We lived on 111th Street off Fifth Avenue. It was a block of mainly three-story buildings – with brick fronts, or brownstone, or limestone imitations of brownstone. Our apartment was a three-room first-floor walk-up. It faced north and had three windows on the street, none in back. There was a master bedroom, a living room, a kitchen-dining room, a foyer with a short hall, and a bathroom. In the kitchen there was an air shaft to evacuate cooking odors and grease – we converted it to a chimney for Santa Claus.

The kitchen was dominated by a large Victorian china closet, and the built-in wall shelves were lined with oilcloth, trimmed with ruffle, both decorated by brilliant and miniature fruits. Prominent on a wall of the kitchen was a large reproduction of a still life, a harvest table full of produce, framed and under glass. From it, I learned to identify apples, pumpkins, bananas, pears, grapes, and melons, and "peaches without worms." A joke between my mother and me. (A peach we had bought in the city market, under the New Haven's elevated tracks, bore, like the trains above, passengers.) [...]

My *madrina* lived on the third floor of our building, and for all practical purposes, her apartment and ours formed a duplex. My godmother really was my second mother. Rocking me to sleep, playing her guitar, and singing me little songs, she used to say, "I'm your real mother, 'cause I love you more." But I knew that wasn't so.

Carmen Diaz, my mother, came to New York in 1931. Her brother, a career soldier, had sent for her with the intention of taking her up to Plattsburg, where he was stationed. Like my father, she arrived in New York on a steamer. My uncle had planned to show his kid sister the big city before leaving for Plattsburg, but during a week in New York my mother was convinced to stay. More opportunities, and other Spanish-speaking people, were the reasons that changed her mind.

Carmen had had a tough time all her life in Puerto Rico. Her mother had died when she was only two. Her father, a wealthy farmer and veterinarian, remarried and began paying less and less attention to his business affairs. The stepmother was not very fond of the children. Thus, when her older sister married a policeman, Carmen accepted the invitation to live with the newlyweds, acting as a sort of housekeeper-governess. After many years in this role, which my mother describes as "rewarding, but not a life for a young girl," came the offer to "go north."

On the island, my mother had two serious suitors. One was a schoolteacher who had an ailing mother and could not afford to marry on his salary. The other was a rookie cop who had arrested her brother-in-law for carrying a concealed weapon. The brother-in-law took the arrest in good humor, and after proving that he was an off-duty cop, invited the rookie home for dinner. The rookie became a frequent visitor, twirling apples for Carmen's delight, but one day he came to visit and said he was going north, to find a good job. He said he would write, but no letter ever came from Joaquin.

Carmen had big plans for her life in America, intending to go to school and study interior decorating. But the Puerto Ricans who came to New York at that time found life in the city tough. It was the Depression, and work was hard to come by. My mother went from job to job for about six months and finally landed a job in the garment district as a seamstress. Twenty years later, she retired from the ILGWU [International Ladies Garment Workers' Union], her dream of becoming a decorator waylaid by bumping into my father on a Manhattan street and reviving the old romance. My father had been back in America since the mid-twenties. In America he remembers working a long day to earn $1.25. After a time, he found a job in a restaurant that paid nine dollars a week and provided two meals a day. That was a good deal, even at a six-day week, twelve to fifteen hours a day.

I am an only child. My parents and I always talked about my becoming a doctor. The law and politics were not highly regarded in my house. Lawyers, my mother would explain, had to defend people whether they were guilty or not, while politicians, my father would say, were all crooks. A doctor helped everybody, rich and poor, white and black. If I became a doctor, I could study hay fever and find a cure for it, my godmother would say. Also, I could take care of my parents when they were old. I liked the idea of helping, and for nineteen years my sole ambition was to study medicine.

My house had books, not many, but my parents encouraged me to read. As I became a good reader they bought books for me and never refused me money for their purchase. My father once built a bookcase for me. It was an important moment, for I had always believed that my father was not too happy about my being a bookworm. The atmosphere at home was always warm. We seemed to be a popular family. We entertained frequently, with two standing parties a year – at Christmas and for my birthday. Parties were always large. My father would dismantle the beds and move all the furniture so that the full two rooms could be used for dancing. My mother would cook up a storm, particularly at Christmas. *Pasteles, lechon asado, arroz con gandules,* and a lot of *coquito* to drink (meat-stuffed plantain, roast pork, rice with pigeon peas, and coconut nog). My father always brought in a band. They played without compensation and were guests at the party. They ate and drank and danced while a victrola covered the intermissions. One year my father brought home a whole pig and hung it in the foyer doorway. He and my mother prepared it by rubbing it down with oil, oregano, and garlic. After preparation, the pig was taken down and carried over to a local bakery where it was cooked and returned home. Parties always went on till daybreak, and in addition to the band, there were always volunteers to sing and declaim poetry.

My mother kept an immaculate household. Bedspreads (chenille seemed to be very in) and lace curtains, washed at home like everything else, were hung up on huge racks with rows of tight nails. The racks were assembled in the living room, and the moisture from the wet bedspreads would fill the apartment. In a sense, that seems to be the lasting image of that period of my life. The house was clean. The neighbors were clean. The streets, with few cars, were clean. The buildings were clean and uncluttered with people on the stoops. The park was clean. The visitors to my house were clean, and the relationships that my family had with other Puerto Rican families, and the Italian families that my father had met through baseball and my mother through the garment center, were clean. Second Avenue was clean and most of the apartment windows had awnings. There was always music, there seemed to be no rain, and snow did not become slush. School was fun, we wrote essays about how grand America was, we put up hunchbacked cats at Halloween, we believed Santa Claus visited everyone. I believed everyone was Catholic. I grew up with dogs, nightingales, my godmother's guitar, rocking chair, cat, guppies, my father's occasional roosters, kept in a cage on the fire escape. Laundry delivered and collected by horse and wagon, fruits and vegetables sold the same way, windowsill refrigeration in winter, iceman and box in summer. The police my friends, likewise the teachers.

In short, the first seven or so years of my life were not too great a variation on Dick and Jane, the school book figures who, if my memory serves me correctly, were blond Anglo-Saxons, not immigrants, not migrants like the Puerto Ricans, and not the children of either immigrants or migrants.

My family moved in 1941 to Lexington Avenue into a larger apartment where I could have my own room. It was a light, sunny, railroad flat on the top floor of a well-kept building. I transferred to a new school, and whereas before my classmates had been mostly black, the new school had few blacks. The classes were made up of Italians, Irish, Jews, and a sprinkling of Puerto Ricans. My block was populated by Jews, Italians, and Puerto Ricans.

And then a whole series of different events began. I went to junior high school. We played in the backyards, where we tore down fences to build fires to cook stolen potatoes. We tore up whole hedges, because the green tender limbs would not burn when they were peeled, and thus made perfect skewers for our stolen "mickies." We played tag in the abandoned buildings, tearing the plaster off the walls, tearing the wire lath off the wooden slats, tearing the wooden slats themselves, good for fires, for kites, for sword fighting. We ran up and down the fire escapes playing tag and over and across many rooftops. The war ended and the heavy Puerto Rican migration began. The Irish and the Jews disappeared from the neighborhood. The Italians tried to consolidate east of Third Avenue.

What caused the clean and open world to end? Many things. Into an ancient neighborhood came pouring four to five times more people than it had been designed to hold. Men who came running at the promise of jobs were jobless as the war ended. They were confused. They could not see the economic forces that ruled their lives as they drank beer on the corners, reassuring themselves of good times to come while they were hell-bent toward alcoholism. The sudden surge in numbers caused new resentments, and prejudice was intensified. Some were forced to live in cellars, and were then characterized as cave dwellers. Kids came who were confused by the new surroundings; their Puerto Ricanness forced us against a mirror asking, "If they are Puerto Ricans, what are we?" and thus they confused us. In our confusion we were sometimes pathetically reaching out, sometimes pathologically striking out. Gangs, Drugs. Wine. Smoking. Girls. Dances and slow-drag music. Mambo. Spics, Spooks, and Wops. Territories, brother gangs, and war councils establishing rules for right of way on blocks and avenues and for seating in the local theater. Pegged pants and zip guns. Slang.

Dick and Jane were dead, man. Education collapsed. Every classroom had ten kids who spoke no English. Black, Italian, Puerto Rican relations in the classroom were good, but we all knew we couldn't visit one another's neighborhoods. Sometimes we could not move too freely within our own blocks. On 109th, from the lamp post west, the Latin Aces, and from the lamp post east, the Senecas, the "club" I belonged to. The kids who spoke no English became known as Marine Tigers, picked up from a popular Spanish song. (The *Marine Tiger* and the *Marine Shark* were two ships that sailed from San Juan to New York and brought over many, many migrants from the island.)

The neighborhood had its boundaries. Third Avenue and east, Italian. Fifth Avenue and west, black. South, there was a hill on 103rd Street known locally as Cooney's Hill. When you got to the top of the hill, something strange happened: America began, because from the hill south was where the "Americans" lived. Dick and Jane were not dead; they were alive and well in a better neighborhood.

When, as a group of Puerto Rican kids, we decided to go swimming to Jefferson Park Pool, we knew we risked a fight and a beating from the Italians. And when we went to La Milagrosa Church in Harlem, we knew we risked a fight and a beating from the blacks. But when we went over Cooney's Hill, we risked dirty looks, disapproving looks, and questions from the police like, "What are you doing in this neighborhood?" and "Why don't you kids go back where you belong?"

Where we belonged! Man, I had written compositions about America. Didn't I belong on the Central Park tennis courts, even if I didn't know how to play? Couldn't I watch Dick play? Weren't these policemen working for me too?

Junior high school was a waste. I can say with 90 per cent accuracy that I learned nothing. The woodshop was used to manufacture stocks for "homemades" after Macy's stopped selling zipguns. We went from classroom to classroom answering "here," and trying to be "good." The math class was generally permitted to go to the gym after roll call. English was still a good class. Partly because of a damn good, tough teacher named Miss Beck, and partly because of the grade-number system (7-1 the smartest seventh grade and 7-12, the dumbest). Books were left in school, there was little or no homework, and the whole thing seemed to be a holding operation until high school. Somehow or other, I passed the entrance exam to Brooklyn Technical High School. But I couldn't cut the mustard, either academically or with the "American" kids. After one semester, I came back to PS 83, waited a semester, and went on to Benjamin Franklin High School.

I still wanted to study medicine and excelled in biology. English was always an interesting subject, and I still enjoyed writing compositions and reading. In the neighborhood it was becoming a problem being categorized as a bookworm and as one who used "Sunday words," or "big words." I dug school, but I wanted to be one of the boys more. I think the boys respected my intelligence, despite their ribbing. Besides which, I belonged to a club with a number of members who were interested in going to college, and so I wasn't so far out. [...]

My mother leads me by the hand and carries a plain brown shopping bag. We enter an immense airplane hangar. Structural steel crisscrosses on the ceiling and walls: large round and square rivets look like buttons or bubbles of air trapped in the girders. There are long metallic counters with people bustling behind them. It smells of C.N. disinfectant. Many people stand on many lines up to these counters; there are many conversations going on simultaneously. The huge space plays tricks with voices and a very eerie combination of sounds results. A white cabbage is rolled down a counter at us. We retaliate by throwing down stamps.

For years I thought that sequence happened in a dream. The rolling cabbage rolled in my head, and little unrelated incidents seemed to bring it to the surface of my mind. I could not understand why I remembered a once-dreamt dream so vividly. I was sixteen when I picked up and read Freud's *The Interpretation of Dreams*. One part I understood immediately and well, sex and symbolism. In no time, I had hung my shingle: Streetcorner Analyst. My friends would tell me their dreams and with the most outrageous sexual explanations we laughed whole evenings away. But the rolling cabbage could not be stopped and neither quack analysis nor serious thought could explain it away. One day I asked my mother if she knew anything about it.

"That was home relief, 1937 or 1938. You were no more than four years old then. Your father had been working at a restaurant and I had a job downtown. I used to take you every morning to Dona Eduvije who cared for you all day. She loved you very much, and she was very clean and neat, but I used to cry on my way to work, wishing I could stay home with my son and bring him up like a proper mother would. But I guess I was fated to be a workhorse. When I was pregnant, I would get on the crowded subway and go to work. I would get on a crowded elevator up. Then down. Then back on the subway. Every day I was afraid that the crowd would hurt me, that I would lose my baby. But I had to work. I worked for the WPA right into my ninth month."

My mother was telling it "like it was," and I sat stupefied, for I could not believe that what she said applied to the time I thought of as open and clean. I had been existing in my life like a small plant in a bell jar, my parents defining my awareness. There were things all around me I could not see.

"When you were born we had been living as boarders. It was hard to find an apartment, even in Harlem. You saw signs that said 'No Renting to Colored or Spanish.' That meant Puerto Ricans. We used to say, 'This is supposed to be such a great country?' But with a new baby we were determined not to be boarders and we took an apartment on 111th Street. Soon after we moved, I lost my job because my factory closed down. Your father was making seven or eight dollars a week in a terrible job in a carpet factory. They used to clean rugs, and your father's hands were always in strong chemicals. You know how funny some of his fingernails are? It was from that factory. He came home one night and he was looking at his fingers, and he started saying that he didn't come to this country to lose his hands. He wanted to hold a bat and play ball and he wanted to work – but he didn't want to lose his hands. So he quit the job and went to a restaurant for less pay. With me out of work, a new apartment and therefore higher rent, we couldn't manage. Your father was furious when I mentioned home relief. He said he would rather starve than go on relief. But I went and filled out the papers and answered all the questions and swallowed my pride when they treated me like an intruder. I used to say to them, 'Find me a job – get my husband a better job – we don't want home relief.' But we had to take it. And all that mess with the stamps in exchange for food. And they used to have weekly 'specials' sort of – but a lot of things were useless – because they were American food. I don't remember if we went once a week or once every two weeks. You were so small I don't know how you remember that place and the long lines. It didn't last long because your father had everybody trying to find him a better job and finally somebody did. Pretty soon I went into the WPA and thank God, we never had to deal with those people again. I don't know how you remember that place, but I wish you didn't. I wish I could forget that home relief thing myself. It was the worst time for your father and me. He still hates it." [. . .]

By sixteen I had my own collection of anecdotes supporting discrimination. Police telling me to "move on" for no reason, to get off the stoop of the building where I lived, being called fag and spic, stopped and searched on the streets, in hallways, in candy stores, and anywhere that we congregated. Called fag because in a time of crew cuts the Puerto Rican male took pride in his long hair. With the postwar movies of American heroes in Germany, Gestapo and Nazi were familiar figures, and for me they were our police. Who could you complain to about police? Hitler?

In school, Mr. Miller, goddamn him to hell forever, took a Puerto Rican boy named Luis and kept him under the teacher's desk during class periods. When Luis would moan, Miller would kick him. Between periods, Miller walked Luis around the school, keeping him in a painful armlock. Mr. Flax, the principal, laughed. And Diamond, the algebra teacher, either sent us to play basketball or asked us to lay our heads on our desks while he checked the stock market reports in the *New York Times*. To whom did you complain about a teacher – a laughing principal? [. . .]

My father and I are walking through East Harlem, south down Lexington from 112th toward 110th, in 1952. Saturday in late spring, I am eighteen years old, sun brilliant on the streets, people running back and forth on household errands. My father is telling me a story about how back in nineteen thirty something, we were very poor and Con Ed light meters were in every apartment. "The Puerto Ricans, maybe everybody else, would hook up a shunt wire around the meter, specially in the evenings when the use was heavy – that way you didn't pay for all the electric you used. We called it '*pillo*' (thief)."

We arrive at 110th Street and all the cart vendors are there peddling plantains, avocados, yams, various subtropical roots. I make a casual remark about how foolish it all seemed, and my father catches that I am looking down on them. "Are they stealing?" he asks. "Are they selling people colored water? Aren't they working honestly? Are they any different from a bank president? Aren't they hung like you and me? They are *machos*, and to be respected. Don't let college go to your head. You think a Ph.D. is automatically better than a peddler? Remember where you come from – poor people. I mopped floors for people and I wasn't ashamed, but I never let them look down on me. Don't you look down on anybody." [. . .]

What is a migration? What does it happen to? Why are the Eskimos still dark after living in that snow all these centuries? Why don't they have a word for snow? What things are around me with such high saturation that I have not named them? What is a migration? If you rob my purse, are you really a fool? Can a poor boy really be president? In America? Of anything? If he is not white? Should one man's achievement fulfill one million people? Will you let us come near your new machine: after all, there is no more ditch digging? What is a migration? What does it happen to?

[. . .] When a Puerto Rican comes to America, he comes looking for a job. He takes the cold as one of a negative series of givens. The mad hustle, the filthy city, filthy air, filthy housing, sardine transportation, are in the series. He knows life will be tough and dangerous. But he thinks he can make a buck. And in his mind, there is only one tableau: himself retired, owner of his home in Puerto Rico, chickens cackling in the back yard.

It startles me still, though it has been five years since my parents went back to the island. I never believed them. My father, driving around New York for the Housing Authority, knowing more streets in more boroughs than I do, and my mother, curious in her later years about museums and theaters, and reading my books as fast as I would put them down, then giving me cryptic reviews. Salinger is really silly (*Catcher in the Rye*), but entertaining. That evil man deserved to die (*Moby Dick*). He's too much (Dostoevski in *Crime and Punishment*). I read this when I was a little girl in school (*Hamlet* and *Macbeth*). It's too sad for me (*Cry, the Beloved Country*).

My father, intrigued by the thought of passing the foreman's exam, sitting down with a couple of arithmetic books, and teaching himself at age fifty-five to do work problems and mixture problems and fractions and decimals, and going into the civil service exam and scoring a seventy-four and waiting up one night for me to show me three poems he had written. These two cosmopolites, gladiators without skills or language, battling hostile environments and prejudiced people and systems, had graduated from Harlem to the Bronx, had risen into America's dream-cherished lower middle class, and then put it down for Puerto Rico after thirty plus years.

What is a migration, when is it not just a long visit?

I was born in Harlem, and I live downtown. And I am a migrant, for if a migration is anything, it is a state of mind. I have known those Eskimos who lived in America twenty and thirty years and never voted, never attended a community meeting, never filed a complaint against a landlord, never informed the police when they were robbed or swindled, or when their daughters were molested. Never appeared at the State or City Commission on Human Rights, never reported a business fraud, never, in other words, saw the snow.

And I am very much a migrant because I am still not quite at home in America. Always there are hills; on the other side – people inclined to throwing cabbages. I cannot "earn and return" – there is no position for me in my father's tableau.

However, I approach the future with optimism. Fewer Puerto Ricans like Eskimos, a larger number of leaders like myself, trained in the university, tempered in the ghetto, and with a vision of America moving from its unexecuted policy to a society open and clean, accessible to anyone.

Dick and Jane? They, too, were tripped by the society, and in our several ways, we are all still migrating.

Study Questions

1   Make a chronology chart for the three generations of family history covered in Agüeros's memoir: his grandparents/parents in Puerto Rico; New York during the Depression and World War II eras; and the 1950s. List one important outside event that influenced the family history for each of these periods.

2   What role does Bodnar's concept of "generational memory" play in the Agüeros family? Identify a passage that captures his parents' or his own generational memory in a way that you find particularly interesting or moving.

3   Why does Agüeros say that his Puerto Rican pilgrimage only brought him "halfway to Dick and Jane"? Who were "Dick and Jane"?

4   Why did Agüeros, a native-born American, feel out of place in his own country? How might Kirk and Okazawa-Rey explain his "social location"?

CHAPTER 13

From *Goodbye, Columbus*

Philip Roth

Philip Roth (1933–) was born in Newark, New Jersey, to Jewish-American parents who were the children of Eastern European immigrants. Roth's father was an insurance manager and his mother a homemaker. Roth spent a year at Newark College of Rutgers University; he received his BA from Bucknell University and his MA in English from the University of Chicago. Roth, whose fiction often focuses on middle-class Jewish families, has published over 20 novels, winning the Pulitzer Prize in 1997 for American Pastoral. Goodbye, Columbus *(1959), which won the National Book Award, was Roth's first novel, written when he was 26. In the opening chapter, reproduced here, Roth explores the worlds of working-class urban Jews and wealthy Jewish families who moved to the suburbs in the post-World War II era.*

The first time I saw Brenda she asked me to hold her glasses. Then she stepped out to the edge of the diving board and looked foggily into the pool; it could have been drained, myopic Brenda would never have known it. She dove beautifully, and a moment later she was swimming back to the side of the pool, her head of shortclipped auburn hair held up, straight ahead of her, as though it were a rose on a long stem. She glided to the edge and then was beside me. "Thank you," she said, her eyes watery though not from the water. She extended a hand for her glasses but did not put them on until she turned and headed away. I watched her move off. Her hands suddenly appeared behind her. She caught the bottom of her suit between thumb and index finger and flicked what flesh had been showing back where it belonged. My blood jumped.

That night, before dinner, I called her.

"Who are you calling?" my Aunt Gladys asked.

"Some girl I met today."

"Doris introduced you?"

"Doris wouldn't introduce me to the guy who drains the pool, Aunt Gladys."

"Don't criticize all the time. A cousin's a cousin. How did you meet her?"

"I didn't really meet her. I saw her."

"Who is she?"

"Her last name is Patimkin."

"Patimkin I don't know," Aunt Gladys said, as if she knew anybody who belonged to the Green Lane Country Club. "You're going to call her you don't know her?"

"Yes," I explained. "I'll introduce myself."

"Casanova," she said, and went back to preparing my uncle's dinner. None of us ate together: my Aunt Gladys ate at five o'clock, my cousin Susan at five-thirty, me at six, and my uncle at six-thirty. There is nothing to explain this beyond the fact that my aunt is crazy.

"Where's the suburban phone book?" I asked after pulling out all the books tucked under the telephone table.

"What?"

"The suburban phone book. I want to call Short Hills."

"That skinny book? What, I gotta clutter my house with that, I never use it?"

"Where is it?"

"Under the dresser where the leg came off."

"For God's sake," I said.

"Call information better. You'll go yanking around there, you'll mess up my drawers. Don't bother me, you see your uncle'll be home soon. I haven't even fed *you* yet."

"Aunt Gladys, suppose tonight we all eat together. It's hot, it'll be easier for you."

"Sure, I should serve four different meals at once. You eat pot roast, Susan with the cottage cheese, Max has steak. Friday night is his steak night, I wouldn't deny him. And I'm having a little cold chicken. I should jump up and down twenty different times? What am I, a workhorse?"

"Why don't we all have steak, or cold chicken – "

"Twenty years I'm running a house. Go call your girl friend."

But when I called, Brenda Patimkin wasn't home. She's having dinner at the club, a woman's voice told me. Will she be home after (my voice was two octaves higher than a choirboy's)? I don't know, the voice said, she may go driving golf balls. Who is this? I mumbled some words – nobody she wouldn't know I'll call back no message thank you sorry to bother...I hung up somewhere along in there. Then my aunt called me and I steeled myself for dinner.

She pushed the black whirring fan up to *High* and that way it managed to stir the cord that hung from the kitchen light.

"What kind of soda you want? I got ginger ale, plain seltzer, black raspberry, and a bottle cream soda I could open up."

"None, thank you."

"You want water?"

"I don't drink with my meals. Aunt Gladys, I've told you that every day for a year already – "

"Max could drink a whole case with his chopped liver only. He works hard all day. If you worked hard you'd drink more."

At the stove she heaped up a plate with pot roast, gravy, boiled potatoes, and peas and carrots. She put it in front of me and I could feel the heat of the food in my face. Then she cut two pieces of rye bread and put that next to me, on the table.

I forked a potato in half and ate it, while Aunt Gladys, who had seated herself across from me, watched. "You don't want bread," she said, "I wouldn't cut it it should go stale."

"I *want* bread," I said.

"You don't like with seeds, do you?"

I tore a piece of bread in half and ate it.

"How's the meat?" she said.

"Okay. Good."

"You'll fill yourself with potatoes and bread, the meat you'll leave over I'll have to throw it out."

Suddenly she leaped up from the chair. "Salt!" When she returned to the table she plunked a salt shaker down in front of me – pepper wasn't served in her home: she'd heard on Galen Drake that it was not absorbed by the body, and it was disturbing to Aunt Gladys to think that anything she served might pass through a gullet, stomach, and bowel just for the pleasure of the trip.

"You're going to pick the peas out is all? You tell me that, I wouldn't buy with the carrots."

"I love carrots," I said, "I love them." And to prove it, I dumped half of them down my throat and the other half onto my trousers.

"Pig," she said.

Though I am very fond of desserts, especially fruit, I chose not to have any. I wanted, this hot night, to avoid the conversation that revolved around my choosing fresh fruit over canned fruit, or canned fruit over fresh fruit; whichever I preferred, Aunt Gladys always had an abundance of the other jamming her refrigerator like stolen diamonds. "He wants canned peaches, I have a refrigerator full of grapes I have to get rid of..." Life was a throwing off for poor Aunt Gladys, her greatest joys were taking out the garbage, emptying her pantry, and making threadbare bundles for what she still referred to as the Poor Jews in Palestine. I only hope she dies with an empty refrigerator, otherwise she'll ruin eternity for everyone else, what with her Velveeta turning green, and her navel oranges growing fuzzy jackets down below.

My Uncle Max came home and while I dialed Brenda's number once again, I could hear soda bottles being popped open in the kitchen. The voice that answered this time was high, curt, and tired. "Hullo."

I launched into my speech. "Hello-Brenda-Brenda-you-don't-know-me-that-is-you-don't-know-my-name-but-I-held-your-glasses-for-you-this-afternoon-at-the-club... You-asked-me-to-I'm-not-a-member-my-cousin-Doris-is-Doris-Klugman-I-asked-who-you-were..." I breathed, gave her a chance to speak, and then went ahead and answered the silence on the other end. "Doris? She's the one who's always reading *War and Peace*. That's how I know it's the summer, when Doris is reading *War and Peace*." Brenda didn't laugh; right from the start she was a practical girl.

"What's your name?" she said.

"Neil Klugman. I held your glasses at the board, remember?"

She answered me with a question of her own, one, I'm sure, that is an embarrassment to both the homely and the fair. "What do you look like?"

"I'm . . . dark."

"Are you a Negro?"

"No," I said.

"What *do* you look like?"

"May I come see you tonight and show you?"

"That's nice," she laughed. "I'm playing tennis tonight."

"I thought you were driving golf balls."

"I drove them already."

"How about after tennis?"

"I'll be sweaty after," Brenda said.

It was not to warn me to clothespin my nose and run in the opposite direction; it was a fact, it apparently didn't bother Brenda, but she wanted it recorded.

"I don't mind," I said, and hoped by my tone to earn a niche somewhere between the squeamish and the grubby. "Can I pick you up?"

She did not answer a minute; I heard her muttering, "Doris Klugman, Doris Klugman . . ." Then she said, "Yes, Briarpath Hills, eight-fifteen."

"I'll be driving a – " I hung back with the year, "a tan Plymouth. So you'll know me. How will I know you?" I said with a sly, awful laugh.

"I'll be sweating," she said and hung up.

Once I'd driven out of Newark, past Irvington and the packed-in tangle of railroad crossings, switchmen shacks, lumberyards, Dairy Queens, and used-car lots, the night grew cooler. It was, in fact, as though the hundred and eighty feet that the suburbs rose in altitude above Newark brought one closer to heaven, for the sun itself became bigger, lower, and rounder, and soon I was driving past long lawns which seemed to be twirling water on themselves, and past houses where no one sat on stoops, where lights were on but no windows open, for those inside, refusing to share the very texture of life with those of us outside, regulated with a dial the amounts of moisture that were allowed access to their skin. It was only eight o'clock, and I did not want to be early, so I drove up and down the streets whose names were those of eastern colleges, as though the township, years ago, when things were named, had planned the destinies of the sons of its citizens. I thought of my Aunt Gladys and Uncle Max sharing a Mounds bar in the cindery darkness of their alley, on beach chairs, each cool breeze sweet to them as the promise of afterlife, and after a while I rolled onto the gravel roads of the small park where Brenda was playing tennis. Inside my glove compartment it was as though the map of *The City Streets of Newark* had metamorphosed into crickets, for those mile-long tarry streets did not exist for me any longer, and the night noises sounded loud as the blood whacking at my temples.

I parked the car under the black-green canopy of three oaks, and walked towards the sound of the tennis balls. I heard an exasperated voice say, "Deuce *again*." It was Brenda and she sounded as though she was sweating considerably. I crackled slowly up the gravel and heard Brenda once more. "My ad," and then just as I rounded the path, catching a cuff full of burrs, I heard, "Game!" Her racket went spinning up in the air and she caught it neatly as I came into sight.

"Hello," I called.

"Hello, Neil. One more game," she called. Brenda's words seemed to infuriate her opponent, a pretty brown-haired girl, not quite so tall as Brenda, who stopped searching for the ball that had been driven past her, and gave both Brenda and myself a dirty look. In a moment I learned the reason why: Brenda was ahead five games to four, and her cocksureness about there being just one game remaining aroused enough anger in her opponent for the two of us to share.

As it happened, Brenda finally won, though it took more games than she'd expected. The other girl, whose name sounded like Simp, seemed happy to end it at six all, but Brenda, shifting, running, up on her toes, would not stop, and finally all I could see moving in the darkness were her glasses, a glint of them, the clasp of her belt, her socks, her sneakers, and, on occasion, the ball. The darker it got the more savagely did Brenda rush the net, which seemed curious, for I had noticed that earlier, in the light, she had stayed back, and even when she had had to rush, after smashing back a lob, she didn't look entirely happy about being so close to her opponent's racket. Her passion for winning a point seemed outmatched by an even stronger passion for maintaining her beauty as it was. I suspected that the red print of a tennis ball on her cheek would pain her more than losing all the points in the world. Darkness pushed her in, however, and she stroked harder, and at last Simp seemed to be running on her ankles. When it was all over, Simp refused my offer of a ride home and indicated with a quality of speech borrowed from some old Katherine Hepburn movie that she could manage for herself; apparently her manor lay no further than the nearest briar patch. She did not like me and I her, though I worried it, I'm sure, more than she did.

"Who is *she*?"

"Laura Simpson Stolowitch."

"Why don't you call her Stolo?" I asked.

"Simp is her Bennington name. The ass."

"Is that where you go to school?" I asked.

She was pushing her shirt up against her skin to dry the perspiration. "No. I go to school in Boston."

I disliked her for the answer. Whenever anyone asks me where I went to school I come right out with it: Newark Colleges of Rutgers University. I may say it a bit too ringingly, too fast, too up-in-the-air, but I say it. For an instant Brenda reminded me of the pug-nosed little bastards from Montclair who come down to the library during vacations, and while I stamp out their books, they stand around tugging their elephantine scarves until they hang to their ankles, hinting all the while at "Boston" and "New Haven."

"Boston University?" I asked, looking off at the trees.

"Radcliffe."

We were still standing on the court, bounded on all sides by white lines. Around the bushes back of the court, fireflies were cutting figure eights in the thorny-smelling air and then, as the night suddenly came all the way in, the leaves on the trees shone for an instant, as though they'd just been rained upon. Brenda walked off the court, with me a step behind her. Now I had grown accustomed to the dark, and as she ceased being merely a voice and turned into a sight again, some of my anger at her "Boston" remark floated off and I let myself appreciate her. Her hands did not twitch at her bottom, but the form revealed itself, covered or not, under the closeness of her khaki Bermudas. There were two wet triangles on the back of her tiny-collared white polo shirt, right where her wings would have been if she'd had a pair. She wore, to complete the picture, a tartan belt, white socks, and white tennis sneakers.

As she walked she zipped the cover on her racket.

"Are you anxious to get home?" I said.

"No."

"Let's sit here. It's pleasant."

"Okay."

We sat down on a bank of grass slanted enough for us to lean back without really leaning; from the angle it seemed as though we were preparing to watch some celestial event, the christening of a new star, the inflation to full size of a half-ballooned moon. Brenda zipped and unzipped the cover while she spoke; for the first time she seemed edgy. Her edginess coaxed mine back, and so we were ready now for what, magically, it seemed we might be able to get by without: a meeting.

"What does your cousin Doris look like?" she asked.

"She's dark – "

"Is she – "

"No," I said. "She has freckles and dark hair and she's very tall."

"Where does she go to school?"

"Northampton."

She did not answer and I don't know how much of what I meant she had understood.

"I guess I don't know her," she said after a moment. "Is she a new member?"

"I think so. They moved to Livingston only a couple of years ago."

"Oh."

No new star appeared, at least for the next five minutes.

"Did you remember me from holding your glasses?" I said.

"Now I do," she said. "Do you live in Livingston too?"

"No. Newark."

"We lived in Newark when I was a baby," she offered.

"Would you like to go home?" I was suddenly angry.

"No. Let's walk though."

Brenda kicked a stone and walked a step ahead of me.

"Why is it you rush the net only after dark?" I said.

She turned to me and smiled. "You noticed? Old Simp the Simpleton doesn't."

"Why do you?"

"I don't like to be up too close, unless I'm sure she won't return it."

"Why?"

"My nose."

"What?"

"I'm afraid of my nose. I had it bobbed."

"What?"

"I had my nose fixed."

"What was the matter with it?"

"It was bumpy."

"A lot?"

"No," she said, "I was pretty. Now I'm prettier. My brother's having his fixed in the fall."

"Does he want to be prettier?"

She didn't answer and walked ahead of me again.

"I don't mean to sound facetious. I mean why's he doing it?"

"He *wants* to . . . unless he becomes a gym teacher . . . but he won't," she said. "We all look like my father."

"Is he having his fixed?"

"Why are you so nasty?"

"I'm not. I'm sorry." My next question was prompted by a desire to sound interested and thereby regain civility; it didn't quite come out as I'd expected – I said it too loud. "How much does it cost?"

Brenda waited a moment but then she answered. "A thousand dollars. Unless you go to a butcher."

"Let me see if you got your money's worth."

She turned again; she stood next to a bench and put the racket down on it. "If I let you kiss me would you stop being nasty?"

We had to take about two too many steps to keep the approach from being awkward, but we pursued the impulse and kissed. I felt her hand on the back of my neck and so I tugged her towards me, too violently perhaps, and slid my own hands across the side of her body and around to her back. I felt the wet spots on her shoulder blades, and beneath them, I'm sure of it, a faint fluttering, as though something stirred so deep in her breasts, so far back it could make itself felt through her shirt. It was like the fluttering of wings, tiny wings no bigger than her breasts. The smallness of the wings did not bother me – it would not take an eagle to carry me up those lousy hundred and eighty feet that make summer nights so much cooler in Short Hills than they are in Newark.

Study Questions

1   Provide three examples from the chapter that tell you about the differences
    between working-class urban and middle-class suburban family life in New
    Jersey during the 1950s. How important is class in explaining these differ-
    ences?
2   Why is Neil's Aunt Gladys worried about his interest in Brenda Patimkin?
3   What do you learn about 1950s dating patterns, education, work, and
    leisure-time activities from this chapter?
4   How does Roth's portrayal of Jewish migration to the suburbs compare
    with the Chicago Blues' presentation of black migration from the South to
    the North in the postwar era?

PART III

War and Social Movements, 1960–1975

In 1960, the population of the USA was approximately 179,000,0000. During the 1960s, the USA became a "middle-class" nation (median income was $6,000 a year). At the same time, Americans living between 1963 and 1968 experienced more widespread social, racial, ethnic, educational, political, and judicial challenges to mainstream institutions than at any other period in US history since the Great Depression. This historic period saw the culmination of the modern Civil Rights Movement, which inspired a variety of liberation movements for students, women, gays and lesbians, Chicanos, Puerto Ricans, Asian Americans, and Native Americans. It also saw massive US government intervention in the economy and abroad, especially in Cuba and Vietnam. As you read about this extraordinary time of ferment, you might explore which of these movements, reforms, and government interventions had the greatest impact on your family, as well as think about which ones had the most lasting influence in shaping the future of American society and culture.

The decade of the 1960s began with the election of President John F. Kennedy, who announced the formation of a "New Frontier" of economic and technological development, followed, after his assassination in 1963, by President Lyndon Johnson's announcement of his "Great Society." Johnson promised a "War on Poverty" and civil rights legislation that would end economic inequality and racial discrimination in the United States. The federal government invested billions of dollars in job training, public housing, and public education; began the Head Start program for the preschool children of poor families; instituted Medicare (health care for the elderly) and Medicaid (health care for the poor); and ended discriminatory immigration laws. In 1969 the US median income was $10,000.

By 1968, the escalating costs and involvement of the US in the civil war of Vietnam (2,800,000 men and women served in Vietnam between 1964 and 1973), and the increasing strength of conservatives in Congress who disliked Johnson's "welfare" policies, sharply reduced public funding and support for the war on poverty. The war in Vietnam was the most divisive war in US history, having an impact on US elections and foreign relations that has lasted into the twenty-first century. The war was an important stimulus for the various "rights movements" of the time, having a galvanizing effect on college student protest in particular.

The social movements whose letters, essays, and manifestoes you will encounter in this section of the book were deeply grounded in grassroots organizing by ordinary Americans who did not wait for leaders or politicians to tell them what to do. They preached, marched, sang songs, petitioned, organized, fought in the courts and sometimes in the streets, in order to achieve their American dreams of freedom and equality.

CHAPTER 14

Letter from Birmingham City Jail

Martin Luther King, Jr.

Martin Luther King, Jr. (1929–68) was born in Atlanta, Georgia, the eldest son of a Baptist minister, and the grandson of the founder of the Ebenezer Baptist Church in Atlanta, where his father served as pastor. King Jr. graduated from Morehouse College and studied theology at Boston University, before accepting his first pastorate at Dexter Avenue Baptist Church in Montgomery, Alabama, in 1954. Here he found a black community with long-standing resentments over the mistreatment of black passengers on the city's segregated buses. When the arrest of Rosa Parks in November 1955 led to a citywide bus boycott, King was chosen as president of the protest organization, the Montgomery Improvement Association. The boycott's successful challenge to segregation laws started King on his journey to becoming the most influential leader of the Civil Rights Movement, a position he held until his assassination in 1968. In 1961, King joined with other local ministers to organize nonviolent protest campaigns against segregation laws in the South. In the spring of 1963, mass demonstrations of teenagers and schoolchildren in Birmingham, Alabama, were met with attack dogs and high-pressure hoses. Hundreds were arrested, including King. King's response to local white clergymen who criticized the protests was "Letter from Birmingham City Jail," which he wrote while he was in prison, on April 16, 1963.

My Dear Fellow Clergymen,

While confined here in the Birmingham City Jail, I came across your recent statement calling our present activities "unwise and untimely." Seldom, if ever, do I pause to answer criticism of my work and ideas. . . . But since I feel that you are men of genuine good will and your criticisms are sincerely set forth, I would like to answer your statement in what I hope will be patient and reasonable terms.

I think I should give the reason for my being in Birmingham, since you have been influenced by the argument of "outsiders coming in." I have the honor of serving as president of the Southern Christian Leadership Conference, an organization operating in every Southern state with headquarters in Atlanta, Georgia. We have some 85 affiliate organizations all across the South. . . . Several months ago our local affiliate here in Birmingham invited us to be on call to engage in a nonviolent direct action program if such were deemed necessary. We readily consented.

In any nonviolent campaign there are four basic steps: 1) collection of the facts to determine whether injustices are alive; 2) negotiation; 3) self-purification; and 4) direct action. We have gone through all of these steps in Birmingham. . . . Birmingham is probably the most thoroughly segregated city in the United States. Its ugly record of police brutality is known in every section of the country. Its unjust treatment of Negroes in the courts is a notorious reality. There have been more unsolved bombings of Negro homes and churches in Birmingham than in any city in this nation. These are the hard, brutal, and unbelievable facts. On the basis of these conditions Negro leaders sought to negotiate with the city fathers. But the political leaders consistently refused to engage in good faith negotiation.

Then came the opportunity last September to talk with some of the leaders of the economic community. In these negotiating sessions certain promises were made by the merchants – such as the promise to remove the humiliating racial signs from the stores. On the basis of these promises Reverend Shuttlesworth and the leaders of the Alabama Christian Movement for Human Rights agreed to call a moratorium on any type of demonstrations. As the weeks and months unfolded we realized that we were the victims of a broken promise. The signs remained. As in so many experiences of the past, we were confronted with blasted hopes, and the dark shadow of a deep disappointment settled upon us. So we had no alternative except that of preparing for direct action, whereby we would present our very bodies as a means of laying our case before the conscience of the local and national community. We were not unmindful of the difficulties involved. So we decided to go through a process of self-purification. We started having workshops on nonviolence and repeatedly asked ourselves the questions, "Are you able to accept the blows without retaliating?" "Are you able to endure the ordeals of jail?"

You may well ask, "Why direct action? Why sit-ins, marches, etc.? Isn't negotiation a better path?" You are exactly right in your call for negotiation. Indeed, this is the purpose of direct action. Nonviolent direct action seeks to create such a crisis and establish such creative tension that a community that has constantly refused to negotiate is forced to confront the issue.

My friends, I must say to you that we have not made a single gain in civil rights without determined legal and nonviolent pressure. History is the long and tragic story of the fact that privileged groups seldom give up their privileges voluntarily. Individuals may see the moral light and give up their unjust posture; but as Reinhold Niebuhr has reminded us, groups are more immoral than individuals.

We know through painful experience that freedom is never voluntarily given by the oppressor; it must be demanded by the oppressed. Frankly I have never yet engaged in a direct action movement that was "well timed," according to the timetable of those who have not suffered unduly from the disease of segregation. For years now I have heard the word "Wait!" It rings in the ear of every Negro with a piercing familiarity. This "wait" has almost always meant "never." It has been a tranquilizing Thalidomide, relieving the emotional stress for a moment, only to give birth to an ill-formed infant of frustration. We must come to see with the distinguished jurist of yesterday that "justice too long delayed is justice denied." We have waited for more than 340 years for our constitutional and God-given rights. The nations of Asia and Africa are moving with jetlike speed toward the goal of political independence, and we still creep at horse and buggy pace toward the gaining of a cup of coffee at a lunch counter.

I guess it is easy for those who have never felt the stinging darts of segregation to say wait. But when you have seen vicious mobs lynch your mothers and fathers at will and drown your sisters and brothers at whim; when you have seen hate-filled policemen curse, kick, brutalize, and even kill your black brothers and sisters with impunity; when you see the vast majority of your 20 million Negro brothers smothering in an airtight cage of poverty in the midst of an affluent society; when you suddenly find your tongue twisted and your speech stammering as you seek to explain to your six-year-old daughter why she can't go to the public amusement park that has just been advertised on television, and see the tears welling up in her little eyes when she is told that Funtown is closed to colored children, and see the depressing clouds of inferiority begin to form in her little mental sky, and see her begin to distort her little personality by unconsciously developing a bitterness toward white people; when you have to concoct an answer for a five-year-old son who is asking in agonizing pathos: "Daddy, why do white people treat colored people so mean?"; when you take a cross country drive and find it necessary to sleep night after night in the uncomfortable corners of your automobile because no motel will accept you; when you are humiliated day in and day out by nagging signs reading "white" men and "colored"; when your first name becomes "nigger" and your middle name becomes "boy" (however old you are) and your last name becomes "John," and when your wife and mother are never given the respected title of "Mrs."; when you are harried by day and haunted by night by the fact that you are a Negro, living constantly at tip-toe stance, never quite knowing what to expect next, and plagued with inner fears and outer resentments; when you are forever fighting a degenerating sense of "nobodiness" – then you will understand why we find it difficult to wait. There comes a time when the cup of endurance runs over, and men are no longer willing to be plunged into an abyss of injustice where they experience the bleakness of corroding despair. I hope, sirs, you can understand our legitimate and unavoidable impatience.

I must make two honest confessions to you, my Christian and Jewish brothers. First, I must confess that over the last few years I have been gravely disappointed with the white moderate. I have almost reached the regrettable conclusion that the Negroes' great stumbling block in the stride toward freedom is not the White Citizens' "Counciler" or the Ku Klux Klanner, but the white moderate who is more devoted to "order" than to justice; who prefers a negative peace which is the absence of tension to a positive peace which is the presence of justice; who constantly says "I agree with you in the goal you seek, but I can't agree with your methods of direct action"; who paternalistically feels that he can set the timetable for another man's freedom; who lives by the myth of time and who constantly advises the Negro to wait until a "more convenient season." Shallow understanding from people of good will is more frustrating than absolute misunderstanding from people of ill will. Lukewarm acceptance is much more bewildering than outright rejection.

You spoke of our activity in Birmingham as extreme. At first I was rather disappointed that fellow clergymen would see my nonviolent efforts as those of the extremist. I started thinking about the fact that I stand in the middle of two opposing forces in the Negro community. One is a force of complacency made up of Negroes who, as a result of long years of oppression, have been so completely drained of self-respect and a sense of "somebodiness" that they have adjusted to segregation, and of a few Negroes in the middle class who, because of a degree of academic and economic security, and because at points they profit by segregation, have unconsciously become insensitive to the problems of the masses. The other force is one of bitterness and hatred and comes perilously close to advocating violence. It is expressed in the various black nationalist groups that are springing up over the nation, the largest and best known being Elijah Muhammad's Muslim movement. This movement is nourished by the contemporary frustration over the continued existence of racial discrimination. It is made up of people who have lost faith in America, who have absolutely repudiated Christianity, and who have concluded that the white man is an incurable "devil."

The Negro has many pent-up resentments and latent frustrations. He has to get them out. So let him march sometime; let him have his prayer pilgrimages to the city hall; understand why he must have sit-ins and freedom rides. If his repressed emotions do not come out in these nonviolent ways, they will come out in ominous expressions of violence. This is not a threat; it is a fact of history. So I have not said to my people, "Get rid of your discontent." But I have tried to say that this normal and healthy discontent can be channeled through the creative outlet of nonviolent direct action.

In spite of my shattered dreams of the past, I came to Birmingham with the hope that the white religious leadership of this community would see the justice of our cause and, with deep moral concern, serve as the channel through which our just grievances could get to the power structure. I had hoped that each of you would understand. But again I have been disappointed.

I have heard numerous religious leaders of the South call upon their worshippers to comply with a desegregation decision because it is the law, but I have longed to hear white ministers say follow this decree because integration is morally right and the Negro is your brother. In the midst of blatant injustices inflicted upon the Negro, I have watched white churches stand on the sideline and merely mouth pious irrelevancies and sanctimonious trivialities. In the midst of a mighty struggle to rid our nation of racial and economic injustice, I have heard so many ministers say, "Those are social issues with which the Gospel has no real concern," and I have watched so many churches commit themselves to a completely other-worldly religion which made a strange distinction between body and soul, the sacred and the secular.

I hope this letter finds you strong in the faith. I also hope that circumstances will soon make it possible for me to meet each of you, not as an integrationist or a civil rights leader, but as a fellow clergyman and a Christian brother. Let us all hope that the dark clouds of racial prejudice will soon pass away and the deep fog of misunderstanding will be lifted from our fear-drenched communities and in some not too distant tomorrow the radiant stars of love and brotherhood will shine over our great nation with all of their scintillating beauty.

Yours for the cause of Peace and Brotherhood,
M. L. King, Jr.

Study Questions

1   What does Martin Luther King consider to be the chief obstacles to achieving racial equality in the US, and why?
2   How would you describe King's language, tone of voice, and use of argument? Choose a passage you find particularly persuasive and explain why.
3   How do King's arguments for racial justice and equality compare with Malcolm X's in the next reading?
4   How do you think the specific situations in which King and Malcolm X write and speak, and the audiences they are communicating with, shaped their language and argument?

CHAPTER 15

Message to the Grass Roots

Malcolm X

Malcolm Little (1925–65) was born in Omaha, Nebraska, the son of a Baptist minister who was active in Marcus Garvey's Universal Negro Improvement Association. He experienced racist hatred directly when hooded Klansmen burned the family home in Lansing, Michigan. Living with his half-sister in Boston in the early 1940s, Malcolm adopted the style of the zoot suit, popularized by African-American hipsters, and lived off income from petty hustling, drug dealing, and pimping. Arrested for burglary in 1946, he discovered the Nation of Islam in jail and converted to the Muslim faith. In 1952, he took the last name "X" in rejection of the "white man's name." Malcolm X became a minister within the Nation of Islam, his charisma and authority earning him national speaking engagements and television appearances, during which he criticized the Civil Rights leadership's focus on integration into white society instead of on building black institutions. Deeply interested in anticolonial struggles in Africa, he traveled to Egypt, Sudan, Nigeria, and Ghana in 1959. Malcolm X delivered the speech, "Message to the Grass Roots" at the Northern Negro Grass Roots Leadership Conference in Detroit on November 10, 1963, two years before he was assassinated.

We want to have just an off-the-cuff chat between you and me, us. We want to talk right down to earth in a language that everybody here can easily understand. We all agree tonight, all of the speakers have agreed, that America has a very serious problem. Not only does America have a very serious problem, but our people have a very serious problem. The only reason she has a problem is she doesn't want us here. And every time you look at yourself, be you black, brown, red or yellow, a so-called Negro, you represent a person who poses such a serious problem for America because you're not wanted. Once you face this as a fact, then you can start plotting a course that will make you appear intelligent, instead of unintelligent.

What you and I need to do is learn to forget our differences. When we come together, we don't come together as Baptists or Methodists. You don't catch hell because you're a Baptist, and you don't catch hell because you're a Methodist. You don't catch hell because you're a Methodist or Baptist, you don't catch hell because you're a Democrat or Republican, you don't catch hell because you're a Mason or an Elk, and you sure don't catch hell because you're an American; because if you were an American, you wouldn't catch hell. You catch hell because you're a black man. You catch hell, all of us catch hell, for the same reason.

So we're all black people, so-called Negroes, second-class citizens, ex-slaves. You're nothing but an ex-slave. You don't like to be told that. But what else are you? You are ex-slaves. You don't come here on the "Mayflower." You came here on a slave ship. In chains, like a horse, or a cow, or a chicken. And you were brought here by the people who came here on the "Mayflower," you were brought here by the so-called Pilgrims, or Founding Fathers. They were the ones who brought you here.

We have a common enemy. We have this in common: We have a common oppressor, a common exploiter, and a common discriminator. But once we all realize that we have a common enemy, then we unite – on the basis of what we have in common. And what we have foremost in common is that enemy – the white man. He's an enemy to all of us. I know some of you all think that some of them aren't enemies. Time will tell.

In Bandung back in, I think, 1954, was the first unity meeting in centuries of black people. And once you study what happened at the Bandung conference, and the results of the Bandung conference, it actually serves as a model for the same procedure you and I can use to get our problems solved. At Bandung all the nations came together, the dark nations from Africa and Asia. Some of them were Buddhists, some of them were Muslims, some of them were Christians, some were Confucianists, some were atheists. Despite their religious differences, they came together. Some were communists, some were socialists, some were capitalists – despite their economic and political differences, they came together. All of them were black, brown, red or yellow.

The number-one thing that was not allowed to attend the Bandung conference was the white man. He couldn't come. Once they excluded the white man, they found that they could get together. Once they kept him out, everybody else fell right in and fell in line. This is the thing that you and I have to understand. And these people who came together didn't have nuclear weapons, they didn't have jet planes, they didn't have all of the heavy armaments that the white man has. But they had unity. [. . .]

Instead of airing our differences in public, we have to realize we're all the same family. And when you have a family squabble, you don't get out on the sidewalk. If you do, everybody calls you uncouth, unrefined, uncivilized, savage. If you don't make it at home, you settle it at home; you get in the closet, argue it out behind closed doors, and then when you come out on the street, you pose a common front, a united front. And this is what we need to do in the community, and in the city, and in the state. We need to stop airing our differences in front of the white man, put the white man out of our meetings, and then sit down and talk shop with each other. That's what we've got to do.

I would like to make a few comments concerning the difference between the black revolution and the Negro revolution. Are they both the same? And if they're not, what is the difference? What is the difference between a black revolution and a Negro revolution? First, what is a revolution? Sometimes I'm inclined to believe that many of our people are using this word "revolution" loosely, without taking careful consideration of what this word actually means, and what its historic characteristics are. When you study the historic nature of revolutions, the motive of a revolution, the objective of a revolution, the result of a revolution, and the methods used in a revolution, you may change words. You may devise another program, you may change your goal and you may change your mind.

Look at the American Revolution in 1776. That revolution was for what? For land. Why did they want land? Independence. How was it carried out? Bloodshed. Number one, it was based on land, the basis of independence. And the only way they could get it was bloodshed. The French Revolution – what was it based on? The landless against the landlord. What was it for? Land. How did they get it? Bloodshed. Was no love lost, was no compromise, was no negotiation. I'm telling you – you don't know what a revolution is. Because when you find out what it is, you'll get back in the alley, you'll get out of the way.

The Russian Revolution – what was it based on? Land; the landless against the landlord. How did they bring it about? Bloodshed. You haven't got a revolution that doesn't involve bloodshed. And you're afraid to bleed. I said, you're afraid to bleed.

As long as the white man sent you to Korea, you bled. He sent you to Germany, you bled. He sent you to the South Pacific to fight the Japanese, you bled. You bleed for white people, but when it comes to seeing your own churches being bombed and little black girls murdered, you haven't got any blood. You bleed when the white man says bleed; you bite when the white man says bite; and you bark when the white man says bark. I hate to say this about us, but it's true. How are you going to be nonviolent in Mississippi, as violent as you were in Korea? How can you justify being nonviolent in Mississippi and Alabama, when your churches are being bombed, and your little girls are being murdered, and at the same time you are going to get violent with Hitler, and Tōjō, and somebody else you don't even know?

If violence is wrong in America, violence is wrong abroad. If it is wrong to be violent defending black women and black children and black babies and black men, then it is wrong for America to draft us and make us violent abroad in defense of her. And if it is right for America to draft us, and teach us how to be violent in defense of her, then it is right for you and me to do whatever is necessary to defend our own people right here in this country. [. . .]

Of all our studies, history is best qualified to reward our research. And when you see that you've got problems, all you have to do is examine the historic method used all over the world by others who have problems similar to yours. Once you see how they got theirs straight, then you know how you can get yours straight. There's been a revolution, a black revolution, going on in Africa. In Kenya, the Mau Mau were revolutionary; they were the ones who brought the word "Uhuru" to the fore. The Mau Mau, they were revolutionary, they believed in scorched earth, they knocked everything aside that got in their way, and their revolution also was based on land, a desire for land. In Algeria, the northern part of Africa, a revolution took place. The Algerians were revolutionists, they wanted land. France offered to let them be integrated into France. They told France, to hell with France, they wanted some land, not some France. And they engaged in a bloody battle.

So I cite these various revolutions, brothers and sisters, to show you that you don't have a peaceful revolution. You don't have a turn-the-other-cheek revolution. There's no such thing as a nonviolent revolution. The only kind of revolution that is nonviolent is the Negro revolution. The only revolution in which the goal is loving your enemy is the Negro revolution. It's the only revolution in which the goal is a desegregated lunch counter, a desegregated theater, a desegregated park, and a desegregated public toilet; you can sit down next to white folks – on the toilet. That's no revolution. Revolution is based on land. Land is the basis of all independence. Land is the basis of freedom, justice, and equality.

The white man knows what a revolution is. He knows that the black revolution is world-wide in scope and in nature. The black revolution is sweeping Asia, is sweeping Africa, is rearing its head in Latin America. The Cuban Revolution – that's a revolution. They overturned the system. Revolution is in Asia, revolution is in Africa, and the white man is screaming because he sees revolution in Latin America. How do you think he'll react to you when you learn what a real revolution is? You don't know what a revolution is. If you did, you wouldn't use that word.

Revolution is bloody, revolution is hostile, revolution knows no compromise, revolution overturns and destroys everything that gets in its way. And you, sitting around here like a knot on the wall, saying, "I'm going to love these folks no matter how much they hate me." No, you need a revolution. Whoever heard of a revolution where they lock arms, as Rev. Cleage was pointing out beautifully, singing "We Shall Overcome"? You don't do that in a revolution. You don't do any singing, you're too busy swinging. It's based on land. A revolutionary wants land so he can set up his own nation, an independent nation. These Negroes aren't asking for any nation – they're trying to crawl back on the plantation.

When you want a nation, that's called nationalism. When the white man became involved in a revolution in this country against England, what was it for? He wanted this land so he could set up another white nation. That's white nationalism. The American Revolution was white nationalism. The French Revolution was white nationalism. The Russian Revolution too – yes, it was – white nationalism. You don't think so? Why do you think Khrushchev and Mao can't get their heads together? White nationalism. All the revolutions that are going on in Asia and Africa today are based on what? – black nationalism. A revolutionary is a black nationalist. He wants a nation. I was reading some beautiful words by Rev. Cleage, pointing out why he couldn't get together with someone else in the city because all of them were afraid of being identified with black nationalism. If you're afraid of black nationalism, you're afraid of revolution. And if you love revolution, you love black nationalism.

To understand this, you have to go back to what the young brother here referred to as the house Negro and the field Negro back during slavery. There were two kinds of slaves, the house Negro and the field Negro. The house Negroes – they lived in the house with master, they dressed pretty good, they ate good because they ate his food – what he left. They lived in the attic or the basement, but still they lived near the master; and they loved the master more than the master loved himself. They would give their life to save the master's house – quicker than the master would. If the master said, "We got a good house here," the house Negro would say, "Yeah, we got a good house here." Whenever the master said "we," he said "we." That's how you can tell a house Negro.

If the master's house caught on fire, the house Negro would fight harder to put the blaze out than the master would. If the master got sick, the house Negro would say, "What's the matter, boss, *we* sick?" *We* sick! He identified himself with his master, more than his master identified with himself. And if you came to the house Negro and said, "Let's run away, let's escape, let's separate," the house Negro would look at you and say, "Man, you crazy. What you mean, separate? Where is there a better house than this? Where can I wear better clothes than this? Where can I eat better food than this?" That was that house Negro. In those days he was called a "house nigger." And that's what we call them today, because we've still got some house niggers running around here.

This modern house Negro loves his master. He wants to live near him. He'll pay three times as much as the house is worth just to live near his master, and then brag about "I'm the only Negro out here." "I'm the only one on my job." "I'm the only one in this school." You're nothing but a house Negro. And if someone comes to you right now and says, "Let's separate," you say the same thing that the house Negro said on the plantation. "What you mean, separate? From America, this good white man? Where you going to get a better job than you get here?" I mean, this is what you say. "I ain't left nothing in Africa," that's what you say. Why, you left your mind in Africa.

On that same plantation, there was the field Negro. The field Negroes – those were the masses. There were always more Negroes in the field than there were Negroes in the house. The Negro in the field caught hell. He ate leftovers. In the house they ate high up on the hog. The Negro in the field didn't get anything but what was left of the insides of the hog. They call it "chitt'lings" nowadays. In those days they called them what they were – guts. That's what you were – gut-eaters. And some of you are still gut-eaters.

The field Negro was beaten from morning to night; he lived in a shack, in a hut; he wore old, castoff clothes. He hated his master. I say he hated his master. He was intelligent. That house Negro loved his master, but that field Negro – remember, they were in the majority, and they hated the master. When the house caught on fire, he didn't try to put it out; that field Negro prayed for a wind, for a breeze. When the master got sick, the field Negro prayed that he'd die. If someone came to the field Negro and said, "Let's separate, let's run," he didn't say, "Where we going?" He'd say, "Any place is better than here." You've got field Negroes in America today. I'm a field Negro. The masses are the field Negroes. When they see this man's house on fire, you don't hear the little Negroes talking about "*our* government is in trouble." They say, "*The* government is in trouble." Imagine a Negro: "*Our* government"! I even heard one say "*our* astronauts." They won't even let him near the plant – and "*our* astronauts"! "*Our* Navy" – that's a Negro that is out of his mind, a Negro that is out of his mind. [. . .]

When Martin Luther King failed to desegregate Albany, Georgia, the civil-rights struggle in America reached its low point. King became bankrupt almost, as a leader. The Southern Christian Leadership Conference was in financial trouble; and it was in trouble, period, with the people when they failed to desegregate Albany, Georgia. Other Negro civil-rights leaders of so-called national stature became fallen idols. As they became fallen idols, began to lose their prestige and influence, local Negro leaders began to stir up the masses. In Cambridge, Maryland, Gloria Richardson; in Danville, Virginia, and other parts of the country, local leaders began to stir up our people at the grass-roots level. This was never done by these Negroes of national stature. They control you, but they have never incited you or excited you. They control you, they contain you, they have kept you on the plantation. As soon as King failed in Birmingham, Negroes took to the streets. King went out to California to a big rally and raised I don't know how many thousands of dollars. He came to Detroit and had a march and raised some more thousands of dollars. And recall, right after that Roy Wilkins attacked King. He accused King and CORE [Congress of Racial Equality] of starting trouble everywhere and then making the NAACP [National Association for the Advancement of Colored People] get them out of jail and spend a lot of money; they accused King and CORE of raising all the money and not paying it back. This happened; I've got it in documented evidence in the newspaper. Roy started attacking King, and King started attacking Roy, and Farmer started attacking both of them. And as these Negroes of national stature began to attack each other, they began to lose their control of the Negro masses.

The Negroes were out there in the streets. They were talking about how they were going to march on Washington. Right at that time Birmingham had exploded, and the Negroes in Birmingham – remember, they also exploded. They began to stab the crackers in the back and bust them up 'side their head – yes, they did. That's when Kennedy sent in the troops, down in Birmingham. After that, Kennedy got on the television and said "this is a moral issue." That's when he said he was going to put out a civil-rights bill. And when he mentioned civil-rights bill and the Southern crackers started talking about how they were going to boycott or filibuster it, then the Negroes started talking – about what? That they were going to march on Washington, march on the Senate, march on the White House, march on the Congress, and tie it up, bring it to a halt, not let the government proceed. They even said they were going out to the airport and lay down on the runway and not let any airplanes land. I'm telling you what they said. That was revolution. That was revolution. That was the black revolution. [. . .]

Study Questions

1 What does Malcolm X believe to be the chief obstacles to racial equality in the US, and why?

2 What are the political lessons/inspiration Malcolm X takes from the countries of Asia and Africa?

3 How does Malcolm X apply the categories of "house Negro" and "field Negro" to this moment in US history?

4 What are the implications of Martin Luther King's call for racial integration, and Malcolm X's call for racial separation, for your understanding of "American identities"?

CHAPTER 16

Songs of the Civil Rights Movements

Songs narrated and motivated the Civil Rights Movement. Men and women at freedom rallies sang traditional hymns and spirituals, which they transformed with new lyrics that spoke to the current political situation. Songs communicated a sense of unity and hope to the participants' defiance of white supremacy. As Martin Luther King explained, "These songs bind us together, give us courage together, help us march together." The song lyrics reprinted below represent both traditional and new expressions of protest and hope. "Oh Freedom" was first sung by enslaved Africans as they disembarked from a slave ship in Georgia: as they sang, they walked into the water and drowned themselves rather than submit to a lifetime of bondage. Slaves and black soldiers continued the song's legacy of defiance during the Civil War. "Keep Your Eyes on the Prize" and "Ain't Gonna Let Nobody Turn Me Round" put new lyrics to traditional spirituals. One of the most well-known songs of the Civil Rights movement, "We Shall Overcome," had a long history of being sung in protest: slaves had sung "I Will Overcome" to help themselves endure the hardships of forced labor, and the song later became associated with the labor movement in the 1940s. Its message was so powerful that President Johnson quoted from it in his speech introducing the 1965 Civil Rights Bill.

"Oh Freedom"

Oh Freedom, Oh Freedom,
Oh Freedom over me, over me —

Chorus:
And before I'll be a slave
I'll be buried in my grave
And go home to my Lord and be free.

No segregation, no segregation,
No segregation over me, over me —

No more weeping, no more weeping,
No more weeping over me, over me —

No burning churches, no burning churches,
No burning churches over me, over me —

No more Jim Crow, no more Jim Crow,
No more Jim Crow over me, over me —

No more Barnett, no more Barnett,
No more Barnett over me, over me —

No more Pritchett, no more Pritchett,
No more Pritchett over me, over me.

"Keep Your Eyes on the Prize"

Paul and Silas, bound in jail,
Had no money for to go their bail.

Chorus:
Keep your eyes on the prize,
Hold on, hold on,
Hold on, hold on —
Keep your eyes on the prize,
Hold on, hold on.
Paul and Silas begin to shout,
The jail door opened and they walked out.

Freedom's name is mighty sweet —
Soon one of these days we're going to meet.

Got my hand on the Gospel plow,
I wouldn't take nothing for my journey now.

The only chain that a man can stand
Is that chain of hand in hand.

The only thing that we did wrong —
Stayed in the wilderness too long.

But the one thing we did right
Was the day we started to fight.

We're gonna board that big Greyhound,
Carryin' love from town to town.

We're gonna ride for civil rights,
We're gonna ride, both black and white.

We've met jail and violence too,
But God's love has seen us through.

Haven't been to Heaven but I've been told
Streets up there are paved with gold.

"Ain't Gonna Let Nobody Turn Me Round"

Ain't gonna let nobody, Lordy, turn me round,
  Turn me round, turn me round.
Ain't gonna let nobody, Lordy, turn me round.

  Chorus:
  I'm gonna keep on a-walkin', Lord,
  Keep on a-talkin', Lord,
  Marching up to freedom land.

Ain't gonna let Nervous Nelly turn me round, etc.

Ain't gonna let Chief Pritchett turn me round, etc.

Ain't gonna let Mayor Kelly turn me round, etc.

Ain't gonna let segregation turn me round, etc.

Ain't gonna let no jailhouse turn me round, etc.

Ain't gonna let no injunction turn me round, etc.

"We Shall Overcome"

We shall overcome,
    we shall overcome,
We shall overcome some day.
Oh, deep in my heart, I do believe,
We shall overcome some day.

We are not afraid,
    we are not afraid,
We are not afraid today.
Oh, deep in my heart, I do believe,
We shall overcome some day.

We are not alone,
    we are not alone,
We are not alone today.

Oh, deep in my heart, I do believe,
We shall overcome some day.

The truth will make us free,
    the truth will make us free,
The truth will make us free some day.
Oh, deep in my heart, I do believe,
We shall overcome some day.

We'll walk hand in hand,
    we'll walk hand in hand,
We'll walk hand in hand some day.
Oh, deep in my heart, I do believe,
We shall overcome some day.

The Lord will see us through,
    the Lord will see us through,
The Lord will see us through today.
Oh, deep in my heart, I do believe,
We shall overcome some day.

Study Questions

1   Who do you think is the "we" in "We Shall Overcome"?
2   What do you think are the sources of these songs' effectiveness? (Try to list more than one.)
3   How did the songs – both performance and lyrics – enable powerless people to feel powerful and challenge the boundaries of racial segregation?
4   Look up Ross Barnett, Governor of Mississippi; Laurie Pritchett, Chief of Police of Albany, Georgia; and Mayor Kelly of Albany, Georgia. Why are they named in these songs?

CHAPTER 17

Port Huron Statement

Students for a Democratic Society

Founded in 1960 by a small group of white college students, Students for a Democratic Society (SDS) marked a new kind of student activism in the 1960s. Critical of an older generation they believed was steeped in Cold War politics, materialism, and apathy about the state of the nation, they focused on grassroots organizing around civil rights, economic justice, and "participatory democracy," hoping to make radical changes within their universities, their local communities, and the nation. In 1962, 59 members of the group met at a United Auto Workers conference center in Port Huron, Michigan, and produced the "Port Huron Statement," a manifesto that outlined their idealistic agenda for transforming American society and culture. By 1968, SDS was a national organization with some 350 chapters that claimed 100,000 members. SDS disbanded in 1969.

W e are people of this generation, bred in at least modest comfort, housed now in universities, looking uncomfortably to the world we inherit.

When we were kids the United States was the wealthiest and strongest country in the world; the only one with the atom bomb, the least scarred by modern war, an initiator of the United Nations that we thought would distribute Western influence throughout the world. Freedom and equality for each individual, government of, by, and for the people – these American values we found good, principles by which we could live as men. Many of us began maturing in complacency.

As we grew, however, our comfort was penetrated by events too troubling to dismiss. First, the permeating and victimizing fact of human degradation, symbolized by the Southern struggle against racial bigotry, compelled most of us from silence to activism. Second, the enclosing fact of the Cold War, symbolized by the presence of the Bomb, brought awareness that we ourselves, and our friends, and millions of abstract "others" we knew more directly because of our common peril, might die at any time. We might deliberately ignore, or avoid, or fail to feel all other human problems, but not these two, for these were too immediate and crushing in their impact, too challenging in the demand that we as individuals take the responsibility for encounter and resolution. [. . .]

Our work is guided by the sense that we may be the last generation in the experiment with living. But we are a minority – the vast majority of our people regard the temporary equilibriums of our society and world as eternally functional parts. In this is perhaps the outstanding paradox; we ourselves are imbued with urgency, yet the message of our society is that there is no viable alternative to the present. Beneath the reassuring tones of the politicians, beneath the common opinion that America will "muddle through," beneath the stagnation of those who have closed their minds to the future, is the pervading feeling that there simply are no alternatives, that our times have witnessed the exhaustion not only of Utopias, but of any new departures as well. Feeling the press of complexity upon the emptiness of life, people are fearful of the thought that at any moment things might be thrust out of control. They fear change itself, since change might smash whatever invisible framework seems to hold back chaos for them now. For most Americans, all crusades are suspect, threatening. The fact that each individual sees apathy in his fellows perpetuates the common reluctance to organize for change. The dominant institutions are complex enough to blunt the minds of their potential critics, and entrenched enough to swiftly dissipate or entirely repel the energies of protest and reform, thus limiting human expectancies. Then, too, we are a materially improved society, and by our own improvements we seem to have weakened the case for further change.

Some would have us believe that Americans feel contentment amidst prosperity – but might it not better be called a glaze above deeply felt anxieties about their role in the new world? And if these anxieties produce a developed indifference to human affairs, do they not as well produce a yearning to believe that there *is* an alternative to the present, that something *can* be done to change circumstances in the school, the workplaces, the bureaucracies, the government? It is to this latter yearning, at once the spark and engine of change, that we direct our present appeal. The search for truly democratic alternatives to the present, and a commitment to social experimentation with them, is a worthy and fulfilling human enterprise, one which moves us and, we hope, others today. On such a basis do we offer this document of our convictions and analysis: as an effort in understanding and changing the conditions of humanity in the late twentieth century, an effort rooted in the ancient, still unfulfilled conception of man attaining determining influence over his circumstances of life. [. . .]

We regard *men* as infinitely precious and possessed of unfulfilled capacities for reason, freedom, and love. In affirming these principles we are aware of countering perhaps the dominant conceptions of man in the twentieth century: that he is a thing to be manipulated, and that he is inherently incapable of directing his own affairs. We oppose the depersonalization that reduces human beings to the status of things – if anything, the brutalities of the twentieth century teach that means and ends are intimately related, that vague appeals to "posterity" cannot justify the mutilations of the present. We oppose, too, the doctrine of human incompetence because it rests essentially on the modern fact that men have been "competently" manipulated into incompetence – we see little reason why men cannot meet with increasing the skill the complexities and responsibilities of their situation, if society is organized not for minority, but for majority, participation in decision-making. [...]

We would replace power rooted in possession, privilege, or circumstance by power and uniqueness rooted in love, reflectiveness, reason, and creativity. As a social system we seek the establishment of a democracy of individual participation, governed by two central aims: that the individual share in those social decisions determining the quality and direction of his life; that society be organized to encourage independence in men and provide the media for their common participation.

> In a participatory democracy, the political life would be based in several root principles: that decision-making of basic social consequence be carried on by public groupings;
>
> that politics be seen positively, as the art of collectively creating an acceptable pattern of social relations;
>
> that politics has the function of bringing people out of isolation and into community, thus being a necessary, though not sufficient, means of finding meaning in personal life;
>
> that the political order should serve to clarify problems in a way instrumental to their solution; it should provide outlets for the expression of personal grievance and aspiration; opposing views should be organized so as to illuminate choices and facilitate the attainment of goals; channels should be commonly available to relate men to knowledge and to power so that private problems – from bad recreation facilities to personal alienation – are formulated as general issues.

The economic sphere would have as its basis the principles:

> that work should involve incentives worthier than money or survival. It should be educative, not stultifying; creative, not mechanical; self-directed, not manipulated, encouraging independence, a respect for others, a sense of dignity, and a willingness to accept social responsibility, since it is this experience that has crucial influence on habits, perceptions and individual ethics;
>
> that the economic experience is so personally decisive that the individual must share in its full determination;
>
> that the economy itself is of such social importance that its major resources and means of production should be open to democratic participation and subject to democratic social regulation.

Like the political and economic ones, major social institutions – cultural, educational, rehabilitative, and others – should be generally organized with the well-being and dignity of man as the essential measure of success.

In social change or interchange, we find violence to be abhorrent because it requires generally the transformation of the target, be it a human being or a community of people, into a depersonalized object of hate. It is imperative that the means of violence be abolished and the institutions – local, national, international – that encourage non-violence as a condition of conflict be developed.

These are our central values, in skeletal form. It remains vital to understand their denial or attainment in the context of the modern world. [. . .]

Study Questions

1   How do the authors of this statement understand their identity as Americans? What personal and historical factors framed their observations about American society in the 1950s and 1960s? Why do they see themselves as a "generation"?

2   What is their critique of American politics and institutions? What kinds of solutions do they propose? Do any of their critiques/solutions seem applicable to the US today? (See the following reading.)

3   What do the authors mean by "participatory democracy"? Can you give an example of it from your own or your family's experience or knowledge? Do you agree with their arguments about its importance? Why or why not?

4   What does the "Port Huron Statement" have in common with the Civil Rights Movement?

CHAPTER 18

The Port Huron Statement at 40

Tom Hayden and Richard Flacks

Tom Hayden (1939–), the principal author of the "Port Huron Statement," grew up outside Detroit, where his father worked as an accountant, and his mother as a film librarian. A student at University of Michigan when SDS was founded, Hayden was also a member of the Student Non-Violent Coordinating Committee (SNCC) and had recently returned from a summer of registering black voters. Hayden served as a California state representative and senator from 1982 to 1999, and is the author of nine books, including Rebel: A Personal History of the 1960s *(2003). Richard Flacks (1938–), also a founder of SDS and coauthor of "Port Huron Statement," is a political sociologist. His books include* Beyond the Barricades: The 60s Generation Grows Up *(1989). In the following article written for* The Nation *in 2002, Hayden and Flacks reflect on the long-term impact of the student activism that began in the 1960s.*

A glance at the web will show tens of thousands of references to "participatory democracy," the central focus of that document, [. . .] which still appears as a live alternative to the top-down construction of most institutions. Participatory democracy has surfaced in the campaigns of the global justice movement, in utopian visions of telecommunications, in struggles around workplace and neighborhood empowerment, in Paulo Freire's "pedagogy of the oppressed," in grassroots environmental crusades and antipoverty programs, in political platforms from Green parties to the Zapatistas, in participatory management theory, in liberation theology's emphasis on base communities of the poor and even in the current efforts of most Catholics to carve out a participatory role for laity in their church. The Port Huron Statement appears in numerous textbooks and has been the subject of thousands of student papers. This continued interest is the more impressive, since the statement was never marketed or even reissued as a book. It was produced only as a mimeographed pamphlet in 20,000 copies, which sold for 35 cents. We were jaundiced toward the very notion of public relations. [. . .]

This year's occasion of the Port Huron Statement's fortieth anniversary provides a chance to ask whether its importance today is primarily symbolic and nostalgic, or whether, as we believe, the core of the statement is still relevant for all those trying to create a world where each person has a voice in the decisions affecting his or her life. It remains, as we described it then, "a living document open to change with our times and experiences."

The original idea, conceived at a winter meeting in Ann Arbor in 1961, was modest: to produce an organizing tool for the movement we were trying to spread through SDS. Then the statement became more audacious. The roughly sixty young people who finalized the statement during a week at a United Auto Workers retreat in Port Huron, Michigan, experienced what one could only call an inspirational moment. As the words flowed night and day, we felt we were giving voice to a new generation of rebels.

The two of us had arrived in Port Huron from different paths that symbolized the cultural fusion that happened at the beginning of the 1960s. Tom was a Midwestern populist by nature, rebelling apolitically against the boring hypocrisy of suburban life – until the Southern black student sit-in movement showed him that a committed life was possible. Tom was drawn to the mystique of citizen action and away from left ideologies based on systems far different from America, with its vast middle-class status system. Many others at Port Huron were mainstream student leaders inspired by the civil rights movement, the South African antiapartheid movement and even the youthful ideals of John Kennedy's New Frontier. Dick, on the other hand, was a New York "red diaper baby" whose parents had been fired as school-teachers during the McCarthy period. Disillusioned by both Stalinism and the conformity of cold war America, he and his wife, Mickey, questioned whether an effective left could be built at all from its quarrelsome subculture of factions. The fusion of these paths yielded a vision informed by a democratic American radicalism going back to Tom Paine, one that attempted to transcend the stale dogmas of the dying left as well as the liberal celebration of the New Frontier as Camelot. [. . .]

At the time, as disfranchised students, embracing such an expansive idea required a wrenching re-examination of common assumptions. What, for example, was the view of human nature that underlay our assertion that all people had basic rights to participation, or that democracy was the system best suited to respecting human dignity? All-night discussions ensued, often concluding at daybreak. On the one hand, there were followers of the theologian Reinhold Niebuhr, influenced by the atrocities of the Holocaust and Stalinism, who had asserted that "the children of darkness," the political realists, were in their generation wiser than "the foolish children of light," the pacifists and idealists. On the other side were the Englightenment humanists who believed in infinite perfectibility through education and nonviolence as adopted by Gandhi and Martin Luther King Jr. The dominant view was that we were children of light. We chose utopia and rejected cynicism. The statement ended on an apocalyptic note: "If we appear to seek the unattainable, as it has been said, then let it be known that we do so to avoid the unimaginable." But, reflecting our mostly mainstream backgrounds, we also wanted to be relevant, effective. Agreement was reached when Mary Varela, a Catholic Worker activist, inspired by Pope John XXIII, suggested that we follow the doctrine that humans have "unfulfilled" rather than "unlimited" capacities for good, and are "infinitely precious" rather than "infinitely perfectible." The theological amendment drew no objections and was incorporated without citation.

Participatory democracy sought to expand the sphere of public decisions from the mere election of representatives to the deeper role of "bringing people out of isolation and into community" in decentralized forms of decision-making. The same democratic humanism was applied to the economy in calls for "incentives worthier than money," and for work to be "self-directed, not manipulated." The statement was not an endorsement of the liberal welfare state or the managerial democracy of the New Frontier, but a call for a thorough, bottom-up reclaiming of the public sector for public, rather than military, purposes. Only then might corporations be made "publicly responsible." In today's terms, we were trying to transform the mass society into a civic society, spark a social awareness in the vast world of private lives and voluntary associations that most people inhabited far from the centers of power. [. . .]

Perhaps the most important legacy of the Port Huron Statement is the fact that it introduced the concept of participatory democracy to popular discourse and practice. It made sense of the fact that ordinary people were making history, and not waiting for parties or traditional organizations. The notion was used to define modes of organization (decentralization, consensus methods of decision-making, leadership rotation and avoidance of hierarchy) that would lead to social transformation, not simply concessions from existing institutions. It proved to be a contagious idea, spreading from its academic origins to the very process of movement decision-making, to the subsequent call for women's liberation. These participatory practices, which had their roots in the town hall, Quaker meetings, anarchist collectives and even sensitivity training, are carried on today in grassroots movements such as the one against corporate globalization. The strength of organizations like the early SDS or SNCC, or today's Seattle-style direct-action networks, or ACT UP, is catalytic, not bureaucratic. They empower the passion of spontaneous, communal revolt, continue a few years, succeed in achieving reforms and yet have difficulty in becoming institutionalized. But while hierarchical mass organizations boast more staying power, they have trouble attracting the personal creativity or the energy of ordinary people taking back power over their lives. Participatory democracy offers a lens for looking at all hierarchies critically and not taking them as inevitable. Perhaps the two strands – the grassroots radical democratic thrust and the need for an organization with a program – can never be fused, but neither can one live without the other.

The Port Huron Statement claimed to be articulating an "agenda for a Generation." Some of that agenda has been fulfilled: The cold war is no more, voting rights for blacks and youth have been won, and much has changed for the better in the content of university curriculums. Yet our dreams have hardly been realized. The Port Huron Statement was composed in the heady interlude of inspiration between the apathetic 1950s and the 1960s' sudden traumas of political assassinations and body counts. Forty years later, we may stand at a similar crossroads. The war on terrorism has revived the cold war framework. An escalating national security state attempts to rivet our attention and invest our resources on fighting an elusive, undefined enemy for years to come, at the inevitable price of our civil liberties and continued neglect of social justice. To challenge the framework of the war on terrorism, to demand a search for real peace with justice, is as difficult today as challenging the cold war was at Port Huron. Yet there is a new movement astir in the world, against the inherent violence of globalization, corporate rule and fundamentalism, that reminds us strongly of the early 1960s. Is history repeating? If so, "participatory democracy" and the priorities of Port Huron continue to offer clues to building a committed movement toward a society responsive to the needs of the vast majority. Many of those who came to Port Huron have been on that quest ever since.

Study Questions

1   What do Hayden and Flacks argue is the contemporary relevance of the "Port Huron Statement"? Do you agree or disagree and why?
2   What do the authors mean by saying that "mass society" should be transformed into "civic society"? Do you have a "civic identity"? If so, how do you practice it?
3   Should there be an "agenda" for your generation"? If so, what should it be?
4   Identify the ways in which one or two of the "ordinary people" you have read about in this book "made history." What are some of the ways in which your family has "made history"?

CHAPTER 19

From *Working-Class War:*
American Combat Soldiers and Vietnam

Christian G. Appy

Christian G. Appy is an historian of the Vietnam War. He is author of Working Class War: American Combat Soldiers and Vietnam *(1993), and editor of* Cold War Constructions: The Political Culture of United States Imperialism 1945–1966 *(2000) and* Patriots: The Vietnam War Remembered From All Sides *(2003). In this excerpt from* Working Class War, *Appy demonstrates that class background was the most important factor in determining which young American men would serve in Vietnam.*

Mapping the Losses

"We all ended up going into the service about the same time – the whole crowd." I had asked Dan Shaw about himself, why *he* had joined the Marine Corps; but Dan ignored the personal thrust of the question. Military service seemed less an individual choice than a collective rite of passage, a natural phase of life for "the whole crowd" of boys in his neighborhood, so his response encompassed a circle of over twenty childhood friends who lived near the corner of Train and King streets in Dorchester, Massachusetts – a white, working-class section of Boston.[1] [. . .]

Focusing on the world of working-class Boston, Dan has a quiet, low-key manner with few traces of bitterness. But when he speaks of the disparities in military service throughout American society, his voice fills with anger, scorn, and hurt. He compares the sacrifices of poor and working-class neighborhoods with the rarity of wartime casualties in the "fancy suburbs" beyond the city limits, in places such as Milton, Lexington, and Wellesley. If three wounded veterans "wasn't bad" for a streetcorner in Dorchester, such concentrated pain was, Dan insists, unimaginable in a wealthy subdivision. "You'd be lucky to find three Vietnam veterans in one of those rich neighborhoods, never mind three who got wounded."

Dan's point is indisputable: those who fought and died in Vietnam were overwhelmingly drawn from the bottom half of the American social structure. The comparison he suggests bears out the claim. The three affluent towns of Milton, Lexington, and Wellesley had a combined wartime population of about 100,000, roughly equal to that of Dorchester. However, while those suburbs suffered a total of eleven war deaths, Dorchester lost forty-two. There was almost exactly the same disparity in casualties between Dorchester and another sample of prosperous Massachusetts towns – Andover, Lincoln, Sudbury, Weston, Dover, Amherst, and Longmeadow. These towns lost ten men from a combined population of 100,000. In other words, boys who grew up in Dorchester were four times more likely to die in Vietnam than those raised in the fancy suburbs. An extensive study of wartime casualties from Illinois reached a similar conclusion. In that state, men from neighborhoods with median family incomes under $5,000 (about $22,800 in 2005 dollars) were four times more likely to die in Vietnam that men from places with median family incomes above $15,000 ($68,600 in 2005 dollars).[2]

Dorchester, East Los Angeles, the South Side of Chicago – major urban centers such as these sent thousands of men to Vietnam. So, too, did lesser known, midsize industrial cities with large working-class populations, such as Saginaw, Michigan; Fort Wayne, Indiana; Stockton, California; Chattanooga, Tennessee; Youngstown, Ohio; Bethlehem, Pennsylvania; and Utica, New York. There was also an enormous rise in working-class suburbanization in the 1950s and 1960s. The post–World War II boom in modestly priced, uniformly designed, tract housing, along with the vast construction of new highways, allowed many workers their first opportunity to purchase homes and to live a considerable distance from their jobs. As a result, many new suburbs became predominantly working class.

Long Island, New York, became the site of numerous working-class suburbs, including the original Levittown, the first mass-produced town in American history. Built by the Levit and Sons construction firm in the late 1940s, it was initially a middle-class town. By 1960, however, as in many other postwar suburbs, the first owners had moved on, often to larger homes in wealthier suburbs, and a majority of the newcomers were working class.[3] Ron Kovic, author of one of the best-known Vietnam memoirs and films, *Born on the Fourth of July,* grew up near Levittown in Massapequa. His parents, like so many others in both towns, were working people willing to make great sacrifices to own a small home with a little land and to live in a town they regarded as a safe and decent place to raise their families, in hope that their children would enjoy greater opportunity. Many commentators viewed the suburbanization of blue-collar workers as a sign that the working class was vanishing and that almost everyone was becoming middle class. In fact, however, though many workers owned more than ever before, their relative social position remained largely unchanged. The Kovics, for example, lived in the suburbs but had to raise five children on the wages of a supermarket checker and clearly did not match middle-class levels in terms of economic security, education, or social status. [. . .]

A community of only 27,000, Massapequa lost 14 men in Vietnam. In 1969, *Newsday* traced the family backgrounds of 400 men from Long Island who had been killed in Vietnam. "As a group," the newspaper concluded, "Long Island's war dead have been overwhelmingly white, working-class men. Their parents were typically blue collar or clerical workers, mailmen, factory workers, building tradesmen, and so on."[4]

Rural and small-town America may have lost more men in Vietnam, proportionately, than did even central cities and working-class suburbs. You get a hint of this simply by flipping through the pages of the Vietnam Memorial directory. As thick as a big-city phone book, the directory lists the names and hometowns of Americans who died in Vietnam. An average page contains the names of five or six men from towns such as Alma, West Virginia (pop. 296), Lost Hills, California (pop. 200), Bryant Pond, Maine (pop. 350), Tonalea, Arizona (pop. 125), Storden, Minnesota (pop. 364), Pioneer, Louisiana (pop. 188), Wartburg, Tennessee (pop. 541), Hillisburg, Indiana (pop. 225), Boring, Oregon (pop. 150), Racine, Missouri (pop. 274), Hygiene, Colorado (pop. 400), Clayton, Kansas (pop. 127), and Almond, Wisconsin (pop. 440). In the 1960s only about 2 percent of Americans lived in towns with fewer than 1,000 people. Among those who died in Vietnam, however, roughly four times that portion, 8 percent, came from American hamlets of that size. It is not hard to find small towns that lost more than one man in Vietnam. Empire, Alabama, for example, had four men out of a population of only 400 die in Vietnam – four men from a town in which only a few dozen boys came of draft age during the entire war.[5]

There were also soldiers who came from neither cities, suburbs, nor small towns but from the hundreds of places in between, average towns of 15,000 to 30,000 people whose economic life, however precarious, had local roots. Some of these towns paid a high cost in Vietnam. In the foothills of eastern Alabama, for example, is the town of Talladega, with a population of approximately 17,500 (about one-quarter black), a town of small farmers and textile workers. Only one-third of Talladega's men had completed high school. Fifteen of their children died in Vietnam, a death rate three times the national average. Compare Talladega to Mountain Brook, a rich suburb outside Birmingham. Mountain Brook's population was somewhat higher than Talladega's, about 19,500 (with no black residents of draft age). More than 90 percent of its men were high school graduates. No one from Mountain Brook is listed among the Vietnam War dead.[6]

I have described a social map of American war casualties to suggest not simply the geographic origins of US soldiers but their class origins – not simply where they came from but the kinds of places as well. Class, not geography, was the crucial factor in determining which Americans fought in Vietnam. Geography reveals discrepancies in military service primarily because it often reflects class distinctions. Many men went to Vietnam from places such as Dorchester, Massapequa, Empire, and Talladega because those were the sorts of places where most poor and working-class people lived. The wealthiest youth in those towns, like those in richer communities, were far less likely either to enlist or to be drafted. [. . .]

The Vietnam Generation's Military Minority:

A Statistical Profile

Presidents Kennedy, Johnson, and Nixon sent 3 million American soldiers to South Vietnam, a country of 17 million. In the early 1960s they went by the hundreds – helicopter units, Green Beret teams, counterinsurgency hotshots, ambitious young officers, and ordinary infantrymen – all of them labeled military advisers by the American command. They fought a distant, "brushfire war" on the edge of American consciousness. Beyond the secret inner circles of government, few predicted that hundreds of thousands would follow in a massive buildup that took the American presence in Vietnam from 15,000 troops in 1964 to 550,000 in 1968.[7] In late 1969 the gradual withdrawal of ground forces began, inching its way to the final US pullout in January 1973. The bell curve of escalation and withdrawal spread the commitment of men into a decade-long chain of one-year tours of duty.

In the years of escalation, as draft calls mounted to 30,000 and 40,000 a month, many young people believed the entire generation might be mobilized for war. There were, of course, many ways to avoid the draft, and millions of men did just that. Very few, however, felt completely confident that they would never be ordered to fight. Perhaps the war would escalate to such a degree or go on so long that all exemptions and deferments would be eliminated. No one could be sure what would happen. Only in retrospect is it clear that the odds of serving in Vietnam were, for many people, really quite small. The forces that fought in Vietnam were drawn from the largest generation of young people in the nation's history. During the years 1964 to 1973, from the Gulf of Tonkin Resolution to the final withdrawal of American troops from Vietnam, 27 million men came of draft age. The 2.5 million men of that generation who went to Vietnam represent less than 10 percent of America's male baby boomers.[8]

The parents of the Vietnam generation had an utterly different experience of war. During World War II virtually all young, able-bodied men entered the service – some 12 million. Personal connections to the military permeated society regardless of class, race, or gender. Almost every family had a close relative overseas – a husband fighting in France, a son in the South Pacific, or at least an uncle with the Seabees, a niece in the WAVES, or a cousin in the Air Corps. These connections continued well into the 1950s. Throughout the Korean War years and for several years after, roughly 70 percent of the draft-age population of men served in the military; but from the 1950s to the 1960s, military service became less and less universal. During the Vietnam years, the portion had dropped to 40 percent: 10 percent were in Vietnam, and 30 percent served in Germany, South Korea, and the dozens of other duty stations in the United States and abroad. What had been, in the 1940s, an experience shared by the vast majority gradually became the experience of a distinct minority.[9] [. . .]

Study Questions

1　Why does Appy say that for working-class men, service in Vietnam was a "collective" experience? Compare their sense of being a "generation" with that of the students in SDS.

2　How does the social map Appy draws of American war casualties compare with other social maps you have encountered in your reading (e.g., Agüeros, Roth)?

3　How did Vietnam compare with earlier wars in terms of who served in the Armed Forces?

Notes

1.　Dan Shaw interview, 21 July 1982.

2.　Casualties by town were provided by Friends of the Vietnam Memorial (Washington, DC), from software derived from the *Vietnam Veterans Memorial: Directory of Names*; the Illinois study is John Martin Willis, "Who Died in Vietnam: An Analysis of the Social Background of Vietnam War Casualties," PhD diss. (Purdue University, 1975).

3.　On Levittown, NY, see William M. Dobriner, *Class in Suburbia* (Englewood Cliffs, NJ: Prentice-Hall, 1961); also useful is Bennett M. Berger, *Working-Class Suburb: A Study of Auto Workers in Suburbia* (Berkeley: University of California Press, 1960).

4.　The *Newsday* quotation is found in Michael Useem, *Conscription, Protest, and Social Conflict: The Life and Death of a Draft Resistance Movement* (New York: Wiley, 1973), p. 83.

5.　These towns are taken from random pages of the *Vietnam Veterans Memorial: Directory of Names*, pp. 18, 77, 163, 754. Populations are taken from the 1970 census. The 8 percent figure is based on a random sample of 1,200 men listed in the directory.

6.　Information about Talladega and Mountain Brook is from the 1970 federal census.

7.　As early as 1961, Secretary of Defense Robert McNamara and the Joint Chiefs of Staff drafted memos for Kennedy arguing that some 200,000 American troops might be needed in Vietnam. See Senator Mike Gravel, *Pentagon Papers*, Vol. 2 (Boston: Beacon Press, 1971), pp. 78–79, 108.

8.　Lawrence N. Baskir and William A. Strauss, *Chance and Circumstance: The Draft, The War, and the Vietnam Generation* (New York: Knopf, 1978), p. 5.

9.　John Helmer, *Bringing the War Home: The American Soldier in Vietnam* (New York: Free Press, 1974), pp. 4–5.

CHAPTER 20

From *Born on the Fourth of July*

Ron Kovic

Ron Kovic was born on July 4, 1946 to a grocery store cashier father and homemaker mother. He was raised with his five younger siblings in a lower-middle-class suburb of Long Island, New York. A self-described "All-American" boy, he loved sports, toy guns, television, and war movies. Not wanting to spend his life working hard for little money like his father, he joined the US Marines in 1964, and was sent to Vietnam. There he confronted the horrors of the war, which included his accidentally killing a fellow soldier, and his participation in a massacre of unarmed civilians, mostly children and elderly. On January 20, 1968, enemy bullets paralyzed him from the chest down. Disillusioned by the treatment he received in a veterans' hospital after returning home, Kovic began to travel a path that led him to question the US government's role in Vietnam. By 1970 he was participating in antiwar rallies and becoming a vocal opponent of the war. In the following opening chapter of his 1976 memoir, Kovic immerses us in the searing terror of his wounding in Vietnam.

Ask not what your country can do for you – ask what you can do for your country.
            – President John F. Kennedy January 20, 1961

I am the living death
the memorial day on wheels
I am your yankee doodle dandy
your john wayne come home
your fourth of july firecracker
exploding in the grave

The blood is still rolling off my flak jacket from the hole in my shoulder and there are bullets cracking into the sand all around me. I keep trying to move my legs but I cannot feel them. I try to breathe but it is difficult. I have to get out of this place, make it out of here somehow.

Someone shouts from my left now, screaming for me to get up. Again and again he screams, but I am trapped in the sand.

Oh get me out of here, get me out of here, please someone help me! Oh help me, please help me. Oh God oh Jesus!

"Is there a corpsman?" I cry. "Can you get a corpsman?"

There is a loud crack and I hear the guy begin to sob.

"They've shot my fucking finger off! Let's go, sarge! Let's get outta here!"

"I can't move," I gasp. "I can't move my legs! I can't feel anything!"

I watch him go running back to the tree line.

"Sarge, are you all right?" Someone else is calling to me now and I try to turn around. Again there is the sudden crack of a bullet and a boy's voice crying. "Oh Jesus! Oh Jesus Christ!" I hear his body fall in back of me.

I think he must be dead but I feel nothing for him, I just want to live. I feel nothing.

And now I hear another man coming up from behind, trying to save me. "Get outta here!" I scream. "Get the fuck outta here!"

A tall black man with long skinny arms and enormous hands picks me up and throws me over his shoulder as bullets begin cracking over our heads like strings of firecrackers. Again and again they crack as the sky swirls around us like a cyclone. "Motherfuckers motherfuckers!" he screams. And the rounds keep cracking and the sky and the sun on my face and my body all gone, all twisted up dangling like a puppet's, diving again and again into the sand, up and down, rolling and cursing, gasping for breath. "Goddamn goddamn motherfuckers!"

And finally I am dragged into a hole in the sand with the bottom of my body that can no longer feel, twisted and bent underneath me. The black man runs from the hole without ever saying a thing. I never see his face. I will never know who he is. He is gone. And others now are in the hole helping me. They are bandaging my wounds. There is fear in their faces.

"It's all right," I say to them. "Everything is fine."

Someone has just saved my life. My rifle is gone and I don't feel like finding it or picking it up ever again. The only thing I can think of, the only thing that crosses my mind, is living. There seems to be nothing in the world more important than that.

Hundreds of rounds begin to crash in now. I stare up at the sky because I cannot move. Above the hole men are running around in every direction. I see their legs and frightened faces. They are screaming and dragging the wounded past me. Again and again the rounds crash in. They seem to be coming in closer and closer. A tall man jumps in, hugging me to the earth.

"Oh God!" he is crying. "Oh God please help us!"

The attack is lifted. They are carrying me out of the hole now – two, three, four men – quickly they are strapping me to a stretcher. My legs dangle off the sides until they realize I cannot control them. "I can't move them," I say, almost in a whisper. "I can't move them," I'm still carefully sucking the air, trying to calm myself, trying not to get excited, not to panic. I want to live. I keep telling myself, Take it slow now, as they strap my legs to the stretcher and carry my wounded body into an Amtrac packed with other wounded men. The steel trapdoor of the Amtrac slowly closes as we begin to move to the northern bank and back across the river to the battalion area.

Men are screaming all around me. "Oh God get me out of here!" "Please help!" they scream. Oh Jesus, like little children now, not like marines, not like the posters, not like that day in the high school, this is for real. "Mother!" screams a man without a face. "Oh I don't want to die!" screams a young boy cupping his intestines with his hands. "Oh please, oh no, oh God, oh help! Mother!" he screams again.

We are moving slowly through the water, the Amtrac rocking back and forth. We cannot be brave anymore, there is no reason. It means nothing now. We hold on to ourselves, to things around us, to memories, to thoughts, to dreams. I breathe slowly, desperately trying to stay awake.

The steel trapdoor is opening. I see faces. Corpsmen, I think. Others, curious, looking in at us. Air, fresh, I feel, I smell. They are carrying me out now. Over wounded bodies, past wounded screams. I'm in a helicopter now lifting above the battalion area. I'm leaving the war. I'm going to live. I am still breathing, I keep thinking over and over, I'm going to live and get out of here.

They are shoving tubes and needles in my arms. Now we are being packed into planes. I begin to believe more and more as I watch the other wounded packed around me on shelves that I am going to live.

I still fight desperately to stay awake. I am in an ambulance now rushing to some place. There is a man without any legs screaming in pain, moaning like a little baby. He is bleeding terribly from the stumps that were once his legs, thrashing his arms wildly about his chest, in a semiconscious daze. It is almost too much for me to watch.

I cannot take much more of this. I must be knocked out soon, before I lose my mind. I've seen too much today, I think. But I hold on, sucking the air. I shout then curse for him to be quiet. "My wound is much worse than yours!" I scream. "You're lucky," I shout, staring him in the eyes. "I can feel nothing from my chest down. You at least still have part of your legs. Shut up!" I scream again. "Shut the fuck up, you goddamned baby!" He keeps thrashing his arms wildly above his head and kicking his bleeding stumps toward the roof of the ambulance.

The journey seems to take a very long time, but soon we are at the place where the wounded are sent. I feel a tremendous exhilaration inside me. I have made it this far. I have actually made it this far without giving up and now I am in a hospital where they will operate on me and find out why I cannot feel anything from my chest down anymore. I know I am going to make it now. I am going to make it not because of any god, or any religion, but because I want to make it, I want to live. And I leave the screaming man without legs and am brought to a room that is very bright.

"What's your name?" the voice shouts.

"Wh-wh-what?" I say.

"What's your name?" the voice says again.

"K-K-Kovic," I say.

"No!" says the voice. "I want your name, rank, and service number. Your date of birth, the name of your father and mother."

"Kovic. Sergeant. Two-oh-three-oh-two-six-one, uh, when are you going to..."

"Date of birth!" the voice shouts.

"July fourth, nineteen forty-six. I was born on the Fourth of July. I can't feel..."

"What religion are you?"

"Catholic," I say.

"What outfit did you come from?"

"What's going on? When are you going to operate?" I say.

"The doctors will operate," he says. "Don't worry," he says confidently. "They are very busy and there are many wounded but they will take care of you soon."

He continues to stand almost at attention in front of me with a long clipboard in his hand, jotting down all the information he can. I cannot understand why they are taking so long to operate. There is something very wrong with me, I think, and they must operate as quickly as possible. The man with the clipboard walks out of the room. He will send the priest in soon.

I lie in the room alone staring at the walls, still sucking the air, determined to live more than ever now.

The priest seems to appear suddenly above my head. With his fingers he is gently touching my forehead, rubbing it slowly and softly. "How are you," he says.

"I'm fine, Father." His face is very tired but it is not frightened. He is almost at ease, as if what he is doing he has done many times before.

"I have come to give you the Last Rites, my son."

"I'm ready, Father," I say.

And he prays, rubbing oils on my face and gently placing the crucifix to my lips. "I will pray for you," he says.

"When will they operate?" I say to the priest.

"I do not know," he says. "The doctors are very busy. There are many wounded. There is not much time for anything here but trying to live. So you must try to live my son, and I will pray for you."

Soon after that I am taken to a long room where there are many doctors and nurses. They move quickly around me. They are acting very competent. "You will be fine," says one nurse calmly.

"Breathe deeply into the mask," the doctor says.

"Are you going to operate?" I ask.

"Yes. Now breathe deeply into the mask." As the darkness of the mask slowly covers my face I pray with all my being that I will live through this operation and see the light of day once again. I want to live so much. And even before I go to sleep with the blackness still swirling around my head and the numbness of sleep, I begin to fight as I have never fought before in my life.

I awake to the screams of other men around me. I have made it. I think that maybe the wound is my punishment for killing the corporal and the children. That now everything is okay and the score is evened up. And now I am packed in this place with the others who have been wounded like myself, strapped onto a strange circular bed. I feel tubes going into my nose and hear the clanking, pumping sound of a machine. I still cannot feel any of my body but I know I am alive. I feel a terrible pain in my chest. My body is so cold. It has never been this weak. I feels so tired and out of touch, so lost and in pain. I can still barely breathe. I look around me, at people moving in shadows of numbness. There is the man who had been in the ambulance with me, screaming louder than ever, kicking his bloody stumps in the air, crying for his mother, crying for his morphine.

Directly across from me there is a Korean who has not even been in the war at all. The nurse says he was going to buy a newspaper when he stepped on a booby trap and it blew off both his legs and his arm. And all that is left now is this slab of meat swinging one arm crazily in the air, moaning like an animal gasping for its last bit of life, knowing that death is rushing toward him. The Korean is screaming like a madman at the top of his lungs. I cannot wait for the shots of morphine. Oh, the morphine feels so good. It makes everything dark and quiet. I can rest. I can leave this madness. I can dream of my back yard once again.

When I wake they are screaming still and the lights are on and the clock, the clock on the wall, I can hear it ticking to the sound of their screams. I can hear the dead being carted out and the new wounded being brought in to the beds all around me. I have to get out of this place.

"Can I call you by your first name?" I say to the nurse.

"No. My name is Lieutenant Wiecker."

"Please, can I . . ."

"No," she says. "It's against regulations."

I'm sleeping now. The lights are flashing. The black pilot is next to me. He says nothing. He stares at the ceiling all day long. He does nothing but that. But something is happening now, something is going wrong over there. The nurse is shouting for the machine, and the corpsman is crawling on the black man's chest, he has his knees on his chest and he's pounding it with his fists again and again.

"His heart has stopped!" screams the nurse.

Pounding, pounding, he's pounding his fist into his chest.

"Get the machine!" screams the corpsman.

The nurse is pulling the machine across the hangar floor as quickly as she can now. They are trying to put curtains around the whole thing, but the curtains keep slipping and falling down. Everyone, all the wounded who can still see and think, now watch what is happening to the pilot, and it is happening right next to me. The doctor hands the corpsman a syringe, they are laughing as the corpsman drives the syringe into the pilot's chest like a knife. They are talking about the Green Bay Packers and the corpsman is driving his fist into the black man's chest again and again until the black pilot's body begins to bloat up, until it doesn't look like a body at all anymore. His face is all puffy like a balloon and saliva rolls slowly from the sides of his mouth. He keeps staring at the ceiling and saying nothing. "The machine! The machine!" screams the doctor, now climbing on top of the bed, taking the corpsman's place. "Turn on the machine!" screams the doctor.

He grabs a long suction cup that is attached to the machine and places it carefully against the black man's chest. The black man's body jumps up from the bed almost arcing into the air from each bolt of electricity, jolting and arcing, bloating up more and more.

"I'll bet on the Packers," says the corpsman.

"Green Bay doesn't have a chance," the doctor says, laughing.

The nurse is smiling now, making fun of both the doctor and the corpsman. "I don't understand football," she says.

They are pulling the sheet over the head of the black man and strapping him onto the gurney. He is taken out of the ward.

The Korean civilian is still screaming and there is a baby now at the end of the ward. The nurse says it has been napalmed by our own jets. I cannot see the baby but it screams all the time like the Korean and the young man without any legs I had met in the ambulance.

I can hear a radio. It is the Armed Forces radio. The corpsman is telling the baby to shut the hell up and there is a young kid with half his head blown away. They have brought him in and put him where the black pilot has just died, right next to me. He has thick bandages wrapped all around his head till I can hardly see his face at all. He is like a vegetable – a nineteen-year-old vegetable, thrashing his arms back and forth, babbling and pissing in his clean white sheets.

"Quit pissin' in your sheets!" screams the corpsman. But the nineteen-year-old kid who doesn't have any brains anymore makes the corpsman very angry. He just keeps pissing in the sheets and crying like a little baby.

There is a Green Beret sergeant calling for his mother. Every night now I hear him. He has spinal meningitis. He will be dead before this evening is over.

The Korean civilian does not moan anymore. He does not wave his one arm and two fingers above his head. He is dead and they have taken him away too.

There is a nun who comes through the ward now with apples for the wounded and rosary beads. She is very pleasant and smiles at all of the wounded. The corpsman is reading a comicbook, still cursing at the baby. The baby is screaming and the Armed Forces radio is saying that troops will be home soon. The kid with the bloody stumps is getting a morphine shot.

There is a general walking down the aisles now, going to each bed. He's marching down the aisles, marching and facing each wounded man in his bed. A skinny private with a Polaroid camera follows directly behind him. The general is dressed in an immaculate uniform with shiny shoes. "Good afternoon, marine," the general says. "In the name of the President of the United States and the United States Marine Corps, I am proud to present you with the Purple Heart, and a picture," the general says. Just then the skinny man with the Polaroid camera jumps up, flashing a picture of the wounded man. "And a picture to send to your folks."

He comes up to my bed and says exactly the same thing he has said to all the rest. The skinny man jumps up, snapping a picture of the general handing the Purple Heart to me. "And here," says the general, "here is a picture to send home to your folks." The general makes a sharp left face. He is marching to the bed next to me where the nineteen-year-old kid is still pissing in his pants, babbling like a little baby.

"In the name of the President of the United States," the general says. The kid is screaming now almost tearing the bandages off his head, exposing the part of his brain that are still left. "...I present you with the Purple Heart. And here," the general says, handing the medal to the nineteen-year-old vegetable, the skinny guy jumping up and snapping a picture, "here is a picture ...," the general says, looking at the picture the skinny guy has just pulled out of the camera. The kid is still pissing in his white sheets. "...And here is a picture to send home...." The general does not finish what he is saying. He stares at the nineteen-year-old for what seems a long time. He hands the picture back to his photographer and as sharply as before marches to the next bed.

"Good afternoon, marine," he says.

The kid is still pissing in his clean white sheets when the general walks out of the room.

I am in this place for seven days and seven nights. I write notes on scraps of paper telling myself over and over that I will make it out of here, that I am going to live. I am squeezing rubber balls with my hands to try to get strong again. I write letters home to Mom and Dad. I dictate them to a woman named Lucy who is with the USO. I am telling Mom and Dad that I am hurt pretty bad but I have done it for America and that it is worth it. I tell them not to worry. I will be home soon.

The day I am supposed to leave has come. I am strapped in a long frame and taken from the place of the wounded. I am moved from hangar to hangar, then finally put on a plane, and I leave Vietnam forever.

Study Questions

1   Kovic places the reader in the middle of the Vietnam War without providing any specific information about the war, or the time or place the events are taking place. Why do you think he decided to begin his memoir this way?

2   How do the thoughts that run through his head relate to the ideas he had about religion, family, and war when he was growing up?

3   Why does Kovic's experience in the hospital begin to raise doubts for him about the war?

4   How does Kovic fit Christian Appy's profile of the average working-class soldier who fought in Vietnam?

CHAPTER 21

From *Bloods*:
An Oral History of the Vietnam War by Black Veterans

Richard J. Ford III

Richard J. Ford was born in 1947 to a father who managed a halfway house and a mother who worked for Washington, DC's Board of Elections. A year after graduating from high school in 1965, he was drafted. Although African Americans constituted 11 percent of the American population, they represented 20 percent of combat deaths in Vietnam during the time Ford served in Vietnam, from June 1967 to July 1968. A specialist in the LURPs (Long Range Reconnaissance Patrol) of the 25th Infantry Division of the US Army, Ford was awarded two Bronze Stars for heroic conduct. In 1969 he joined the Washington, DC police department as an undercover narcotics agent, earning a gold medal, as well as the American Legion Award. Ford joined the FBI in 1971. He was injured on duty and retired on disability. In the following oral history, excerpted from Wallace Terry's Bloods *(1984) Ford tries to make sense of what happened to him in Vietnam.*

I should have felt happy I was goin' home when I got on that plane in Cam Ranh Bay to leave. But I didn't exactly. I felt – I felt – I felt very insecure 'cause I didn't have a weapon. I had one of them long knives, like a big hacksaw knife. I had that. And had my cane. And I had a couple of grenades in my bag. They took them from me when I got to Washington, right? And I felt insecure. I just felt real bad.

You know, my parents never had a weapon in the house. Rifle, shotgun, pistol, nothing. Never had one. Never seen my father with one. And I needed a weapon. 'Cause of that insecurity. I never got over it.

It was Saturday evening when we landed. Nineteen sixty-eight. I caught a cab from Dulles and went straight to my church. The Way of the Cross Church. It's a Pentecostal [Holiness] church. I really wasn't active in the church before I went overseas. But a lot of people from the church wrote me, saying things like "I'm praying for you." There was a couple of peoples around there. They had a choir rehearsal. And they said they were glad to see me. But I went to the altar and stayed there from seven o'clock to about eleven-thirty. I just wanted to be by myself and pray. At the altar.

I was glad to be home. Just to be stateside. I was thankful that I made it. But I felt bad because I had to leave some friends over there. I left Davis there. I couldn't say a prayer for people that was already gone. But I said a prayer for them guys to come back home safely. For Davis. Yeah, for Davis.

The first nights I came home I couldn't sleep. My room was the back room of my parents' house. I couldn't sleep in the bed, so I had to get on the floor. I woke up in the middle of the night, and looking out my back window, all you see is trees. So I see all these trees, and I'm thinkin' I'm still in Vietnam. And I can't find my weapon. And I can't find Davis. I can't find nobody. And I guess I scared my mother and father half to death 'cause I got to hollering, "Come on, where are you? Where are you? Davis. Davis. SIR DAVIS." I thought I had got captured or something.

The first thing I did Monday was went to the store and bought me a .38. And bought me a .22.

It was right after the Fourth of July, and kids were still throwing firecrackers. I couldn't deal with it. Hear the noise, I hit the ground. I was down on 7th and F, downtown. I had this little .22. A kid threw firecrackers, and I was trying to duck. And some guys laughed at me, right? So I fired the pistol back at them and watched them duck. I said, "It's not funny now, is it?" I didn't go out of my way to mess with nobody, but I demanded respect.

One day, me and my mother and my wife were coming home from church, up Illinois Avenue. I made a left turn, and four white guys in a car cut in front of me and blew the horn. They had been drinking. They gave me the finger. And, man, I forgot all about my mother and wife was in the car. I took off after them. I had the .22 and was firing out the window at them. I just forgot where – and Vietnam does that to you – you forget where you are. It was open season. I'm shooting out the window. My mother said, "Oh, my God. Please, please help him."

Got home and it was, "You need help. You need help." But I was like that. I just couldn't adjust to it. Couldn't adjust to coming back home, and people think you dirty 'cause you went to Vietnam.

The Army sent me to Walter Reed Hospital for therapy. For two weeks. It was for guys who had been involved in a lot of combat. They said that I was hyper. And they pumped me up with a whole bunch of tranquilizers.

I'll never forget this goddamn officer. I'm looking at him. He's got a Good Conduct ribbon on. He's a major. He's reading my jacket, and he's looking with his glasses at me. I'm just sitting there. So he says, "Ford, you were very lucky. I see you got these commendations. You were very lucky to come back." So I told him, "No, I'm not lucky. You're lucky. You didn't go. You sitting there with a Good Conduct Medal on your chest and haven't been outside the States. You volunteered for service. You should have went. I didn't volunteer for Vietnam. They made me go." [...]

I graduated from Roosevelt High School in 1966 and was working for the Food and Drug Administration as a lab technician when I was drafted. My father was administrator of a half-way house for Lorton, and my mother was on the Board of Elections in DC. I was nineteen, and they took me to Fort Bragg. Airborne.

We were really earmarked for Vietnam. Even the drill sergeant and the first sergeant in basic told us that we was going to Vietnam. From basic we went straight to jungle warfare AIT [Administrator-in-Training] in South Carolina. Before I went to Vietnam, three medical doctors at Fort Dix examined my knees. They trained us so hard in Fort Bragg the cartilages were roughed up. The doctors signed the medical record. It was a permanent profile. Said they would find something in the rear for you. A little desk job, clerk, or medic aid. But they didn't. I was sent straight to the infantry.

I really thought Vietnam was really a civil war between that country, and we had no business in there. But it seems that by the Russians getting involved and supplying so many weapons to the North Vietnamese that the United States should send troops in.

When I stepped off the plane in Tan Son Nhut, that heat that was coming from the ground hit me in the face. And the odor from the climate was so strong. It hit me. I said, Goddamn, where am I? What is this?

While we was walking off the plane, guys were coming toward the plane. And guys said, "Happy Birthday, Merry Christmas, Happy Easter. I'll write your mom." They kept going. In other words, you gon' have Easter here, gonna have a birthday here, and you gonna have Christmas here. And good luck.

It was in June 1967. My MOS [military occupational specialty] was mortarman, but they made me be a rifleman first and sent me to Company C, 3rd Brigade, 25th Infantry Division. We was operating in Chu Lai, but we was a floatin' battalion.

It was really weird how the old guys would ask you what you want to carry. It wasn't a thing where you get assigned an M-14, M-16. If you want to carry an M-16, they say how many rounds of ammo do you want to carry? If you want to carry 2,000, we got it for you. How many grenades do you want? It was really something. We were so in the spirit that we hurt ourself. Guys would want to look like John Wayne. The dudes would just get in the country and say, "I want a .45. I want eight grenades. I want a bandolier. I want a thousand rounds ammo. I want ten clips. I want the works, right?" We never knew what the weight of this ammo is gon' be.

A lot of times guys be walkin' them hills, choppin' through them mountains, and the grenades start gettin' heavy. And you start throwin' your grenades under bushes and takin' your bandoliers off. It wasn't ever questioned. We got back in the rear, and it wasn't questioned if you felt like goin' to get the same thing again next time.

Once I threw away about 200 rounds of ammo. They designated me to carry ammo for the M-60 machine gun. We was going through a stream above Chu Lai. I'm carrying my C rations, my air mattress, poncho, five quarts of water, everything that you own. The ammo was just too heavy. I threw away the ammo going through the river. I said it got lost. The terrain was so terrible, so thick, nobody could question that you lost it.

I come from a very religious family. So I'm carrying my sister's Bible, too. All my letters that I saved. And a little bottle of olive oil that my pastor gave me. Blessed olive oil. But I found it was a lot of guys in basic with me that were atheist. When we got to Vietnam there were no atheist. There was not one atheist in my unit. When we got hit, everybody hollered, "Oh, God, please help, please." And everybody want to wear a cross. Put a cross on their helmet. Something to psych you up.

Black guys would wear sunglasses, too. We would put on sunglasses walking in the jungle. Think about it, now. It was ridiculous. But we want to show how bad we are. How we're not scared. We be saying, "The Communists haven't made a bullet that can kill me." We had this attitude that I don't give a damn. That made us more aggressive, more ruthless, more careless. And a little more luckier than the person that was scared.

I guess that's why I volunteered for the LURPs and they brought me into Nha Trang. And it was six other black fellas to go to this school at the 5th Special Forces. And we would always be together in the field. Sometimes it would be Captain Park, this Korean, with us. Most of the time it was us, five or six black dudes making our own war, doing our thing alone.

There was Larry Hill from New York. Garland from Baltimore. Holmes from Georgia. Louis Ford from New Orleans. Moon from Detroit, too. They called him Sir Drawers, 'cause he wouldn't wear underwear. Said it gave him a rash. And this guy from Baton Rouge named Albert Davis. He was only 5 feet 9. Only 120 pounds. He was a terrific soldier. A lot of guts, a lot of heart. He was Sir Davis. I was Sir Ford. Like Knights of the Round Table. We be immortal. No one can kill us. [...]

In the field most of the guys stayed high. Lot of them couldn't face it. In a sense, if you was high, it seemed like a game you was in. You didn't take it serious. It stopped a lot of nervous breakdown.

See, the thing about the field that was so bad was this. If I'm working on the job with you stateside and you're my friend, if you get killed, there's a compassion. My boss say, "Well, you better take a couple of days off. Get yourself together." But in the field, we can be the best of friends and you get blown away. They put a poncho around you and send you back. They tell 'em to keep moving.

We had a medic that give us a shot of morphine anytime you want one. I'm not talkin' about for wounded. I'm talkin' about when you want to just get high. So you can face it.

In the rear sometimes we get a grenade, dump the gunpowder out, break the firing pin. Then you'll go inside one of them little bourgeois clubs. Or go in the barracks where the supply guys are, sitting around playing bid whist and doing nothing. We act real crazy. Yell out, "Kill all y'all motherfuckers." Pull the pin and throw the grenade. And everybody would haul ass and get out. It would make a little pop sound. And we would laugh. You didn't see anybody jumpin' on them grenades.

One time in the field, though, I saw a white boy jump on a grenade. But I believe he was pushed. It ain't kill him. He lost both his legs.

The racial incidents didn't happen in the field. Just when we went to the back. It wasn't so much that they were against us. It was just that we felt that we were being taken advantage of, 'cause it seemed like more blacks in the field than in the rear.

In the rear we saw a bunch of rebel flags. They didn't mean nothing by the rebel flag. It was just saying we for the South. It didn't mean that they hated blacks. But after you in the field, you took the flags very personally.

One time we saw these flags in Nha Trang on the MP barracks. They was playing hillbilly music. Had their shoes off dancing. Had nice, pretty bunks. Mosquito nets over top the bunks. And had the nerve to have this camouflaged covers. Air conditioning. Cement floors. We just came out the jungles. We dirty, we smelly, hadn't shaved. We just went off. Said, "Y'all the real enemy. We stayin' here." We turned the bunks over, started tearing up the stereo. They just ran out. Next morning, they shipped us back up.

In the field, we had the utmost respect for each other, because when a fire fight is going on and everybody is facing north, you don't want to see nobody looking around south. If you was a member of the Ku Klux Klan, you didn't tell nobody. [...]

I remember February 20. Twentieth of February. We went to this village outside Duc Pho. Search and destroy. It was suppose to have been VC sympathizers. They sent fliers to the people telling them to get out. Anybody else there, you have to consider them as a VC.

It was a little straw-hut village. Had a little church at the end with this big Buddha. We didn't see anybody in the village. But I heard movement in the rear of this hut. I just opened up the machine gun. You ain't wanna open the door, and then you get blown away. Or maybe they booby-trapped.

Anyway, this little girl screamed. I went inside the door. I'd done already shot her, and she was on top of the old man. She was trying to shield the old man. He looked like he could have been about eighty years old. She was about seven. Both of them was dead. I killed an old man and a little girl in the hut by accident.

I started feeling funny. I wanted to explain to someone. But everybody was there, justifying my actions, saying, "It ain't your fault. They had no business there." But I just – I ain't wanna hear it. I wanted to go home then.

It bothers me now. But so many things happened after that, you really couldn't lay on one thing. You had to keep going.

The flame throwers came in, and we burnt the hamlet. Burnt up everything. They had a lot of rice. We opened the bags, just throw it all over the street. Look for tunnels. Killing animals. Killing all the livestock. Guys would carry chemicals that they would put in the well. Poison the water so they couldn't use it. So they wouldn't come back to use it, right? And it was trifling.

They killed some more people there. Maybe 12 or 14 more. Old people and little kids that wouldn't leave. I guess their grandparents. See, people that were old in Vietnam couldn't leave their village. It was like a ritual. They figured that this'll pass. We'll come and move on.

Sometimes we went in a village, and we found a lot of weapons stashed, little tunnels. On the twentieth of February we found nothing.

You know, it was a little boy used to hang around the base camp. Around Hill 54. Wasn't no more than about eight years old. Spoke good English, a little French. Very sharp. His mother and father got killed by mortar attack on his village. I thought about that little girl. And I wanted to adopt him. A bunch of us wanted to. And we went out to the field, and then came back and he was gone. [...]

Our main function was to try to see can we find any type of enemy element. They gave us a position, a area, and tell us to go out there and do the recon. We alone – these six black guys – roamin' miles from the base camp. We find them. We radio helicopter pick us up, take us to the rear. We go and bring the battalion out and wipe 'em out. You don't fire your weapon. That's the worse thing you do if you a LURP. Because if it's a large unit and it's just six of y'all, you fire your weapon and you by yourself. You try to kill 'em without firing your weapon. This is what they taught us in Nha Trang. Different ways of killing a person without using your weapon. Use your weapon, it give you away. [...]

Davis would do little crazy things. If they had gold in their mouth, he'd knock the gold out 'cause he saved gold. He saved a little collection of gold teeth. Maybe 50 or 60 in a little box. And he went and had about 100 pictures made of himself. And he used to leave one in the field. Where he got the gook.

One day we saw two gooks no more than 50 yards away. They was rolling cigarettes. Eating. Davis said, "They mine. Y'all just stay here and watch." He sneaked up on 'em real fast, and in one swing he had them. Hit one with the bayonet, hit the other one with the machete.

Wherever he would see a gook, he would go after 'em. He was good. [...]

Before I went home, the company commanders in Bravo and Echo got killed. And rumor said their own men did it. Those companies were pressed because the captains do everything by the book. And the book didn't work for Vietnam. They had this West Point thing about you dug a foxhole at night. Put sandbags around it. You couldn't expect a man to cut through that jungle all day, then dig a hole, fill up the sandbags, then in the morning time dump the sandbags out, fill your foxhole back up, and then cut down another mountain. Guys said the hell with some foxhole. And every time you get in a fire fight, you looking for somebody to cover your back, and he looking around to see where the captain is 'cause he gon' fire a couple rounds at him. See, the thing about Vietnam, your own men could shoot you and no one could tell, because we always left weapons around and the Viet Congs could get them. [...]

When I got out of the service, I went back to Food and Drug, the lab technician thing. But I was carrying this pistol all the time, so people come up and say, "Why don't you go in the police department?"

I joined in December '69. And because I was a LURP and had these medals, they figured I wasn't scared of anything. So they asked me to work undercover in narcotics. I did it for 19 months. Around 7th and T, 9th and U, all in the area. The worst in DC. I would try to buy drugs on a small scale, like $25. Heroin and cocaine. Then I gradually go up to where I could buy a spoon, $100. Then I could buy a ounce for a $1,000. I got robbed three times, hit in the head with a gun once. But my investigation was so successful that they didn't lock anybody up until it was all over.

I threw a great big party at the Diplomat Motel. I had 34 arrest warrants. I invited all the guys that I bought dope from. About 20 of them showed up. All dressed up, and everybody had Cadillacs and Mercedes. We had agents everywhere outside. Then I told them, "I am not a dope pusher like y'all scums." They laughed. I said, "Y'all scums of the earth selling dope to your own. Take the dope up in Georgetown if you want to do something with it. Heroin. Cocaine. Get rid of it." All of them laughed and laughed. And I said, "When I call your name, just raise your hand, 'cause you'll be under arrest for selling these heroins." And they laughed. And I call their names, and they raise their hand. Then these uniforms came in, and it wasn't funny anymore.

But they put out a $25,000 contract on me. [...]

I was a federal agent until this thing went down in Jersey. We was working police corruption. This lieutenant was stealing dope out the property office and selling it back on the street. But somethin' told me the investigation just wasn't right. We had a snitch telling us about the lieutenant. But he had all the answers. He knew everything. He knows too much. I think he's playing both ends against the middle. So one night, my partner and me are walking down this street going to meet the lieutenant to buy these heroins. This scout car comes driving down on us, hits us both, and the lieutenant jumps out and shoots me in the head. He knows that even if he didn't sell no dope, we gon' nab him. I didn't have no gun, but I reach like I do from instinct. And the lieutenant took off. He went to jail, and the prisoners tried to rape him, kill him.

I retired on disability, because the wound gives me headaches. I do a little private security work now for lawyers, and I try to keep in touch with Davis and the other guys.

Davis tried to get a job with the New Orleans police, but they said he was too short. When it comes to weapons, Sir Davis is terrific. But he's been in trouble. A drug thing, two assaults. He writes me sometimes. Tells me his light bulb is out. They trained us for one thing. To kill. Where is he gonna get a job? The Mafia don't like blacks.

Hill went home first. Said send him all our grenades. He was on his way to Oakland to join the Panthers. Never heard nothin' about him again.

Fowler got shot through the chest with a BAR [Browning automatic rifle]. But he got home. He stays in trouble. He's serving 15–45 in Lewisburg for armed robbery.

Holmes got to computer school. He's doing okay in San Diego. I don't know what happened to Ferguson and Taylor.

Sir Drawers came over to see me for the Vietnam Veterans Memorial. He is still out of work. We marched together. When we got to the memorial, I grabbed his hand. Like brothers do. It was all swollen up.

We looked for one name on the memorial. Louis. We found it, and I called his mother. I told her it was nice, and she said she might be able to see it one day.

But I think the memorial is a hole in the ground. It makes me think they ashamed of what we did. You can't see it from the street. A plane flying over it can't see nothing but a hole in the ground.

And it really hurt me to see Westmoreland at the memorial, 'cause he said that we had no intentions of winning the war. What the hell was we over there for then? And the tactical thing was we fought it different from any way we was ever trained to fight in the States. They tell you about flanks, platoons, advance this. It wasn't none of that. It was just jungle warfare. You jumped up and ran where you could run.

We went to church on the Sunday after the memorial thing. I was doing pretty good about Vietnam the last five years, 'cause I was active a whole lot. If I ever sit down and really think about it, it's a different story.

My sister's husband was with me. He got shrapnel in his eye. His vision is messed up. There were 2,000 people in the church. And the pastor gave us space to talk, 'cause we were the only two that went to Vietnam. My brother-in-law is a correction officer at the jail. So we've always been kind of aggressive. Ain't scared that much. But we got up there to talk, and we couldn't do nothing but cry. My wife cried. My children cried. The whole church just cried.

I thought about Louis and all the people that didn't come back. Then people that wasn't even there tell us the war was worthless. That a man lost his life following orders. It was worthless, they be saying.

I really feel used. I feel manipulated. I feel violated.

Study Questions

1   What kinds of relationships sustained and troubled Ford in the military?
2   How did his experiences in the military affect Ford's experiences when he returned home? How do his experiences compare with those of Maria Tymoczko's father?
3   How did Ford see the Vietnamese people he came into contact with (soldiers and civilians)? Why do you think he saw them this way?

CHAPTER 22

'Black Power:
Its Need and Substance

Stokely Carmichael and Charles V. Hamilton

Born in Port-of-Spain, Trinidad, in 1941, Stokely Carmichael emigrated with his family to a mostly white neighborhood in the Bronx, New York, in 1952, becoming a naturalized citizen of the US in 1954. He graduated from Bronx High School of Science in 1960, and earned a degree in philosophy from Howard University, Washington, DC, in 1964, the year he joined the Student Nonviolent Coordinating Committee (SNCC), where he worked as a field organizer registering black voters in Lowndes County, Alabama. Because established political parties showed little interest in the newly registered black voters, Carmichael organized the all-black Lowndes County Freedom Organization. Arrested numerous times for nonviolent protests, he watched peaceful protesters in the South being beaten and sometimes killed for seeking the ordinary rights of citizens. In 1966, as chairman of SNCC, he raised the call for black power, signaling a new insistence on black pride, black leadership, and black unity, and a new direction for civil rights demands. In the 1967 book he wrote with political scientist Charles Hamilton, from which the following selection is excerpted, they explained "black power" and its implications for civil rights strategy.

"To carve out a place for itself in the politico-social order," V. O. Key, Jr. wrote in *Politics, Parties and Pressure Groups*, "a new group may have to fight for reorientation of many of the values of the old order" (p. 57). This is especially true when that group is composed of black people in the American society – a society that has for centuries deliberately and systematically excluded them from political participation. Black people in the United States must raise hard questions, questions which challenge the very nature of the society itself: its long-standing values, beliefs and institutions.

To do this, we must first redefine ourselves. Our basic need is to reclaim our history and our identity from what must be called cultural terrorism, from the depredation of self-justifying white guilt. We shall have to struggle for the right to create our own terms through which to define ourselves and our relationship to the society, and to have these terms recognized. This is the first necessity of a free people, and the first right that any oppressor must suspend. [. . .]

"Integration" is a current example of a word which has been defined according to the way white Americans see it. To many of them, it means black men wanting to marry white daughters; it means "race mixing" – implying bed or dance partners. To black people, it has meant a way to improve their lives – economically and politically. But the predominant white definition has stuck in the minds of too many people.

Black people must redefine themselves, and only *they* can do that. Throughout this country, vast segments of the black communities are beginning to recognize the need to assert their own definitions, to reclaim their history, their culture; to create their own sense of community and togetherness. There is a growing resentment of the word "Negro," for example, because this term is the invention of our oppressor; it is *his* image of us that he describes. Many blacks are now calling themselves African-Americans, Afro-Americans or black people because that is *our* image of ourselves. When we begin to define our own image, the stereotypes – that is, lies – that our oppressor has developed will begin in the white community and end there. The black community will have a positive image of itself that *it* has created. This means we will no longer call ourselves lazy, apathetic, dumb, good-timers, shiftless, etc. Those are words used by white America to define us. If we accept these adjectives, as some of us have in the past, then we see ourselves only in a negative way, precisely the way white America wants us to see ourselves. Our incentive is broken and our will to fight is surrendered. From now on we shall view ourselves as African-Americans and as black people who are in fact energetic, determined, intelligent, beautiful and peace-loving.

There is a terminology and ethos peculiar to the black community of which black people are beginning to be no longer ashamed. Black communities are the only large segments of this society where people refer to each other as brother – soul-brother, soul-sister. Some people may look upon this as *ersatz*, as make-believe, but it is not that. It is real. It is a growing sense of community. It is a growing realization that black Americans have a common bond not only among themselves, but with their African brothers. [. . .]

More and more black Americans are developing this feeling. They are becoming aware that they have a history which pre-dates their forced introduction to this country. African-American history means a long history beginning on the continent of Africa, a history not taught in the standard textbooks of this country. It is absolutely essential that black people know this history, that they know their roots, that they develop an awareness of their cultural heritage. Too long have they been kept in submission by being told that they had no culture, no manifest heritage, before they landed on the slave auction blocks in this country. If black people are to know themselves as a vibrant valiant people, they must know their roots. [. . .]

The next step is what we shall call the process of political modernization – a process which must take place if the society is to be rid of racism. "Political modernization" includes many things, but we mean by it three major concepts: (1) questioning old values and institutions of the society; (2) searching for new and different forms of political structure to solve political and economic problems; and (3) broadening the base of political participation to include more people in the decision-making process. [...]

The values of this society support a racist system; we find it incongruous to ask black people to adopt and support most of those values. We also reject the assumption that the basic institutions of this society must be preserved. The goal of black people must *not* be to assimilate into middle-class America, for that class – as a whole – is without a viable conscience as regards humanity. The values of the middle class permit the perpetuation of the ravages of the black community. The values of that class are based on material aggrandizement, not the expansion of humanity. The values of that class ultimately support cloistered little closed societies tucked away neatly in tree-lined suburbia. The values of that class do *not* lead to the creation of an open society. That class *mouths* its preference for a free, competitive society, while at the same time forcefully and even viciously denying to black people as a group the opportunity to compete. [...]

Thus we reject the goal of assimilation into middle-class America because the values of that class are in themselves anti-humanist and because that class as a social force perpetuates racism. We must face the fact that, in the past, what we have called the movement has not really questioned the middle-class values and institutions of this country. If anything, it has accepted those values and institutions without fully realizing their racist nature. Reorientation means an emphasis on the dignity of man, not on the sanctity of property. It means the creation of a society where human misery and poverty are repugnant to that society, not an indication of laziness or lack of initiative. The creation of new values means the establishment of a society based, as Killens expresses it in *Black Man's Burden*, on "free people," not "free enterprise" (p. 167). To do this means to modernize – *indeed, to civilize* – this country. [...]

The two major political parties in this country have become non-viable entities for the legitimate representation of the real needs of masses – especially blacks – in this country. [...]

Black people have seen the city planning commissions, the urban renewal commissions, the boards of education and the police departments fail to speak to their needs in a meaningful way. We must devise new structures, new institutions to replace those forms or to make them responsive. There is nothing sacred or inevitable about old institutions; the focus must be on people, not forms.

Existing structures and established ways of doing things have a way of perpetuating themselves and for this reason, the modernizing process will be difficult. Therefore, timidity in calling into question the boards of education or the police departments will not do. They must be challenged forcefully and clearly. If this means the creation of parallel community institutions, then that must be the solution. If this means that black parents must gain control over the operation of the schools in the black community, then that must be the solution. The search for new forms means the search for institutions that will, for once, make decisions in the interest of black people. It means, for example, a building inspection department that neither winks at violations of building codes by absentee slumlords nor imposes meaningless fines which permit them to continue their exploitation of the black community.

Essential to the modernization of structures is a broadened base of political participation. More and more people must become politically sensitive and active (we have already seen this happening in some areas of the South). People must no longer be tied, by small incentives or handouts, to a corrupting and corruptible white machine. Black people will choose their own leaders and hold those leaders responsible to *them*. A broadened base means an end to the condition described by James Wilson in *Negro Politics*, whereby "Negroes tended to be the objects rather than the subjects of civic action. Things are often done for, or about, or to, or because of Negroes, but they are less frequently done *by* Negroes" (p. 133). Broadening the base of political participation, then, has as much to do with the quality of black participation as with the quantity. We are fully aware that the black vote, especially in the North, has been pulled out of white pockets and "delivered" whenever it was in the interest of white politicians to do so. That vote must no longer be controllable by those who have neither the interests nor the demonstrated concern of black people in mind.

As the base broadens, as more and more black people become activated, they will perceive more clearly the special disadvantages heaped upon them as a group. They will perceive that the larger society is growing more affluent while the black society is retrogressing, as daily life and mounting statistics clearly show. [. . .]

The adoption of the concept of Black Power is one of the most legitimate and healthy developments in American politics and race relations in our time. The concept of Black Power speaks to all the needs mentioned in this chapter. It is a call for black people in this country to unite, to recognize their heritage, to build a sense of community. It is a call for black people to begin to define their own goals, to lead their own organizations and to support those organizations. It is a call to reject the racist institutions and values of this society.

The concept of Black Power rests on a fundamental premise: *Before a group can enter the open society, it must first close ranks.* By this we mean that group solidarity is necessary before a group can operate effectively from a bargaining position of strength in a pluralistic society. Traditionally, each new ethnic group in this society has found the route to social and political viability through the organization of its own institutions with which to represent its needs within the larger society. Studies in voting behavior specifically, and political behavior generally, have made it clear that politically the American pot has not melted. Italians vote for Rubino over O'Brien; Irish for Murphy over Goldberg, etc. This phenomenon may seem distasteful to some, but it has been and remains today a central fact of the American political system. [. . .]

The point is obvious: black people must lead and run their own organizations. Only black people can convey the revolutionary idea – and it is a revolutionary idea – that black people are able to do things themselves. Only they can help create in the community an aroused and continuing black consciousness that will provide the basis for political strength. In the past, white allies have often furthered white supremacy without the whites involved realizing it, or even wanting to do so. Black people must come together and do things for themselves. They must achieve self-identity and self-determination in order to have their daily needs met.

Black Power means, for example, that in Lowndes County, Alabama, a black sheriff can end police brutality. A black tax assessor and tax collector and county board of revenue can lay, collect, and channel tax monies for the building of better roads and schools serving black people. In such areas as Lowndes, where black people have a majority, they will attempt to use power to exercise control. This is what they seek: control. When black people lack a majority, Black Power means proper representation and sharing of control. It means the creation of power bases, of strength, from which black people can press to change local or nation-wide patterns of oppression – instead of from weakness.

It does not mean *merely* putting black faces into office. Black visibility is not Black Power. Most of the black politicians around the country today are not examples of Black Power. The power must be that of a community, and emanate from there. The black politicians must start from there. The black politicians must stop being representatives of "downtown" machines, whatever the cost might be in terms of lost patronage and holiday handouts.

Black Power recognizes – it must recognize – the ethnic basis of American politics as well as the power-oriented nature of American politics. Black Power therefore calls for black people to consolidate behind their own, so that they can bargain from a position of strength. But while we endorse the *procedure* of group solidarity and identity for the purpose of attaining certain goals in the body politic, this does not mean that black people should strive for the same kind of rewards (i.e., end results) obtained by the white society. The ultimate values and goals are not domination or exploitation of other groups, but rather an effective share in the total power of the society.

Nevertheless, some observers have labeled those who advocate Black Power as racists; they have said that the call for self-identification and self-determination is "racism in reverse" or "black supremacy." This is a deliberate and absurd lie. There is no analogy – by any stretch of definition or imagination – between the advocates of Black Power and white racists. Racism is not merely exclusion on the basis of race but exclusion for the purpose of subjugating or maintaining subjugation. The goal of the racists is to keep black people on the bottom, arbitrarily and dictatorially, as they have done in this country for over three hundred years. The goal of black self-determination and black self-identity – Black Power – is full participation in the decision-making processes affecting the lives of black people, and recognition of the virtues in themselves as black people. The black people of this country have not lynched whites, bombed their churches, murdered their children and manipulated laws and institutions to maintain oppression. White racists have. Congressional laws, one after the other, have not been necessary to stop black people from oppressing others and denying others the full enjoyment of their rights. White racists have made such laws necessary. The goal of Black Power is positive and functional to a free and viable society. No white racist can make this claim. [. . .]

It is a commentary on the fundamentally racist nature of this society that the concept of group strength for black people must be articulated – not to mention defended. No other group would submit to being led by others. Italians do not run the Anti-Defamation League of B'nai B'rith. Irish do not chair Christopher Columbus Societies. Yet when black people call for black-run and all-black organizations, they are immediately classed in a category with the Ku Klux Klan. This is interesting and ironic, but by no means surprising: the society does not expect black people to be able to take care of their business, and there are many who prefer it precisely that way. [. . .]

One of the tragedies of the struggle against racism is that up to this point there has been no national organization which could speak to the growing militancy of young black people in the urban ghettos and the black-belt South. There has been only a "civil rights" movement, whose tone of voice was adapted to an audience of middle-class whites. It served as a sort of buffer zone between that audience and angry young blacks. It claimed to speak for the needs of a community, but it did not speak in the tone of that community. None of its so-called leaders could go into a rioting community and be listened to. In a sense, the blame must be shared – along with the mass media – by those leaders for what happened in Watts, Harlem, Chicago, Cleveland and other places. Each time the black people in those cities saw Dr. Martin Luther King get slapped they became angry. When they saw little black girls bombed to death *in a church* and civil rights workers ambushed and murdered, they were angrier; and when nothing happened, they were steaming mad. We had nothing to offer that they could see, except to go out and be beaten again. We helped to build their frustration.

We had only the old language of love and suffering. And in most places – that is, from the liberals and middle class – we got back the old language of patience and progress. The civil rights leaders were saying to the country: "Look, you guys are supposed to be nice guys, and we are only going to do what we are supposed to do. Why do you beat us up? Why don't you give us what we ask? Why don't you straighten yourselves out?" For the masses of black people, this language resulted in virtually nothing. In fact, their objective day-to-day condition worsened. The unemployment rate among black people increased while that among whites declined. Housing conditions in the black communities deteriorated. Schools in the black ghettos continued to plod along on outmoded techniques, inadequate curricula, and with all too many tired and indifferent teachers. Meanwhile, the President picked up the refrain of "We Shall Overcome" while the Congress passed civil rights law after civil rights law, only to have them effectively nullified by deliberately weak enforcement. "Progress is being made," we were told. [. . .]

When the concept of Black Power is set forth, many people immediately conjure up notions of violence. The country's reaction to the Deacons for Defense and Justice, which originated in Louisiana, is instructive. Here is a group which realized that the "law" and law enforcement agencies would not protect people, so they had to do it themselves. If a nation fails to protect its citizens, then that nation cannot condemn those who take up the task themselves. The Deacons and all other blacks who resort to self-defense represent a simple answer to a simple question: what man would not defend his family and home from attack?

But this frightened some white people, because they knew that black people would now fight back. They knew that this was precisely what *they* would have long since done if *they* were subjected to the injustices and oppression heaped on blacks. Those of us who advocate Black Power are quite clear in our own minds that a "non-violent" approach to civil rights is an approach black people cannot afford and a luxury white people do not deserve. It is crystal clear to us – and it must become so with the white society – *that there can be no social order without social justice*. White people must be made to understand that they must stop messing with black people, or the blacks *will* fight back! [. . .]

The racial and cultural personality of the black community must be preserved and that community must win its freedom while preserving its cultural integrity. Integrity includes a pride – in the sense of self-acceptance, not chauvinism – in being black, in the historical attainments and contributions of black people. No person can be healthy, complete and mature if he must deny a part of himself; this is what "integration" has required thus far. This is the essential difference between integration as it is currently practiced and the concept of Black Power.

The idea of cultural integrity is so obvious that it seems almost simple-minded to spell things out at this length. Yet millions of Americans resist such truths when they are applied to black people. Again, that resistance is a comment on the fundamental racism in the society. Irish Catholics took care of their own first without a lot of apology for doing so, without any dubious language from timid leadership about guarding against "backlash." Everyone understood it to be a perfectly legitimate procedure. Of course, there would be "backlash." Organization begets counterorganization, but this was no reason to defer.

The so-called white backlash against black people is something else: the embedded traditions of institutional racism being brought into the open and calling forth overt manifestations of individual racism. In the summer of 1966, when the protest marches into Cicero, Illinois, began, the black people knew they were not allowed to live in Cicero and the white people knew it. When blacks began to demand the right to live in homes in that town, the whites simply reminded them of the status quo. Some people called this "backlash." It was, in fact, racism defending itself. In the black community, this is called "White folks showing their color." It is ludicrous to blame black people for what is simply an overt manifestation of white racism. Dr. Martin Luther King stated clearly that the protest marches were not the cause of the racism but merely exposed a long-term cancerous condition in the society. [. . .]

Study Questions

1   According to Carmichael and Hamilton, what are the key words of American political ideology?

2   On what grounds do Carmichael and Hamilton reject assimilation into the white middle class? What new words do they propose to define the black experience in its own, rather than in white, terms?

3   Why do Carmichael and Hamilton propose the term "black power"? What advantage does it hold for them over the term "civil rights"? How does the term "black power" challenge Martin Luther King's program of nonviolence"?

References

Key, V. O., Jr. (1964). *Politics, Parties and Pressure Groups*. New York: Thomas Y. Crowell.

Killens, J. O. (1965). *Black Man's Burden*. New York: Trident Press.

Wilson, J. (1960). *Negro Politics*. Glencoe, IL: The Free Press.

CHAPTER 23

"Respect"

Aretha Franklin

Aretha Franklin, the daughter of a celebrity minister who sold thousands of his sermons on records, was born in Memphis in 1942 and raised in Detroit. She began her singing career as a young child in church gospel choirs, and was able to parlay her father's friendship with gospel superstars like Mahalia Jackson and Dinah Washington into private musical tutoring. The first woman to be inducted into the Rock and Roll Hall of Fame in 1987, Franklin remains a powerful voice in contemporary music. "Respect" was written and first recorded by the rhythm and blues giant Otis Redding, in 1965. But it was Franklin's cover version, recorded in 1967, that made "Respect" into one of the best-selling and most influential recordings of the civil rights era. The song's powerful lyrics were quickly interpreted as a demand for black civil rights, and, after Franklin recorded her woman-narrated version, for women's equality as well.

(oo) What you want
(oo) Baby, I got
(oo) What you need
(oo) Do you know I got it?
(oo) All I'm askin'
(oo) Is for a little respect when you come home (just a little bit)
Hey baby (just a little bit) when you get home
(just a little bit) mister (just a little bit)

I ain't gonna do you wrong while you're gone
Ain't gonna do you wrong (oo) 'cause I don't wanna (oo)
All I'm askin' (oo)
Is for a little respect when you come home (just a little bit)
Baby (just a little bit) when you get home (just a little bit)
Yeah (just a little bit)

I'm about to give you all of my money
And all I'm askin' in return, honey
Is to give me my propers

When you get home (just a, just a, just a, just a)
Yeah baby (just a, just a, just a, just a)
When you get home (just a little bit)
Yeah (just a little bit)

Ooo, your kisses (oo)
Sweeter than honey (oo)
And guess what? (oo)
So is my money (oo)
All I want you to do (oo) for me
Is give it to me when you get home (re, re, re, re)
Yeah baby (re, re, re, re)
Whip it to me (respect, just a little bit)
When you get home, now (just a little bit)

R-E-S-P-E-C-T
Find out what it means to me
R-E-S-P-E-C-T
Take care, TCB
Oh (sock it to me, sock it to me, sock it to me, sock it to me)
A little respect (sock it to me, sock it to me, sock it to me, sock it to me)
Whoa, babe (just a little bit)
A little respect (just a little bit)
I get tired (just a little bit)
Keep on tryin' (just a little bit)
You're runnin' out of fools (just a little bit)
And I ain't lyin' (just a little bit)
(re, re, re, re) 'spect
When you come home (re, re, re, re)
Or you might walk in (respect, just a little bit)
And find out I'm gone (just a little bit)
I got to have (just a little bit)
A little respect (just a little bit)

Study Questions

1 One of the changes Aretha Franklin made in her version of "Respect" was to spell out the word "respect" toward the end of the song, which Otis Redding did not do in the original. Why do you think Franklin did this? How does it change the sound of the song?
2 Who is the "I" in the song, and who is the "you"? Consider that there is more than one way to answer this question.

CHAPTER 24

"Say It Loud (I'm Black and I'm Proud)"

James Brown

Widely referred to as "The Godfather of Soul," James Joe Brown was born in 1928 in Barnwell, South Carolina, and raised by his aunt in a Georgia brothel. As a young boy, he helped his aunt drum up business by running errands for soldiers at a nearby military base; he also entertained them by singing and playing piano, drums, and guitar. Brown left school in the seventh grade and found work picking cotton, shining shoes, and washing cars. As a young man, he joined a gospel quartet, which became a popular rhythm and blues act. Brown's solo career, and his experiments with funk and soul music, made him a superstar. He remains one of the strongest and most influential voices in America popular music. Brown was among the first group of musicians to be inducted into the Rock and Roll Hall of Fame, in 1986; in 1992, he was honored with a lifetime achievement Grammy.

Say it loud (I'm black and I'm proud)
Say it loud (I'm black and I'm proud)

Some people say we got a lot of malice
Some say we got a lot of nerve
I say we won't quit moving until we get what we deserve

We've been 'buked, and we've been scorned,
We've been treated bad, talked about sure as you're born
Just as sure as it takes two eyes to make a pair
Brother we can't quit until we get our share

Say it loud (I'm black and I'm proud)
Say it loud (I'm black and I'm proud)
Say it loud (I'm black and I'm proud)

I worked on jobs
With my feet and my hands

And all the work I did
Was for the other man.

Now we demand a chance
To do things for ourself
We're tired of beatin' our head against the wall
And workin' for someone else

Say it loud
Say it loud
Say it loud
Say it loud

Now we demand a chance
To do things for ourself
We're tired of beatin' our head against the wall
And workin' for someone else

We're people, we're like the birds and the bees
We'd rather die on our feet
Than be livin' on our knees
Say it loud, I'm black and I'm proud

Say it loud (I'm black and I'm proud)
Say it loud (I'm black and I'm proud)
Say it loud (I'm black and I'm proud)
Say it loud (I'm black and I'm proud)

Study Questions

1   Throughout the song, Brown's spoken line, "Say it loud," is answered by a group of African-American schoolchildren who say, "I'm black and I'm proud." Why do you think Brown includes the children's voices in the song?

2   How do you think the song defines the idea of "freedom" or "liberation"? Would Stokely Carmichael approve of the lyrics? Explain.

3   Compare Franklin's and Brown's songs with the songs of the Civil Rights Movement? What is similar about them? What is new and different?

CHAPTER 25

13-Point Program and Platform

Young Lords Party

The Young Lords Party emerged as an important political organization of mainland-born Puerto Ricans in the late 1960s. The group began as a street gang. One of its members, Jose "Cha Cha" Jimenez, met Black Panther Party members while in jail and was inspired by their work in civil rights activism. He took their political ideas to other Young Lords, and the group subsequently transformed itself into a human rights organization, joining the Black Panther Party's Rainbow Coalition, which also included the Young Patriots, a former white street gang turned political. Centered in the Bronx by 1969 and expanded to include branches in several US cities and Puerto Rico, the Young Lords made their arguments through a newspaper and radio show, both called Palante *("Forward") and through street-level direct action. The group's early activities included public health programs, community education, cultural events, prison reform, women's rights, and a host of community services for the urban poor. The Young Lords also participated in the opposition to the Vietnam War, and called for the independence of Puerto Rico, which had been colonized first by Spain (in 1508) and then by the United States (in 1898). The goals and political philosophy of the Young Lords Party are outlined in their "13-Point Program and Platform," written in 1969, which calls for economic and social justice across the US.*

The Young Lords Party Is a Revolutionary Political Party Fighting for the Liberation of All Oppressed People

1. WE WANT SELF-DETERMINATION FOR PUERTO RICANS – LIBERATION ON THE ISLAND AND INSIDE THE UNITED STATES.

    For 500 years, first spain and then united states have colonized our country. Billions of dollars in profits leave our country for the united states every year. In every way we are slaves of the gringo. We want liberation and the Power in the hands of the People, not Puerto Rican exploiters.

    QUE VIVA PUERTO RICO LIBRE!

2. WE WANT SELF-DETERMINATION FOR ALL LATINOS.

   Our Latin Brothers and Sisters, inside and outside the united states, are oppressed by amerikkkan business. The Chicano people built the Southwest, and we support their right to control their lives and their land. The people of Santo Domingo continue to fight against gringo domination and its puppet generals. The armed liberation struggles in Latin America are part of the war of Latinos against imperialism.
   QUE VIVA LA RAZA!

3. WE WANT LIBERATION OF ALL THIRD WORLD PEOPLE.

   Just as Latins first slaved under spain and the yanquis, Black people, Indians, and Asians slaved to build the wealth of this country. For 400 years they have fought for freedom and dignity against racist Babylon (decadent empire). Third World people have led the fight for freedom. All the colored and oppressed peoples of the world are one nation under oppression.
   NO PUERTO RICAN IS FREE UNTIL ALL PEOPLE ARE FREE!

4. WE ARE REVOLUTIONARY NATIONALISTS AND OPPOSE RACISM.

   The Latin, Black, Indian and Asian people inside the u.s. are colonies fighting for liberation. We know that washington, wall street, and city hall will try to make our nationalism into racism; but Puerto Ricans are of all colors and we resist racism. Millions of poor white people are rising up to demand freedom and we support them. These are the ones in the u.s. that are stepped on by the rulers and the government. We each organize our people, but our fights are the same against oppression and we will defeat it together.
   POWER TO ALL OPPRESSED PEOPLE!

5. WE WANT COMMUNITY CONTROL OF OUR INSTITUTIONS AND LAND.

   We want control of our communities by our people and programs to guarantee that all institutions serve the needs of our people. People's control of police, health services, churches, schools, housing, transportation and welfare are needed. We want an end to attacks on our land by urban removal, highway destruction, universities and corporations.
   LAND BELONGS TO ALL THE PEOPLE!

6. WE WANT A TRUE EDUCATION OF OUR CREOLE CULTURE AND SPANISH LANGUAGE.

   We must learn our history of fighting against cultural, as well as economic genocide by the yanqui. Revolutionary culture, culture of our people, is the only true teaching.

7. WE OPPOSE CAPITALISTS AND ALLIANCES WITH TRAITORS.

   Puerto Rican rulers, or puppets of the oppressor, do not help our people. They are paid by the system to lead our people down blind alleys, just like the thousands of poverty pimps who keep our communities peaceful for business, or the street workers who keep gangs divided and blowing each other away. We want a society where the people socialistically control their labor.
   VENCEREMOS!

8. WE OPPOSE THE AMERIKKKAN MILITARY.

    We demand immediate withdrawal of u.s. military forces and bases from Puerto Rico, Vietnam, and all oppressed communities inside and outside the u.s. No Puerto Rican should serve in the u.s. army against his Brothers and Sisters, for the only true army of oppressed people is the people's army to fight all rulers.

    U.S. OUT OF VIETNAM, FREE PUERTO RICO!

9. WE WANT FREEDOM FOR ALL POLITICAL PRISONERS.

    We want all Puerto Ricans freed because they have been tried by the racist courts of the colonizers, and not by their own people and peers. We want all freedom fighters released from jail.

    FREE ALL POLITICAL PRISONERS!

10. WE WANT EQUALITY FOR WOMEN. MACHISMO MUST BE REVOLU-TIONARY...NOT OPPRESSIVE.

    Under capitalism, our women have been oppressed by both the society and our own men. The doctrine of machismo has been used by our men to take out their frustrations against their wives, sisters, mothers, and children. Our men must support their women in their fight for economic and social equality, and must recognize that our women are equals in every way within the revolutionary ranks.

    FORWARD, SISTERS, IN THE STRUGGLE!

11. WE FIGHT ANTI-COMMUNISM WITH INTERNATIONAL UNITY.

    Anyone who resists injustice is called a communist by "the man" and condemned. Our people are brainwashed by television, radio, newspapers, schools, and books to oppose people in other countries fighting for their freedom. No longer will our people believe attacks and slanders, because they have learned who the real enemy is and who their real friends are. We will defend our Brothers and Sisters around the world who fight for justice against the rich rulers of this country.

    VIVA CHE! [Guevara]

12. WE BELIEVE ARMED SELF-DEFENSE AND ARMED STRUGGLE ARE THE ONLY MEANS TO LIBERATION.

    We are opposed to violence – the violence of hungry children, illiterate adults, diseased old people, and the violence of poverty and profit. We have asked, petitioned, gone to courts, demonstrated peacefully, and voted for politicians full of empty promises. But we still ain't free. The time has come to defend the lives of our people against repression and for revolutionary war against the businessman, politician, and police. When a government oppresses our people, we have the right to abolish it and create a new one.

    BORICUA [i.e., Puerto Rico] IS AWAKE! ALL PIGS BEWARE!

13. WE WANT A SOCIALIST SOCIETY.

    We want liberation, clothing, free food, education, health care, transportation, utilities, and employment for all. We want a society where the needs of

our people come first, and where we give solidarity and aid to the peoples of
the world, not oppression and racism.
HASTA LA VICTORIA SIEMPRE!

—*Palante*, Latin Revolutionary News Service

Study Questions

1 How might Jack Agüeros respond to the Young Lords Party program?
2 History has shown us that many leaders of the civil rights movements of the
   1960s – Malcolm X, Cesar Chavez, and others, as well as early leaders of
   the Young Lords – came to political activity through street culture. Why do
   you think this might be so?
3 How does the manifesto define "violence"?
4 What are the international implications of the Young Lords Party's platform? How are they related to the international implications of Stokely
   Carmichael's statement on Black Power?

CHAPTER 26

Sources of the Second Wave:
The Rebirth of Feminism

Sara M. Evans

Sara M. Evans (1943–), a professor of history, is the daughter of a Methodist minister and a mother she describes as "a radical egalitarian in her bones." Evans became involved in the Civil Rights Movement as an undergraduate student and was an early activist in the Women's Liberation Movement. One of the first historians to focus on women's history, she helped to shape the field. Her books include Personal Politics: The Roots of Women's Liberation in the Civil Rights Movement and the New Left *(1979) and* Born for Liberty: A History of Women in America *(1989). In the following essay, published in 2001, Evans analyzes the complex roots of the modern women's movement.*

A ll of the social movements of the 1960s – civil rights, student New Left, antiwar, counterculture – emphasized the personal nature of political action. They expressed the existential yearning for authenticity and meaning of a generation raised in postwar affluence, and idealistic rage at the betrayals of the American dream: hunger in the midst of plenty, racism in a democracy, and imperialism by the leader of the "free" world. The women's liberation movement burst on the scene in the late 1960s to take this yet one step further by declaring that "the personal is political." With this critical insight, women challenged the ways power and sexism shaped relationships from the bedroom to the boardroom, and they demanded that American society redefine the meanings of masculinity and femininity.

The 1960s were the launching pad for a massive feminist movement that matched in size and fervor the suffrage movement half a century earlier. To understand the energy feminism unleashed in the 1970s, we need to understand how the turbulence of the 1960s stirred up deep contradictions in women's lives, while at the same time providing a free space in which women could challenge both cultural and legal expectations and develop the skills to build a movement for change.

The Setting

Throughout the 1950s US popular culture was suffused with images of and paeans to – domesticity. [. . .]

The assumption that women's proper place was in the home undergirded the legal reality that women had few protections in public. Employment want ads routinely listed jobs separately for men and women. The labor force was extremely segregated, with women crowded into a small number of lower-paid occupations primarily in the service sector. When they did do the same work, women could be paid less than men, as many employers had separate pay scales. Professional schools in law and medicine set restrictive quotas to limit the proportion of female students to as low as 5 percent. In many states married women could not even obtain credit in their own names or without their husband's signature.

In this case, domestic ideology, later called "feminine mystique" by author Betty Friedan, served to obscure and temporarily contain dramatic changes. Since the Second World War, during which women had broken through many of the traditional barriers to work outside the home, American women's entry into the labor force accelerated dramatically as did their access to higher education. Within racial minority groups, women had of necessity traditionally worked outside the home, and they took leading roles in the upsurge against discrimination and segregation. Yet, such changes remained obscured and denied by a popular culture of family sitcoms such as *Father Knows Best* and *Leave It to Beaver*, which portrayed a placid, all-white, suburban, middle-class world.[1]

The rumblings of the civil rights movement signaled new – but still unrecognized – possibilities. For example, in 1955, Rosa Parks, secretary of the Montgomery, Alabama, NAACP, was arrested for refusing to move to the back of a segregated city bus. Black women in Montgomery had been organizing and planning behind the scenes for some time, and they seized on Parks's arrest as the moment to initiate a boycott of the city bus system. The story of the Montgomery bus boycott has entered American mythology in a way that obscures the work of the Montgomery Women's Political Council. The boycott, called by the local NAACP chapter, was effective because the Women's Political Council – an organization of middle-class African American women, parallel to the League of Women Voters in the white community – was able, overnight, to print and distribute literally thousands of fliers at every bus stop in the black community. Most of the riders were women who used buses to get to their jobs as domestics in white neighborhoods. The buses remained empty for months, as women walked and carpooled to work and gathered with others in community churches to hear the inspiring rhetoric of Dr. Martin Luther King, Jr., and other civil rights leaders.[2] [. . .]

Another early sign of renewed activism was the emergence of a peace movement that challenged the nuclear arms race in the name of motherhood. Five women who had been active in the Committee for a SANE Nuclear Policy started Women Strike for Peace in 1960 to raise "mothers' issues" like the dangers of nuclear testing to children through the radioactive contamination of milk. They called for a one-day "strike" on November 1, 1961, as a radioactive cloud from a Russian test floated across the United States. Using female networks in PTAs, the League of Women Voters, peace organizations, and personal contacts, leaders of Women Strike for Peace spread the word. Fifty thousand turned out to lobby government officials to "End the Arms Race – Not the Human Race." Women Strike for Peace activists (61 percent of whom were housewives) were intellectuals and civic-minded women who were increasingly concerned about the dangers of nuclear war. Inspired by the courageous examples of civil rights activists in the South, and drawing on their own histories of involvement during the war years of the 1940s, they insisted that their point of view as mothers deserved recognition. Leader Dagmar Wilson, conscious that "the housewife was a downgraded person," set out to show "that this was an important role and that it was time we were heard."[3] [...]

Mobilization

The mobilization of professional women was the first tremor in the quake that set off the second wave of women's rights activism in the twentieth century. Its beginnings can be traced to the President's Commission on the Status of Women, established in 1961. Esther Peterson, Kennedy's appointee to head the Women's Bureau, formulated the idea for the commission, chaired by Eleanor Roosevelt, that would reexamine women's place in the economy, the family, and the legal system. The commission, its staff, and seven technical committees were drawn from labor unions, women's organizations, and governmental agencies.

Lawyers, government officials, union organizers, academics, commission members, and their staff documented in great detail the ongoing realities of employment discrimination, unequal pay, legal inequities, and lack of child care and other social services. They were stunned by their findings. Individually they had all experienced the problems, but the pervasiveness of discrimination and the hardships that accompanied women's "double burden" of household and labor force responsibilities validated that experience. The study allowed them to develop a set of shared goals and gave them a sense of mission.[4]

The President's Commission on the Status of Women put women's issues back on the national political agenda, and the publication of the commission's report in 1963 resulted in two immediate policy changes. The president issued an order requiring the federal civil service to hire for career positions "solely on the basis of ability to meet the requirements of the position, and without regard to sex." Congress then passed the 1963 Equal Pay Act, making it illegal to set different rates of pay for women and men for equal (i.e., the same) work.[5] The pressure for change broadened as governors in virtually every state appointed commissions on the status of women to conduct similar state-level investigations.

Nineteen sixty-three was also the year that Betty Friedan published *The Feminine Mystique*. In a brilliant and thoroughly researched polemic, Friedan gave a name to the malaise of housewives and the dilemma of those who did not fit the mold.

Popular culture, psychologists, and educators, she argued, defined women in a way that excluded them from public life (and paid work) and coerced them into a passive and childlike domesticity. Thousands of letters flooded Friedan's mailbox, as women poured out the stories they had thought no one would ever understand. "My undiluted wrath," wrote one, "is expended on those of us who were educated and therefore privileged, who put on our black organza nightgowns and went willingly, joyfully, without so much as a backward look at the hard-won freedoms handed down to us by the feminists (men and women)."[6] Others turned their anger inward, resulting in depression and despair.

Despite the ripples from the commission report and publication of *The Feminine Mystique*, Congress was surprised when, during the debate on the 1964 Civil Rights Act, Representative Howard Smith of Virginia suggested that the Title VII prohibition against employment discrimination on the basis of race, creed, and national origin should also include "sex." As an ardent segregationist, his primary motive may have been to kill the bill. Ironically, as a longtime supporter of the Equal Rights Amendment (ERA), he was also quite serious about the amendment itself.[7] His efforts drew a chuckle from his male colleagues, but Senator Margaret Chase Smith of Maine was not amused. She and Congresswoman Martha Griffiths of Michigan set to work to ensure that the amendment passed. When their bipartisan effort (Smith was a Republican; Griffiths, a Democrat) succeeded, women suddenly had a potentially powerful and far-reaching legal tool.

Title VII provided an outlet for the thousands of women who knew that they faced discrimination but previously had no place to file their grievances. The Equal Employment Opportunity Commission (EEOC) received a flood of complaints against employers (and also against unions). But the bureaucrats were slow to take them seriously. Most, including those at the EEOC, still considered the inclusion of sex a bit of a joke. The *New York Times* referred to it as the "bunny law," on the theory that a Playboy Club might be sued for refusing to hire a male applicant as a bunny/waitress.[8]

The rumbles were beginning to be audible, but women still had no organized force to demand the enforcement of laws like Title VII. At a 1966 conference of State Commissions on the Status of Women, several women gathered in Betty Friedan's hotel room to discuss the situation. They submitted a resolution to the conference but were told that action of any kind was not permitted. They decided on the spot that they had to form a new organization. On the last day, Betty Friedan recalled, they "cornered a large table at the luncheon, so that we could start organizing before we had to rush for planes. We all chipped in $5.00, began to discuss names. I dreamed up NOW on the spur of the moment." The National Organization for Women was born with a clear statement of purpose: "To take action to bring women into full participation in the mainstream of American society now, assuming all the privileges and responsibilities thereof in truly equal partnership with men."[9]

The organization challenged the assumptions of the feminine mystique head-on and demanded full and equal access for women to education, work, and political participation. "It is no longer either necessary or possible," NOW's organizers argued in their founding statement, "for women to devote the greater part of their lives to child-rearing."[10] Using the United Auto Workers Women's Department as its headquarters, NOW sparked pickets and demonstrations across the country against sex-segregated want ads and "men only" clubs. They pressured the government to enforce antidiscrimination laws, especially Title VII. By 1968, the membership insisted on an endorsement of the ERA, which forced UAW women to withdraw from NOW until their union changed its position. The adoption by NOW of a strong position in support of legalizing abortion precipitated another split. A number of lawyers who wanted to focus on legal and economic issues felt that abortion was too controversial and would hamper their efforts. They broke away from NOW to found the Women's Equity Action League (WEAL).

Women's Liberation

While professional women's networks began to mobilize – building organizations and legal challenges to inequality – the foundation for an even more explosive challenge to women's place in American culture was being laid among the younger activists in the civil rights, student, and antiwar movements.

First in the civil rights movement and then in the student New Left, young women encountered a set of radically egalitarian ideas. Visions of the "beloved community" and of "participatory democracy" were not distant images but rather were understood to be the realities of life in the movement. Members acted on an idealized vision of what the world should be. In the civil rights movement, that meant a belief that every individual regardless of race should be treated with dignity and equality, and that every person should be admitted to full citizenship and have access to the American dream. When participants sang – and lived – the dream of "black and white together" they *were* the beloved community, and they showed the world that it was possible.

Similarly, in New Left organizations like Students for a Democratic Society (SDS), the ideal of participatory democracy asserted that everyone should participate in "the decisions that affect their lives." They adopted and adapted the consensus model of decision making that had developed in SNCC (Student Nonviolent Coordinating Committee) in which groups would debate all night if necessary before reaching a conclusion. If that is what it took to live out these ideals, then so be it.

Finally, young, usually middle-class women, both black and white, found inspiring models of courageous womanhood in the lives of local black women in the civil rights movement such as Fannie Lou Hamer, Ella Baker, Septima Clarke, and Rosa Parks. On a local level there were "the Mamas," the backbones of their communities, who took young civil rights workers into their homes at the risk of their own lives and livelihoods, who urged and cajoled and shamed their neighbors into registering to vote, and who defied the worst violence southern whites could bring down on their communities. From them, younger women in the movement learned that being female and being a leader were not antithetical. From their lives young women saw examples of nurturing, courage, power, and indomitable self-respect. If they needed new models of womanhood to replace the feminine mystique, they had them close at hand.[11]

For women, it seems in retrospect a short step – ideologically – from "freedom now" to "women's liberation." But that was actually not an easy step to take. On the one hand, young women in the civil rights movement and the student New Left generally believed that they were already liberated. Their participation required them to break many of the social rules with which they had been raised. They risked their lives, sometimes in defiance of their frightened parents. They developed powerful organizational skills when they taught in freedom schools and organized in poor northern communities. When the movement was small and human scale, they felt visible and valued, and joyfully joined in the personal and erotic intensity of building this new community and new movement. Sexual liberation was another of the boundary breaking aspects of this generation, and women certainly participated.

Yet, both women and men in the civil rights movement had also been deeply socialized to think in terms of traditional sex roles, and even as they broke many traditional rules they also bumped up against expectations which put them back "in their place." Ironically, when people returned from jail, women found that they were still expected to clean up the "freedom house," do most of the cooking and laundry, and, of course, the typing. Both men and women generally expected that visible leadership would be male. Men overwhelmingly dominated the heated ideological debates (which were frequently also contests over leadership) excluding all but a few women in tone and style. Even when women spoke up, they frequently were not taken seriously. [. . .]

Making the Personal Political

The contagiousness of feminism lay in its ability to touch women at a deeply personal level, giving political voice to issues that had gone unchallenged and bringing new opportunities for action. When *Newsweek* published a cover story on the women's movement, it hired a freelance writer, having rejected versions by one of the few females in its ranks of reporters and editors. The day the cover story reached the newsstands, however, a group of women on the staff called a press conference to announce that they had filed a sex-discrimination complaint with the EEOC. At that time all but one of *Newsweek*'s research staff were women, and all but one of its fifty-two writers were men.[12]

Women responded to the movement's ideals even though the media's presentation of this new movement was decidedly hostile. For example, the epithet "bra burners" was a media fabrication. No bras were actually burned at the Miss America Pageant demonstration in August 1968, though one of the organizers suggested ahead of time to a journalist that they might be. Instead, participants tossed "objects of female torture" – girdles, bras, curlers, issues of the *Ladies Home Journal* – into a "freedom trash can," auctioned off an effigy of Miss America ("Gentlemen, I offer you the 1969 model. She's better in every way. She walks. She talks. AND she does housework"), and crowned a live sheep.[13]

In general, media coverage sensationalized and mocked women's liberation with nicknames like "women's lib" and "libbers."[14] One editor was known to have instructed a journalist to "get the bra-burning and karate up front."[15] It did not matter. For a few years, positive or negative publicity served to bring women out in droves.

When NOW called for a "women's strike" on August 26, 1970 in commemoration of the fiftieth anniversary of the passage of the Nineteenth Amendment to the Constitution, which granted women the right to vote, the national scope of this new movement became visible to activists and observers alike. Its insistence on the politics of personal life was likewise on display as women took action under the slogan "Don't iron while the strike is hot." *Life* magazine reported that

> in Rochester, NY, women shattered teacups. In Syracuse they dumped 50 children in the city hall. In New York City, Boston, and Washington thousands marched and rallied and hundreds more held teach-ins and speech-ins in dozens of other cities. Women's liberation is the liveliest conversational topic in the land, and last week, all across it, the new feminists took their argument for sexual equality into the streets.[16]

In New York City, between twenty thousand and fifty thousand women staged the largest women's rights rally since the suffrage movement, completely blocking Fifth Avenue during rush hour. Branches of a movement springing from different roots intertwined in theatrical and humorous actions: guerrilla theater in Indianapolis portrayed the middle-class female life cycle, from "sugar and spice" to "Queen for a Day"; Boston women chained themselves to a huge typewriter; women in Berkeley marched with pots and pans on their backs; New Orleans reporters ran engagement announcements under photos of future grooms; flight attendants carried posters challenging discriminatory airlines rules: "Storks Fly – Why Can't Mothers?"[17]

Coverage of the women's strike gave the nation a glimpse of the surge of creative energy (driven by a powerful combination of anger and high expectations) that flowed into the movement. Consciousness-raising groups were seed-beds for what grew into diverse movements around issues ranging from women's health, child care, violence, and pornography to spirituality and music. The groups formed child-care centers, bookstores, coffeehouses, shelters for battered women, and rape crisis hot lines – new institutions they could wholly own. At the same time, other feminists built enclaves within mainstream institutions – unions, churches and synagogues, and professional associations.

Consciousness-raising meant, from the outset, that feminist deliberation would center on the most intimate aspects of personal life. As groups analyzed childhood experiences for clues to the origins of women's oppression in relations with men, marriage, motherhood, and sex, discussion led to action, and action on one topic led to another. For example, in an early meeting of New York Radical Women, several women described their experiences with illegal abortions. For most it was the first time they had told anyone beyond a close friend or two. The power of this revelation, however, contrasted sharply with the current debates surrounding proposed liberalization of the abortion law in New York, which were conducted with clinical detachment. A group of women – subsequent founders of Redstockings – decided to disrupt a legislative hearing scheduled to hear testimony from fourteen men and one woman (a nun). Women who had undergone abortions were the "real experts," the feminists argued, and they went to Albany to tell their stories. When the committee declined to hear them, they held a public "speak-out" on March 21, 1969, drawing an audience of three hundred. Thousands of women, hearing about such speak-outs, experienced a release from lonely silence. Journalist Gloria Steinem recalled, "For the first time, I understood that the abortion I had kept so shamefully quiet about for years was an experience I had probably shared with at least one out of four American women of every race and group."[18]

With this and numerous other actions and demonstrations women's liberation groups made themselves the "shock troops" of abortion rights, joining an already active abortion law reform movement. For the most part, they sought to intervene directly, offering services, public education, and assistance to women rather than lobbying for reform. In Chicago, a group within the Chicago Women's Liberation Union called "Jane," which began doing counseling and referrals in the late 1960s, shifted in 1971 to performing the abortions themselves. Between 1971 and 1973, Jane performed eleven thousand illegal abortions with a safety record that matched that of doctor-performed legal abortions.[19] Sarah Weddington, an unemployed law school graduate who belonged to a consciousness-raising group in Austin, Texas, investigated the legal risks of providing an underground abortion referral service. Her research revealed the possibility of a legal challenge to laws against abortion based on the right to privacy. Thus began the process that ended in the landmark Supreme Court case *Roe v. Wade*, in which Sarah Weddington argued her very first case at the age of twenty-six.[20]

Similar processes led to the creation of the first shelters for battered women, rape crisis hot lines, and women's health clinics. As women focused on personal issues and the body, they forced new issues on the political agenda and set out to provide immediate responses to women in need. A Boston group offered a course on women's health and wrote *OurBodies/OurSelves*, thereby inventing a new form of self-help literature designed to empower women to take charge of their own health. Twenty-five years and many editions later, it is still in print. [...]

The Golden Years: Women as a Political Force

[...] With the passage of the Equal Pay Act in 1963 and Title VII of the Civil Rights Act in 1964, working women had new legal tools, which they proceeded to employ with vigor. In the EEOC's first year, more than a third of the complaints submitted concerned sex discrimination. Though these complaints, which numbered in the hundreds, were independent from the organized women's movement, they came in response to the same social pressures and expectations and led commissioners like Aileen Hernandez and Richard Graham to articulate the need for an "NAACP for women." Even progressive unions like the United Auto Workers and the International Union of Electrical Workers, whose leaders had been involved in the President's Commission on the Status of Women and had a history of attention to women's issues, found their members restless and willing to use governmental remedies when local leaders did not take them seriously. Unions and corporations alike argued that they were required by state protective laws to deny women access to overtime or higher paying jobs.[21] In turn, courts, prodded by feminist lawyers, began to rule that protective laws were discriminatory and thereby in violation of Title VII of the Civil Rights Act.

The landmark employment sex discrimination case began when Lorena Weeks sued Southern Bell Telephone Company for refusing to promote her to a job she had handled many times as a substitute and instead hiring a man with less seniority. When Weeks lost her case in 1967, Marguerite Rawalt of the NOW legal committee offered assistance on appeal. Attorney Sylvia Roberts of Baton Rouge prepared the case with Rawalt and argued it before the Appeals Court. Standing only five feet tall, Roberts marched around the courtroom carrying the equipment required for the job in one hand, while arguing that the weight-lifting restrictions the company placed on women's jobs did not constitute a "bona fide occupational qualification."[22] The decision handed down in March 1969, in *Weeks v. Southern Bell*, denied the validity of the exemption for Bell's weight-lifting restrictions and set a new standard of proof. No longer would a demonstration that many, or even most, women could not perform a specific job requirement justify such a restriction. Instead, employers (and states) would have to show that all or "substantially all" women could not perform the required task. The choice of whether to accept a particularly difficult job would rest with the woman, as it already did with men.[23]

The idea of an Equal Rights Amendment (ERA), which would provide simple constitutional equality on the basis of sex, had long been opposed by supporters of protective laws for women. The *Weeks* decision and similar cases, executive orders forbidding discrimination, and the many EEOC complaints under Title VII began in the 1960s to convince key union leaders and other former opponents of the ERA that the protective laws unfairly prevented women from access to higher paying jobs.[24] By 1970, the ranks of ERA supporters included the League of Women Voters, Business and Professional Women, the YWCA, the American Association of University Women, Common Cause, and the United Auto Workers. Together they formed a coalition that succeeded in mounting a massive two-year campaign that generated more mail on Capitol Hill than the Vietnam War.

In 1970 the ERA received its first committee hearing in decades. The hearing was the result of a NOW demonstration in February during which twenty women from the Pittsburgh chapter, led by Wilma Scott Heide, disrupted a hearing on the eighteen-year-old voting age to demand immediate action on the ERA. By July 20, a constant flow of letters and telegrams to reluctant congressmen had helped Representative Martha Griffiths collect the 218 signatures needed to bring the ERA to the House floor. On August 10 (after a debate in which Emanuel Celler of New York argued that there was "as much difference between a male and a female as between a horse chestnut and a chestnut horse"), it passed the House 350 to 15.[25] By

March 22, 1972, both houses of Congress finally had approved the ERA. By the end of the year, twenty-two of the needed thirty-five states had ratified it.

Through the 1970s ERA became the symbolic focal point for social debates over women's rights and the place of women in American society, the rallying point for antifeminists. Ratification stalled in the face of enormous social anxieties about the transformations in gender roles and expectations that the women's movement had wrought. After 1975, antifeminist forces mobilized with great effect, finally defeating the ERA in 1982. Yet by that time, most discriminatory laws had already been changed legislatively or declared unconstitutional. Underlying structural changes – in labor force participation, in family composition, in sexual norms, in access to education – could not be rolled back.

It is a sign of continued ambivalence about female equality that the United States has yet to grant it in our founding document, but the forces unleashed by the eruption of women's liberation in the late 1960s continue to transform life in this country, and neither politics nor personal life will ever be quite the same again. Feminism erupted onto the landscape of American life during a time that was already turbulent with social movements: conflict over the Vietnam War, racial strife, and a national crisis over the meaning and inclusiveness of democracy. It challenged Americans to rethink the most fundamental aspects of personal as well as political life, indeed of human identity. As it did so, it mobilized a new kind of political power that could be felt in the bedroom as well as in the courtroom, the boardroom, and the halls of Congress.

Study Questions

1   According to Evans, what are the most important causes and accomplish-
    ments of the "second wave" of the women's rights movement?
2   Where does Betty Friedan's "feminine mystique" fit in to Evans's analysis?
3   What does it mean to say "the personal is the political"? Give an example
    from the reading or from your own or your family's experiences.
4   How do the key issues of "women's liberation" relate to other liberation
    movements of the late 1960s and early 1970s, such as Gay Liberation, Black
    Power, and the American Indian Movement? What similarities and differ-
    ences do you find?

Notes

1.   On the family in the 1950s, see Elaine Tyler May, *Homeward Bound: American Families in the Cold War Era* (New York: Basic Books, 1988).
2.   Jo Ann Gibson Robinson, *The Montgomery Bus Boycott and the Women Who Started It: The Memoir of Jo Ann Gibson Robinson*, edited with a foreword by David G. Garrow (Knoxville: University of Tennessee Press, 1987).

3.   Amy Swerdlow, "Ladies Day at the Capitol: Women Strike for Peace versus HUAC," *Feminist Studies* 8 (fall 1983): 510.

4.   See Jo Freeman, *The Politics of Women's Liberation: A Case Study of an Emerging Social Movement and Its Relation to the Policy Process* (New York: McKay, 1975).

5.   Cynthia E. Harrison, "A 'New Frontier' for Women: The Public Policy of the Kennedy Administration," *Journal of American History* 67 (December 1980): 630–35.

6.   Betty Friedan, *The Feminine Mystique* (New York: W.W. Norton, 1963). Letter quoted in May, *Homeward Bound*, p. 210.

7.   Leila Rupp and Verta Taylor, *Survival in the Doldrums: The American Women's Rights Movement, 1945 to the 1960s* (New York: Oxford University Press, 1987).

8.   "Desexing the Job Market," *New York Times*, 21 August 1965, p. A20.

9.   Judith Hole and Ellen Levine, *Rebirth of Feminism* (New York: Quadrangle Books, 1971), p. 84.

10. Freeman, *Politics of Women's Liberation*, p. 74.

11. Sara M. Evans, *Personal Politics: The Roots of Women's Liberation in the Civil Rights Movement and the New Left* (New York: Knopf, 1979).

12. Freeman, *Politics of Women's Liberation*; Sandie North, "Reporting the Movement," *Atlantic*, March 1970, pp. 105–106.

13. See Evans, *Personal Politics*, chapter 8; Alice Echols, *Daring to Be Bad: Radical Feminism in America, 1967–1975* (Minneapolis: University of Minnesota Press, 1989), pp. 92–96.

14. *The Reader's Guide to Periodical Literature* first listed "women's liberation" as a subtopic under "women" in Volume 29, March 1969–February 1970, with three entries. The next year there were more than 75 entries under "Women's liberation."

15. Susan Brownmiller, *Against Our Will: Men, Women and Rape* (New York: Simon and Schuster, 1975), p. 27.

16. "Women Arise," *Life* 69, 4 September 1970, B16.

17. See Flora Davis, *Moving the Mountain: The Women's Movement in America Since 1960* (New York: Simon & Schuster, 1991), pp. 114–16; Georgia Painter Nielsen, *From Sky Girl to Flight Attendant* (New York: ILR Press, 1982).

18. Suzanne Levine and Harriet Lyons, *The Decade of Women: A Ms. History of the Seventies in Words and Pictures* (New York: Paragon, 1980), p. 9.

19. Laura Kaplan, *The Story of Jane: The Legendary Underground Feminist Abortion Service* (New York: Pantheon Books, 1996).

20. See Sarah Weddington, *A Question of Choice* (New York: G. P. Putnam's Sons, 1992); see also David J. Garrow, *Liberty and Sexuality: The Right to Privacy and the Making of Roe v. Wade* (New York: Macmillan Publishing Co., 1994).

21. Susan M. Hartmann, "Allies of the Women's Movement: Origins and Strategies of Feminist Activists in Male Dominated Organizations in the 1970s: The Case of the International Union of Electrical Workers," Paper presented at the 1993 Berkshire Conference on the History of Women, Vassar College, Poughkeepsie, N.Y., June 1993. This material was subsequently published in Susan Hartmann, *The Other Feminists: Activists in the Liberal Establishment* (New Haven, Ct.: Yale University Press, 1998).

22. Since the Georgia legislature had repealed its weight-limitations law, the company's only defense lay in the Title VII exemption for "bona fide occupational qualification."

23. See Davis, *Moving the Mountain*; Hole and Levine, *Rebirth of Feminism; Weeks v. Southern Tel. & Tel. Co.* (CA-5, 3-4-69) 408 F. 2d rev. & rem. S.D. Ga 277 F. Supp. 117.

24. Interviews with Olga Madar, Detroit, 10 December 1982; Dorothy Haener, Detroit, 21 January 1983; and Millie Jeffry, Detroit, 11 December 1982.

25. Davis, *Moving the Mountain*, pp. 121–27; Hole and Levine, *Rebirth of Feminism*; Marguerite Rawalt, "The Equal Rights Amendment" in *Women in Washington: Advocates for Public Policy*, ed. Irene Tinker (Beverly Hills, Calif.: Sage Publications, 1983), pp. 49–78.

CHAPTER 27

NOW Bill of Rights

National Organization for Women

The National Organization for Women was founded in 1966 at a meeting of the National Conference of State Commissions on the Status of Women, which grew out of John F. Kennedy's 1961 appointment of the Commission on the Status of Women. Twenty-eight of the commissioners, Betty Friedan and Pauli Murray among them, decided that women needed a national lobbying organization similar in purpose to such civil rights organizations as the NAACP (The National Association for the Advancement of Colored People). The largest women's rights organization in the United States, NOW has lobbied for passage of the Equal Rights Amendment to the Constitution (ERA), nationalized day care, and access to birth control and abortion services. Many of the demands listed in their "Bill of Rights," adopted at their first national conference in Washington, DC, 1967, do not seem surprising today because organizations like NOW helped to improve the status of women in the US.

    I.   Equal Rights Constitutional Amendment
   II.   Enforce Law Banning Sex Discrimination in Employment
  III.   Maternity Leave Rights in Employment and in Social Security Benefits
  IV.   Tax Deduction for Home and Child Care Expenses for Working Parents
   V.   Child Day Care Centers
  VI.   Equal and Unsegregated Education
 VII.   Equal Job Training Opportunities and Allowances for Women in Poverty
VIII.   The Right of Women to Control Their Reproductive Lives

WE DEMAND:

I.   That the US Congress immediately pass the Equal Rights Amendment to the Constitution to provide that "Equality of rights under the law shall not be denied or abridged by the United States or by any State on account of sex," and that such then be immediately ratified by the several States.

II.   That equal employment opportunity be guaranteed to all women, as well as men, by insisting that the Equal Employment Opportunity Commission enforces the prohibitions against racial discrimination.

III.   That women be protected by law to ensure their rights to return to their jobs within a reasonable time after child-birth without loss of seniority or other accrued benefits, and be paid maternity leave as a form of social security and/ or employee benefit.

IV.   Immediate revision of tax laws to permit the deduction of home and child-care expenses for working parents.

V.   That child-care facilities be established by law on the same basis as parks, libraries, and public schools, adequate to the needs of children from the pre-school years through adolescence, as a community resource to be used by all citizens from all income levels.

VI.   That the right of women to be educated to their full potential equally with men be secured by Federal and State legislation, eliminating all discrimination and segregation by sex, written and unwritten, at all levels of education, including colleges, graduate and professional schools, loans and fellowships, and Federal and State training programs such as the Job Corps.

VII.   The right of women in poverty to secure job training, housing, and family allowances on equal terms with men, but without prejudice to a parent's right to remain at home to care for his or her children; revision of welfare legislation and poverty programs which deny women dignity, privacy, and self-respect.

VIII.   The right of women to control their own reproductive lives by removing from the penal code laws limiting access to contraceptive information and devices, and by repealing penal laws governing abortion.

Study Questions

1   Which of the demands in the NOW Bill of Rights have been accomplished? Which haven't?

2   Which of the demands that haven't been accomplished do you think should be and why?

CHAPTER 28

The Liberation of Black Women

Pauli Murray

Anna Pauline Murray (1910–85) was born in Baltimore, Maryland, where her father was a high school principal and her mother a nurse. After her mother died and her father entered a mental hospital, three-year-old Pauli was raised by her mother's sisters and parents in Durham, North Carolina, a family whose interwoven black and white heritage Murray would detail in Proud Shoes: the Story of an American Family *(1956). Murray graduated from Hunter College, New York, in 1933, one of four black students out of a class of 247 women. Murray mounted challenges to racial and gender boundaries that constrained her, including being arrested and jailed for refusing to move to the back of a bus in 1940. When she applied to the all-male 'Harvard Law School in 1944, she was denied admission on the grounds of her gender. As a legal scholar, Murray was one of the first to theorize the connections between race and gender discrimination, which she named "Jane Crow." In 1966 she was one of the cofounders, along with Betty Friedan, of the National Organization for Women. The following excerpt from her essay, "The Liberation of Black Women," was published in the 1970 anthology,* Voices of the New Feminism.

B
lack women, historically, have been doubly victimized by the twin immoralities of Jim Crow and Jane Crow. Jane Crow refers to the entire range of assumptions, attitudes, stereotypes, customs, and arrangements which have robbed women of a positive self-concept and prevented them from participating fully in society as equals with men. Traditionally, racism and sexism in the United States have shared some common origins, displayed similar manifestations, reinforced one another, and are so deeply intertwined in the country's institutions that the successful outcome of the struggle against racism will depend in large part upon the simultaneous elimination of all discrimination based upon sex. Black women, faced with these dual barriers, have often found that sex bias is more formidable than racial bias. If anyone should ask a Negro woman in America what has been her greatest achievement, her honest answer would be, "I survived!"

Negro women have endured their double burden with remarkable strength and fortitude. With dignity they have shared with black men a partnership as members of an embattled group excluded from the normal protections of the society and engaged in a struggle for survival during nearly four centuries of a barbarous slave trade, two centuries of chattel slavery, and a century or more of illusive citizenship. Throughout this struggle, into which has been poured most of the resources and much of the genius of successive generations of American Negroes, these women have often carried a disproportionate share of responsibility for the black family as they strove to keep its integrity intact against a host of indignities to which it has been subjected. Black women have not only stood shoulder to shoulder with black men in every phase of the struggle, but they have often continued to stand firmly when their men were destroyed by it. Few Blacks are unfamiliar with that heroic, if formidable, figure exhorting her children and grandchildren to overcome every obstacle and humiliation and to "Be somebody!"

In the battle for survival, Negro women developed a tradition of independence and self-reliance, characteristics which according to the late Dr. E. Franklin Frazier, Negro sociologist, have "provided generally a pattern of equalitarian relationship between men and women in America." The historical factors which have fostered the black women's feeling of independence have been the economic necessity to earn a living to help support their families – if indeed they were not the sole breadwinners – and the need for the black community to draw heavily upon the resources of all of its members in order to survive.

Yet these survival values have often been distorted, and the qualities of strength and independence observable in many Negro women have been stereotyped as "female dominance" attributed to the "matriarchal" character of the Negro family developed during slavery and its aftermath. The popular conception is that because society has emasculated the black male, he has been unable to assume his economic role as head of the household and the black woman's earning power has placed her in a dominant position. The black militant's cry for the retrieval of black manhood suggests an acceptance of this stereotype, an association of masculinity with male dominance and a tendency to treat the values of self-reliance and independence as purely masculine traits. Thus, while Blacks generally have recognized the fusion of white supremacy and male dominance (note the popular expressions "The Man" and "Mr. Charlie"), male spokesmen for Negro rights have sometimes pandered to sexism in their fight against racism. When nationally known civil rights leader James Farmer ran for Congress against Mrs. Shirley Chisholm in 1968, his campaign literature stressed the need for a "strong male image" and a "man's voice" in Washington. [...]

Yet, despite the crucial role which Negro women have played in the struggle, in the great mass of magazine and newspaper print expended on the racial crisis, the aspirations of the black community have been articulated almost exclusively by black males. There has been very little public discussion of the problems, objectives, or concerns of black women. [...]

In *Black Rage*, psychiatrists Greer and Cobbs devote a chapter to achieving woman-hood. While they sympathetically describe the traumatic experience of self-depreci-ation which a black woman undergoes in a society in which the dominant standard of beauty is "the blond, blue-eyed, white-skinned girl with regular features," and make a telling point about the burden of the stereotype that Negro women are available to white men, they do not get beyond a framework in which the Negro woman is seen as a sex object. Emphasizing her concern with "feminine narcissism" and the need to be "lovable" and "attractive," they conclude: "Under the sign of discouragement and rejection which governs so much of her physical operation, she is inclined to organize her personal ambitions in terms of her achievements serving to compensate for other losses and hurts." Nowhere do the authors suggest that Negro women, like women generally, might be motivated to achieve as *persons*. Implied throughout the discus-sion is the sexuality of Negro females.

The ultimate expression of this bias is the statement attributed to a black militant male leader: "The position of the black woman should be prone." Thus, there appears to be a distinctly conservative and backward-looking view in much of what black males write today about black women, and many black women have been led to believe that the restoration of the black male to his lost manhood must take precedence over the claims of black women to equalitarian status. Consequently, there has been a tendency to acquiesce without vigorous protest to policies which emphasize the "underemployment" of the black male in relation to the black female and which encourage the upgrading and education of black male youth while all but ignoring the educational and training needs of black female youth, although the highest rates of unemployment today are among black female teenagers. A parallel tendency to concentrate on career and training opportunities primarily for black males is evident in government and industry. [...]

Cognizant of the similarities between paternalism and racial arrogance, black women are nevertheless handicapped by the continuing stereotype of the black "matriarchy" and the demand that black women now step back and push black men into positions of leadership. They are made to feel disloyal to racial interests if they insist upon women's rights. Moreover, to the extent that racial polarization often accompanies the thrust for Black Power, black women find it increasingly difficult to make common cause with white women. These developments raise several questions. Are black women gaining or losing in the drive toward human rights? As the movement for women's liberation becomes increasingly a force to be reckoned with, are black women to take a backward step and sacrifice their egalitarian tradition? What are the alterna-tives to matriarchal dominance on the one hand or male supremacy on the other? [...]

When we compare the position of the black woman to that of the white woman, we find that she remains single more often, bears more children, is in the labor market longer and in greater proportion, has less education, earns less, is widowed earlier, and carries a relatively heavier economic responsibility as family head than her white counterpart. [...]

Black women also carry heavy responsibilities as family heads. In 1966, one-fourth of all black families were headed by a woman as compared with less than one-tenth of all white families. The economic disabilities of women generally are aggravated in the case of black women. Moreover, while all families headed by women are more vulnerable to poverty than husband–wife families, the black woman family head is doubly victimized. For example, the median wage or salary income of all women workers who were employed full time the year round in 1967 was only 58 per cent of that of all male workers, and the median earnings of white females was less than that of black males. The median wage of nonwhite women workers, however, was $3,268, or only 71 per cent of the median income of white women workers. In 1965, one-third of all families headed by women lived in poverty, but 62 per cent of the 1,132,000 nonwhite families with a female head were poor.

A significant factor in the low economic and social status of black women is their concentration at the bottom rung of the employment ladder. More than one-third of all nonwhite working women are employed as private household workers. The median wages of women private household workers who were employed full time the year round in 1968 was only $1,701. Furthermore, these workers are not covered by the Federal minimum wage and hours law and are generally excluded from state wage and hours laws, unemployment compensation, and workmen's compensation.

The black woman is triply handicapped. She is heavily represented in nonunion employment and thus has few of the benefits to be derived from labor organization or social legislation. She is further victimized by discrimination because of race and sex. Although she has made great strides in recent decades in closing the educational gap, she still suffers from inadequate education and training. In 1966, only 71.1 per cent of all Negro women had completed eight grades of elementary school compared to 88 per cent of all white women. Only one-third (33.2 per cent) of all Negro women had completed high school as compared with more than one-half of all white women (56.3). More than twice as many white women, proportionally, have completed college (7.2 per cent) as black women (3.2 per cent). [. . .]

In the face of their multiple disadvantages, it seems clear that black women can neither postpone nor subordinate the fight against sex discrimination to the Black Revolution. Many of them must expect to be self-supporting and perhaps to support others for a considerable period or for life. In these circumstances, while efforts to raise educational and employment levels for black males will ease some of the economic and social burdens now carried by many black women, for a large and apparently growing minority these burdens will continue. As a matter of sheer survival black women have no alternative but to insist upon equal opportunities without regard to sex in training, education, and employment. Given their heavy family responsibilities, the outlook for their children will be bleak indeed unless they are encouraged in every way to develop their potential skills and earning power.

Because black women have an equal stake in women's liberation and black liberation, they are key figures at the juncture of these two movements. White women feminists are their natural allies in both causes. Their own liberation is linked with the issues which are stirring women today: adequate income maintenance and the elimination of poverty, repeal or reform of abortion laws, a national system of child-care centers, extension of labor standards to workers now excluded, cash maternity benefits as part of a system of social insurance, and the removal of all sex barriers to educational and employment opportunities at all levels. Black women have a special stake in the revolt against the treatment of women primarily as sex objects, for their own history has left them with the scars of the most brutal and degrading aspects of sexual exploitation.

The middle-class Negro woman is strategically placed by virtue of her tradition of independence and her long experience in civil rights and can play a creative role in strengthening the alliance between the Black Revolution and Women's Liberation. Her advantages of training and her values make it possible for her to communicate with her white counterparts, interpret the deepest feelings within the black community, and cooperate with white women on the basis of mutual concerns as women. The possibility of productive interchange between black and white women is greatly facilitated by the absence of power relationships which separate black and white males as antagonists. By asserting a leadership role in the growing feminist movement, the black woman can help to keep it allied to the objectives of black liberation while simultaneously advancing the interests of all women. [...]

Study Questions

1   What does Murray mean by the phrase "Jane Crow"?
2   What does Murray claim were important roles that black women have played in the struggle for African-American rights?
3   Which concerns and issues do black and white women feminists share? Which are particular to black women?

CHAPTER 29

Jessie Lopez de la Cruz:
The Battle for Farmworkers' Rights

Ellen Cantarow

Trade union organizer Jessie Lopez de la Cruz was born in Anaheim, California, in 1919. She was raised by her Mexican-born grandmother and railroad worker and miner grandfather in a multigenerational home. When her grandfather lost his job after an industrial accident, the family moved to the United States and became migrant farm laborers. The women and children worked alongside the men, picking fruit, vegetables, and cotton by hand and living in labor camps. Jessie married her childhood sweetheart, Arnold, in 1938 at the age of 19. She met Cesar Chavez working in the fields of Fresno, California, in 1962 and joined the National Farmworkers' Association in 1966, organizing around the inequities that women faced both at home and on the farms. She was the "first woman organizer out in the fields." Ellen Cantarow interviewed Jessie Lopez de la Cruz for her 1980 book Moving the Mountain: Women Working for Social Change.*

Rootedness and Uprooting

M y grandmother was born in Mexico in Aguas Callentes, near Guada-
lajara. She was raised by a very strict father and she married at
[...] thirteen. That was the custom. The girls, as soon as they were old
enough to learn cooking and sewing, would get married. Most married at twelve or
thirteen. My grandmother married and she was left out in a little shack by herself. She
was so young, so afraid....

She had my mother and my oldest brother when she and my grandfather came
across.[1] My grandfather worked for the rail-road laying the ties and tracks. Then he
worked for a mining company. After that we moved to Anaheim. We lived in a big four-
bedroom house my grandfather built. With my grandparents and their children, three
children of my mother's sister who had died, and the three of us, that made a big crowd.

My grandfather would get up Sunday mornings and start the fire in a great big wood-burning stove. He would wrap us up in blankets and seat us around that stove on chairs and say, "Now, don't get too close to the stove. Take care of the younger children." Then he would go out to the store and get bananas and oranges and cereal that he'd cook for us to eat, and milk, and he would feed us Sunday mornings. [. . .]

Then my grandfather had an accident. The middle finger of his right hand was crushed, and he couldn't work for about two weeks. When he went back he was told that he'd already been replaced by another worker. So he was out of a job. He decided we'd better go on and pick the crops. We had done that before, during the summer. But this time we went for good.

We came north. The families got together; the women would start cooking at night, boiling eggs and potatoes and making piles of tortillas and tacos, and these lunches would be packed in pails and boxes. There was as much fruit as they could get together, and roasted pumpkin seeds. My uncle had a factory where he made Mexican candy in East Los Angeles. And he used to give us a lot of pumpkin seeds. So my mother dried these, and she roasted and salted them for the trip to keep the drivers awake. We'd start in a car caravan, six or seven families together, one car watching for the other, and when it got a little dark they'd pull onto the roadside and build a fire and start some cooking to feed us. Then they'd spread blankets and quilts on the ground, and we would sleep there that night. The next morning, the women and older children would get up first and start the breakfast. And we smaller children, it was our job to fold the blankets and put them back in the cars and trucks. Then my brothers and the men would check the cars over again, and after breakfast all the women would wash the dishes and pack them, get 'em in the cars, and we'd start again.

We'd finally get to Delano and we would work there a little.[2] If work was scarce, we would keep on going till San José. I did the same thing my mother and my grandfather and my uncles did, picking prunes on our hands and knees off the ground, and putting them in the buckets. We were paid four dollars a ton, and we had to fill forty boxes to make it a ton. They made us sign a contract that we would stay there until all the prunes were picked. When we would finish the prunes, in early September, we would start back. And stop on the way to Mendota to pick cotton.

When I was about thirteen, I used to lift a twelve-foot sack of cotton with 104 or 112 pounds. When you're doing this work, you get to be an expert. I could get that sack and put it on my shoulder, and walk with that sack for about a city block or maybe a little less, to where the scale was. I could hook this sack up on the scale, have it weighed, take it off the hook, and put it back on my shoulder; and walk up a ladder about eight-feet high and dump all that cotton in the trailer.

My brothers taught me how to do it. When I first started picking cotton, they had to untie their sack and go on my side of the row and help me put this sack on my shoulder, so they taught me how to do it when it was full. It's stiff. My brother said, "Just walk over it, pick up one end, and sort of pull it up, up, and then bend, and when the middle of the sack hits your shoulder, you just stand up slowly. Then put your arm on your waist, and the sack will sit on your shoulder and you can just walk with it." At thirteen, fourteen, I was lifting 104 and 112 pounds. I weighed ninety-five, I guess!

As a child, I remember we had tents without any floors. It was Giffen's Camp Number Nine. I remember the water coming from under the tent at night to where we were sleeping. My brothers would get up with shovels and put mud around the tent to keep the water out. But our blankets and our clothes were always damp during the winter. [...]

There was a lot of disease. I don't remember two weeks out of my life: I had typhoid fever. I was put in the hospital in Bakersfield. At that time, we lived in some kind of tin building where they stored grain and apricot after it's been dried, and raisins. During the winter, I recall, I'd get up in the morning and want to wash my hands and face. We had to run quite a distance to the water faucet. I'd open the faucet and no water would come out: It was frozen. There was a barrel underneath with just a block of ice on the top. I would break this with my hands and wash my face and hands in a hurry and run back to the house and get ready for school. And in this water you'd see little things crawling up and going down. I don't know what they're called. But the typhoid is from water that's standing too long in one place, like this barrel, where my brothers and sisters and the other kids washed. [...]

In '33, we came up north to follow the crops because my brothers couldn't find any work in Los Angeles during the Depression. I remember going hungry to school. I didn't have a sweater. I had nothing. I'd come to school and they'd want to know, "What did you have for breakfast?" They gave us a paper, to write down what we had! I *invented* things! We had eggs and milk, I'd say, and the same things the other kids would write, I'd write. There weren't many Mexican people at school, mostly whites, and I'd watch to see what they were writing or the pictures that they'd show. You know: glasses of milk, and toast, and oranges and bananas and cereal. I'd never had *anything*. My grandmother couldn't work, we couldn't work, so we went hungry. One of my friends at school said, "Jessie, why don't you eat with us?" And I said, "I don't have any money. So they talked to the teacher, and the teacher called me one day during recess. She said, "Jessie, where's your father?"

"I don't have one."

"Where's your mother?"

"I don't have one." Then she wanted to know who did I live with. I said my grandmother and my uncles and aunts. She said, "Did you eat any breakfast?"

"No."

"Did your brothers and sisters eat breakfast?"

"No."

"Did you bring a lunch?"

"No." So she said, "Well, you help us in the kitchen. You can help us clear the tables after all the children eat, and you and your brothers and sisters can come and eat." It got to where after school, everything that was left in those big pots they'd put in those gallon cans for tomato sauce or canned peaches, and say, "You can take these home with you." And I'd take them home and we'd have a party – my grandmother and everybody. [. . .]

Courtship, Marriage, and Childrearing

[. . .] I was fourteen when I met Arnold, In 1933. We lived next door to his family, which was a big one. I'd go there and help Arnold's mother make stacks of tortillas. She didn't have time enough to do all the work for the little children. I'd go and help her. When she went to the hospital in 1935, when Arnold's younger brother was born, I cared for the whole family. I'd make tortillas and cook. The little ones we kept in our house, and the rest of them stayed in their cabin.

Arnold and I got married in 1938 in Firebaugh, where we'd all moved. We had a big party with an orchestra: some of Arnold's friends played the violin and guitar. But we had no honeymoon. On the second day after our wedding, he went back to his job – irrigating. I'd get up at four o'clock in the morning to fix his breakfast and his lunch. He'd start the fire for me. I did the cooking in his mother's kitchen. We had three cabins in all by this time. His mother had one cabin that was used as a bedroom. There was ours. And the other cabin in front was used as the kitchen for all of us. So in the morning I'd get up and run across and I'd fix his breakfast and his lunch and he'd go off and I'd go back to bed. He'd come home about four or five o'clock and there would be ice around his ears. It didn't come from the irrigating. It came from riding in the pickup. They were going fast, and the wind was that cold! He'd come home and get next to the stove where the fire was burning and have something hot to eat. He worked twelve hours a day. [. . .]

After I was married, sometime in May, my husband was chopping cotton and I said, "I want to go with you."

"You can't! You have to stay at home!"

"I just feel like going outside somewhere. I haven't gone anyplace. I want to at least go out to the fields. Take another hoe and I'll help you." I went, but only for one or two days. Then he refused to take me. He said, "You have to stay home and raise children." I was pregnant with my first one. "I want you to rest," he said. "You're not supposed to work. You worked ever since I can remember. Now that you're married, you are going to rest." So I stayed home, but I didn't call it rest doing all the cooking for his mother.

Arnold was raised in the old Mexican custom – men on the one side, women on the other. Women couldn't do anything. Your husband would say, "Go here," you'd do it. You didn't dare go out without your husband saying you could.

Arnold never beat me, or anything like that. But every time I used to talk to him he didn't answer, even if I asked a question. He'd say, "Well, you don't have to know about it." If I asked, "Arnold, has the truck been paid for?" he wouldn't answer. Or I would ask him, "Did you pay the loan company?" he wouldn't answer. Then I'd get kind of mad and say, "Why can't you tell me?" and he'd say, "What do you want to know about it, are you going to pay for it, or what? Let me do the worrying." Now that is all changed; we talk things over. But in the beginning it was different.

The first year we were married, he was home every night. After the first year was up, I guess that was the end of the honeymoon. He would just take off, and I wouldn't see him for three or four days, even more. I didn't even ask, "Where were you?" I accepted it. I wasn't supposed to question him. He would come in and take his dirty clothes off, pile them up, and when I did the wash the next day I'd look through his pockets and find bus ticket stubs of where he'd been to – Santa Maria, miles and miles away from home. He would be home for about two days and then take off again with his friends, his pals who were gambling. I really couldn't blame him that much, because when he was young, before we were married, he was never even allowed to go to a dance. So he was trying out his wings.

After a time I said, "I have really had it. Why do you have to go with your friends all the time when I'm being left alone?"

"Well, what's wrong with that? You can go visit my mother." I said, "Big deal, you want me to go visit your mother and help make some tortillas." So he finally started giving me money, five or six dollars. He'd say, "My mother's going to Fresno. If you want to go with them you can go." Or he would say, "Doña Genoveva," a friend of ours, "is going to Fresno and she said you can come along." I'd get my kids – I had two of them – ready early in the morning and we'd go to Fresno or to visit her husband, who was up in the mountains in the hospital for TB. One day I just said, "Why do I have to depend on other people to take me out somewhere? I'm married, I have a husband – who should be taking me out." The next time he was home and said, "Here's the money," I said, "I don't want to go." He let it go at that, and I did, too. I didn't say another word. The following weekend he said, "Do you want to go to a show? My mother's going. They're going to Fresno." I said, "No." Then about the third time this happened he said, "Why don't you want to go anymore?"

"I do, I do want to go. I want to go somewhere, but not with anyone else. I want to go with you." So then he started staying home and he'd say, "Get ready, we're going into Fresno." And both of us would come in, bring the children, go to a show and eat, or just go to the park.

We'd come in about once a month and bring the children with us. They just loved that, and now they're always talking about it, how Arnold would sing funny songs for them all the way from camp to town, and we'd all have a good time. This began happening around 1942, when I was in my twenties. [. . .]

My first child was born in 1939, Ray. I had five more. I also took Susan, the girl my sister left when she died. Now I have fourteen grandchildren, and this spring it will be fifteen, sometime in May.

I stopped working toward the last months of my pregnancies, but I would start again after they were born. When I was working and I couldn't find somebody, I would take them with me. I started taking Ray with me when he wasn't a year old yet. I'd carry one of those big washtubs and put it under the vine and sit him there. I knew he was safe; he couldn't climb out. Arnold and I would move the tub along with us as we worked. I hated to leave him with somebody that probably wouldn't take care of him the way I could. [...]

There was a lot of sickness. I remember when my kids got whooping cough. Arnold would come back late in the evening and wet, and the children were coughing and coughing. Arnold was sick, too, he was burning hot. During this time instead of staying in my own cabin at night I'd go to my mother-in-law's. The children would wake up at night coughing and there was blood coming out of their noses. I cried and cried, I was afraid they'd choke. I went to the clinic and they told me the children had whooping cough. That cough lasted six months.

I had a little girl who died in '43. She was so tiny...only five months. The cause was the way we were living, under the tree, with only chicken wire to separate us from the cows and horses. There were thousands of flies. I didn't have a refrigerator, no place to refrigerate the milk. She got sick. I couldn't stop the diarrhea. They told me she had a brain infection. And so I had to leave her, and my little girl died. We were so poor and I felt so helpless – there was nothing I could do.

It was like that for all of us. I would see babies who died. It was claimed if you lifted a young baby up fast, the soft spot would cave in and it would get diarrhea and dehydrate and die. After all these years I know it wasn't that that killed them. It was hunger, malnutrition, no money to pay the doctors. When the union came, this was one of the things we fought against.

Work in the Fields

[...] From 1939 until 1944, we stayed at Giffen's camp number three. We were still following the crops. We would go out to pick cotton or apricots or grapes here near Fresno, or we would go farther north to Tracey to pick peas. When there was no work chopping or picking cotton, we'd go to Patterson or San José to pick apricots. Arnold did the picking and I did cutting for the drying-out in the sheds. The apricots would be picked out in the field or in the orchard. They'd bring 'em in, in trucks, and they'd just set them beside us. They always had a boy or two that would dump these apricots on a table. We would have a knife, and we'd cut around it and take out the pit, and just spread them out on top of big trays. After we filled all these trays, they would come and take these out where they were dried. And they'd put some more on the table on the trays for us to cut.

We always went where the women and men were going to work, because if it were just the men working it wasn't worth going out there because we wouldn't earn enough to support a family. In one camp we were living at, the camp was at the edge of a cotton patch and the cotton needed to be thinned. We would start early. It was May. It got so hot, we would start around 6:30 A.M. and work for four or five hours, then walk home and eat and rest until about three-thirty in the afternoon when it cooled off. We would go back and work until we couldn't see. Then we'd get home and rest, visit, talk. Then I'd clean up the kitchen. I was doing the housework and working out in the fields and taking care of the kids. I had two children by this time. [. . .]

The hardest work we did was thinning beets. You were required to use a short-handled hoe. The cutting edge is about seven- to eight-inches wide, and the handle is about a foot long. You have to be bent over with the hoe in one hand. You walk down the rows stooped over. You have to work hard, fast, as fast as you can because you were paid by the row, not by the hour. I learned how to do it without straining my back too much. I put my hand on my left knee, and I got so good at it that I'd leave one beet on each stroke. You're supposed to pull one off with your hand if you leave two. I'd go as fast as I could and I'd always leave one and one. Most of them would be chopping, and then picking and separating with two hands. But I was walking backward and going fast. But when I wanted to stand up, I'd have to go very slow and I couldn't stand up straight. I still have a bad back, and I think I got it from the short-handled hoe. [. . .]

Out in the fields there were never any restrooms. We had to go eight or ten hours without relief. If there wasn't brush or a little ditch, we were forced to wait until we got home! Just the women. The men didn't need to pull their clothes down. Later, when I worked for the Farmworkers, in a hearing I said, "I was working for Russell Giffen, the biggest grower in Huron. These big growers have a lot of money because we earned all that money for them. Because of our sweat and our labor that we put on the land. What they do instead of supplying restrooms and clean water where we can wash our hands, is put posts on the ground with a piece of gunny sack wound around them." That's where we went. And that thing was moved along with us. It was just four stakes stuck in the ground, and then there was canvas or a piece of gunny sack around it. You would be working, and this restroom would be right there. The canvas didn't come up high enough in front for privacy. We made it a practice to go two at a time. One would stand outdoors and watch outside that nobody came along. And then the other would do the same for the one inside. Then we'd go back to work.

La Causa

[. . .] Growing up, I could see all the injustices and I would think, "If only I could do something about it! If only there was somebody who could do something about it! That was always in the back of my mind. And after I was married, I cared about what was going on, but I felt I couldn't do anything. So I went to work, and I came home to clean the house, and I fixed the food for the next day, took care of the children and the next day went back to work. The whole thing over and over again. Politics to me was something foreign, something I didn't know about. I didn't even listen to the news. I didn't read the newspapers hardly at all. *True Romance* was my thing!

But then late one night in 1962, there was a knock at the door and there were three men. One of them was Cesar Chavez. And the next thing I knew, they were sitting around our table talking about a union. I made coffee. Arnold had already told me about a union for the farmworkers. He was attending their meetings in Fresno, but I didn't. I'd either stay home or stay outside in the car. But then Cesar said, "The women have to be involved. They're the ones working out in the fields with their husbands. If you can take the women out to the fields, you can certainly take them to meetings." So I sat up straight and said to myself, *"That's* what I want!"

When I became involved with the union, I felt I had to get other women involved. Women have been behind men all the time, always. Just waiting to see what the men decide to do, and tell us what to do. In my sister-in-law and brother-in-law's families, the women do a lot of shouting and cussing and they get slapped around. But that's not standing up for what you believe in. It's just trying to boss and not knowing how. I'd hear them scolding their kids and fighting their husbands and I'd say, "Gosh! Why don't you go after the people that have you living like this? Why don't you go after the growers that have you tired from working out in the fields at low wages and keep us poor all the time? Let's go after them! *They're* the cause of our misery! Then I would say we had to take a part in the things going on around us. "Women can no longer be taken for granted – that we're just going to stay home and do the cooking and cleaning. It's way past the time when our husbands could say, 'You stay home! You have to take care of the children! You have to do as I say!'"

Then some women I spoke to started attending the union meetings, and later they were out on the picket lines.

I think I was made an organizer because in the first place I could relate to the farmworkers, being a lifelong farmworker. I was well-known in the small towns around Fresno. Wherever I went to speak to them, they listened. I told them about how we were excluded from the NLRB in 1935, how we had no benefits, no minimum wage, nothing out in the fields – no restrooms, nothing.[3] I would talk about how we were paid what the grower wanted to pay us, and how we couldn't set a price on our work. I explained that we could do something about these things by joining a union, by working together. I'd ask people how they felt about these many years they had been working out in the fields, how they had been treated. And then we'd all talk about it. They would say, "I was working for so-and-so, and when I complained about something that happened there, I was fired." I said, "Well! Do you think we should be putting up with this in this modern age? You know, we're not back in the twenties. We can stand up! We can talk back! It's not like when I was a little kid and my grandmother used to say, 'You have to especially respect the Anglos,' 'Yessir,' 'Yes, Ma'am!' That's over. This country is very rich, and we want a share of the money these growers make of our sweat and our work by exploiting us and our children!" I'd have my sign-up book and I'd say, "If anyone wants to become a member of the union, I can make you a member right now." And they'd agree!

So I found out that I could organize them and make members of them. Then I offered to help them, like taking them to the doctor's and translating for them, filling out papers that they needed to fill out, writing their letters for those that couldn't write. A lot of people confided in me. Through the letter-writing, I knew a lot of the problems they were having back home, and they knew they could trust me, that I wouldn't tell anyone else about what I had written or read. So that's why they came to me. [. . .]

It was very hard being a woman organizer. Many of our people my age and older were raised with the old customs in Mexico: where the husband rules, he is king of his house. The wife obeys, and the children, too. So when we first started it was very, very hard. Men gave us the most trouble – neighbors there in Parlier! They were for the union, but they were not taking orders from women, they said. When they formed the ranch committee at Christian Brothers – that's a big wine company, part of it is in Parlier – the ranch committee was all men.[4] We were working under our first contract in Fresno County. The ranch committee had to enforce the contract. If there are any grievances they meet with us and the supervisors. But there were no women on the first committee.

That year, we'd have a union meeting every week. Men, women, and children would come. Women would ask questions and the men would just stand back. I guess they'd say to themselves, "I'll wait for someone to say something before I do." The women were more aggressive than the men. And I'd get up and say, "Let's go on, let's do it!" [. . .]

The second year we had a contract I started working for Christian Brothers. The men were doing the pruning on the grape vines. After they did the pruning, the women's crew would come and tie the vines – that was something we got changed. We made them give pruning jobs to women.

I was made a steward on the women's crew.[5] If there were any grievances, it was up to me to listen and then enforce the contract. For example, the first time we were paid when I started working, during the break the supervisor would come out there with our checks. It was our fifteen-minute break, which the contract gave us the right to. He always came then! We had to walk to the other end of the row, it took us about five minutes to get there, the rest of the fifteen to get our checks, and walk back, and we'd start working. This happened twice. The third time I said, "We're not going to go after our checks this time. They always come during our break and we don't get to rest." So when we saw the pickup coming with the men who had the checks I said, "Nobody move. You just sit here." I walked over to the pickup. I said to the man inside, "Mr. Rager, these women refuse to come out here on their break time. It's their time to rest. So we're asking you, If you must come during our rest period, you take the checks to these ladies." From that day on, every payday he would come to us. That was the sort of thing you had to do to enforce the contract.

I became involved in many of the activities in the community – school board meetings, city council meetings, everything that I could get into. For example, I began fighting for bilingual education in Parlier, went to a lot of meetings about it and spoke about it. [. . .]

Fresno County didn't give food stamps to the people – only surplus food.[6] There were no vegetables, no meat, just staples like whole powdered milk, cheese, butter. At the migrant camp in Parlier, the people were there a month and a half before work started, and since they'd borrowed money to get to California, they didn't have any food. I'd drive them into Fresno to the welfare department and translate for them, and they'd get food, but half of it they didn't eat. We heard about other counties where they had food stamps to go to the store and buy meat and milk and fresh vegetables for the children. So we began talking about getting that in Fresno. Finally, we had Senate hearings at the Convention Center in Fresno. There were hundreds of people listening. A man I know comes to me and says, "Jessie, you're next." He'd been going to speak, but he said he wanted me to speak in his place. I started in Spanish, and the senators were looking at each other, you know, saying, "What's going on?" So then I said, "Now, for the benefit of those who can't speak Spanish, I'll translate. They tell us there's no money for food stamps for poor people. But if there is money enough to fight a war in Vietnam, and if there is money enough for Governor Reagan's wife to buy a three-thousand-dollar dress for the inauguration Ball, there should be money enough to feed these people. The nutrition experts say surplus food is full of vitamins. I've taken a look at that food, this cornmeal, and I've seen them come up and down. But you know, we don't call them vitamins, we call them weevils!" Everybody began laughing and whistling and shouting. In the end, we finally got food stamps for the people in Fresno County.

Sometimes I'd just stop to think: what if our parents had done what we were doing now? My grandparents were poor. They were humble. They never learned to speak English. They felt God meant them to be poor. It was against their religion to fight. I remember there was a huge policeman named Marcos, when I was a child, who used to go around on a horse. My grandmother would say, "Here comes Marcos," and we just grew up thinking, "He's law and order." But during the strikes I stood up to them. They'd come up to arrest me and I'd say, "O.K., here I come if you want. Arrest me!"

Study Questions

1 Trace the influences of class, ethnicity, and gender on Lopez's ideas about family, work, and women.
2 How was Lopez affected by her extended family network? How was she affected by mainstream American culture?
3 How did Lopez's sense of identity shift when Cesar Chavez knocked on her door in 1962? Why did "La Causa" provide a framework for rethinking what she could accomplish as a woman, as a farmworker, and as an American citizen?
4 Compare Pauli Murray's and Lopez's ideas on women roles in their respective movements.

Notes

1. Jessie De La Cruz calls her uncles "brothers." After the age of ten, she was raised by her grandmother, and some of her mother's brothers weren't much older than she was.
2. Dclano is northeast of Los Angeles near the bottom of the San Joaquin Valley. It was in Delano that the great grape strike called by Cesar Chavez's National Farmworkers' Association, together with Larry Itliong's United Farmworkers' Organizing Committee, began in 1965.
3. The National Labor Relations Board (NLRB) was established by President Franklin Delano Roosevelt in 1933. Its purpose was to settle differences between employers and employees. The board was set up under the National Labor Relations Act, which made union negotiations between employers and employees legal for the first time in the United States. The act, and the board set up to implement it, were historical landmarks in the history of unionism. But two major groups of workers were excluded by the act and its board – domestic workers (who were mostly women) and farmworkers (who were mainly Chicanos, Filipinos, and blacks). Both major groups were among the poorest of the United States working class.
4. On every farm, the union created a ranch committee elected by the workers. The committee is the grassroots base of the union. If you have an on-the-job complaint, you bring it to the ranch committee, which then discusses the complaint with the supervisor. Before the ranch committee was introduced by the union, individual workers had to get up nerve to complain about abuses on their own – and often they were fired on the spot when they dared speak up. The ranch committee put the union behind them and gave them a democratically-elected group for support.
5. Every union has its workers elect "shop stewards" from their midst. These officially-elected union representatives remain on the job, working side-by-side with the other employees. Their responsibility is to provide information to their co-workers about the union, and to deal with any complaints – "grievances" – workers may have. The steward is empowered to go to the manager or boss on the workers' behalf, and to consult with other union officials about on-the-job problems.
6. In 1964, Congress established a program under which low-income people could "pay" for food at stores by using stamps issued by the government. Your eligibility for food stamps depended on your income. When the Welfare office sent you surplus food, you had to eat what you got: you had no choice. But you could take food stamps to your local store, and buy what you wanted.

CHAPTER 30

This Country Was a Lot Better Off When the Indians Were Running It

Vine Deloria, Jr.

Raised as a Standing Rock Sioux in a family with a long history of activism, Vine Deloria, Jr. was the most influential Native American spokesman of his generation. Born 1933 in South Dakota, he is the son of a Protestant Indian minister, the grandson of a missionary, and the great-grandson of a medicine man and leader of the Yankton Sioux. Deloria, Jr. earned his BS from Iowa State University in 1958, and a Master's degree from the Lutheran School of Theology, in 1962. Frustrated by Indians' lack of legal representation and understanding of American law, he took a law degree at the University of Colorado in 1970. Deloria's first book, Custer Died for Your Sins: An Indian Manifesto *(1969), established his argument for Native American sovereignty and self-determination. It was followed by other influential titles, including* God is Red *(1973), and* Red Earth, White Lies: Native Americans and the Myth of Scientific Fact *(1995). In the following essay, Deloria displays his comic eloquence as he defends Indians' rights to their land. His essay is followed by the Indians of All Tribes' account of their three-year occupation of Alcatraz Island (a federal penitentiary), which began in 1969, and marked the beginning of radical Indian activism.*

O n Nov. 9, 1969, a contingent of American Indians, led by Adam Nordwall, a Chippewa from Minnesota, and Richard Oakes, a Mo-
[. . .] hawk from New York, landed on Alcatraz Island in San Francisco Bay and claimed the 13-acre rock "by right of discovery." The island had been abandoned six and a half years ago, and although there had been various suggestions concerning its disposal nothing had been done to make use of the land. Since there are Federal treaties giving some tribes the right to abandoned Federal property within a tribe's original territory, the Indians of the Bay area felt that they could lay claim to the island.

For nearly a year the United Bay Area Council of American Indians, a confederation of urban Indian organizations, had been talking about submitting a bid for the island to use it as a West Coast Indian cultural center and vocational training headquarters. Then, on Nov. 1, the San Francisco American Indian Center burned down. The center had served an estimated 30,000 Indians in the immediate area and was the focus of activities of the urban Indian community. It became a matter of urgency after that and, as Adam Nordwall said, "it was GO." Another landing, on Nov. 20, by nearly 100 Indians in a swift midnight raid secured the island.

The new inhabitants have made "the Rock" a focal point symbolic of Indian people. Under extreme difficulty they have worked to begin repairing sanitary facilities and buildings. The population has been largely transient, many people have stopped by, looked the situation over for a few days, then gone home, unwilling to put in the tedious work necessary to make the island support a viable community.

The Alcatraz news stories are somewhat shocking to non-Indians. It is difficult for most Americans to comprehend that there still exists a living community of nearly one million Indians in this country. For many people, Indians have become a species of movie actor periodically dispatched to the Happy Hunting Grounds by John Wayne on the "Late, Late Show." Yet there are some 315 Indian tribal groups in 26 states still functioning as quasi-sovereign nations under treaty status; they range from the mammoth Navajo tribe of some 132,000 with 16 million acres of land to tiny Mission Creek of California with 15 people and a tiny parcel of property. There are over a half a million Indians in the cities alone, with the largest concentrations in San Francisco, Los Angeles, Minneapolis and Chicago.

The take-over of Alcatraz is to many Indian people a demonstration of pride in being Indian and a dignified, yet humorous protest against current conditions existing on the reservations and in the cities. It is this special pride and dignity, the determination to judge life according to one's own values, and the unconquerable conviction that the tribes will not die that has always characterized Indian people as I have known them.

I was born in Martin, a border town on the Pine Ridge Indian Reservation in South Dakota, in the midst of the Depression. My father was an Indian missionary who served 18 chapels on the eastern half of the reservation. In 1934, when I was 1, the Indian Reorganization Act was passed, allowing Indian tribes full rights of self-government for the first time since the late eighteen-sixties. Ever since those days, when the Sioux had agreed to forsake the life of the hunter for that of the farmer, they had been systematically deprived of any voice in decisions affecting their lives and property. Tribal ceremonies and religious practices were forbidden. The reservation was fully controlled by men in Washington, most of whom had never visited a reservation and felt no urge to do so.

The first years on the reservations were extremely hard for the Sioux. Kept confined behind fences they were almost wholly dependent upon Government rations for their food supply. Many died of hunger and malnutrition. Game was scarce and few were allowed to have weapons for fear of another Indian war. In some years there was practically no food available. Other years rations were withheld until the men agreed to farm the tiny pieces of land each family had been given. In desperation many families were forced to eat stray dogs and cats to keep alive.

By World War I, however, many of the Sioux families had developed prosperous ranches. Then the Government stepped in, sold the Indians' cattle for wartime needs, and after the war leased the grazing land to whites, creating wealthy white ranchers and destitute Indian landlords. [. . .]

The most memorable event of my early childhood was visiting Wounded Knee where 200 Sioux, including women and children, were slaughtered in 1890 by troopers of the Seventh Cavalry in what is believed to have been a delayed act of vengeance for Custer's defeat. The people were simply lined up and shot down much as was allegedly done, according to newspaper reports, at Songmy. The wounded were left to die in a three-day Dakota blizzard, and when the soldiers returned to the scene after the storm some were still alive and were saved. The massacre was vividly etched in the minds of many of the older reservation people, but it was difficult to find anyone who wanted to talk about it.

Many times, over the years, my father would point out survivors of the massacre, and people on the reservation always went out of their way to help them. For a long time there was a bill in Congress to pay indemnities to the survivors, but the War Department always insisted that it had been a "battle" to stamp out the Ghost Dance religion among the Sioux. This does not, however, explain bayoneted Indian women and children found miles from the scene of the incident.

Strangely enough, the Depression was good for Indian reservations, particularly for the people at Pine Ridge. Since their lands had been leased to non-Indians by the Bureau of Indian Affairs, they had only a small rent check and the contempt of those who leased their lands to show for their ownership. But the Federal programs devised to solve the national economic crisis were also made available to Indian people, and there was work available for the first time in the history of the reservations. [. . .]

World War II ended this temporary prosperity. The [. . .] reservation programs were cut to the bone and social services became virtually nonexistent; "Victory gardens" were suddenly the style, and people began to be aware that a great war was being waged overseas.

The war dispersed the reservation people as nothing ever had. Every day, it seemed, we would be bidding farewell to families as they headed west to work in the defense plants on the Coast.

A great number of Sioux people went west and many of the Sioux on Alcatraz today are their children and relatives. There may now be as many Sioux in California as there are on the reservations in South Dakota because of the great wartime migration. [. . .]

After the war Indian veterans straggled back to the reservations and tried to pick up their lives. It was very difficult for them to resume a life of poverty after having seen the affluent outside world. Some spent a few days with the old folks and then left again for the big cities. Over the years they have emerged as leaders of the urban Indian movement. Many of their children are the nationalists of today who are adamant about keeping the reservations they have visited only on vacations. Other veterans stayed on the reservations and entered tribal politics. [. . .]

I left the reservation in 1951 when my family moved to Iowa. I went back only once for an extended stay, in the summer of 1955, while on a furlough, and after that I visited only occasionally during summer vacations. In the meantime, I attended college, served a hitch in the Marines, and went to the seminary. After I graduated from the seminary, I took a job with the United Scholarship Service, a private organization devoted to the college and secondary-school education of American Indian and Mexican students. I had spent my last two years of high school in an Eastern preparatory school and so was probably the only Indian my age who knew what an independent Eastern school was like. As the program developed, we soon had some 30 students placed in Eastern schools.

I insisted that all the students who entered the program be able to qualify for scholarships as students and not simply as Indians. I was pretty sure we could beat the white man at his own educational game, which seemed to me the only way to gain his respect. I was soon to find that this was a dangerous attitude to have. The very people who were supporting the program – non-Indians in the national church establishments – accused me of trying to form a colonialist "élite" by insisting that only kids with strong test scores and academic patterns be sent east to school. They wanted to continue the ancient pattern of soft-hearted paternalism toward Indians. I didn't feel we should cry our way into the schools; that sympathy would destroy the students we were trying to help.

In 1964, while attending the annual convention of the National Congress of American Indians, I was elected its executive director. I learned more about life in the NCAI in three years than I had in the previous 30. Every conceivable problem that could occur in an Indian society was suddenly thrust at me from 315 different directions. I discovered that I was one of the people who were supposed to solve the problems. The only trouble was that Indian people locally and on the national level were being played off one against the other by clever whites who had either ego or income at stake. While there were many feasible solutions, few could be tried without whites with vested interests working night and day to destroy the unity we were seeking on a national basis.

In the mid-nineteen sixties, the whole generation that had grown up after World War II and had left the reservations during the fifties to get an education was returning to Indian life as "educated Indians." But we soon knew better. Tribal societies had existed for centuries without going outside themselves for education and information. Yet many of us thought that we would be able to improve the traditional tribal methods. We were wrong. [. . .]

By 1967 there was a radical change in thinking on the part of many of us. Conferences were proving unproductive. Where non-Indians had been pushed out to make room for Indian people, they had wormed their way back into power and again controlled the major programs serving Indians. The poverty programs, reservation and university technical assistance groups were dominated by whites who had pushed Indian administrators aside.

Reservation people, meanwhile, were making steady progress in spite of the numerous setbacks suffered by the national Indian community. So, in large part, younger Indian leaders who had been playing the national conference field began working at the local level to build community movements from the ground up. By consolidating local organizations into power groups they felt that they would be in a better position to influence national thinking. [. . .]

By the fall of 1967, it was apparent that the national Indian scene was collapsing in favor of strong regional organizations, although the major national organizations such as the National Congress of American Indians and the National Indian Youth Council continued to grow. There was yet another factor emerging on the Indian scene: the old-timers of the Depression days had educated a group of younger Indians in the old ways and these people were now becoming a major force in Indian life. Led by Thomas Banyaca of the Hopi, Mad Bear Anderson of the Tuscaroras, Clifton Hill of the Creeks, and Rolling Thunder of the Shoshones, the traditional Indians were forcing the whole Indian community to rethink its understanding of Indian life.

The message of the traditionalists is simple. They demand a return to basic Indian philosophy, establishment of ancient methods of government by open council instead of elected officials, a revival of Indian religions and replacement of white laws with Indian customs; in short, a complete return to the ways of the old people. In an age dominated by tribalizing communications media, their message makes a great deal of sense. [. . .]

I did not run for re-election as executive director of the NCAI in the fall of 1967, but entered law school at the University of Colorado instead. It was apparent to me that the Indian revolution was well under way and that someone had better get a legal education so that we could have our own legal program for defense of Indian treaty rights. Thanks to a Ford Foundation program, nearly 50 Indians are now in law school, assuring the Indian community of legal talent in the years ahead. Within four years I foresee another radical shift in Indian leadership patterns as the growing local movements are affected by the new Indian lawyers.

There is an increasing scent of victory in the air in Indian country these days. The mood is comparable to the old days of the Depression when the men began to dance once again. As the Indian movement gathers momentum and individual Indians cast their lot with the tribe, it will become apparent that not only will Indians survive the electronic world of Marshall McLuhan, they will thrive in it. At the present time everyone is watching how mainstream America will handle the issues of pollution, poverty, crime and racism when it does not fundamentally understand the issues. Knowing the importance of tribal survival, Indian people are speaking more and more of sovereignty, of the great political technique of the open council, and of the need for gaining the community's consensus on all programs before putting them into effect. [. . .]

In 1965 I had a long conversation with an old Papago. I was trying to get the tribe to pay its dues to the National Congress of American Indians and I had asked him to speak to the tribal council for me. He said that he would but that the Papagos didn't really need the NCAI. They were like, he told me, the old mountain in the distance. The Spanish had come and dominated them for 300 years and then left. The Mexicans had come and ruled them for a century, but they also left. "The Americans," he said "have been here only about 80 years. They, too, will vanish but the Papagos and the mountain will always be here."

This attitude and understanding of life is what American society is searching for.

Indian people have managed to maintain a viable and cohesive social order in spite of everything the non-Indian society has thrown at them in an effort to break the tribal structure. At the same time, non-Indian society has created a monstrosity of a culture where people starve while the granaries are filled and the sun can never break through the smog.

By making Alcatraz an experimental Indian center operated and planned by Indian people, we would be given a chance to see what we could do toward developing answers to modern social problems. Ancient tribalism can be incorporated with modern technology in an urban setting. Perhaps we would not succeed in the effort, but the Government is spending billions every year and still the situation is rapidly growing worse. It just seems to a lot of Indians that this continent was a lot better off when we were running it.

★ ★ ★ ★ ★ ★ ★ ★ ★ ★ ★ ★ ★

The Occupation of Alcatraz Island

Indians of All Tribes

November 1969

Proclamation:

To the Great White Father and All His People:

We, the native Americans, re-claim the land known as Alcatraz Island in the name of all American Indians by right of discovery.

We wish to be fair and honorable in our dealings with the Caucasian inhabitants of this land, and hereby offer the following treaty:

We will purchase said Alcatraz Island for twenty-four dollars ($24) in glass beads and red cloth, a precedent set by the white man's purchase of a similar island about 300 years ago. We know that $24 in trade goods for these 16 acres is more than was paid when Manhattan Island was sold, but we know that land values have risen over the years. Our offer of $1.24 per acre is greater than the 47 cents per acre the white men are now paying the California Indians for their land.

We will give to the inhabitants of this island a portion of that land for their own, to be held in trust by the American Indian Government – for as long as the sun shall rise and the rivers go down to the sea – to be administered by the Bureau of Caucasian Affairs (BCA). We will further guide the inhabitants in the proper way of living. We will offer them our religion, our education, our life-ways, in order to help them achieve our level of civilization and thus raise them and all their white brothers up from their savage and unhappy state. We offer this treaty in good faith and wish to be fair and honorable in our dealings with all white men.

We feel that this so-called Alcatraz Island is more than suitable for an Indian Reservation, as determined by the white man's own standards. By this we mean that this place resembles most Indian reservations, in that:

1. It is isolated from modern facilities, and without adequate means of transportation.
2. It has no fresh running water.
3. It has inadequate sanitation facilities.
4. There are no oil or mineral rights.
5. There is no industry so unemployment is great.
6. There are no health care facilities.
7. The soil is rocky and non-productive; and the land does not support game.
8. There are no educational facilities.
9. The population has always exceeded the land base.
10. The population has always been held as prisoners and kept dependent upon others.

Further, it would be fitting and symbolic that ships from all over the world, entering the Golden Gate, would first see Indian land, and thus be reminded of the true history of this nation. This tiny island would be a symbol of the great lands once ruled by free and noble Indians.

Use to be Made of Alcatraz Island

What use will be made of this land?

Since the San Francisco Indian Center burned down, there is no place for Indians to assemble and carry on our tribal life here in the white man's city. Therefore, we plan to develop on this island several Indian institutes:

1. A Center for Native American Studies will be developed which will train our young people in the best of our native cultural arts and sciences, as well as educate them to the skills and knowledge relevant to improve the lives and spirits of all Indian peoples. Attached to this center will be traveling universities, managed by Indians, which will go to the Indian Reservations in order to learn the traditional values from the people, which are now absent in the Caucasian higher educational system.

2.   An American Indian Spiritual center will be developed which will practice our ancient tribal religious ceremonies and medicine. Our cultural arts will be featured and our young people trained in music, dance, and medicine.

3.   An Indian center of Ecology will be built which will train and support our young people in scientific research and practice in order to restore our lands and waters to their pure and natural state. We will seek to de-pollute the air and the water of the Bay Area. We will seek to restore fish and animal life, and to revitalize sea life which has been threatened by the white man's way. Facilities will be developed to desalt sea water for human use.

4.   A Great Indian Training School will be developed to teach our peoples how to make a living in the world, improve our standards of living, and end hunger and unemployment among all our peoples. This training school will include a center for Indian arts and crafts, and an Indian Restaurant serving native foods and training Indians in culinary arts. This center will display Indian arts and offer the Indian foods of all tribes to the public, so they all may know of the beauty and spirit of the traditional Indian ways.

5.   Some of the present buildings will be taken over to develop an American Indian Museum, which will depict our native foods and other cultural contributions we have given to all the world. Another part of the Museum will present some of the things the white man has given to the Indians, in return for the land and the life he took: disease, alcohol, poverty, and cultural decimation (as symbolized by old tin cans, barbed wire, rubber tires, plastic containers, etc.). Part of the museum will remain a dungeon, to symbolize both Indian captives who were incarcerated for challenging white authority, and those who were imprisoned on reservations. The Museum will show the noble and the tragic events of Indian history, including the broken treaties, the documentary of the Trail of Tears, the Massacre of Wounded Knee, as well as the victory over Yellow-Hair Custer and his army.

In the name of all Indians, therefore, we re-claim this island for Indian nations, for all these reasons. We feel this claim is just and proper, and that this land should rightfully be granted to us for as long as the rivers shall run and the sun shall shine.

SIGNED,

INDIANS OF ALL TRIBES

November 1969

San Francisco, California

Study Questions

1   Why was it difficult for most Americans to recognize that there were nearly one million Indians living in the US in 1970?
2   How does the history of the Sioux people that Deloria recounts help to explain the rise of the modern American Indian Rights Movement? What role did "generational memory" play in that history (see John Bodnar)? How did tribal history shape Deloria's "social location"?
3   What does Deloria mean when he says of the old Papago man's statement: "This attitude and understanding of life is what American society is searching for"?
4   Why was the takeover of Alcatraz Island so important to Native Americans?
5   Compare the Alcatraz "Proclamation" to SDS's "Port Huron Statement" or to the Young Lords' "Thirteen Point Program and Platform."

CHAPTER 31

Gay Liberation

John D'Emilio and Estelle B. Freedman

John D'Emilio (1948–) is a professor of US history, with specialties in the history of homosexual rights movements, civil rights movements, and the history of sexuality. His books include Sexual Politics, Sexual Communities: The Making of a Homosexual Minority in the US, 1940–1970 *(1983). Estelle B. Freedman (1947–) is a professor of US history, with specialties in women's history, the history of sexuality, and the history of feminism. Her books include* No Turning Back: the History of Feminism and the Future of Women *(2002). The following reading was excerpted from their coauthored book,* Intimate Matters: A History of Sexuality in America *(1988).*

[...] Few social movements can trace their birth to an event as unexpected and dramatic as the one which gave life to gay liberation. On Friday, June 27, 1969, a group of Manhattan police officers set off to close the Stonewall Inn, a gay bar in the heart of Greenwich Village. Raids of gay bars were common enough occurrences in the 1960s, and the police must have viewed their mission as a routine part of their weekend duties. But the patrons of the Stonewall Inn refused to behave according to script. As the officers hauled them one by one into police vans, a crowd of onlookers assembled on the street, taunting the cops. When a lesbian in the bar put up a struggle, the *Village Voice* reported,

> the scene became explosive. Limp wrists were forgotten. Beer cans and bottles were heaved at the windows and a rain of coins descended on the cops. . . . Almost by signal the crowd erupted into cobblestone and bottle heaving. . . . From nowhere came an uprooted parking meter – used as a battering ram on the Stonewall door. I heard several cries of "let's get some gas," but the blaze of flame which soon appeared in the window of the Stonewall was still a shock.

Although the police officers were rescued from the torched bar, their work had just begun. Rioting continued far into the night, as crowds of angry homosexuals battled the police up and down the streets of Greenwich Village. The following day, graffiti proclaiming "Gay Power" was scribbled on walls and pavements in the area. The rioting that lasted throughout the weekend signaled the start of a major social movement. Within weeks, gay men and lesbians in New York had formed the Gay Liberation Front (GLF), a self-proclaimed revolutionary organization in the style of the New Left, seeking justice for homosexuals. As word of the Stonewall riots circulated among radical gay youth and other disaffected homosexuals, the gay liberation impulse took root across the country, spawning scores of similar groups.[1]

Dramatic as the rioting was, it was not sufficient to spark a nationwide grass-roots movement. The speed with which gay liberation grew testified to equally profound changes in the structure of gay life and the consciousness of homosexuals in the preceding years. Throughout the 1950s and 1960s, a gay subculture had been growing, providing the setting in which homosexuals might develop a group consciousness. The weakening of taboos against the public discussion of homosexuality, the pervasive police harassment of the era, and the persistent work of a small coterie of pre-Stonewall activists combined to make many lesbians and gay men receptive to the message of "gay power."

The collapse in the 1960s of strictures against the portrayal of sexual matters gave the media license to turn its attention to homosexuality. Though much of the information presented was negative – highlighting medical theories that emphasized pathology, reporting police campaigns against "deviants," or casting pitying glances at the lives of sexual outlaws – the articles in newspapers and magazines also provided welcome clues to the existence of a gay world. Magazines such as *Life* and *Look* printed photo essays of the gay subculture, alerting their audience to the concentration of homosexuals in cities such as New York, Los Angeles, and San Francisco. Series in local newspapers served much the same function as they unwittingly instructed isolated gay readers about where they might find others. A spate of Hollywood movies in the 1960s – *The Children's Hour, Advise and Consent, Walk on the Wild Side*, among others – treated gay themes. Many writers included homosexual characters and subplots in their novels, and a number of journalists published exposés of gay life in modern America. Taken together, these forays into the world of homosexuals served as mapping expeditions that made exploration and discovery easier for countless numbers of gay men and lesbians.[2]

Meanwhile, some gay men and women were mounting a response to the repressive public policies that had characterized the Cold War era. In Los Angeles, in 1950, a group of gay men associated with the Communist party founded the Mattachine Society, a gay rights organization. A few years later, they were joined by a lesbian counterpart, the Daughters of Bilitis. During the fifties, these groups struggled to exist, as they operated with scanty resources, no models for how to proceed, and the ever-present threat of police harassment. But they did survive, establishing chapters in several cities, publishing their own magazines, and projecting, however faintly, a point of view about same-gender relationships that departed from the consensus of sin, sickness, and criminality.

During the 1960s, this pre-Stonewall generation of "homophile" leaders, as they called themselves, became bolder. Inspired by the model of the civil rights movement, activists such as Frank Kameny in New York and Barbara Gittings in Philadelphia moved beyond the task of education and shaped a more direct challenge to the laws and public policies that denied gays equality. Homophile organizations staffed picket lines around government buildings in the nation's capital to protest the ban on federal employment and the exclusion from military service. They initiated court cases to challenge discriminatory statutes, lobbied successfully to win the support of the American Civil Liberties Union, and monitored police practices. A dialogue was opened with liberal Protestant clergy, and a campaign begun within the medical establishment to have homosexuality removed from the list of mental disorders. Perhaps most importantly, these ventures made the movement newsworthy. Television cameras filmed the picketing in front of the White House, while print journalists incorporated the views of activists into their articles on gay life. By the end of the 1960s, this pioneering band had succeeded in disseminating widely a point of view that diverged sharply from the dominant consensus about homosexuality.

As consciousness within the gay subculture slowly altered, the protests of the 1960s were creating another – radicalized – gay cohort. When black power advocates proclaimed that "black is beautiful," they provided the model of an oppressed group that inverted the negative values of the society. The student movement spread skepticism toward middle-class values among white college youth and led to an alienation from mainstream America that encouraged a cavalier disregard for social respectability. The hippie counterculture urged the young to drop out and "do your own thing." Finally, the women's liberation movement launched an ideological attack on sex-role constructs while popularizing the slogan "the personal is political." Taken together, these movements offered another lens through which radical gay youth, who were keeping their homosexuality secret, might view their sexual preferences. After the Stonewall riot of 1969, when some of them gathered to form the Gay Liberation Front in New York City, they were well situated to launch a major social movement.

The culture of protest that existed at the time provided opportunities to spread the gay liberation impulse widely. Activists appeared with gay banners at the many antiwar demonstrations that erupted during the fall of 1969. At colleges and universities, gay students rallied openly alongside other campus radicals. Soon, these young gay militants were taking the message of their movement into the heart of the gay subculture. Seeing the Mafia-run bars as oppressive institutions that reinforced self-hatred and encouraged a dehumanizing sexual objectification, gay activists in many cities "liberated" the bars for an evening, and urged patrons to join the struggle for freedom.

Appearing as it did at the end of the 1960s, gay liberation adopted much of the revolutionary rhetoric of the New Left. GLF's statement of purpose announced that "we are a revolutionary homosexual group of men and women formed with the realization that complete sexual liberation for all people cannot come about unless existing social institutions are abolished. We reject society's attempt to impose sexual roles and definitions of our nature. . . . Babylon has forced us to commit ourselves to one thing . . . revolution!"[3] Rather than fight the ban on homosexuals in the military, radical gays urged resistance to the Vietnam War. They marched in solidarity with groups such as the Black Panther party, and saw themselves as an integral part of the larger movement of oppressed minorities seeking the overthrow of a destructive social order. [. . .]

As one of its chief tactics for accomplishing its goals, gay liberation adopted the notion of "coming out." In its older, original meaning, "coming out" referred to the acknowledgment of one's homosexuality to oneself and other gay people. Gay liberationists transformed it into a public avowal. A critical step on the road to freedom, coming out implied a rejection of the negative social meaning attached to homosexuality in favor of pride and self-acceptance. The men and women who took the plunge had to overcome the fear of punishment and be willing to brave the ostracism of society that might result. In the process, they would also shed much of the self-hatred that they had internalized. Thus, the act became both a marker of liberation and an act of resistance against an oppressive society. As the banner of New York GLF's newspaper exhorted, "Come Out For Freedom! Come Out Now! . . . - Come Out of the Closet Before the Door Is Nailed Shut!"[4]

This deceptively simple proposition was both a unique product of its time and an important roadmark in the history of sexuality. At a moment when the hippie counterculture was urging the young to "do your own thing," and feminists were redefining the personal as political, coming out seemed perfectly to embody both. Moreover, it was precisely adapted to the immediate constituency and needs of the movement. With the range of penalties that exposure promised to homosexuals, it was radical youth, contemptuous of the rewards that American society offered for conformity, who were most likely to rally to the banner of gay liberation. Exclusion from the military or a civil service career, ostracism by society, and the threat of arrest held little power over these self-styled revolutionaries. And, coming out promised the movement an army of permanent recruits. By discarding the protection that came from hiding, gay men and lesbians invested heavily in the successful outcome of their struggle.

But coming out signified something more. As the gay movement grew and gathered strength in the 1970s, the example of radical activists proved infectious, and many conventional homosexuals imitated this simple act of pride. Coming out of the closet was incorporated into the basic assumptions of what it meant to be gay. As such, it came to represent not simply a single act, but the adoption of an identity in which the erotic played a central role. Sexuality became emblematic of the person, not as an imposed medical label connoting deviance, but as a form of self-affirmation. No longer merely something you did in bed, sex served to define a mode of living, both private and public, that encompassed a wide range of activities and relationships. The phenomenon of coming out highlighted just how far the erotic had moved from the previous century when it was still embedded in a web of marital duties and procreative responsibilities. And the concept of gay identity placed in sharper relief alternative self-conceptions: heterosexuality or bisexuality, "straight" or "swinger." Thus gay liberation confirmed the growing significance of the erotic in modern life, even as it seemed to break with the assumptions of sexual liberalism. [. . .]

By 1973, almost eight hundred gay and lesbian organizations had formed; by the end of the decade their numbers reached into the thousands. Alongside the proliferating bars sprang churches, synagogues, health clinics, community centers, law offices, travel agencies, restaurants, and a host of other businesses and nonprofit services. Lesbians formed record companies to market the music they were creating; gay men formed choruses that sang in some of the most prominent performance halls in the country. In many large cities, gay men and lesbians supported their own newspapers. Gays formed Democratic and Republican clubs, and ran for office. In Massachusetts Elaine Noble was elected to the state assembly; in Minnesota, Karen Clark and Allen Spear had similar successes; and in San Francisco, Harvey Milk became the city's first openly gay supervisor. Various constituencies within the gay population – blacks, Hispanics, Asians, youth, elders – staffed their own organizations. Gay teachers, nurses, doctors, bankers, and others created caucuses within their professions. In less than a decade, American society had witnessed, in the words of one commentator, "an explosion of things gay."[5] What had been an underground sexual subculture increasingly came to resemble an urban community.

The gay movement also made some progress in chipping away at the institutional structures, public policies, and cultural attitudes that sustained a system of oppression. In the course of the 1970s, half the states eliminated the sodomy statute from the penal code. In 1974, the American Psychiatric Association removed homosexuality from its list of mental disorders, and the following year the US Civil Service Commission lifted its ban on the employment of gay men and lesbians. Several dozen cities, including populous ones such as Detroit, Boston, Los Angeles, San Francisco, Houston, and Washington, DC, incorporated sexual preference into their municipal civil rights laws. Gay activists lobbied in many legislatures for similar statewide protections, and in Congress the movement found sponsors for a federal civil rights law. Candidates for elective office sought the endorsement of gay organizations; the national Democratic party, at its 1980 convention, for the first time included a gay rights plank in its platform. A number of liberal Protestant denominations created task forces on homosexuality, initiating the revision of Christian teachings that had remained fixed since the thirteenth century. In most large cities, police harassment, though not eliminated, declined sharply, allowing many gay men and lesbians greater freedom from fear than they had ever enjoyed. Newspapers, magazines, book publishers, and television offered positive portrayals of gay life. Perhaps most importantly, countless numbers of lesbians and gay men were coming out to their families, friends, co-workers, and neighbors, defusing the fear that attached to popular conceptions of homosexuality, humanizing the stereotypical images that most Americans held, and making possible a permanent alteration of attitudes. Equality had not been achieved. Indeed, by the late 1970s a vocal, well-organized resistance to gay liberation had emerged, demonstrating how deeply rooted in American culture the fear of homosexuality was. But the gay movement had set in motion profound changes in America's sexual mores. [. . .]

Study Questions

1 According to the authors, what is the relationship between the emergence of gay liberation and the other social movements of the 1960s and early 1970s?

2 Explain some of the most important ways that the gay liberation movement challenged older ways of thinking about gender and sexuality.

3 What historical information do D'Emilio and Freedman provide that helps you better understand the memoirs of Damien Martin and Sylvia Rivera that follow their essay?

Notes

1 *Village Voice*, July 3, 1969, p. 18; John D'Emilio, *Sexual Politics, Sexual Communities: The Making of a Homosexual Minority in the United States, 1940–1970* (Chicago: University of Chicago Press, 1983), pp. 231–37.

2 The discussion of pre-Stonewall gay activism comes from D'Emilio, *Sexual Politics, Sexual Communities*.

3 *Ibid.*, p. 234.

4 Donn Teal, *The Gay Militants* (New York: Stein and Day, 1971), p. 61.

5 The phrase is used by Toby Marotta in *The Politics of Homosexuality* (Boston: Houghton Mifflin, 1981).

CHAPTER 32

The Fighting Irishman

A. Damien Martin

A. Damien Martin (1934–91) grew up in Philadelphia, one of seven children. A self-described "devout Catholic" in childhood, he spent some time on the streets and in Catholic foster care. Martin served six years in the Air Force, including the Korean War. After graduating from Northwestern University, he became a professor of speech pathology. Martin and his partner, Emery Hetrick, a psychiatrist, organized the Institute for the Protection of Gay and Lesbian Youth (now called the Hetrick–Martin Institute) in 1979. Martin was also a founder of the Harvey Milk High School, an alternative public high school in New York City created because antigay violence made it impossible for some gay and lesbian youth to remain in other schools. Until his death from complications of AIDS, he remained active with many gay rights organizations. In the following excerpt, Martin describes his evolution as a gay rights activist and public figure to journalist Eric Marcus, who published it in his book, Making History: The Struggle for Gay and Lesbian Rights, 1945–1990: An Oral History *(1992).*

G rowing up, I was a devout Catholic – in fact, I wanted to be a priest. But I was suffering tremendous turmoil because I was gay. How could I have these feelings and be Catholic? The fact that I was a real horny kid and was very sexually active just intensified the conflict. I was out there on the streets from the time I was twelve or thirteen years old. I would go out, commit the act, have terrible, terrible guilt, and go running to confession. I'd swear never to do it again, but five days later I would go running back to the streets. It was incredibly destructive for me.

That cycle ended at about age sixteen, when I finally stayed overnight with somebody. The next day was a Sunday, and I was going to go to mass. As I was laying there in bed with this man next to me, I started to think about what we had been taught in school concerning what that idiot Paul said about how if you pray long and hard enough you can get enough grace to resist any temptation. I thought to myself *I know I've been praying as hard as I can, but I'm not getting the grace to resist the temptation. If I'm already doomed to hell, why should I go through such agony with the church?* That broke my tie to the church. I stopped going to mass. I figured that since I was going to hell anyway, I would do whatever I wanted. So I got involved in some very self-destructive behavior, including drinking.

I was a street kid, basically, but I was one of those street kids who was able to maintain some sort of home base so he could stay in school. I had enough sense to know that the one hope for a kid like me was to get a high school education and further education after that. I was very lucky because a lot of nuns drummed that into me.

When I graduated from high school, I went into the air force for six years, became a navigator, and flew in Korea, the Far East, and here in this country. I was sexually active the whole time I was in the service, but I was careful. This was the McCarthy period, and if you even associated with someone gay or were seen going near a gay place, you could be kicked out.

One time they had a big lecture about security. They talked about homosexuality and security risks. I said to myself, *Suppose somebody came up to you and said, "Betray the secrets of your country, or I will reveal you to be a faggot."* I asked myself what I would do in this situation. The answer was that I'd go to the FBI. I remember thinking that it would be terribly embarrassing and I'd hate it, but I wouldn't do anything like betray the secrets of my country. Looking back, it's so stupid that you even had to ask yourself a question like that. But we all accepted it back then.

When I think of the orgies that used to go on at air force bases, it's a wonder more people weren't caught. There was always this underground. People knew; there were certain codes. I very seldom did anything on the base. Most of the time I would go away to areas where people weren't likely to know me. I also had certain rules, like I would never approach somebody I was interested in. I would wait until somebody I was interested in approached me, which didn't always work because everyone was afraid. You have to understand that I was in the middle of some of the worst antigay purges the air force has ever known. I remember in about 1952 at Biloxi, Mississippi, there was a purge where people were committing suicide. The air force finally had to stop because people were turning people in just to get revenge for one thing or another. It's a little hard to comprehend the mentality of that time.

From the air force I went to Northwestern University. I worked part time at the library, where I used to read the *Mattachine Review* and *ONE*. They were locked in the pornography department. You had to have a key to get in, but I had access to the key because I worked there. I would feel a sort of guilty thrill reading those magazines because people were saying positive things about being gay. I was a little surprised. I remember reading in *ONE* that we were perfectly normal. I said to myself, *That's stupid!*

I think I had difficulty handling material like that because it was threatening. So much of your person gets tied up in the act of hiding that any effort made by people not hiding is seen as a threat. Like so many gay men of my generation, I developed two lives. I had a sexual life, which occurred in the bars and so forth, and I had another life with my straight friends. The issue of sexuality never came up, except that I would tell fag jokes just like everybody else.

The first time I met gay people where sex wasn't the basis of the relationship was when I joined a group in New York in 1960 to stop drinking. I'd been drinking very,

very heavily since I was a teenager. This group was made up of about eighteen people – sixteen women and two men. All the women were lesbians. Through these women, many of whom are still friends, I started developing some interaction skills that were homosexually based, but not erotically based. I don't want to say these women were like mothers, but they were peers who were not peers, who sort of guided me. Meeting them was the important turning point for me.

At these meetings I was very open about being gay, but I was not at all involved in the gay movement during the 1960s. In fact, I was rather hostile to the few things I'd heard about. My feeling was, *Why cause trouble?*

The Stonewall riot in June 1969 provoked the same kind of feeling I'd had when I read the *Mattachine Review* and *ONE* in the library. I was thrilled, but a little fearful. I wasn't at the Stonewall that first night, but for some reason, on the second night, I had to go up Sixth Avenue in a cab. I passed right by where the old Women's House of Detention used to be, and there were these gay and lesbian people chanting. The police were out in force keeping the crowds back. I'll never forget the look on the cops' faces. They looked like someone who has just been bitten by a trusted pet, a look of astonishment and fear at the same time.

I finally got hooked into the movement around 1972. My ex-lover said, "You ought to go to Dignity." I said, "What's Dignity?" and he told me it was a group for gay Catholics. As far as I was concerned, the last thing in the world I needed was a bunch of Irish Catholics sitting around beating their breasts and saying, "Why did God make me like this?" So I said, "Forget it!" But he kept pushing, so I thought, *What the hell? I'll go. Maybe there'll be some cute Jesuits.* And there were!

I'll never forget walking into this room where they were having a business meeting. I was overwhelmed. It was the first time I had been in a room with a bunch of gay men where sex was not the issue. I immediately joined, but I kept saying, "I'm an atheist! It's just an ethnic identification, that's all."

Dignity was very good for me. For the first time I got involved in a gay rights activity, one in which people were really working together for a common goal. I ended up not agreeing with Dignity's goals. I was much more interested in political issues than in religion.

Something very important happened to me when I was a member of Dignity. It was right around the time of the vote on the New York City Gay Rights Bill in 1972. A majority of Dignity members decided they couldn't demonstrate in favor of the bill, but that they could pray for its passage. So they went to a Catholic church down near City Hall to pray. I got very snotty and said, "I don't believe in prayer, and I'm not going!" When they needed someone to bring some leaflets down to the church, though, I volunteered.

When I got to the church, everyone was praying outside on the steps, rather than inside. I just stood watching from across the street. One of the guys came over to get the flyers from me. He said that the pastor threw them out of the church and locked the doors when he found out what they were praying for, so they decided to have the vigil outside. He asked me to come over and I said that I couldn't. Thank God I had enough self-honesty to know that what was keeping me from going had nothing to do with the fact that I didn't believe in prayer. The truth was that I was scared to death to go across the street. I suddenly realized that although I thought I was out, it was absolutely not true. I was still just as afraid as that kid I was in high school.

I went home and got very depressed. I realized how afraid and closeted I still was even though I had been sneering at these people about their prayer vigil. As much as I pooh-poohed them, they were much braver than I was. I was a coward, and it was unjust to expect them to put their necks out for me. It was almost like I was committing a sin by not coming out. I felt very guilty, very depressed, and very ashamed.

To get out of the depression, I said to myself, *All right, the next time anybody asks me to participate in anything public, I'll do it!* Before long, I got a call from Ron Gold, from the National Gay Task Force [NGTF]. Ron told me that an antigay episode of "Marcus Welby, M.D." was about to air on television. He asked me to spread the word that at a specific time people should call the television station carrying the show to tie up the phones for two days.

I had no problem calling the station. They were clever there because they said, "All the lines are busy. Leave your name and number, and we'll call you back." I got this sharp pain in my stomach remembering what I'd said to myself about being public the next time I had the opportunity. I gave my name and address. "And besides," I said, "here's my office number." I worked at the Veterans Administration at the time. The station called me back later at the office, and I raised all kinds of hell on the phone and felt marvelous! Wonderful! I remember not caring if something bad happened. I was ready to bust a few noses!

When I met Emery Hetrick, I soon discovered we had different views about what it meant to be gay. We had met in 1974 at one of the meetings for people with alcohol problems. Very soon after we got involved – I think we had just had marvelous sex – I said, "Gee, isn't it great to be gay!" He started bouncing off the walls; he was enraged. "What do you mean? We're no different from anyone else! The only thing is we do something slightly different in bed! We're entirely like everyone else!" For once in my life, I didn't react with anger. I shrugged and said, "Well, you obviously need a consciousness-raising group if you think you're the same as everybody else." He didn't know what I was talking about, but when I explained to him what a consciousness-raising group was, he became intrigued. The next night he said, "Let's start one." So we did.

The CR group had a tremendous impact on Emery. He suddenly became aware of all the restrictions on his life and how different he really was. We formed other CR groups, stayed for about three weeks, left, and then let them start their own groups. We were like Johnny Appleseed. That first CR group was what really got Emery involved in gay rights. He had always been involved in social causes setting up organizations of one kind or another, so he was no novice. He looked like such a part of the Establishment that he could say the most radical things and people would think it was the Daughters of the American Revolution talking. That's how he got things done.

About this time, after we had started several of the CR groups, we became involved in the National Gay Task Force. This was one of the few organizations around for people like Emery and me to get involved in. We were not into the left-wing radical political thing, and NGTF sort of appealed to middle-class squares like us. And even then, we only participated in a fund-raising capacity at first.

The level of our involvement changed after we went to a Task Force meeting and met Barbara Gittings. Barbara came over to us and said, "I'm glad you belong to the Task Force. What do you do?" And Emery said, "I'm a psychiatrist." Womp! She zeroed in on him. Well, you know, Barbara was very instrumental in the whole battle with the American Psychiatric Association [APA] over the listing of homosexuality as a mental illness. At the point we met her, she wanted to get psychiatrists themselves more involved in it. Well, she started working on Emery – the charm and everything else came through.

At the 1978 APA convention down in Atlanta, Barbara was going to do a booth with the theme, "Gay Love: Good Medicine." She wanted to have pictures of psychiatrists with their lovers as part of the display. So she asked Emery and me for a photo. After a little hemming and hawing, Emery said yes. Then she said, "Why don't you come down and be at the booth?" After more hesitation he agreed.

The experience was great for Emery. He called me from Atlanta and said, "You have to come down here!" It was the only time in my life I ever lied by calling in sick to cancel a class. I flew down to Georgia and found Emery transformed. He was standing there by the booth grabbing psychiatrists he knew were homophobic and saying, "Hi! Let's go look at the exhibit." He confronted them not with the fact that they were homophobic but with the truth about himself: "I'm gay. I'm open. I'm a psychiatrist. I'm as good as you are." After that, he just took off with the movement. He started the gay psychiatrists group here in New York. He got very involved with the national gay psychiatric group. Then he got involved in starting SAGE, Senior Action in a Gay Environment, a support and social organization for older gays and lesbians. He paid SAGE's expenses for one year, which I didn't find out about until afterwards. There was a little heavy breathing over that one.

SAGE was well on its way when we went to a political meeting where we heard about a fifteen-year-old boy who had been gang-raped and beaten up at one of the city's youth shelters. This boy was the one who was thrown out because he was gay – as if it was his fault. I went into one of my typical Irish hysterical snits and got very angry. Emery, who was much calmer and more focused, said, "Let's see what we can do about this." After helping start several different organizations, it wasn't surprising that Emery's approach was to see how we could organize to address this issue.

This was around 1979. We got together a group of about forty people here at our apartment. Emery asked a lot of psychiatrists and social workers to come. Most of them agreed that there was a real need for an organization to address the problems of gay and lesbian youth. [. . .]

We realized from the beginning that to do this we had to have credentials. This need was met, in part, by our professional titles. Emery was a psychiatrist. I was an associate professor of speech pathology and audiology at New York University. We had another psychiatrist and someone who was about to become a social worker. And so on.

At one particularly big meeting we decided on a name, The Institute for the Protection of Lesbian and Gay Youth. This was actually an awful name, but we had reasons for it, one of which was Anita Bryant's antigay Save Our Children campaign. Our argument always was, "Ours are the ones who need protection!" We wanted the name to say up front who we were and what we were about.

People started to hear about us and, unfortunately, called up and said, "I have this gay kid, and I don't know what to do with him. Can you help me?" We quickly made the decision not to get involved in anything we weren't prepared to handle at that time. We simply were not prepared to get involved in offering direct services. Some people were very upset about this decision, and a few even stopped coming to meetings. They said, "You're not doing anything! You're just talking!" And in a way they were right.

But, of course, we didn't just talk during that first year. When we heard of specific instances where government agencies were not providing the services they were supposed to provide for our kids, we would go out and ask what happened. We learned a lot from these interventions. We began to find many individual professionals out there, primarily straight professionals, who wanted to work with gay and lesbian kids. They didn't want to discriminate against them, but they were working under impossible circumstances. First of all, they had had no training to deal with gay kids, so they didn't understand a lot of the issues involved. They had to deal with hostile administrators who were afraid they'd lose their funding by trying to help these kids. They were afraid of community reactions. And they had to deal with the straight kids in the agency, who would react in all sorts of ways to the gay kids.

Meeting these professionals changed our understanding of what the problem was and what we were going to do about it. We could no longer view ourselves as knights and amazons on white horses going out to conquer discrimination, violence, and oppression. So rather than just checking out instances of discrimination or exploitation, we moved into a kind of educational, case-management mode, where we would help various agencies solve specific problems.

I remember the first agency we met with. It was a settlement house in Brooklyn that dealt primarily with black kids. They had a boy there who was sort of swish. He dropped out of high school because he got beaten up all the time. The teachers were not protecting him. This settlement house called us and said, "You've got to come! He's disrupting the whole agency." So we went and we listened. Everybody liked the kid. The disruption was a result of a disagreement between the staff. One group of professionals wanted to get him to macho it up a bit – they wanted to teach him how to box and to walk differently. Another group wanted to let him do what he wanted to do, which was to run the fashion show for the settlement house.

I wish we could have said this for most of the agencies we went to, but we found no real homophobia among those people. They really wanted to help this kid, but they were fighting among themselves because they disagreed about how to handle him. So we spent five or six sessions with the staff discussing issues related to homosexuality. We happened to agree with the staff people who wanted to let him do the fashion show, but at the same time we didn't dismiss what the others were saying. We spent time explaining why the macho approach didn't quite work. I'm a firm believer in teaching gay kids self-defense, but self-defense wasn't going to make him macho.

During this whole period, Emery kept saying, "We're going to have to move into direct social services." And I said, "Oh no we're not! It's going to eat us alive. It's going to take all our time." We were both right.

What eventually convinced me that we needed to provide direct services was the fact that we were getting more and more calls for help. People would call and say they had a fifteen year old and they didn't know what to do with him. Others would call to complain about how a particular agency was handling gay kids. Most of the complaints related to a group called Gay and Young. Gay and Young was supposedly a gay youth group, but it was run by a guy who was more interested in the kids than he should have been. It was complicated because everyone in the community was afraid of a scandal involving kids. Joyce Hunter, who was a social work student at that time, brought this situation to our attention. We tried to make some government officials aware of the problem, but they didn't want to touch it with a ten-foot pole.

The vice squad got involved. They came up to see us here in this living room. You could tell the police were wondering, "Who are these people, and what are they doing?" But pretty soon they were very open with us. One of the policemen finally got sort of irritated and said, "We don't know what to do with these kids. Do you people expect us to come up with solutions? We have no solutions to this. We already know that what we do doesn't work. Why don't you do something?" [...]

The kids get to you in different ways, but I always remember this one kid who came in after we had been in existence for about a year. We were still in the one room, where we did everything from administrative work to the support groups. This young man was fourteen years old. He came from a Hispanic family. His father brought him in. The father had gone to court to try to get the kid placed somewhere, not because he wanted to get rid of his kid, but because the kid had been identified as gay in his neighborhood and was constantly getting beaten up. The father was heartsick and didn't know what to do. He was actually willing to give up his kid for the kid's safety.

Joyce was doing the interview and then she sent the father off to get some coffee. She was talking to the boy by himself. He was a shy kid, a tiny little thing. He suddenly said to Joyce, "Are you gay?" And she said, "Yes." He said, "Is everybody here gay?" She said, "Well, not everybody, but most of us." And then I walked by, and he said, "Is he gay?" She said, "Yes." And he said, "That old man?" Now that's not the reason I remember the kid – I remember him because of the heartbreaking circumstances.

There was another case involving a young girl that got to me. As far as we knew, she didn't think of herself as a lesbian – or she hadn't identified as a lesbian yet. But she had a crush on her gym teacher and had sent her a note. I don't know what the gym teacher's problem was, but she took the note to the principal, who called in the parents and said, "We can't keep a child like this here. She could corrupt all the others. If you can't find any other place for her, put her in a school for the learning disabled." That's how we got her because one of the counselors at the school knew about us and brought her over. This kid just didn't know what had happened; she had no idea what she had done wrong. She was just being a teenager. The parents were ashamed. It was one of these horrendous things that came from ignorance. It was one of the times when I could understand violent revolutionaries. I really wanted to go out and just punch that principal right in the mouth. I am very much an Establishment person, but there does come a point, by golly, when you just don't take it anymore.

It's ironic that I got involved in starting this agency because I don't particularly like kids. One of the reasons I'm glad I'm on the administrative end of it is because kids get on my nerves. I probably never would have been a good father. I don't like the noise. I find kids silly. But they have a right to be noisy. They have a right to be silly. They have a right to be teenagers. And that's one of the things that's been denied to our kids. They're denied the right to be teenagers, to be pains in the ass without being beaten up or thrown out of school or thrown into the street.

At the Institute we give them the opportunity to be teenagers – and that includes disciplining them. We're very strict about certain things. For many of the kids who come here, this is the first place where they feel they don't have to hide. They think all the rules go by the wayside, that they can do anything they want. Part of what our kids have to learn is that freedom in one area does not mean anarchy in another. In some ways, I suppose I'm very much a traditionalist, and certainly my Catholic background comes through in this work. I remember one of the things the nuns used to say, that I believe very firmly, "For every right there's a corresponding responsibility." I hope it's one of the things we teach the kids at the Institute.

I think that the Institute is probably one of the most – if not *the* most – radical things that the movement has done. We took what was the most defective political charge against us, the biggest hate campaign, that we are a danger to children and to families, and we've turned it around. We've said, "No, that's not true. What *you* people are doing is a danger to children, and to *our* children in particular." But we often make the point that it's a danger to straight kids, too. You don't teach straight kids to hate without damaging them. What the Institute says is that gay and lesbian people are nurturing people who are just as interested in caring for kids as straight people. [. . .]

Study Questions

1 What does Martin mean when he says that in his young adulthood he "developed two lives"?
2 What led to Martin's involvement with direct social services?
3 How did "consciousness raising" affect Martin's conception of what it means to be gay?
4 How does the "consciousness raising" that Martin experienced resemble, or differ from, the "consciousness raising" experienced by Sylvia Rivera?

CHAPTER 33

The Drag Queen

Rey "Sylvia Lee" Rivera

Born in the South Bronx, Rivera (1951–2002) identified as Puerto Rican, Venezuelan, and female. Raised by her grandmother from 1954, Rivera had a childhood that was characterized by conflict. A committed activist in the black liberation and peace movements of the 1960s, she participated in the 1969 Stonewall uprising (some credit her with leading the charge), which marked the beginning of a new generation of gay rights activism. Rivera cofounded Street Transvestite Action Revolutionaries (STAR), a group that took in homeless teenage cross-dressers. She joined the Gay Liberation Front, the Gay Activists Alliance, and the Young Lords, successfully lobbying for the gay rights bill in New York. When journalist Eric Marcus interviewed Rivera, she was living with her long-term partner and working at a halfway home for children. In the following account, Rivera names some of the turning points in her struggle toward self-acceptance. Rivera told her story to Eric Marcus, who published it in his book, Making History: The Struggle for Gay and Lesbian Rights, 1945–1990: An Oral History *(1992).*

I was born at two-thirty in the morning on July 2, 1951, in a taxi cab in the old Lincoln Hospital parking lot in the South Bronx. I came out feet first. This old queen couldn't wait. She says, "I'm ready to hit the streets!" My grandmother always used to joke about that. I says, "Yeah, you see why I'm always standing out on the street corner?"

I didn't choose to be effeminate. It wasn't something that you just decided to do. I really believe I was born to be an effeminate child. My grandmother used to come home and find me all dressed up. My grandmother raised me because my mother died when I was three years old. She'd whip my ass, of course, for dressing up. "We don't do this. You're one of the boys. I want you to be a mechanic." And I says, "No, I want to be a hairdresser. And I want to wear these clothes."

From day one I was like this. I remember sitting down with my grandmother sewing and knitting when I was seven years old. I said, "Would you teach me?" And she'd sit there and just say, "Okay, we'll do this." After I left home she couldn't understand why I came out this way. "But don't we remember sitting down and doing everything together?" We used to sew and cook. We used to wash clothes. And she'd say, "No, you're supposed to be one of the boys." And I'd say, "No, I'm one of the girls." She couldn't stand that.

I remember in 1961, on July 2, when I turned ten years old, I had such a bad feeling about everything that was going on in my life and what my grandmother was going through – she took shit because I was an effeminate boy – that I attempted to commit suicide. I almost killed myself. I took all her pills. After I started getting the effect, I went upstairs and told my aunt, who wasn't really my aunt, and she rushed me to Bellevue Hospital.

You feel so afraid. I thought there was nobody out there. As far as I was concerned, I was the only one that was different. I just felt that I was the only gay person, the only faggot in the world, the only person that felt the way that I felt, that was attracted to men. I couldn't discuss it with my grandmother, even though she knew where I was coming from. There was nobody to talk to. I couldn't deal with school. I was a great student as far as certain things were concerned, but *we* will *not* play football. And *we* will *not* go in the locker room. We won't!

School was hard: "You fuckin' fag." When I used to go to Coney Island with Granny, I remember that as soon as that subway train would stop on Forty-Second Street, the queens would get on. And everyone would say, "Look at the *maricónes*. Look at the *maricónes*." I'd sit there and I knew I was part of them. The other kids from the neighborhood would say, "Oh, look, Rey, isn't that funny?" And I would turn my head and look at the wall and think to myself, *Why do people have to do this?*

A few months after I tried to kill myself, I left home. I was grown by then. I thought I was grown. I knew I had to leave because of life, because of what my being gay was doing to my grandmother. She came home crying one day. She says, with tears in her eyes, "They're calling you *pato*." That means "faggot" in the Spanish language. It hurt her so bad because they were doing this to me. She knew where I was coming from. She knew. But it hurt her. I didn't want her to suffer. It wasn't my suffering. I was worrying about her suffering. That's why I left. I went to Times Square. I became a streetwalker. You stand out on the street and you make money. At that age it was easy to make money.

Every dirty old man that called himself straight picked me up. I remember playing psychiatrist to a lot of them. "If my wife knew that I was laying with a man...." Give me a break! I don't want to hear this. Are you paying me? Fine. Then I have to deal with it. This is when I was dressed as a boy. A year or two later I started living in drag. These people who picked me up were sick. They would say, "My wife would never appreciate the fact that I was laying with a man that dresses in women's clothes." And I said, "Just give me the money. Don't worry about it."

You can sell anything out on the streets. You can sell men, young boys, and young women. There's always a customer out there, and they are the ones that are sick. They are the ones that have the problem.

I remember going home and just scrubbing myself in a tub of hot water. "Oh, these people touched me. This sleaze." Even if they weren't old, I felt that way. They could have been young. When I was thirteen and fourteen years old, I remember sleeping with guys that were twenty and twenty-one. They were paying me. And they had their hang-ups. I'd screw them up the ass and whatnot. That's what I was getting paid for. But I'd go home and clean myself. I didn't understand then and I still don't really, why people have to go through all them problems.

I thought I had my head together because I could sit there and talk to somebody for a half an hour. If you paid me fifty dollars, oh, I'd tell you anything, honey. And if my alarm clock went off, give me some more money, or you've got to go out the door. I knew I was a whore. I was out to make money.

When I was growing up, if you walked down Forty-Second Street and even looked like a faggot, you were going to jail. I went to jail a lot of times. I remember the first time I got arrested. I was walking down the street with this other queen, and she said, "We got to move it! We got to move it!" I asked, "Why?" She says, "The *camarónes* are coming! They're coming to get us!" I'm like, "What the fuck are you talking about?" So she explained to me that *camarónes* was slang for plainclothes cops. With that, I'm like, "Okay, I'll walk, I'll walk!" We did triple steps.

The police didn't get us from behind, though, they got us from the front. [...]

I don't know how many times my grandmother had to come and bail me out of jail. She always came and got me. She would say, "That's my grandson. I have to take him out." She loved me very dearly.

Before gay rights, before the Stonewall riot, I was involved in the black liberation movement and the peace movement. I felt I had the time and I knew that I had to do something. Back then, my revolutionary blood was going. I did a lot of marches. I had to do something back then to show everyone that the world was changing.

I got involved with a lot of different things because I had so much anger about the world, the way it was, the way they were treating people. When the Stonewall happened, it was fabulous. Actually, it was the first time that I had been to the friggin' Stonewall. It was like a God-sent thing. I just happened to be there when it all jumped off.

The Stonewall wasn't a bar for drag queens. Everybody keeps saying it was. The drag-queen spot was a bar called the Washington Square Bar, at Third Street and Broadway. This is where I get into arguments with people. They say, "Oh, no, it was a drag-queen bar, it was a black bar." No, Washington Square Bar was the drag-queen bar.

If you were a drag queen, you could get into the Stonewall if they knew you. And only a certain number of drag queens were allowed into the Stonewall at that time. I wasn't in full drag that night anyway. I was dressed very pleasantly. When I dressed up, I always tried to pretend that I was a white woman. I always like to say that, but really I'm Puerto Rican and Venezuelan. That night I was wearing this fabulous woman's suit I had made at home. It was light beige – very summery. Bell bottoms were in style then. I had my hair out. Lots of makeup and lots of hair. I was wearing boots. I don't know why I was wearing boots.

We had just come back in from Washington, DC, my first lover and I. At that time we were passing bad paper around and making lots of money. And I said, "Let's go to the Stonewall." So I was drinking at the bar, and the police came in to get their payoff as usual. They were the same people who always used to come into the Washington Square Bar.

I don't know if it was the customers or if it was the police, but that night everything just clicked. Everybody was like, "Why the fuck are we doing all this for? Why should we be chastised? Why do we have to pay the Mafia all this kind of money to drink in a lousy fuckin' bar? And still be harassed by the police?" It didn't make any sense. The people at them bars, especially at the Stonewall, were involved in other movements. And everybody was like, "We got to do our thing. We're gonna go for it!"

When they ushered us out, they very nicely put us out the door. Then we were standing across the street in Sheridan Square Park. But why? Everybody's looking at each other. "Why do we have to keep on putting up with this?" Suddenly, the nickels, dimes, pennies, and quarters started flying. I threw quarters and pennies and whatnot. "You already got the payoff, and here's some more!"

To be there was so beautiful. It was so exciting. I said, "Well, great, now it's my time. I'm out there being a revolutionary for everybody else, and now it's time to do my thing for my own people." It was like, "Wow, we're doing it! We're doing it! We're fucking their nerves!" The police thought that they could come in and say, "Get out," and nothing was going to happen. They could padlock the door and they knew damn well like everybody else knew that as soon as the police were gone, the Mafia would be there cutting the door. They had a new cash register. They had more money and they had more booze. This is what we learned to live with at that time. Until that day.

So we're throwing the pennies, and everything is going off really fab. The cops locked themselves in the bar. It was getting vicious. Then someone set fire to the Stonewall. The cops, they just panicked. They had no backup. They didn't expect any of this retaliation. But they should have. People were very angry for so long. How long can you live in the closet like that? I listen to the stories of my brothers and sisters who are older than I am. I could never have survived the lives that my brothers and sisters from the 1940s and 1950s did. Because I have a mouth. I would never have made it. Somebody would have killed me.

That night I got knocked around a bit by a couple of plainclothes cops. I didn't really get hurt. I was very careful that night, thank God. But I saw other people being hurt by the police. There was one drag queen, I don't know what she said, but they just beat her into a bloody pulp. There were a couple of dykes they took out and threw in a car. The dykes got out the other side. It was inhumane, senseless bullshit. They called us animals. We were the lowest scum of the Earth at that time.

Even though I was at the Stonewall riot, I didn't join the movement per se until February 1970. I didn't feel like I wanted to be bothered with anything organized. Then I joined the Gay Activists Alliance, GAA. That first year after Stonewall, we were petitioning for a gay rights bill for New York City, and I got arrested for petitioning on Forty-Second Street. I was asking people to sign the petition. I was dressed casually – makeup, hair, and whatnot. The cops came up to me and said,

"You can't do this." I said, "My constitution says that I can do anything that I want." "No, you can't do this. Either you leave, or we're going to arrest you." I said, "Fine, arrest me." They very nicely picked me up and threw me in a police car and took me to jail.

When I got to the precinct, I called GAA to see if they could get me out of this bind. When I went in front of the judge, he looked at the two arresting officers and he's like, "Don't you realize what's going on?" I could see the look in his face. He said, "Number one, I'm letting him go." He says to the policemen, "Don't you realize what you just did? The whole country is in an uproar, and you're messing with a person who's circulating a petition?" They let me go home.

I testified for the gay rights bill at City Hall. It was hard to get up there to testify because the City Council tried to push the drag queens into the background. There was this councilman who said, "Why should I have my children being taught by them, men that dress in women's clothing?" I testified a couple of times. It was not a very agreeable experience. I am the straight person's stereotype of the gay community. They don't want their children to be exposed to someone like me. Even my own community, the gay community, doesn't want to be bothered with people like me. Nobody wanted us queens there.

When the bill was finally passed, in 1986, I was living up here, and this man came to me in a bar and kissed me. My straight friends were coming up to me and kissing me because we finally did it. That bill was mine. I worked very hard for it. The fucking community has no respect for the people that really did it, the drag queens. We did it for our own brothers and sisters. Don't keep shoving us in the fuckin' back and stabbing us in the back! You get beaten up by your own, and that hurts. We're just the low trash of life. I'm tired of being the bottom of the heap. I want to be the top of the heap.

I also went to protest demonstrations, like the one in the fall of 1970, when we did a sit-in at New York University. At that time I was sleeping in the park, in Sheridan Square. I had given up my job, given up everything, for gay liberation. Bob Kohler from the Gay Liberation Front (GLF) came and says to me, "Sylvia, come on, let's go, we're having a sit-in." New York University didn't want us to have a dance there. So, okay, we won't have any dances there, but we took over the basement of the building where we would have had the dance. It was a nice sit-in for three or four days. Here again, my brothers and sisters from the gay community were not very supportive of anything that went down. They just did not react properly.   [. . .]

Out of that NYU protest, STAR was born, the Street Transvestite Action Revolutionaries. We formed STAR because my brothers and sisters kept using us when they needed us, but they weren't treating us fairly. So we wanted to be by ourselves. Myself, Marsha Johnson, Bambi Lamour, Endora, Bebe, and a few others were involved in STAR. Marsha Johnson and I fought for the liberation of our people. We did a lot back then. We had a building on Second Street, which we called STAR House. When we asked the community to help us, there was nobody to help us. We were nothing. We were nothing! We were taking care of kids that were younger than us. Marsha and I were young, and we were taking care of them. And organizations like GAA had teachers and lawyers, and all we asked was for them to help us teach our own, so we could all become a little bit better. There was nobody there to help us. They left us hanging.

There was only one person that came and helped us: Bob Kohler. Bob helped paint and put wires together. We didn't know what the fuck we were doing, but we tried. We really did. Marsha and I and a few of the other older drag queens, we took this slum building and kept it going for about a year or two. We went out and made money off the streets to keep these kids off the streets. We already went through it. We wanted to protect them, to show them that there was a better life.

Our kids came from everywhere. We had kids from Boston, California. They were good kids. I've seen a couple of them since the movement. The ones that I've seen, they've done very well. It makes you feel good.

But we just didn't have the money. The community was not going to help us. The community is always embarrassed by the drag queens because straight society says, "A faggot always dresses in drag, or he's effeminate." But you've got to be who you are. Passing for straight is like a light-skinned black woman or man passing for white. I refuse to pass. I couldn't have passed, not in this lifetime.

Except for GLF, who made us the vanguard of the revolution, everyone else left us in the dark. They pushed us aside. Actually, it was not even the men that pushed aside the drag queens. It was the gay women from this radical group. One of them was Jean O'Leary. We hated each other from day one and always will. She has her own political view. I have my political view. But do not put me down. We were all put down as human beings for being gay, but she always put down the gay male and she always put down the drag queen because she hated men. And that's not right.

Basically, a lot of the women I knew in the movement appreciated the fact that I was bold. Women like Martha Shelley, from GLF. We got along very well. But Jean O'Leary was a bitch, a bitch in plain English. She was the one who had the hatred not just toward the drag queens but toward men in general. We did a lecture together one time at Queens College, me and Jean, and I was in full fuckin' drag sitting there looking fabulous. She got very nasty as I was speaking and jumped up and says, "You are a genital male." And I'm like, "Who the fuck asked you?" I says, "We're here telling college students where we come from, and this is your attitude?" Why was she putting me down? We were supposed to be a part of each other.

A lot of times I just sit here and I hurt. I hurt for the simple fact that the movement never recognized the drag queen until this year [1989], twenty years after Stonewall. It was always, "We must wear a suit and tie. We have to look part of their world. We can't be different." But the whole world is different from one another. It just so happened that for the first part of the movement, the drag queen was part of the vanguard of the revolution. We were the front liners. And we didn't take no shit from nobody back then.

I don't condemn the rest of the community for not being as bold as some of my sisters and some of my brothers. Because I do understand. You do have a family. You do have a job. And back then you did have to hide. But when you were obvious back then, the effeminate male or the butch woman, there was nothing to hold you back.

I like being myself. It's fun being Sylvia. It's fun playing the game. I've been up here in this town for a lot of years. I'm proud of what I am, and they respect me for that. We've done drag shows up here, and this whole community loves it. Curiosity will always kill the cat, so they always want to see something different. And when they see something different, they freak out.

The years that I've lived up here I feel that I've liberated a lot of people just by living here and by being myself, just by being a campy queen. Of course, when you go to a local bar, you get some strange looks, but eventually you become friends with everybody. I'm not saying that I haven't had people try to attack me, but when that happens, I have these other people who sit at the bar with me and they'll say, "You can't touch her. She is our friend. If you touch her, you've got to take on the whole bar." These are women that are jumping to back me up. "Oh, no, we do not touch her. You want to fight her, you're coming through us first."

You know, I'd still like to do a lot more for the movement, but the movement just doesn't want to deal with me.

The place where I work now, my boss knows where I'm coming from. I work with food and always wear a baseball cap because I have so much hair. I work at a home for children who come from problem homes. Actually, they're a terror.

Study Questions

1 How did Rivera's childhood experiences shape her adult identity and values?
2 What kind of resources could Rivera count on from her community and family?
3 Why was Rivera marginalized by the mainstream gay rights movement?
4 When did the "personal" come to feel "political" to Rivera? Discuss two moments from other readings when political organizing or activity happened around personal issues.

CHAPTER 34

From *Suburban Warriors:*
The Origins of the New American Right

Lisa McGirr

Lisa McGirr is an historian who specializes in twentieth-century social movements and political cultures, and has published on conservative politics and labor history in the US. Her 2001 book, Suburban Warriors: The Origins of the New American Right *is a study of the rise of the national conservative movement from its grassroots base in Orange County, California, during the 1960s and 1970s. Ch. 6, "New Social Issues and Resurgent Evangelicalism," from which the following excerpt is taken, discusses the role that Christian evangelicalism played in the consolidation of New Right conservatism, leading up to the election of President Ronald Reagan.*

New Social Issues and Resurgent Evangelicalism

By the late 1960s, the Right had made important political gains in both California and the nation. Ronald Reagan, an unabashed conservative ideologue, had won a resounding victory in his run for governor. Richard Nixon, a centrist Republican who courted the Republican Right, had become his party's presidential nominee and won the election through an embrace of a new middle-class conservatism, even while George Wallace, a law-and-order populist, had garnered 13.5 percent of the national vote on a third-party ticket. Building on new opportunities, the Right had refashioned itself, gaining new political respectability. As the late 1960s witnessed antiwar protests, a flourishing counterculture, and riots in the nation's inner cities, the conservative critique of liberalism resonated with an increasing number of Americans. [. . .]

As conservative elites moved closer to the halls of power, the grassroots activists invigorated their movement by increasingly focusing on single-issue campaigns. These new issues expressed some of the same general concerns over moral corruption and traditional values that previously had been subsumed under the rubric of anti-communism. But these concerns now took on new dimensions, in large part in reaction to changes in family life, sexual liberation, a growing youth culture, and liberal Supreme Court decisions that expanded the scope of personal freedoms. As a result, various forms of "domestic corruption" – obscenity, sex education, abortion, and, by the late 1970s, an ever more assertive gay liberation movement – became the new targets of attack. And the enemy responsible for such ills was no longer an international, public, and political opponent, but the secular humanists in one's own community. These new issues drew in activists from among discontented Democrats who had previously been part of the liberal coalition. [. . .]

The late 1960s and early 1970s witnessed the reorientation of the conservative move-ment away from its earlier focus on anti-communism. Seismic changes rocked the country; assertive liberalism, sexual liberation, the prominence of black and youth cultures, and changes in family life hit ever closer to home, promoting a cultural backlash. Even in the suburban enclaves of affluent Orange County, middle-class men and women could not shut out these changes; their children, influenced by the vibrant youth culture, literally brought them home. In the nearby seaside communities of Newport Beach and Laguna, a thriving hippie culture flourished. Orange County's burgeoning institutions of higher learning, including California State University, Full-erton, and the spanking new University of California, Irvine, became sites of protest, sprouting their own SDS [Students for a Democratic Society] chapters (as well as Young Americans for Freedom).[1] Even Disneyland, that sacred symbol of safety, certainty, and Americana, was, on August 6, 1970, taken over by an unruly group of about 300 yippies, who raised a Viet Cong flag on Tom Sawyer's Island.[2] Throughout the country, old certainties were giving way under pressure from newly assertive groups. As the women's and minority rights movements blossomed and gay liber-ationists became ever more assertive, religious and cultural conservatives became increasingly anxious. With the economic crisis of the 1970s, these concerns fused with a growing economic preservationism, the combination with which the Right would move into national political power in 1980.

This reaction to the social changes of the 1960s is vividly illustrated by the fantastic growth, in the late 1960s and 1970s, of born-again evangelical Christianity in Orange County and nationally.[3] [. . .]

In Orange County, these churches mushroomed with the in-migration of the 1950s and 1960s.[4] In a land where businessmen of all varieties made their starts and their fortunes, religious entrepreneurs had also come to build their kingdoms for God on earth. With rapid population growth, fueled by migrants from Bible Belt states, and the lack of an organic community in the newly built environment, they found plenty of recruits for God's army. Already during the early 1960s, the community provided by the conservative churches, the firm moorings they advocated, their simple doctrines of right living, and their apocalyptic messages had resonated among many Orange Countians and had established an institutional base for the county's conservative mobilization.[5] One religious conservative, Bee Gathright, argued that the "Christian movement" and the conservative movement "grew at the same time."[6] [. . .] But while the conservative religious influence was important earlier, it took on vastly new proportions in the late 1960s.[7] Fundamentalist and evangelical sects, associated in the public imagination with rural, poor, and backward folk of the Deep South, boomed in the new technocratic Sunbelt suburbs in regions like Cobb County, Georgia; Orange County; and Dallas, Texas.[8] These religious conservatives, in contrast to popular perceptions, were prosperous suburban middle-class men and women, both young and old.

The burgeoning counterculture of the late 1960s pointed to deep dissatisfaction among the nation's youth with the empty materialism, affluence, and pragmatic middle-class lifestyle of their parents. The growth of evangelical Christianity – which, at its heart, also represented a rejection of liberal secular pragmatism – suggested that these currents of discontent could be channeled in many directions, by very different social groups.[9] A search for authenticity and for meaning, along with dissatisfaction with the emptiness of modern consumer society no doubt contributed to the evangelical revival, just as it had to the counterculture.[10] But also at the heart of this movement's growth was an effort by middle-class men and women to assert their sense of a properly ordered world – one they felt was threatened by sexual liberation, the women's movement, the burgeoning Left, and the youth culture movements – by championing family values, authority, and tradition backed by the authority of the "word of God."[11] [. . .]

What were the implications of the growth of conservative religious Christianity for the national political Right? Mark Hertel, the manager of Maranatha Village in Costa Mesa, made clear the profoundly political, as well as social, meaning of these beliefs in 1978, when he said:

> . . . This country is in serious trouble right now. . . . I can't see God left with any other choice than to bring judgment on the United States. . . . The only thing holding back God's hand right now is the body of believers in this country. . . . United, we could have a tremendous effect on this government . . . we could fill Congress with Christians. We could pass legislation that would get the smut out of every store you walk into, that would clean up dope.[12]

And organize they did, joining the Religious Right's political crusade for a more "Godly nation."[13] The opening salvo was fired against the growing gay rights movement. Rather than seeing homosexuality as an alternative lifestyle, born-again Christians saw it as a challenge to biblical precepts of right and wrong, a threat to the traditional family, and one more sign of the moral corruption of American society. Following on the heels of Anita Bryant's successful 1977 campaign to overturn Miami–Dade County's inclusion of gays in the local antidiscrimination laws, John Briggs, the state senator from Orange County and a self-proclaimed born-again Christian, placed on his state's 1978 ballot a referendum that would have allowed public school boards to ban teachers "who publicly admit being homosexual or who promote homosexuality as a life-style."[14] He became the first politician to tap the region's growing evangelical movement, claiming the support of about 500, mostly fundamentalist, churches.[15] Hymn-singing rallies in the southland in support of the amendment, according to the *Los Angeles Times*, "resembled revival meetings more than political assemblies."[16] Symbolizing the national networks of the newly politicized evangelicals, the Reverend Jerry Falwell, of the 16,000-strong Thomas Road Baptist Church in Virginia, attended a rally held at the San Diego Convention Center in favor of the measure, thundering that Proposition 6 was needed to save California's children "from homosexuals." Falwell urged born-again Christians to political involvement. "The government calls this political," he railed "we call it moral."[17] [...]

Out of the evangelical churches' deepening concerns over new social issues came an ever more organized voice in politics. The southland was the site of the first national Christian Right organization, the Christian Voice.[18] It circulated Christian morality scorecards on the voting records of legislators and actively raised funds and advertised for Ronald Reagan's presidential campaign.[19] By 1981, the organization boasted 200,000 members, tens of thousands of them ministers, and it remained a "major Christian Right electoral vehicle" in the 1980s.[20] In Orange County, Jim Willems, owner of Maranatha Village, moreover, established a newspaper, *Contemporary Christian Acts*, a publication for and about the fundamentalist community that offered its followers advice on "the caliber of men Christians should vote for."[21]

These newly politicized Christian voters helped elect Ronald Reagan in 1980. In Orange County, the votes they cast, along with those of conservatives of other stripes, brought Reagan 68 percent of the county's vote, nearly three times as many as Jimmy Carter received. In no other large county in the nation was Reagan's victory as overwhelming.[22] But while Orange County's vote, just like that fourteen years earlier, made it the heart of "Reagan Country," Reagan appealed broadly across the nation. The conservative stalwart, who had gotten his political start in the southland's conservative movement, had not only made it onto the national stage, but American voters, hearing his message of freedom from government, firm nationalism, and the support of "traditional values," had also chosen, in a landslide vote, to make him their national leader.[23]

With Reagan's election came a new seat at the table of national power not only for conservative economic elites who had established a growing number of think tanks in the 1970s to assert their cause, but also for the mass of religious Christians who had provided the social base for the movement and who now descended on Washington, lobbying to make their voices heard.[24] Conservatism, refashioned and newly respectable, had emerged from its days of communist-hunting fervency and arrived in the halls of power. The sense of elation and triumph conservatives felt in their victory was expressed by Reagan himself, in the wake of his inauguration: "Fellow citizens, fellow conservatives . . . our time has come . . . our moment has arrived."[25]

This moment had been more than twenty years in the making. The seeds of Reagan's victory were planted with the organizational networks, ideas, and strategies of the conservative movement of the 1960s. That movement, which first mobilized middle-class men and women to action against the communist menace, had reconstructed itself, earning a new political respectability. The Right had not strayed from its long-standing core concerns over "social planners" and government waste, but with new opportunities, it had abandoned the conspiratorial, apocalyptic language in which these concerns had been couched earlier. While "moral" issues had long been part of a broader conservative package, these concerns gained a new prominence. At the same time, anticommunism receded to the background, no longer providing the glue uniting economic and religious conservatives. Gone were the educational meetings and "Freedom" study groups, and in their place stood Bible study groups, evangelical tent meetings, pro-life and "pro-family" organizations, along with a more organized and separate libertarian movement, symbolized best by the Libertarian Party.

The reworked conservative package, voiced ever more in the language of the "people," resonated with growing numbers of Americans, bringing conservatives to a position of power that they had previously enjoyed only prior to the New Deal. With their new power, conservatives began to dismantle what they had long perceived as the nightmarish collectivism of the "New Deal order." In so doing, they hoped to bring late twentieth-century Americans into a world with parallels to an earlier time in American life, when government responsibilities in the lives of citizens were minimal and a staunch moral Protestantism reigned supreme. Yet [. . .] conservatives were not seeking a wholesale return to a rural life of simpler times. They reveled in the world of consumer culture, and were part of the bureaucratized, skilled, and technological modern America. They found the principles of an earlier time, a staunch laissez-faire capitalism often linked with a belief in absolute moral values, relevant to their very modern lives and communities. The economic and social settings that have fostered thriving conservative cultures, like that in Orange County, suggest not only that "it is possible to live in the modern world and enjoy its largess without absorbing modern values" but also, and even more, that modernity itself may foster values often considered incompatible with it: a militant religiosity, an unbending belief in the fundamental truth of the "rock of ages," and a strident laissez-faire individualism.[26] If this is the case, then we can expect the Right to have a vibrant place in American life in the years to come.

Study Questions

1   According to McGirr, what was the conservative critique of liberalism? What were conservatives' specific concerns? Were any of their concerns similar to those of liberals? Which ones?

2   What was the "social location" of members of the Christian Right and how did their social location help to shape their politics?

3   How does conservative activism compare to the activism of the liberal social movements you have read about?

4   Create a dialogue about gay rights between Rey "Sylvia Lee" Rivera or Damien Martin and one of the religious conservatives that McGirr quotes in this chapter.

Notes

1. *Register*, 8 August 1970, 6 June 1970.
2. *Los Angeles Times*, 6 August 1970.
3. Jeffrey K. Hadden, "Religious Broadcasting and the Mobilization of the New Christian Right," in *Fundamentalism and Evangelicalism*, ed. Martin E. Marty (Munich: K. G. Saur, 1993), 295; James Davison Hunter, *American Evangelicalism: Conservative Religion and the Quandary of Modernity* (New Brunswick, NJ: Rutgers University Press, 1983); Steve Bruce, *The Rise and Fall of the New Christian Right: Conservative Protestant Politics in America, 1978–1988* (Oxford: Clarendon Press, 1988); Bruce B. Lawrence, *Defenders of God: The Fundamentalist Revolt Against the Modern Age* (San Francisco: Harper and Row, 1989).
4. See Lisa McGirr, *Suburban Warriors: The Origins of the New American Right* (Princeton, NJ: Princeton University Press, 2001), chapter 1.
5. See McGirr, *Suburban Warriors*, chapter 2.
6. Gathright, interview.
7. By 1975, according to a survey conducted by the Orange County Human Relations Commission, 17 percent of Orange County churches belonged to the theologically and socially conservative National Association of Evangelicals.
8. "Megachurches," huge congregations sharing a conservative theology, have mushroomed in these suburban regions. See *New York Times*, 16 April 1995.
9. E. J. Dionne, Jr., *Why Americans Hate Politics: The Impact of Race, Rights, and Taxes on American Politics* (New York: Simon and Schuster, 1991), 219–21.
10. Donald Miller, who has closely examined the draw of what he terms "new paradigm churches," offers support for this argument. He contends that they are successful in part because of their emphasis on emotional expressiveness, authenticity, and immediacy, as well as picking up on the anti-establishment themes of the counterculture. See Donald E. Miller, *Reinventing American Protestantism: Christianity in the New Millennium* (Berkeley: University of California Press, 1997), 1–20.
11. Leonard I. Sweet, "The 1960s: The Crisis of Liberal Christianity and the Public Emergence of Evangelicalism," in *Evangelicalism and Modern America*, ed. George Marsden (Grand Rapids, Mich.: William B. Eerdmans, 1984), 29–45.
12. Hertel was converted to fundamentalist Christianity by a fellow officer while serving in the Marine Corps; Michael Smith, "Apocalypse Now," *New West*, 12 March 1979, Sc-2–Sc-3.
13. Michael Lienesch, "Right-Wing Religion: Christian Conservatism as a Political Movement," *Political Science Quarterly*, 97 (fall 1982): 403–406; James L. Guth, "The New Christian Right," *The New Christian Right: Mobilization and Legitimization*, ed. Robert C. Liebman and Robert Wuthnow (Hawthorne, N.Y.: Aldine, 1983), 31–45; Perry Deane Young, *God's Bullies: Native Reflections on Preachers and Politics* (New York: Holt, Rinehart and Winston, 1982); Robert Zwier, *Born Again Politics: The New Christian Right in America* (Downers Grove, Ill.: InterVarsity Press, 1982).
14. *Los Angeles Times*, 6 October 1978, 1.
15. *Christianity Today*, 1 December 1978, 40; *Los Angeles Times*, 2 March 1979.
16. *Los Angeles Times*, 31 October 1978.
17. Ibid.
18. Young, *God's Bullies*.
19. James Davison Hunter, "In the Wings," *American Evangelicalism: Conservative Religion and the Quandary of Modernity* (Newark: Rutgers University Press, 1983), 124–125; Young, *God's Bullies*, 101–106.
20. Sara Diamond, *Roads to Dominion: Right-Wing Movements and Political Power in the United States* (New York: Guilford Press, 1994), 171.
21. Smith, "Apocalypse Now."

22. California Secretary of State, *Statement of Vote*, General Election, 4 November 1980. "Large" is defined here as a county of more than 250,000 residents. Many small counties surpassed Orange County.

23. In the general election in November, Reagan won handily, with 51 percent of the popular vote to Carter's 41 percent. The Republican landslide also gave that party control of the Senate for the first time since 1954.

24. On the strengthening of older think tanks and the establishment of new ones, see Diamond, *Roads to Dominion*, 199–205. See also Sanford M. Jacoby, *Modern Manors: Welfare Capitalism since the New Deal* (Princeton, N.J.: Princeton University Press, 1997). On the Christian Right's focus on Washington lobbying and its relationship to the Reagan administration, see Diamond, *Roads to Dominion*, 234–36.

25. *Conservative Digest*, 26 April 1981, quoted in Jerome Himmelstein, *To the Right. The Transformation of American Conservatism* (Berkeley: *University of California Press, 1989*).

26. Alan Brinkley has made this argument, but I would take it one step further and argue that there is a causal link between modern cultures and staunch fundamentalist morality. Brinkley, "The Problem of American Conservatism," *American Historical Review* 99 (April 1994): 427.

PART IV

A Postindustrial and Global Society, 1975–2000

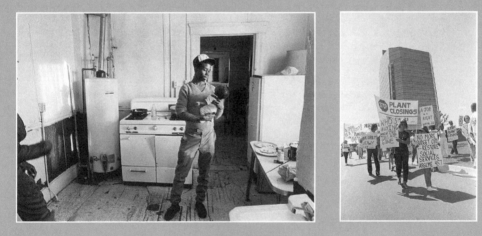

I n 2000, the population of the United States was approximately 281,000,000. During the last quarter of the twentieth century, the country experienced enormous upheavals in its economic, social, and cultural spheres, as an increasingly global and service economy, new technologies such as the personal computer and the internet, massive legal and illegal immigration from Latin America and Asia, and a growing number of interracial marriages began to change the "complexion" of the nation. Scholars and journalists increasingly began to describe the US as a "borderlands" society because of the ways in which it was cross-pollinated by cultural influences and economic markets from all over the globe, which influenced the growth of everything from the "postmodern" family to rap music.

The period from 1974 to 1993 saw a "U-turn" in the distribution of wealth in the US upward, which primarily benefited the wealthiest Americans, as well as an increasing population shift from the North and Midwest to the South and West. President Ronald Reagan's tax cuts and deregulation of the economy (1980–88) were accompanied by deindustrialization (increased automation and the movement of many American factory jobs to Third World countries where labor was cheaper). In a backlash against abortion, affirmative action, and the anti-Vietnam war movement, many Americans supported a conservative coalition that became a powerful presence in American politics until the end of the century, including the years of President William Clinton's presidency (1992–2000).

During this same time period, however, Americans continued to work on issues of social and economic inequality and injustice, organizing to stop the escalation of nuclear weapons within the US and abroad, providing sanctuary for illegal immigrants who were fleeing brutal dictatorships, holding concerts to help the thousands of Americans in danger of losing their farms, organizing shelters for the homeless and for battered women, and calling national attention to the growing AIDS crisis. During the 1980s, students on several college campuses successfully convinced their universities to divest their stock in South Africa as a protest against its apartheid policies. During the 1990s, students fought to ensure that university labels did not appear on apparel made in sweatshops at home or abroad.

As you read the articles, stories, and songs in this section of the textbook, you might want to think about the ways in which work, family, and community values and practices changed (or remained the same) between World War II and the end of the twentieth century. Did it mean the same to be an American in 2000 as it did in 1940?

CHAPTER 35

From *The Great U-Turn:*
Corporate Restructuring and the Polarizing of America

Bennett Harrison and Barry Bluestone

Bennett Harrison (1942–99) and Barry Bluestone (1944–) are political economists whose work focuses on economic disparities in the US. Harrison was the son of a salesman and a teacher, and taught economics, politics, and urban policy at a number of universities. Bluestone grew up in Detroit, where his father worked in leadership positions with the United Auto Workers. He has taught political economy and consulted with trade unions and state and city governments. Harrison and Bluestone coauthored The Deindustrialization of America: Plant Closings, Community Abandonment, and the Dismantling of Basic Industry *(1982), and* Growing Prosperity: The Battle for Growth with Equality in the Twenty-First Century *(2000). The following excerpt is taken from their book,* The Great U-Turn: Corporate Restructuring and the Polarizing of America *(1988).*

The standard of living of American workers – and a growing number of their families – is in serious trouble. For every affluent "yuppie" in an expensive big-city condominium, working as a white-collar professional for a high-flying high-technology concern or a multibillion dollar insurance company, there are many more people whose wages have been falling and whose families are finding it more and more difficult to make ends meet:

For more than a decade, the United States has been evolving as an increasingly unequal society. This development has been hidden by the ability of consumers, government, and business to maintain their accustomed spending by accumulating more and more debt. Now, on the eve of the 1990s, the underlying weaknesses of the economy are finally becoming apparent, while the assurance of a new era of stable economic growth and vitality is being challenged by debt and global competition. The time has come for a serious reappraisal of just how poorly the economy has performed under the conservative business and government policies of the last decade, and how the prospects for average American workers and their families have actually worsened.

The story is one of a series of changes in direction – reversals in course, great U-turns if you will – in the strategic policies of both business and the government, and as a consequence, a great U-turn in our material well-being. Between the end of World War II and a watershed that dates to a time between the late 1960s and the mid-1970s, the standard of living of the average American worker rose steadily. Adjusted for inflation, average family incomes were on the rise. Hourly, weekly, and annual wages and salaries were trending upward. The share of the work force whose wages were at or below the poverty level fell sharply. The numbers earning high wages rose rapidly. More and more workers could count on such basic benefits as unemployment and health insurance, paid vacations, and sick leave. This was especially true in the goods-producing industries, but even in the burgeoning service sector, the trend was toward a higher standard of living. [...]

Not only was the pie growing, but especially during the 1960s, the shares were becoming more equally distributed among working people and their families. At the same time, greater income equality itself contributed to the more rapid economic growth out of which public expenditures (and even further redistribution, for example, through the War on Poverty) could be financed. Most important of all, more and more parents could realistically expect that their children would eventually be better off financially and less insecure than they had been. That belief in the future in turn brought about a greater commitment to work, saving, and investment in the present.[1]

After about 1973, the direction changed. Wages, adjusted for inflation, began a long downward trend [...]. Median annual family income stopped growing, even though more family members were working than ever before [...].[2] And, by the latter half of the decade, even the most stable "core" workers in the economy – the roughly three-fifths of the labor force working year round and full time (YRFT) – were becoming more and more likely to earn low wages. [...]

What caused this dramatic reversal in the fortunes and expectations of American workers and their families – this great U-turn in the structure of economic opportunity in the United States?

The explanation lies not in bad luck or in something out of our control. It cannot be blamed on the Japanese or the Europeans, or on unions, or on the "social welfare state." The real explanation, we believe, lies in a more fundamental set of dramatic shifts in direction, taken first by the leaders of American business in the early 1970s and then ratified by policies of the government, beginning in the latter half of that decade, even before the election of Ronald Reagan. What ultimately motivated these shifts, which add up to an across-the-board U-turn in managerial, economic, and social policy, was what happened to corporate profits – private enterprise's bottom line. While wages and family incomes continued to grow for another eight years after the midpoint of the decade of the '60s, corporate profits did not.

The Profit Squeeze

Whether measured as business owners' share of the total national income or by the conventional rate of return on investment, profits peaked in the mid-1960s and continued to fall or stagnate for the next fifteen years. From a peak of nearly 10 percent in 1965, the average net after tax profit rate of domestic nonfinancial corporations plunged to less than 6 percent during the second half of the 1970s – a decline of more than a third [. . .].

What caused the profit squeeze was mainly the sudden emergence of heightened international economic competition – a competition to which US business leaders were initially blind. [. . .]

For the first time in modern economic history, all of the major industrialized countries (as well as the NICs [newly industrialized countries]) were producing very much the same collection of products and were engaged in "intraindustry trade" – the trading back and forth of essentially the same products. The United States now both buys steel from *and* sells it to the United Kingdom, while Mexico both imports and exports auto parts. Along with the two-way movement of commodities came two-way investment in factories and equipment, and the composition of both inward and outward foreign direct investments became increasingly similar.[3] The United States once built auto plants in Germany, France, England, and Mexico; now the Koreans and Japanese build them here. This complementarity led to the emergence on a global scale of chronic excess capacity in one mass-production industry after another.[4] With every country attempting to supply its neighbors with computers, let alone shoes, each country found its corporations operating their own plants at well below full capacity.[5] This necessarily eroded productivity and raised the unit cost of production. Nowhere was this more true than in the United States. And to make matters worse, while foreign competition raised unit costs, it simultaneously made it more difficult for firms in any one country to pass these higher costs onto their own citizens in the form of inflated prices. As a result, profits were squeezed – on the one side by rising costs; on the other by constrained prices. [. . .]

The Response of Business to the Crisis

And what were the new strategies? How did American business respond to these new competitive pressures? [. . .]

Specifically, the vast majority of American businesses have undertaken a series of experiments in what can best be described as *corporate restructuring*. [. . .]

Consider the restructuring of the organization of work and of the deployment of finances. Managers have increasingly reallocated the capital at their disposal, directing it into different industries, different regions of the country, and different nations. In doing so, corporate leaders have introduced new technologies – especially in transportation and communications – to facilitate the coordination and control of the far-flung activities of their home offices.[6] At the same time, corporations began a dramatic restructuring of their internal hierarchies. They moved toward "vertical disintegration" of their large, highly centralized industrial organizations, with their characteristic "internal labor markets." In doing so, they removed many of the career ladders that had provided well-defined paths of upward mobility for a significant fraction of the work force.

While such changes in work organization may provide "flexibility" for management, they tend to bring with them increased instability and insecurity for employees. In the course of this restructuring, managers have pared employment and increased their use of "contingent" labor, leasing more of their employees from agencies that supply temporary employees and putting more of their own workers on part-time schedules – increasingly, against their wishes. Much more blatantly, more and more managers have simply "frozen" wages, imposed outright reductions in pay, or unilaterally introduced two-tiered pay systems to reduce the cost of labor by paying different wages for essentially the same work. With the threat of layoffs and plant closings all around them, labor unions found it difficult, if not impossible, to contest these actions. Lee Iacocco's famous remark during the Chrysler crisis – "It's freeze time, boys. I've got plenty of jobs at seventeen dollars an hour; I don't have any at twenty" – haunted labor in virtually every industry.[7]

In the financial sphere, investors – especially those responsible for managing pension funds and other large pools of finance capital – accelerated the shift from productive investment to investment, often overtly speculative, primarily for short-term financial gain, while free-wheeling and well-heeled "entrepreneurs" pursued "hostile takeovers" and "forced mergers." In the colorful language of British political economist Susan Strange, language later popularized by *Business Week*, America became a "casino society."[8] One indicator of this trend – the volume of futures trading in stocks and bonds – rose ninefold between 1973 and 1985 in contrast to only a threefold increase in the nation's total output.[9]

Government to the Rescue

For a short period between the mid-1970s and the early 1980s, there was intense debate about whether the government should play a more constructive role in mediating the relationship between business and labor. Various corporate, labor, and academic circles called for the federal government to adopt a domestic industrial policy and intervene more actively in foreign trade. Guaranteed federal loans that saved both Lockheed and Chrysler from bankruptcy were the two best-known instances of an industrial policy in actual practice.

But beginning in 1978, and increasingly after the election of President Ronald Reagan, the administration and the Congress intervened in a very different way. Washington began to adopt policies that effectively forced workers to accept wage concessions, discredited the trade-union movement, and reduced the cost to business of complying with government regulations. Social programs were either restricted to their present levels or, like publicly assisted housing, actually cut back. A restrictive monetary regime introduced in 1979 by Paul Volcker, chair of the Federal Reserve Board, was indeed successful in curtailing inflation, but only by creating the worst recession since the 1930s. With more than one out of ten Americans unemployed by 1982, the government supported management's demand for a docile work force that would swallow wage concessions without a major fight.

The deep recessions of 1980 and 1981–82 were, by their nature, two-edged swords for the corporate sector. The drastic drop in consumer demand obviously cut into short-term profits. But at the same time, the recessions established the foundation for greater long-term returns by undercutting organized labor and by forcing workers to choose between a modicum of job security and higher wages. In the end, the recessions contributed handsomely to the corporations' bottom line.

The federal government's curtailment of its regulation of business also promoted corporate restructuring. Responding to deregulation, leaders in the airlines, trucking, and telecommunications industries were forced to devise strategies for responding to more intense competition. Virtually all of them turned to their work forces to bail them out. Management demanded wholesale wage concessions from their employees and increased pressure on the job to squeeze out more productivity from them. In some industries, especially the airlines, the quality of the deregulated service seems to have deteriorated, often dangerously, in the face of heightened competition.[10] At the same time, government entered into more contracts with ununionized outside companies – so-called "privatization" – eroding civil-service wage standards. The growing inclination of the government to sell off what had previously been publicly owned and operated services (Conrail, for example) had the same effect.

For the first time since the 1920s, direct attacks on labor emanated from the White House. The assault began with the disbanding of the air traffic controllers' union and the appointment of conservative members to the National Labor Relations Board (NLRB). These highly publicized acts of the president contributed to shifting the balance of power between labor and management toward business, implicitly legitimating "union avoidance" as a socially acceptable posture for even the most "liberal" of managements.[11] Unions were deliberately made the scapegoat of an economy that increasingly seemed unable to perform acceptably at home or abroad.

Lurking not far below the surface of all of these particular policies was the growing dominance of a conservative ideology that pinned the blame for the profit squeeze on "big government" itself. It followed that the most appropriate public policy for the 1980s was, to quote Reagan's campaign rhetoric, to "get the government off the backs of the people." Translated into budgetary terms, this meant cuts in social legislation, but not in the size or influence of government per se. In fact, after eight years of "Reaganomics," the public sector's influence on the economy on the eve of the 1990s is greater than ever, as evidenced by the explosive growth of military spending and the stubbornly mushrooming budget deficit. The federal government takes a larger share of the gross national product (GNP) today than when Reagan took office in 1981. Nevertheless, even middle-of-the-road Democrats and Republicans have accepted the new conventional wisdom that government spending, regulation, and redistribution of income are somehow "bad for business."[12] What could not be sold at any price to the voters by presidential candidate Barry Goldwater in the go-go days of 1964 became the coin of the realm a mere twenty years later.

These public policies of government-induced deflation, deregulation, regressive tax reform, privatization, and out-right union-bashing have contributed directly to corporate strategies that single-mindedly concentrate on cost containment, especially the cost of labor, as the principal basis for meeting the global economic challenge. They have created a new civil war among firms and among regions of the country competing for job-creating investments, and they have pitted worker against worker. This, we believe, is what is mainly responsible for reducing both the standard of living and the economic security of the average family. It is the main reason for the great U-turn in the distribution of income since the 1970s – what Lester Thurow has aptly called the "surge in inequality"[13] – and what we see as the growing polarization of our society. [...]

Reversing the Great U-Turn

Given the increasingly competitive – and, as we shall see, fragile – international environment, and in light of such domestic constraints as the daunting federal debt, is there room for a progressive restructuring of the economy, aimed toward achieving stable economic growth, more equitably shared? We believe there is.

Essentially, the nation must move forward in at least seven areas: (1) industrial (and related educational) policy; (2) democracy in the workplace; (3) renewed public support for the right of unorganized workers to be represented by unions of their choosing; (4) managed international trade; (5) the reconstruction of the nation's physical infrastructure; (6) reregulation of specific private market activities, especially in the runaway financial sector; and (7) public fulfillment of the promise of universal social benefits, including health insurance, child care, and care of the aging. It is at least possible to imagine political and economic conditions under which a combination of programs in these areas might reverse the calamitous U-turn that America has taken since the 1970s. [...]

Study Questions

1   According to Harrison and Bluestone, what were the most important economic factors that affected American families in the period from the end of World War II up to the early 1970s?
2   What was "The Great U-Turn"? What role did the government play in it? How did American families' economic circumstances change as a result of it?
3   What impact did "corporate restructuring" have on employment patterns?

Notes

1. We know all too well that these gains were never equally shared. Men of color and women of all races were systematically crowded into the least attractive jobs. They faced the greatest difficulties in obtaining government services to which they were entitled by law. And, too often, they were excluded altogether from the "social contract" between business and labor that implicitly governed a growing proportion of American workplaces in the prosperous years after World War II. Nevertheless, the promise was there, the basic economic possibilities for more widespread participation were present, and in fact, as we shall demonstrate, the economic conditions of the "minorities" improved greatly during the last years of the great postwar expansion, and continued to do so through most of the 1970s.

2. Family income would have plummeted even further had it not been for the growth of two-earner couples. By 1984, 70 percent of all employed husband-wife households had both spouses holding down jobs outside the home. See Lester C. Thurow, "Middle Class Lifestyles," *Boston Globe*, 26 August 1986, 44.

3. John F. Dunning, *International Production and the Multinational Enterprise* (London: Allen and Unwin, 1981).

4. On global excess capacity as a contributor to the profit squeeze, see Philip Armstrong, Andrew Glyn, and John Harrison, *Capitalism Since World War II* (London: Fontana, 1984), esp. chap. 11.

5. This does not mean, of course, that there is literally too much productive capacity in the world. Obviously even more capacity is needed in a world where so many still go ill, hungry, and homeless. The point is that, given the uses to which profit-seeking private business is prepared to direct its investments, by the 1970s there were more suppliers of those "profitable" goods and services than there were paying customers.

6. A dramatic example comes from the motion picture industry. It used to take Paramount Pictures up to 36 hours to distribute film clips ("coming attractions") and print advertisements from offices in New York and Los Angeles to field agencies in thirty-two American cities. The parent conglomerate, Gulf and Western, now uses satellites to transmit the same information from a microwave relay mounted on the roof of its headquarters building in New York City. It takes roughly 30 minutes to get the job done – 1 percent of the original time! Gulf and Western, *1981 Corporate Report* (New York) 34.

7. Quoted in Robert B. Reich and John D. Donahue, *New Deals: The Chrysler Revival and the American System* (New York: Penguin Books, 1986), 219. Iacocco was referring to total hourly compensation, including the value of all job benefits, not merely straight time hourly wages.

8. Susan Strange, *The Casino Society* (London: Basil Blackwell, 1984); and "Playing With Fire: Games the Casino Society Plays," *Business Week*, 16 September 1985, 78ff.

9. See "Review of the Month," *Monthly Review*, October 1986, 16.

10. "Is Deregulation Working?" *Business Week*, 22 December 1986, 50–55.

11. Mike Davis, *Prisoners of the American Dream* (London: New Left Books, 1986); and Richard Edwards and Michael Podgursky, "The Unraveling Accord: U.S. Unions in Crisis," in *Unions in Crisis and Beyond: Perspectives from Six Countries*, Richard Edwards, Paolo Garonna, and Franz Todtling, eds. (Dover, Mass.: Auburn House, 1986).

12. Thomas Ferguson and Joel Rogers, *Right Turn: The Decline of the Democrats and the Future of American Politics* (New York: Hill and Wang, 1986). The proposition that an active national government is "bad for business" is thoroughly and systematically refuted in a comparison of the recent histories of the United States, Germany, Sweden, and Japan in Lucy Gorham, *No Longer Leading: A Comparative Study of the U.S., Germany, Sweden, and Japan* (Washington, DC: Economic Policy Institute, 1986).

13. Lester Thurow, "A Surge in Inequality," *Scientific American*, May 1987.

CHAPTER 36

From *"It Ain't No Sin to Be Glad You're Alive":*
The Promise of Bruce Springsteen

Eric Alterman

Born in Queens, New York, in 1960, Eric Alterman is a journalist and English professor who has written books on US foreign policy and on the US news media. He has also published articles and columns in many magazines and newspapers, such as Rolling Stone, Elle, The New York Times, *and* The Nation. *With "It Ain't No Sin to Be Glad You're Alive": The Promise of Bruce Springsteen (1999), Alterman brought his political commentary to popular culture analysis. In this excerpt, he introduces Springsteen's 1982 album* Nebraska *as an important artistic response to the conditions of Ronald Reagan's America.*

[...] **N**ebraska, according to Springsteen, tells the story of people who are "isolated from their jobs, from their friends, from their family, from their fathers, mothers, not being connected to anything that's going on.... When you lose that sense of community, there's some spiritual sense of breakdown that occurs. You just get shot off somewhere where nothing really matters." For Bruce, the songs on the album are also connected to his early childhood, when his family was forced to live with his grandparents. He could smell the kerosene stove in the living room that was the source of heat for the entire house, and he recalled the power of the photograph of his father's sister, who had died at age five in an accident at the gas station around the corner: "Her ethereal presence from this 1920s portrait gave the room a feeling of being lost in time."

Nebraska feels as if it, too, is lost in time. Musically, it belongs to pre-rock 'n' roll America. Bryan Garman, writing in *Popular Music and Society,* tied the album to the history of the "hurt song": "Written in working-class language, hurt songs express the collective pain, suffering, and injustice working people have historically suffered, and articulate their collective hopes and dreams for a less oppressive future." By resurrecting the tradition of the hurt song, *Nebraska* not only gives voice to Springsteen's own battered psyche but also connects to a thread of social dislocation he sensed around him.

Consider the cultural and economic circumstances surrounding Springsteen's bedroom recording. The United States entered a deep recession in 1982, and many workers who saw their jobs go overseas felt an even more hopeless form of displacement than that experienced during the Depression. Unemployment reached 11 percent in 1982, but President Reagan still complained that he was tired of hearing about it every time someone lost his job in "South Succotash." In contrast to FDR, moreover, Reagan set out to destroy the union movement's power. Under his presidency, union membership dropped by 29 percent in the years leading up to the economic crisis, with the United Auto Workers alone seeing 250,000 workers lose their jobs. Those workers who remained unemployed grew increasingly quiescent, agreeing to corporate givebacks and less autonomy in the manufacturing process. An entire way of life – a way of life that had sustained the American Dream for generations – appeared to be crumbling. [. . .]

While writing *Nebraska*, Springsteen had been reading Flannery O'Connor, whose brilliant fiction frequently deals with grotesque, occasionally freakish characters, without ever mocking their longings. O'Connor had an uncanny ability to merge the deeply religious sensibility of her characters with the profane desires of their hearts in a gritty, personalized setting. These stories, Springsteen averred, reminded him of "the unknowability of God and contained a dark spirituality that resonated with my own feelings at the time." A second powerful influence on him during this period was a film he saw on television: Terrence Malick's *Badlands*, which tells the story of Charlie Starkweather and Caril Fugate and their 1958 killing spree across the Great Plains. Like a good Bruce Springsteen song, the film makes a seamless transition from the mundane details of the lives of inarticulate people to an epic commentary on inherent violence lurking in the banality of everyday life. Malick's characters, played by Martin Sheen and Sissy Spacek, seem wholly unconcerned with the moral consequences of their actions. Shooting innocents disturbs these two teenage runaways no more (or less) than Sheen's decision to shoot a football. Springsteen saw in the film a "stillness on the surface" that masked beneath it "a world of moral ambiguity and violence."

Musically, these notions swirled inside Springsteen's imagination and connected to his growing fascination with old-fashioned folk and country-and-western music. Having whetted his taste recording *The River*, Springsteen went deeper into the music, turning to the famous six-record *Anthology of American Folk Music* collected by the musical archivist Harry Smith and released on Moses Asch's Folkways label in 1952. The collection, released at the height of the McCarthy era, is an attempt by two left-wing bohemians to tell the story of another America, one that lived outside the mainstream of history and national politics. Both Asch and Smith were obsessed with the possibilities of political and cultural syncretism that folk music seemed to offer. Although the *Anthology*'s sales were small, its influence was enormous. It helped inspire the folk explosion of the early sixties, which in turn gave rock its social and intellectual edge. When Bob Dylan made history by plugging in an electric guitar at the 1965 Newport Folk Festival, horrifying his audience but redirecting the slow train of American popular culture, the song he chose was "Maggie's Farm," itself an homage to the Bently Boys' "Down on Penny's Farm," number twenty-five on the *Anthology*.

Though its cultural impact cannot be compared with Dylan's "going electric" at Newport, *Nebraska* nevertheless stands as a key moment in American cultural history. Virtually alone in the mass culture of the period, the record provides stark human testimony to the destruction of all forms of communal, psychological, and political support for workingpeople in Ronald Reagan's America. Like Dylan, Springsteen drew directly on Harry Smith's anthology. Song number seventy-four on the collection is a bluesy dirge called "Ninety-Nine-Year Blues" recorded by a North Carolina native named Julius Daniels in February 1927. The song concerns a young black man who is arrested while visiting a new town under the "poor boy law." (In other words, he is guilty of being poor and black.) The judge sentences him to ninety-nine years in "Joe Brown's coal mine," and the injustice inspires the boy to express a desire to "kill everybody" in town.

Springsteen's response is "Johnny 99," which tells the story of a man named Ralph who loses his job when "they closed down the auto plant in Mahwah" and cannot find another. (Springsteen's songs may derive from the "hurt song" tradition, but they are grounded in the events of the day. In June 1980 Ford did close its twenty-five-year-old plant in Mahwah, New Jersey.) Facing foreclosure on his house, Ralph snaps, shoots a night clerk, and is charged with murder. When brought before Judge "Mean John Brown," Ralph does not try to shirk responsibility for what he's done, but he also notes that what drove him to the edge was a crisis not of his making. Told that he can expect to spend the rest of his life in prison, Ralph asks for the death penalty instead. There is no place in society for a man who cannot keep a job, feed his family, or maintain his dignity and the respect of his peers.

E. L. Doctorow has observed that whenever a novel features poor or working-class people as its protagonists, it is judged to be "political" and, therefore, not art. This is in part a comment on the prejudices of the critical elite in the United States, but it is also a reflection of the relative rarity, in recent years, of artistic attention paid to workingpeople. In November 1969 President Nixon gave a speech hailing the so-called silent majority – conservative Americans who disapproved of the increasing cultural liberalism of the youth culture, the entertainment industry, and the media world that surrounded them. The White House then secretly engineered tens of thousands of supportive telegrams in response, and newspapers and television stations were flooded with letters. The mainstream media discovered workingpeople as if for the first time. *Newsweek* professed to observe a "pendulum swing" back toward the silent majority in national politics and culture. *U.S. News* reported that "the common man is beginning to look like a Very Important Person indeed." *Time*'s editors concluded that "above all, Middle America is a state of mind."

As Barbara Ehrenreich demonstrates in her perceptive *Fear of Falling: The Inner Life of the Middle Class* (1985), film and television writers also lavished considerable attention on blue-collar workers during this period, but it was attention of the most condescending kind. Two months after Nixon's election, CBS introduced us to the racist Archie Bunker and *All in the Family.* The hero of the film *Joe* (1970) complained: "The niggers are getting all the money. Why work? You tell me – why the fuck work when you can screw, have babies and get paid for it?" *Joe* was followed on the big screen by one working-class psychotic after another. *Taxi Driver's* (1976) Travis Bickle was a crazy killer. In *Saturday Night Fever* (1977), working-class kids literally fall off the Brooklyn Bridge while fooling around; the romantic lead, John Travolta's Tony Manero, dreams of leaving these tawdry types behind and entering the world of glamour and romance in Manhattan. The three small-time workers/hoods in *Blue Collar* (1978) are out to rip off their union as it had done to them. The dumb working stiffs in *The Deer Hunter* (1979) draw guns against one another in a fight over hunting boots and eat their Twinkies with mustard. [...]

Class was hardly a new subject for Springsteen, for even his early records are filled with young people yearning for escape into a better life. And certainly no one in a Bruce Springsteen song spoke college-educated English. With *Darkness,* however, the terms of the discourse began to change; characters now referred angrily to persons of authority ("Mister, I ain't a boy" in "Promised Land" or "Mister, when you're young" from "The River.") By *Nebraska,* virtually every song is addressed to the impersonal, unapproachable authority of a "mister," a "sir," a "judge," a "Mister State Trooper," or some combination thereof. The songs all take place in factories, mines, mills, convenience stores, kitchens, front porches, and VFW and union halls. But now decay infiltrates the workingman's life and refuges in the form of crime, drugs, and danger. Ralph gets into trouble at the Club Tip Top, located in a part of town "where when you hit a red light you don't stop."

What Springsteen accomplished with *Nebraska* was more than just forcing the subject of class into the mainstream cultural discourse. He also forged his own emotional confusion and political depression with his deepening mastery of literary and cinematic narrative. As Alan Rauch wrote in the journal *American Studies*: "Springsteen lets us hear the voice of someone who has been humbled far more than we have, even in the wide range of most of our experiences. . . . So intensely personal is the monologue of the narrator that it forces even the most sympathetic listener to step outside of the context of this monologue in order to see whether there are any valid connections with his or her own life." Nowhere is this power more evident than on the album's opening cut, "Nebraska," Charlie Starkweather's story told from the perspective of the mass murderer.

Springsteen does not falsely ennoble his working-class characters but humanizes them instead, demonstrating the complexity of their moral choices. For instance, the "good" brother in "Highway Patrolman," Joe Roberts, is forever trying to get the "bad" one, Frankie, out of trouble, even if it means bending the law a little. Joe is certainly the more socially responsible of the two, but he is also the one who received a farm deferment and married the girl they both loved. Frankie ended up in Vietnam and came back a lost soul. For Joe, who loves his fallen brother, "nothin' feels better than blood on blood." In "Used Cars," a young man walks down "the same dirty streets where I was born" as his father "sweats the same job from mornin' to morn."

He is shamed by his father's inability to buy a new car, but the only hope of escape he himself can imagine is winning the lottery. In "Reason to Believe," a would-be groom stands alone, jilted and humiliated before his friends and family following a wedding ceremony that never took place. Still, he finds a "reason to believe" no more convincing, Springsteen avers, than that of a man poking a dead dog with a stick trying to make it run.

Released without much fanfare, critics nevertheless stood in awe of Springsteen's brave accomplishment. Mikal Gilmore writing in the *Los Angeles Herald Examiner*, called *Nebraska* "the most successful attempt at making a sizable statement about American life that popular music has yet produced." Greil Marcus observed that in Springsteen's portrayal of a society where "social and economic function have become the measure of all things and have dissolved all values beyond money and status," honest work becomes trivialized, honest goals reduced to a bet on the state lottery, and murder, however nihilistic, the only recognizable form of rebellion." Springsteen had fashioned "the most complete and probably the most convincing statement of resistance and refusal that Ronald Reagan's USA has elicited from any artist or politician."

Study Questions

1 Why, according to Alterman, did "folk" music matter so much to Springs-teen?
2 What specific examples can you find in the three songs from *Nebraska* included in the following reading to support Alterman's claim that the album is a response to Reagan's economic policies?

CHAPTER 37

A Musical Representation of Work in Postindustrial America
Bruce Springsteen's *Nebraska*, Shelley Thunder's "Working Girl", and Canibus's "Shove That Jay-Oh-Bee"

New Jersey's Bruce Springsteen (1949–), whose father was a bus driver and mother was a legal secretary, emerged as one of the most popular rock and roll musicians of the 1980s. Springsteen sang about small-town existence, plant closings, and the often-thwarted dreams of a better life. "Johnny 99," "Highway Patrolman," and "Atlantic City" are from his 1982 album Nebraska.

As Springsteen's enormously popular songs on Nebraska *and future albums issued a kind of epitaph for blue-collar optimism, hip hop and rap artists were finding cultural possibility and creative materials in the shift to new technologies. Originally an underground phenomenon of New York's South Bronx, this music claimed national attention in the early 1980s. Shelley Thunder, born Michelle Harrison in Jamaica in 1965, responds in "Working Girl" (Fresh Out the Pack, 1989) to the overt machismo of hip hop's reigning male performers, while connecting rap music to a work-based identity. Like Shelley Thunder, Jamaican-born rapper Canibus (born Germaine Williams, in 1974) is part of the "new immigration" from the Caribbean, Asia, and Latin America. With Harlem's Biz Markie (born Marcel Hall, in 1964), he reworked the refrain of country singer Johnny Paycheck's 1978 hit "Take This Job and Shove It" in their rap "Shove This Jay-Oh-Bee" (Office Space: The Motion Picture Soundtrack, 1999). In the following songs, Bruce Springsteen's, Shelley Thunder's, and Canibus's comments on the technological changes that were restructuring the economy are clearly audible.*

From *Nebraska* by Bruce Springsteen (1982)

"Johnny 99"

Well they closed down the auto plant in
Mahwah late that month
Ralph went out lookin' for a job but he
couldn't find none
He came home too drunk from mixin'
Tanqueray and wine
He got a gun shot a night clerk now they
call 'im Johnny 99

Down in the part of town where when you
hit a red light you don't stop
Johnny's wavin' his gun around and
threatenin' to blow his top
When an off-duty cop snuck up on him
from behind
Out in front of the Club Tip Top they
slapped the cuffs on Johnny 99

Well the city supplied a public defender
but the judge was Mean John Brown
He came into the courtroom and stared
poor Johnny down
Well the evidence is clear gonna let the
sentence son fit the crime
Prison for 98 and a year and we'll call it
even Johnny 99

A fist-fight broke out in the courtroom they
had to drag Johnny's girl away
His mamma stood up and shouted "Judge
don't take my boy this way"
Well son you got a statement you'd like to
make before the bailiff comes to forever
take you away

Now judge I got debts no honest man could
pay
The bank was holdin' my mortgage and
they was takin' my house away
Now I ain't saying that makes me an
innocent man
But it was more'n all this that put that gun
in my hand

Well your honor I do believe I'd be better
off dead
And if you can take a man's life for the
thoughts that's in his head
Then won't you sit back in that chair and
think it over judge one more time
And let 'em shave off my hair and put me
on that execution line.

"Highway Patrolman"

My name is Joe Roberts I work for the
state
I'm a sergeant out of Perrineville
barracks number 8
I always done an honest job, as honest as I
could
I got a brother named Frankie and
Frankie ain't no good

Now ever since we was young kids it's
been the same come down
I get a call over the radio Frankie's in
trouble downtown
Well if it was any other man, I'd put him
straight away
But when it's your brother sometimes you
look the other way

CHORUS

Me and Frankie laughin' and drinkin'
nothin' feels better than blood on blood
Takin' turns dancing with Maria as the
band played "Night of the Johnstown
Flood"
I catch him when he's strayin' like any
brother would
Man turns his back on his family well he
just ain't no good

Well Frankie went in the army back in
1965
I got a farm deferment settled down took
Maria for my wife
But them wheat prices kept on droppin' till
it was like we were gettin' robbed
Frankie came home in '68 and me I took
this job

CHORUS

Yeah we're laughin' and drinkin' nothin'
feels better than blood on blood
Takin' turns dancin' with Maria as the
band played "Night of the Johnstown
Flood"
I catch him when he's strayin', teach him
how to walk that line
Man turns his back on his family he ain't
no friend of mine

That night was like any other, I got a call
'bout quarter to nine
There was trouble in a roadhouse out on
the Michigan line
There was a kid lyin' on the floor lookin'
bad, bleedin' hard from his head,
There was a girl cryin' at a table, it was Frank
they said
Well I went out and I jumped in my car
and I hit the lights
I must of done 110 through Michigan
county that night

It was out at the crossroads down round
Willow Bank
Seen a Buick with Ohio plates behind the
wheel was Frank
Well I chased him through them county
roads till a sign said Canadian border 5
miles from here
I pulled over the side of the highway and
watched his tail-lights disappear

CHORUS

Me and Frankie laughin' and drinkin'
nothin' feels better than blood on blood
Takin' turns dancin' with Maria as the
band played "Night of the Johnstown
Flood"
I catch him when he's strayin' like any
brother would
Man turns his back on his family well he
just ain't no good

"Atlantic City"

Well they blew up the chicken man in
Philly last night now they blew up his
house too
Down on the boardwalk they're gettin'
ready for a fight gonna see what them
racket boys can do

Now there's trouble busin' in from outta
state and the DA can't get no relief
Gonna be a rumble out on the promenade
and the gamblin' commission's hangin'
on by the skin of its teeth

CHORUS

Everything dies baby that's a fact
But maybe everything that dies someday
comes back
Put your makeup on fix your hair up pretty
And meet me tonight in Atlantic City

Well I got a job and I tried to put my
money away
But I got debts no honest man could pay
So I drew what I had from the Central
Trust
And I bought us two tickets on that Coast
City bus

CHORUS

Now our luck may have died and our love
may be cold but with you forever I'll stay
We're goin' out where the sands turnin' to
gold
so put your stockin's on baby cause the nights
gettin' cold and maybe everything dies
That's a fact but maybe everything that
dies someday comes back

Now I been lookin' for a job but it's hard to
find
Down here it's just winners and losers
and don't get caught on the wrong side of
that line

Well I'm tired of comin' out on the losin'
end
So honey last night I met this guy and I'm
gonna do a little favor for him

CHORUS

Well I guess everything dies baby that's a
fact
But maybe everything that dies someday
comes back
Put your makeup on fix your hair up
pretty and
Meet me tonight in Atlantic City

Shelley Thunder, "Working Girl" (1989)

Work and work
Work and work
Work and work

I'm a working girl
I don't waste my time to get mine in this world
You see I do what I want to, I don't answer to no one
Believe me, I get the job done
Some people wonder, then try to understand why they call me MC Shelly Thunder
I ain't about posing fronts
I just stopped by to get paid for months
It don't make a difference, Yardie or Yankee
Just give me the mike and I bet you're gonna thank me
For giving you the cold rock stuff
I'm a working girl, and I'm rugged and rough
A fiend for the mike, as long as I hold it
I'm a take it, and I control it
And it don't make a difference what some people say
I must get a check on pay day.

'Cause I'm a working girl
(Well, that cash never seems to stop coming)
I'm a working girl
(Keep those sucker MCs coming)
I'm a working girl
(My fingers to the bone
Shelley keep on and don't stop cause it's time to get paid)

I'm a career girl in a man's world
The more I sweat the more money I get
So when it's time to do work I don't like to joke around

Rappers that play me, get broken down
I'm serious, I live up to my rep and I never half-step
I get totally aggressive and I couldn't care less if you don't think my rap is impressive
I kick it live, I must survive,
Shelley wasn't made for no nine to five,
No way, I got to have all the cash
Strictly one hundred dollar bills in my stash
Why? Because I get paid to rap
I go for broke if the crowd don't clap.
It don't matter what some people say
I must get a check on payday

'Cause I'm a working girl
(Well, that cash never seems to stop coming)
I'm a working girl
(Keep those sucker MCs coming)
I'm a working girl
(My fingers to the bone
Shelley keep on and don't stop cause it's time to get paid)

I'm a working girl
Seven days a week I get paid when I speak
Ten times out of the year I go on trips
Come back to New York and I flip on these suckers
As is my witness
I don't only do work, I do business
So when there's work to be done, I gets chosen
I react like an atomic explosion
'Cause I master rhyming as a pastime
Treat me like a kid, and that'll be the last time
I bet you don't brag no more
I'm not the herb that you're looking for
I get the feeling like the eye of the tiger
I grab the mike and watch the people get hyper
It don't matter what some punks say
I must get a check on pay day

'Cause I'm a working girl
(That cash never seems to stop coming)
I'm a working girl
(Keep those sucker MCs coming)
I'm a working girl
(My fingers to the bone
Shelley keep on and don't stop 'cause it's time to get paid)

I'm a working girl
(Well, that cash never seems to stop coming)
I'm a working girl
(Keep those sucker MCs coming)
I'm a working girl
(My fingers to the bone
Shelley keep on and don't stop 'cause it's time to get paid)

Canibus and Biz Markie, "Shove This Jay-Oh-Bee" (1999)

[Canibus]
Yo 6 o'clock every morning you waking up yawning
To the sound of your alarm clock alarming
About an hour from now
You should be at the place of employment
Which is annoying cause it's so boring
Your co-workers are talking too loud for you to ignore them
It affects your occupational performance
You wonder why your work load is so enormous
Because your boss just laid off three quarters of the whole office
People get depressed, they get ulcers
From the stress that the corporate environment causes
Regardless of how you ultimately wanna solve this
Seems to me like you've got one of four choices:
You could take a new job offer for more chips
Stick it out a little longer or forfeit
But my advice to anybody that wants to quit
It'll feel much better if you say it like this:

[Biz Markie]
Take this job and shove it
I ain't workin here no more
Take this job and shove it
I ain't workin' here no more
Take this job and shove it
I ain't workin' here no more
Take this job, take this job, take this job and shove it

[Canibus]
Yo, if your boss is a S-O-B
Tell him to S-H-O-V-E the J-O-B
Put your middle finger up slowly
Put it close enough to his face so he can examine it closely
Say I ain't workin' here no more
Who do you think you are?
Rip your apron off, throw it on the floor
Run to the door, to the payphone
Make a toll-free call
Tell your spouse what happened and where you are
So they can come and get you in the car later on
And help you search for a new 9 to 5 job
If the unemployment line ain't that long

You can take your time printin' out W-9 forms
Eventually, you'll get on if you try hard enough
And you'll get money if you keep punchin' your time card enough
Maybe you hate it, maybe you love it
But if you hate it all you gotta do is get mad and tell the boss to:

[Biz Markie]
Take this job and shove it
I ain't workin' here no more
Take this job and shove it
I ain't workin' here no more
Take this job and shove it
I ain't workin' here no more
Take this job, take this job, take this job and shove it

[Canibus]
Yo, some occupations are like slave gigs
The boss's favorite gets placed in something spacious
While the most hated get placed in some small cubicle spaces
Or get thrown down in the basement, get your stapler confiscated
You constantly waitin' for a paycheck
Twelve months passed by and you still ain't get paid yet
Here's a optimistic motto
If you ever late for today you could say you early for tomorrow
Most 9 to 5's are hard
Cause the description in the job ain't no picnic in the park
People get hired
Drink coffee to stay wired
So they don't get tired, sleep late, and get fired

[Biz Markie]
You came in late, you already ate,
nowww, you wanna take a lunch break!??!

[Canibus]
Ay, yo bust it, ain't no need to discuss it
Just take this job and shove it, right between your buttocks

[Biz Markie]
Take this job and shove it
I ain't workin' here no more
Take this job and shove it
I ain't workin' here no more
Take this job and shove it
I ain't workin' here no more
Take this job, take this job, take this job and shove it
Take this job and shove it
I ain't workin' here no more
Ah Ah ah ah ahahah ah
I ain't workin' here no more
Take this job and shove it
I ain't workin' here no more
Ay Ay Ay ayee ay

I ain't workin' here no more
[Canibus and the Biz]
It's comin from Canibus and the Biz
It's comin from Canibus and the Biz
From, from Canibus and the Biz

Study Questions

1   In the Springsteen songs, which line is repeated in more than one song? What is the most important word in that line? Why?

2   Which song(s) seem to have the most complex arrangements of instruments? Which have the most stripped-down sound? How do these choices contribute to the songs' meanings? How do they affect you as a listener?

3   Over the course of all five songs, what kinds of jobs are mentioned or alluded to?

4   How can Harrison and Bluestone's historical and economic analysis in *The Great U-Turn* be used to shed light on the three Springsteen songs? Can it be used to explain anything about the songs by Shelley Thunder and Canibus? Why or why not?

CHAPTER 38

Class in America:
Myths and Realities (2000)

Gregory Mantsios

Gregory Mantsios (1950–) is a specialist in labor studies and worker education. Trained in sociology, he writes extensively on issues of poverty, inequality, and education. Mantsios is the publisher o New Labor Forum: A Journal of Ideas, Analysis and Debate *and has edited the anthology* A New Labor Movement for the New Century *(1998). In the following essay, Mantsios argues that class is the single most important predictor of success and quality of life in the US.*

People in the United States don't like to talk about class. Or so it would seem. We don't speak about class privileges, or class oppression, or the class nature of society. These terms are not part of our everyday vocabulary, and in most circles they are associated with the language of the rhetorical fringe. Unlike people in most other parts of the world, we shrink from using words that classify along economic lines or that point to class distinctions: phrases like "working class," "upper class," and "ruling class" are rarely uttered by Americans.

For the most part, avoidance of class-laden vocabulary crosses class boundaries. There are few among the poor who speak of themselves as lower class; instead, they refer to their race, ethnic group, or geographic location. Workers are more likely to identify with their employer, industry, or occupational group than with other workers, or with the working class.[1]

Neither are those at the other end of the economic spectrum likely to use the word "class." In her study of thirty-eight wealthy and socially prominent women, Susan Ostrander asked participants if they considered themselves members of the upper class. One participant responded, "I hate to use the word 'class.' We are responsible, fortunate people, old families, the people who have something." Another said, "I hate [the term] upper class. It is so non-upper class to use it. I just call it 'all of us,' those who are wellborn."[2]

It is not that Americans, rich or poor, aren't keenly aware of class differences – those quoted above obviously are; it is that class is not in the domain of public discourse. Class is not discussed or debated in public because class identity has been stripped from popular culture. The institutions that shape mass culture and define the parameters of public debate have avoided class issues. In politics, in primary and secondary education, and in the mass media, formulating issues in terms of class is unacceptable, perhaps even un-American.

There are, however, two notable exceptions to this phenomenon. First, it is acceptable in the United States to talk about "the middle class." Interestingly enough, such references appear to be acceptable precisely because they mute class differences. References to the middle class by politicians, for example, are designed to encompass and attract the broadest possible constituency. Not only do references to the middle class gloss over differences, but these references also avoid any suggestion of conflict or exploitation.

This leads us to the second exception to the class-avoidance phenomenon. We are, on occasion, presented with glimpses of the upper class and the lower class (the language used is "the wealthy" and "the poor"). In the media, these presentations are designed to satisfy some real or imagined voyeuristic need of "the ordinary person." As curiosities, the ground-level view of street life and the inside look at the rich and the famous serve as unique models, one to avoid and one to aspire to. In either case, the two models are presented without causal relation to each other: one is not rich because the other is poor. Similarly, when social commentators or liberal politicians draw attention to the plight of the poor, they do so in a manner that obscures the class structure and denies class exploitation. Wealth and poverty are viewed as one of several natural and inevitable states of being: differences are only differences. One may even say differences are the American way, a reflection of American social diversity.

We are left with one of two possibilities: either talking about class and recognizing class distinctions are not relevant to US society, or we mistakenly hold a set of beliefs that obscure the reality of class differences and their impact on people's lives.

Let us look at four common, albeit contradictory, beliefs about the United States.

Myth 1: The United States is fundamentally a classless society. Class distinctions are largely irrelevant today, and whatever differences do exist in economic standing are, for the most part, insignificant. Rich or poor, we are all equal in the eyes of the law, and such basic needs as health care and education are provided to all regardless of economic standing.

Myth 2: We are, essentially, a middle-class nation. Despite some variations in economic status, most Americans have achieved relative affluence in what is widely recognized as a consumer society.

Myth 3: We are all getting richer. The American public as a whole is steadily moving up the economic ladder, and each generation propels itself to greater economic well-being. Despite some fluctuations, the US position in the global economy has brought previously unknown prosperity to most, if not all, North Americans.

Myth 4: Everyone has an equal chance to succeed. Success in the United States requires no more than hard work, sacrifice, and perseverance: "In America, anyone can become a millionaire; it's just a matter of being in the right place at the right time."

In trying to assess the legitimacy of these beliefs, we want to ask several important questions. Are there significant class differences among Americans? If these differences do exist, are they getting bigger or smaller, and do these differences have a significant impact on the way we live? Finally, does everyone in the United States really have an equal opportunity to succeed?

The Economic Spectrum

We will begin by looking at differences. An examination of available data reveals that variations in economic well-being are in fact immense. Consider the following:

- The wealthiest 20 percent of the American population holds 85 percent of the total household wealth in the country. That is, they own nearly seven-eighths of all the consumer durables (such as houses, cars, and stereos) and financial assets (such as stocks, bonds, property, and savings accounts).[3]
- Approximately 144,000 Americans, or 0.1 percent of the adult working population, earn more than $1 million annually, with many of these individuals earning over $10 million and some earning over $100 million annually. It would take the average American, earning $34,000 per year, more than 65 lifetimes to earn $100 million.[4]

Affluence and prosperity are clearly alive and well in certain segments of the United States population. However, this abundance is in contrast to the poverty and despair that is also prevalent in the United States. At the other end of the spectrum:

- A total of 13 percent of the American population – that is, one of every eight[5] – live below the government's official poverty line (calculated in 1999 at $8,500 for an individual and $17,028 for a family of four).[6] These poor include a significant number of homeless people – approximately two million Americans.
- Approximately one out of every five children in the United States under the age of eighteen lives in poverty.[7]

The contrast between rich and poor is sharp, and with nearly one-third of the American population living at one extreme or the other, it is difficult to argue that we live in a classless society. The income gap between rich and poor in the United States (measured as the percentage of total income held by the wealthiest 20 percent of the population versus the poorest 20 percent) is approximately 11 to 1, one of the highest ratios in the industrialized world. The ratio in Japan and Germany, by contrast, is 4 to 1.[8]

Reality 1: There are enormous differences in the economic status of American citizens. A sizable proportion of the US population occupies opposite ends of the economic spectrum.

In the middle range of the economic spectrum:

- Sixty percent of the American population hold less than 4 percent of the nation's wealth.[9]
- While the real income of the top 1 percent of US families skyrocketed by 89 percent during the economic growth period from 1977 to 1995, the income of the middle fifth of the population actually declined by 13 percent during that same period.[10] This led one prominent economist to describe economic growth as a "spectator sport for the majority of American families."[11]

The level of inequality is sometimes difficult to comprehend fully with dollar figures and percentages. To help his students visualize the distribution of income, the well-known economist Paul Samuelson asked them to picture an income pyramid made of children's blocks, with each layer of blocks representing $1,000. If we were to construct Samuelson's pyramid today, the peak of the pyramid would be much higher than the Eiffel Tower, yet almost all of us would be within six feet of the ground.[12] In other words, the distribution of income is heavily skewed; a small minority of families take the lion's share of national income, and the remaining income is distributed among the vast majority of middle-income and low-income families. Keep in mind that Samuelson's pyramid represents the distribution of income, not wealth. The distribution of wealth is skewed even further.

Reality 2: The middle class in the United States holds a very small share of the nation's wealth, and its income – in constant dollars – is declining.

Lottery millionaires and celebrity salaries notwithstanding, evidence suggests that the level of inequality in the United States is getting higher. Census data show the gap between the rich and the poor to be the widest since the government began collecting information in 1947. Furthermore, the percentage of households earning between $25,000 and $75,000 has been falling steadily since 1969, while the percentage of households earning less than $25,000 has actually increased between 1989 and 1997.[13] And economic polarization is expected to increase over the next several decades.[14]

Reality 3: The middle class is shrinking in size, and the gap between rich and poor is bigger than it has ever been.

American Lifestyles

At last count, nearly 35 million Americans across the nation lived in unrelenting poverty.[15] Yet, as political scientist Michael Harrington once commented, "America has the best dressed poverty the world has ever known."[16] Clothing disguises much of the poverty in the United States, and this may explain, in part, its middle-class image. With increased mass marketing of "designer" clothing and with shifts in the nation's economy from blue-collar (and often better-paying) manufacturing jobs to white-collar and pink-collar jobs in the service sector, it is becoming increasingly difficult to distinguish class differences based on appearance.[17] [...]

Reality 4: Even ignoring the extreme poles of the economic spectrum, we find enormous class differences in the lifestyles among the haves, the have-nots, and the have-littles.

Class affects more than lifestyle and material well-being. It has a significant impact on our physical and mental well-being as well.

Researchers have found an inverse relationship between social class and health. Lower-class standing is correlated to higher rates of infant mortality, eye and ear disease, arthritis, physical disability, diabetes, nutritional deficiency, respiratory disease, mental illness, and heart disease.[18] In all areas of health, poor people do not share the same life chances as those in the social class above them. Furthermore, lower-class standing is correlated with a lower quality of treatment for illness and disease. The results of poor health and poor treatment are borne out in the life expectancy rates within each class. Researchers have found that the higher your class standing, the higher your life expectancy. Conversely, they have also found that within each age group, the lower one's class standing, the higher the death rate; in some age groups, the figures are as much as two and three times as high.[19]

Reality 5: From cradle to grave, class standing has a significant impact on our chances for survival.

The lower one's class standing, the more difficult it is to secure appropriate housing, the more time is spent on the routine tasks of everyday life, the greater is the percentage of income that goes to pay for food and other basic necessities, and the greater is the likelihood of crime victimization.[20] Class can predict chances for both survival and success.

Class and Educational Attainment

School performance (grades and test scores) and educational attainment (level of schooling completed) also correlate strongly with economic class. Furthermore, despite some efforts to make testing fairer and schooling more accessible, current data suggest that the level of inequity is staying the same or getting worse.

In his study for the Carnegie Council on Children 15 years ago, Richard De Lone examined the test scores of over half a million students who took the College Board exams (SATs). His findings were consistent with earlier studies that showed a relationship between class and scores on standardized tests; his conclusion: "the higher the student's social status, the higher the probability that he or she will get higher grades."[21] Fifteen years after the release of the Carnegie report, College Board surveys reveal data that are no different; test scores still correlate strongly with family income.

A little more than 20 years ago, researcher William Sewell showed a positive correlation between class and overall educational achievement. In comparing the top quartile (25%) of his sample to the bottom quartile, he found that students from upper-class families were twice as likely to obtain training beyond high school and four times as likely to attain a postgraduate degree. Sewell concluded: "Socioeconomic background ... operates independently of academic ability at every stage in the process of educational attainment."[22]

Today, the pattern persists. There are, however, two significant changes. On the one hand, the odds of getting into college have improved for the bottom quartile of the population, although they still remain relatively low compared to the top. On the other hand, the chances of completing a college degree have deteriorated markedly for the bottom quartile. Researchers estimate the chances of completing a four-year college degree (by age 24) to be 19 times as great for the top 25 percent of the population as it is for the bottom 25 percent. "Those from the bottom quartile of family income ... are faring worse than they have at any time in the 23 years of published Current Population Survey data."[23]

Reality 6: Class standing has a significant impact on chances for educational attainment.

Class standing, and consequently life chances, are largely determined at birth. Although examples of individuals who have gone from rags to riches abound in the mass media, statistics on class mobility show these leaps to be extremely rare. In fact, dramatic advances in class standing are relatively few. One study showed that fewer than one in five men surpass the economic status of their fathers.[24] For those whose annual income is in six figures, economic success is due in large part to the wealth and privileges bestowed on them at birth. Over 66 percent of the consumer units with incomes of $100,000 or more have some inherited assets. Of these units, over 86 percent reported that inheritances constituted a substantial portion of their total assets.[25]

Economist Harold Wachtel likens inheritance to a series of Monopoly games in which the winner of the first game refuses to relinquish his or her cash and commercial property for the second game. "After all," argues the winner, "I accumulated my wealth and income by my own wits." With such an arrangement, it is not difficult to predict the outcome of subsequent games.[26]

Reality 7: All Americans do not have an equal opportunity to succeed. Inheritance laws ensure a greater likelihood of success for the offspring of the wealthy.

Study Questions

1   What is Mantsios's argument about the role that class plays in American society? How does it affect life chances and lifestyles? Give three examples. Why are Americans reluctant to talk about class?
2   What are the "myths and realities" of class? What evidence does Mantsios provide for the realities? Explain why you find his evidence convincing and/ or unconvincing.
3   How do you define your class position? How does your family? What are your/their criteria for this definition/identification?
4   Trace the trajectory of your family's class position since 1945.

Notes

1. See Jay MacLead, *Ain't No Makin' It: Aspirations and Attainment in a Lower-Income Neighborhood* (Boulder, Colo.: Westview Press, 1995); Benjamin DeMott, *The Imperial Middle* (New York: Morrow, 1990); Ira Katznelson, *City Trenches: Urban Politics and Patterning of Class in the United States* (New York: Pantheon Books, 1981); Charles W. Tucker, "A Comparative Analysis of Subjective Social Class: 1945–1963," *Social Forces*, no. 46, June 1968, pp. 508–514; Robert Nisbet, "The Decline and Fall of Social Class," *Pacific Sociological Review*, vol. 2, Spring 1959, pp. 11–17; and Oscar Glantz, "Class Consciousness and Political Solidarity," *American Sociological Review*, vol. 23, August 1958, pp. 375–382.

2. Susan Ostander, "Upper-Class Women: Class Consciousness as Conduct and Meaning," in G. William Domhoff, *Power Structure Research*, Beverly Hills, CA, Sage Productions, 1980, pp. 78–79. Also see, Stephen Birmingham, *America's Secret Aristocracy*, Boston, Little Brown, 1987.

3. Jared Bernstein, Lawrence Hishel, and John Schmitt, *The State of Working America: 1998–99*, ILR Press, Cornell University Press, 1998, p. 262.

4. The number of individuals filing tax returns showing a gross adjusted income of $1 million or more in 1997 was 144,459 (Internal Revenue Service, *Statistics of Income Bulletin, Summer 1999*, Washington, DC, 1999, p. 268). The total civilian employment in 1997 was 129,588,000 (US Bureau of Labor Statistics, 1997).

5. Joseph Dalaker, US Bureau of the Census, "Current Population Reports," series pp. 60–207, *Poverty in the United States: 1998*. Washington, DC, US Government Printing Office, 1999, p. v.

6. "Preliminary Estimates of Weighted Average Poverty Thresholds in 1999," Department of Commerce, Bureau of Census, 2000.

7. Ibid, p. v.

8. See The Center on Budget and Policy Priorities, Economic Policy Institute, "Pulling Apart: State-by-State Analysis of Income Trends," January 2000, fact sheet; US Department of Commerce, "Current Population Reports: Consumer Income," Washington, DC, 1993; The World Bank, "World Development Report: 1992," Washington, DC, International Bank for Reconstruction and Development, 1992; The World Bank "World Development Report 1999/2000," pp. 238–239.

9. Jared Bernstein et al., op. cit., p. 262.

10. Derived from Ibid, p. 95.

11. Alan Blinder, quoted by Paul Krugman, in "Disparity and Despair," *U.S. News and World Report*, March 23, 1992, p. 54.

12. Paul Samuelson, *Economics*, 10th ed., New York, McGraw-Hill, 1976, p. 84.

13. "Money Income of Households, Families, and Persons in the United States: 1992," U.S. Department of Commerce, "Current Population Reports: Consumer Income" series P60–184, Washington, DC, 1993, p. B6. Also, Jared Bernstein et al., op. cit., p. 61.

14. Paul Blumberg, *Inequality in an Age of Decline*, New York, Oxford University Press, 1980.

15. US Census Bureau, 1999, op. cit., p. v.

16. Michael Harrington, *The Other America*, New York, Macmillan, 1962, p. 12–13.

17. Stuart Ewen and Elizabeth Ewen, *Channels of Desire: Mass Images and the Shaping of American Consciousness*, New York, McGraw-Hill, 1982.

18. E. Pamuk, D. Makuc, K. Heck, C. Reuben, and K. Lochner, *Socioeconomic Status and Health Chartbook, Health, United States, 1998*, Hyattsville, MD, National Center for Health Statistics, 1998, pp. 145–159; Vincente Navarro "Class, Race, and Health Care in the United States," in Bersh Berberoglu, *Critical Pespectives in Sociology*, 2nd ed., Dubuque, IA, Kendall/Hunt, 1993, pp. 148–156; Melvin Krasner, *Poverty and Health in New York City*, United Hospital Fund of New York, 1989. See also US Dept. of Health and Human Services, *Health Status of Minorities and Low Income Groups*, 1985; and Dan Hughes, Kay

Johnson, Sara Rosenbaum, Elizabeth Butler, and Janet Simons, *The Health of America's Children,* The Children's Defense Fund, 1988.

19.   E. Pamuk et al., op. cit.; Kenneth Neubeck and Davita Glassberg, *Sociology: A Critical Approach,* New York, McGraw-Hill, 1996, pp. 436–438; Aaron Antonovsky, "Social Class, Life Expectancy, and Overall Mortality," in *The Impact of Social Class,* New York, Thomas Crowell, 1972, pp. 467–491. See also Harriet Duleep, "Measuring the Effect of Income on Adult Mortality Using Longitudinal Administrative Record Data," *Journal of Human Resources,* vol. 21, no. 2, Spring 1986.

20.   E. Pamuk et al., op. cit., fig. 20; Dennis W. Roncek, "Dangerous Places: Crime and Residential Environment," *Social Forces,* vol. 60, no. 1, September 1981, pp. 74–96.

21.   Richard De Lone, *Small Futures,* New York, Harcourt Brace Jovanovich, 1978.

22.   William H. Sewell, "Inequality of Opportunity for Higher Education," *American Sociological Review,* vol. 36, no. 5, 1971, pp. 793–809.

23.   The Mortenson Report on Public Policy Analysis of Opportunity for Postsecondary Education, "Postsecondary Education Opportunity," Iowa City, IA, September 1993, no. 16.

24.   De Lone, op. cit., pp. 14–19.

25.   Howard Tuchman, *Economics of the Rich,* New York, Random House, 1973, p. 15.

26.   Howard Wachtel, *Labor and the Economy,* Orlando, FL, Academic Press, 1984, pp. 161–162.

CHAPTER 39

From *Abortion and the Politics of Motherhood*

Kristin Luker

Kristin Luker (1946–) was born in San Francisco to a father who was a colonel in the US Air Force and a mother who was an herbalist. She specializes in the sociology of medicine and the family, with a focus on issues related to contraception and abortion. Her books include Taking Chances: Abortion and the Decision Not to Contracept *(1975), and* Dubious Conceptions: The Politics of Teenage Pregnancy *(1996). The following reading is excerpted from* Abortion and the Politics of Motherhood *(1984), which was nominated for a Pulitzer Prize. In the excerpt, Luker examines the different views of motherhood and family expressed by women on opposite sides of the abortion debate.*

This chapter will argue that all the previous rounds of the abortion debate in America were merely echoes of the issue as the nineteenth century [...] defined it: a debate about the medical profession's right to make life-and-death decisions. In contrast, the most recent round of the debate is about something new. By bringing the issue of the moral status of the embryo to the fore, the new round focuses on the relative rights of women and embryos. Consequently, the abortion debate has become a debate about women's contrasting obligations to themselves and others. New technologies and the changing nature of work have opened up possibilities for women outside of the home undreamed of in the nineteenth century; together, these changes give women – for the first time in history – the option of deciding exactly how and when their family roles will fit into the larger context of their lives. In essence, therefore, this round of the abortion debate is so passionate and hard-fought *because it is a referendum on the place and meaning of motherhood.*

Motherhood is at issue because two opposing visions of motherhood are at war. Championed by "feminists" and "housewives," these two different views of motherhood represent in turn two very different kinds of social worlds. The abortion debate has become a debate among women, women with different values in the social world, different experiences of it, and different resources with which to cope with it. How the issue is framed, how people think about it, and, most importantly, where the passions come from are all related to the fact that the battlelines are increasingly drawn (and defended) by women. [. . .]

Who Are the Activists?

On almost every social background variable we examined, pro-life and pro-choice women differed dramatically. For example, in terms of income, almost half of all pro-life women (44 percent) in this study reported an income of less than $20,000 a year, but only one-fourth of the pro-choice women reported an income that low, and a considerable portion of those were young women just starting their careers. On the upper end of the income scale, one-third of the pro-choice women reported an income of $50,000 a year or more compared with only one pro-life woman in every seven.

These simple figures on income, however, conceal a very complex social reality, and that social reality is in turn tied to feelings about abortion. The higher incomes of pro-choice women, for example, result from a number of intersecting factors. Almost without exception pro-choice women work in the paid labor force, they earn good salaries when they work, and if they are married, they are likely to be married to men who also have good incomes. An astounding 94 percent of all pro-choice women work, and over half of them have incomes in the top 10 percent of all working women in this country. Moreover, one pro-choice woman in ten has an annual *personal* income (as opposed to a family income) of $30,000 or more, thus putting her in the rarified ranks of the top 2 percent of all employed women in America. Pro-life women, by contrast, are far less likely to work: 63 percent of them do not work in the paid labor force, and almost all of those who do are unmarried. Among pro-life married women, for example, only 14 percent report any personal income at all, and for most of them, this is earned not in a formal job but through activities such as selling cosmetics to groups of friends. Not surprisingly, the personal income of pro-life women who work outside the home, whether in a formal job or in one of these less-structured activities, is low. Half of all pro-life women who do work earn less than $5,000 a year, and half earn between $5,000 and $10,000. Only two pro-life women we contacted reported a personal income of more than $20,000. Thus pro-life women are less likely to work in the first place, they earn less money when they do work, and they are more likely to be married to a skilled worker or small businessman who earns only a moderate income.

These differences in income are in turn related to the different educational and occupational choices these women have made along the way. Among pro-choice women, almost four out of ten (37 percent) had undertaken some graduate work beyond the BA degree, and 18 percent had an MD, a law degree, a PhD., or a similar postgraduate degree. Pro-life women, by comparison, had far less education: 10 percent of them had only a high school education or less; and another 30 percent never finished college (in contrast with only 8 percent of the pro-choice women). Only 6 percent of all pro-life women had a law degree, a PhD., or a medical degree.

These educational differences were in turn related to occupational differences among the women in this study. Because of their higher levels of education, pro-choice women tended to be employed in the major professions, as administrators, owners of small businesses, or executives in large businesses. The pro-life women tended to be housewives or, of the few who worked, to be in the traditional female jobs of teaching, social work, and nursing. (The choice of home life over public life held true for even the 6 percent of pro-life women with an advanced degree: of the married women who had such degrees, at the time of our interviews only one of them had not retired from her profession after marriage.)

These economic and social differences were also tied to choices that women on each side had made about marriage and family life. For example, 23 percent of pro-choice women had never married, compared with only 16 percent of pro-life women; 14 percent of pro-choice women had been divorced, compared with 5 percent of pro-life women. The size of the families these women had was also different. The average pro-choice family had between one and two children and was more likely to have one; pro-life families averaged between two and three children and were more likely to have three. (Among the pro-life women, 23 percent had five or more children; 16 percent had seven or more children.) Pro-life women also tended to marry at a slightly younger age and to have had their first child earlier.

Finally, the women on each side differed dramatically in their religious affiliation and in the role that religion played in their lives. Almost 80 percent of the women active in the pro-life movement at the present time are Catholics. The remainder are Protestants (9 percent), persons who claim no religion (5 percent), and Jews (1 percent). In sharp contrast, 63 percent of pro-choice women say that they have no religion, 22 percent think of themselves as vaguely Protestant, 3 percent are Jewish, and 9 percent have what they call a "personal" religion. We found no one in our sample of pro-choice activists who claimed to be a Catholic at the time of the interviews.

When we asked activists what religion they were raised in as a child, however, a different picture emerged. For example, 20 percent of the pro-choice activists were raised as Catholics, 42 percent were raised as Protestants, and 15 percent were raised in the Jewish faith. In this group that describes itself as predominantly without religious affiliation, therefore, only 14 percent say they were not brought up in any formal religious faith. By the same token, although almost 80 percent of present pro-life activists are Catholic, only 58 percent were raised in that religion (15 percent were raised as Protestants and 3 percent as Jews). Thus, almost 20 percent of the pro-life activists in this study are converts to Catholicism, people who have actively chosen to follow a given religious faith, in striking contrast to pro-choice people, who have actively chosen not to follow any.

Perhaps the single most dramatic difference between the two groups, however, is in the role that religion plays in their lives. Almost three-quarters of the pro-choice people interviewed said that formal religion was either unimportant or completely irrelevant to them, and their attitudes are correlated with behavior: only 25 percent of the pro-choice women said they *ever* attend church, and most of these said they do so only occasionally. Among pro-life people, by contrast, 69 percent said religion was important in their lives, and an additional 22 percent said that it was very important. For pro-life women, too, these attitudes are correlated with behavior: half of those pro-life women interviewed said they attend church regularly once a week, and another 13 percent said they do so even more often. Whereas 80 percent of pro-choice people never attend church, only 2 percent of pro-life advocates never do so.

Keeping in mind that the statistical use of averages has inherent difficulties, we ask, who are the "average" pro-choice and pro-life advocates? When the social background data are looked at carefully, two profiles emerge. The average pro-choice activist is a forty-four-year-old married woman who grew up in a large metropolitan area and whose father was a college graduate. She was married at age twenty-two, has one or two children, and has had some graduate or professional training beyond the BA degree. She is married to a professional man, is herself employed in a regular job, and her family income is more than $50,000 a year. She is not religiously active, feels that religion is not important to her, and attends church very rarely if at all.

The average pro-life woman is also a forty-four-year-old married woman who grew up in a large metropolitan area. She married at age seventeen and has three children or more. Her father was a high school graduate, and she has some college education or may have a BA degree. She is not employed in the paid labor force and is married to a small businessman or a lower-level white-collar worker; her family income is $30,000 a year. She is Catholic (and may have converted), and her religion is one of the most important aspects of her life: she attends church at least once a week and occasionally more often.

Interests and Passions

To the social scientist (and perhaps to most of us) these social background characteristics connote lifestyles as well. We intuitively clothe these bare statistics with assumptions about beliefs and values. When we do so, the pro-choice women emerge as educated, affluent, liberal professionals, whose lack of religious affiliation suggests a secular, "modern," or (as pro-life people would have it) "utilitarian" outlook on life. Similarly, the income, education, marital patterns, and religious devotion of pro-life women suggest that they are traditional, hard-working people ("polyester types" to their opponents), who hold conservative views on life. We may be entitled to assume that individuals' social backgrounds act to shape and mold their social attitudes, but it is important to realize that the relationship between social worlds and social values is a very complex one.

Perhaps one example will serve to illustrate the point. A number of pro-life women in this study emphatically rejected an expression that pro-choice women tend to use almost unthinkingly – the expression *unwanted pregnancy*. Pro-life women argued forcefully that a better term would be a *surprise* pregnancy, asserting that although a pregnancy may be momentarily unwanted, the child that results from the pregnancy almost never is. Even such a simple thing – what to call an unanticipated pregnancy – calls into play an individual's values and resources. Keeping in mind our profile of the average pro-life person, it is obvious that a woman who does not work in the paid labor force, who does not have a college degree, whose religion is important to her, and who has already committed herself wholeheartedly to marriage and a large family is well equipped to believe that an unanticipated pregnancy usually becomes a beloved child. Her life is arranged so that for her, this belief is true. This view is consistent not only with her values, which she has held from earliest childhood, but with her social resources as well. It should not be surprising, therefore, that her world view leads her to believe that everyone else can "make room for one more" as easily as she can and that therefore it supports her in her conviction that abortion is cruel, wicked, and self-indulgent.

It is almost certainly the case that an unplanned pregnancy is never an easy thing for anyone. Keeping in mind the profile of the average pro-choice woman, however, it is evident that a woman who is employed full time, who has an affluent lifestyle that depends in part on her contribution to the family income, and who expects to give a child as good a life as she herself has had with respect to educational, social, and economic advantages will draw on a different reality when she finds herself being skeptical about the ability of the average person to transform unwanted pregnancies into well-loved (and well-cared-for) children.

The relationship between passions and interests is thus more dynamic than it might appear at first. It is true that at one level, pro-choice and pro-life attitudes on abortion are self-serving: activists on each side have different views of the morality of abortion because their chosen lifestyles leave them with different needs for abortion; and both sides have values that provide a moral basis for their abortion needs in particular and their lifestyles in general. But this is only half the story. The values that lead pro-life and pro-choice women into different attitudes toward abortion are the same values that led them at an earlier time to adopt different lifestyles that supported a given view of abortion.

For example, pro-life women have *always* valued family roles very highly and have arranged their lives accordingly. They did not acquire high-level educational and occupational skills, for example, because they married, and they married because their values suggested that this would be the most satisfying life open to them. Similarly, pro-choice women postponed (or avoided) marriage and family roles because they chose to acquire the skills they needed to be successful in the larger world, having concluded that the role of wife and mother was too limited for them. Thus, activists on both sides of the issue are women who have a given set of values about what are the most satisfying and appropriate roles for women, and they have made *life commitments that now limit their ability to change their minds.* Women who have many children and little education, for example, are seriously handicapped in attempting to become doctors or lawyers; women who have reached their late forties with few children or none are limited in their ability to build (or rebuild) a family. For most of these activists, therefore, their position on abortion is the "tip of the iceberg," a shorthand way of supporting and proclaiming not only a complex set of values but a given set of social resources as well.

To put the matter differently, we might say that for pro-life women the traditional division of life into separate male roles and female roles still works, but for pro-choice women it does not. Having made a commitment to the traditional female roles of wife, mother, and homemaker, pro-life women are limited in those kinds of resources – education, class status, recent occupational experiences – they would need to compete in what has traditionally been the male sphere, namely, the paid labor force. The average pro-choice woman, in contrast, is comparatively well endowed with exactly those resources: she is highly educated, she already has a job, and she has recent (and continuous) experience in the job market.

In consequence, anything that supports a traditional division of labor into male and female worlds is, broadly speaking, in the interests of pro-life women because that is where their resources lie. Conversely, such a traditional division of labor, when strictly enforced, is against the interests of pro-choice women because it limits their abilities to use the valuable "male" resources that they have in relative abundance. It is therefore apparent that attitudes toward abortion, even though rooted in childhood experiences, are also intimately related to present-day interests. Women who oppose abortion and seek to make it officially unavailable are declaring, both practically and symbolically, that women's reproductive roles should be given social primacy. Once an embryo is defined as a child and an abortion as the death of a person, almost everything else in a woman's life must "go on hold" during the course of her pregnancy: any attempt to gain "male" resources such as a job, an education, or other skills must be subordinated to her uniquely female responsibility of serving the needs of this newly conceived person. Thus, when personhood is bestowed on the embryo, women's nonreproductive roles are made secondary to their reproductive roles. The act of conception therefore creates a pregnant woman rather than a woman who is pregnant; it creates a woman whose life, in cases where roles or values clash, is defined by the fact that she is – or may become – pregnant. [...]

Thus, the sides are fundamentally opposed to each other not only on the issue of abortion but also on what abortion *means*. Women who have many "human capital" resources of the traditionally male variety want to see motherhood recognized as a private, discretionary choice. Women who have few of these resources and limited opportunities in the job market want to see motherhood recognized as the most important thing a woman can do. In order for pro-choice women to achieve their goals, therefore, they *must* argue that motherhood is not a primary, inevitable, or "natural" role for all women; for pro-life women to achieve their goals, they *must* argue that it is. In short, the debate rests on the question of whether women's fertility is to be socially recognized as a resource or as a handicap. [...]

Abortion [...] strips the veil of sanctity from motherhood. When pregnancy is discretionary – when people are allowed to put anything else they value in front of it – then motherhood has been demoted from a sacred calling to a job. In effect, the legalization of abortion serves to make men and women more "unisex" by deemphasizing what makes them different – the ability of women to visibly and directly carry the next generation. Thus, pro-choice women are emphatic about their right to compete equally with men without the burden of an unplanned pregnancy, and pro-life women are equally emphatic about their belief that men and women have different roles in life and that pregnancy is a gift instead of a burden. [...]

Abortion also has a symbolic dimension that separates the needs and interests of homemakers and workers in the paid labor force. In sofar as abortion allows a woman to get a job, to get training for a job, or to advance in a job, it does more than provide social support for working women over homemakers; it also seems to support the value of economic considerations over moral ones. Many pro-life people interviewed said that although their commitment to traditional family roles meant very real material deprivations to themselves and their families, the moral benefits of such a choice more than made up for it.

> My girls babysit and the boys garden and have paper routes and things like that. I say that if we had a lot of money that would still be my philosophy, though I don't know because we haven't been in that position. But it's a sacrifice to have a larger family. So when I hear these figures that it takes $65,000 from birth to [raise a child], I think that's ridiculous. That's a new bike every year. That's private colleges. That's a complete new outfit when school opens. Well, we've got seven daughters who wear hand-me-downs, and we hope that sometime in their eighteen years at home each one has a new bike somewhere along the line, but otherwise it's hand-me-downs. Those figures are inflated to give those children everything, and I think that's not good for them.

For pro-life people, a world view that puts the economic before the noneconomic hopelessly confuses two different kinds of worlds. For them, the private world of family as traditionally experienced is the one place in human society where none of us a price tag. Home, as Robert Frost pointed out, is where they have to take you in, whatever your social worth. Whether one is a surgeon or a rag picker, the family is, at least ideally, the place where love is unconditional.

Pro-life people and pro-life women in particular have very real reasons to fear such a state of affairs. Not only do they see an achievement-based world as harsh, superficial, and ultimately ruthless; they are relatively less well-equipped to operate in that world. A considerable amount of social science research has suggested, at least in the realm of medical treatment, that there is an increasing tendency to judge people by their official (achieved) worth.[1] Pro-life people have relatively fewer official achievements in part because they have been doing what they see as a moral task, namely, raising children and making a home; and they see themselves as becoming handicapped in a world that discounts not only their social contributions but their personal lives as well.

It is relevant in this context to recall the grounds on which pro-life people argue that the embryo is a baby: that it is genetically human. To insist that the embryo is a baby because it is genetically human is to make a claim that it is both wrong and impossible to make distinctions between humans at all. Protecting the life of the embryo, which is by definition an entity whose social worth is all yet to come, means protecting others who feel that they may be defined as having low social worth; more broadly, it means protecting a legal view of personhood that emphatically rejects social worth criteria. [...]

The Core of the Debate

In summary, women come to be pro-life and pro-choice activists as the end result of lives that center around different definitions of motherhood. They grow up with a belief about the nature of the embryo, so events in their lives lead them to believe that the embryo is a unique person, or a fetus; that people are intimately tied to their biological roles, or that these roles are but a minor part of life; that motherhood is the most important and satisfying role open to a woman, or that motherhood is only one of several roles, a burden when defined as the only role. These beliefs and values are rooted in the concrete circumstances of women's lives – their educations, incomes, occupations, and the different marital and family choices they have made along the way – and they work simultaneously to shape those circumstances in turn. Values about the relative place of reason and faith, about the role of actively planning for life versus learning to accept gracefully life's unknowns, of the relative satisfactions inherent in work and family – all of these factors place activists in a specific relationship to the larger world and give them a specific set of resources with which to confront that world.

The simultaneous and on-going modification of both their lives and their values by each other finds these activists located in a specific place in the social world. They are financially successful, or they are not. They become highly educated, or they do not. They become married and have a large family, or they have a small one. And at each step of the way, both their values and their lives have undergone either ratification or revision.

Pro-choice and pro-life activists live in different worlds, and the scope of their lives, as both adults and children, fortifies them in their belief that their own views on abortion are the more correct, more moral, and more reasonable. When added to this is the fact that should "the other side" win, one group of women will see the very real devaluation of their lives and life resources, it is not surprising that the abortion debate has generated so much heat and so little light.

Study Questions

1 What is the "social location" of a self-described "prochoice" activist? What is the "social location" of a self-described "prolife" activist?

2 Explain how the different social backgrounds and life commitments of these two groups of activists lead to different social constructions of family life and motherhood in terms of the following issues: thinking about "unplanned pregnancies," thinking about a traditional sexual division of labor, thinking about equality of roles vs. equality of status, thinking about sexuality and contraception.

3 How does Lisa McGirr's analysis of the Christian Right provide further insight into the position that prolife activists have taken on abortion?

Note

1. See, e.g., Victor Fuchs, *Who Shall Live? Health, Economics, and Social Choice* (New York: Basic Books, 1974); H. Tristam Engelhardt, Jr., ed., *Science, Ethics, and Medicine* (Hasting-on-Hudson, NY: Hastings Center, Institute of Society, Ethics, and Life Sciences, 1976); Diana Crane, *Sanctity of Social Life* (New York: Russell Sage, 1975); and Paul Ramsey, *Ethics at the Edges of Life: Medical and Legal Intersections* (New Haven, CT: Yale University Press, 1978).

CHAPTER 40

The Making and Unmaking
of Modern Families

Judith Stacey

*Professor of gender studies and sociology, Judith Stacy (1945–) was born in Irvington, New
Jersey, to a meat dealer and a decorator. Noted for her expertise on contemporary gender,
family, and sexuality issues, she has consulted on five documentary films, appeared on TV,
and contributed numerous articles to newspapers and magazines. Her books include* In the
Name of the Family: Rethinking Family Values in a Postmodern Age *(1996) and* Brave
New Families: Stories of Domestic Upheaval in Late Twentieth-Century America
(1991), from which the "Introduction" is excerpted here.

*On a spring afternoon half a century from today, the Joneses are gathering to sing
"Happy Birthday" to Junior.*

*There's Dad and his third wife, Mom and her second husband, Junior's two half
brothers from his father's first marriage, his six stepsisters from his mother's spouse's
previous unions, 100-year-old Great-Grandpa, all eight of Junior's current "grandparents," assorted aunts, uncles-in-law and stepcousins.*

*While one robot scoops up the gift wrappings and another blows out the candles,
Junior makes a wish – that he didn't have so many relatives.*

*The family tree by the year 2033 will be rooted as deeply as ever in America's social
landscape, but it will be sprouting some odd branches.*

– U.S. News & World Report[1]

In the summer of 1986 I attended a wedding ceremony in a small Christian pentecostal church in the Silicon Valley. The service celebrated the same "traditional"
family patterns and values that two years earlier had inspired a "profamily" movement to assist Ronald Reagan's landslide reelection to the presidency of the United
States. At the same time, however, the pastor's rhetoric displayed substantial sympathy with feminist criticisms of patriarchal marriage. "A ring is not a shackle, and

marriage is not a relationship of domination," he instructed the groom. Moreover, complex patterns of divorce, remarriage, and stepkinship linked the members of the wedding party and their guests. The group bore far greater resemblance to the postmodern family of the imaginary twenty-first-century Joneses than it did to the image of "traditional" family life that arouses the nostalgic fantasies so widespread among critics of contemporary family practices.

In the final decades before the twenty-first century, passionate contests over changing family life in the United States have polarized vast numbers of citizens. Outside the Supreme Court of the United States, righteous, placard-carrying Right-to-Lifers square off against feminists and civil libertarians demonstrating their anguish over the steady dismantling of women's reproductive freedom. On the same day in July 1989 when New York's highest court expanded the legal definition of a family to extend rent-control protection to gay couples, a coalition of conservative clergymen in San Francisco blocked implementation of their city's new "domestic partners" ordinance. "It is the totality of the relationship," proclaimed the New York judge, "As evidenced by the dedication, caring and self-sacrifice of the parties which should, in the final analysis, control" the definition of family.[2] But just this concept of family is anathema to "profamily" activists. Declaring that the attempt by the San Francisco Board of Supervisors to grant legal status to unmarried heterosexual and homosexual couples "arbitrarily redefined the time-honored and hallowed nature of the family," the clergymen's petition was signed by sufficient citizens to force the ordinance into a referendum battle.[3] The reckoning came in November 1989, when the electorate of the city many consider to be the national capital of family change narrowly defeated the domestic partners law.

Most popular, as well as many scholarly, assessments of family change anxiously and misguidedly debate whether "the family" will survive the twentieth century at all.[4] Anxieties like these are far from new. "For at least 150 years," historian Linda Gordon writes, "there have been periods of fear that 'the family' – meaning a popular image of what families were supposed to be like, by no means a correct recollection of any actual 'traditional' family – was in decline; and these fears have tended to escalate in periods of social stress."[5] The actual subject of this recurring, fretful discourse is a historically specific form and concept of family life, one that most historians identify as the "modern" family. Students in a course I teach called "The Making and Unmaking of Modern Families" helped me realize that many of us who write and teach about American family life have not abetted public understanding of family change with our counterintuitive use of the concept, the "modern" family. The "modern" family of sociological theory and historical convention designates a form no longer prevalent in the United States – an intact nuclear household unit composed of a male breadwinner, his full-time homemaker wife, and their dependent children. This is precisely the form of family life that many mistake for an ancient, essential, and now-endangered institution.

"How many of you grew up in a modern family?" I used to ask my students at the beginning of each term. I expected the proportion of raised hands to decline, like the modern family, with the years. It baffled me at first to receive precisely the inverse response. Just when demographers were reporting that twice as many American households were headed by divorced, separated, and never-married individuals as were occupied by "modern" families, increasing numbers of my students claimed to have grown up in "modern" ones. This seemingly anomalous finding was the product, of course, of my poorly conceived survey question. Just as I had anticipated, over the years fewer and fewer of my students were coming of age in Ozzie and Harriet families. Quite sensibly, however, unlike me, they did not regard such families as "modern"; to them they were archaic "traditional" ones. Those contemporary family relationships that my students took to be modern comprise the "post-modern" family terrain that is the central subject of this book. [...]

Feminism as Midwife to Postindustrial Society

Feminists intentionally accelerated the modern family's demise. *The Feminine Mystique*, Betty Friedan's best-selling critique of "the problem that has no name," inspired the awakening women's movement to launch a full-scale attack on the exploitative and stultifying effects of women's confinement and dependency as homemaker. Soon feminist scholars were warning women that "in truth, being a housewife makes women sick."[6] This backward-looking critique of a declining institution and culture, one that I personally embraced wholeheartedly and helped to disseminate, colluded unwittingly in postindustrial processes, and at considerable political cost to the feminist movement. Although we intended the institutions of domesticity and their male beneficiaries to be the targets of our critique, we placed housewives on the defensive just when sizable numbers of working-class women were attaining this long-denied status. Feminists provided ideological support for divorce and for the soaring rates of female-headed households. Feminist enthusiasm for female autonomy encouraged women's massive entry into the postindustrial labor market. This, in turn, abetted the corporate deunionization strategies that have accompanied the reorganization of the US economy.

Millions of women like myself, derived enormous, tangible benefits from the changes in postindustrial home and work life and from the ways in which feminist ideology encouraged us to initiate and cope with such changes.[7] The lioness's share of these benefits, however, fell to privileged women. As postindustrial society became entrenched, many women, perhaps the majority, found their economic and personal conditions worsening. While unionized occupations and real wages began to decline, women were becoming the postindustrial "proletariat," performing most of the nation's low-skilled, poorly paid jobs. As the overall percentage of jobs that were secure and well paying declined, particularly within blue-collar occupations, increasing numbers of even white men swelled the ranks of the under- and unemployed. Nonetheless, most white male workers still labored at jobs that were skilled and comparatively well paid.[8] The devastating economic effects on women and children of endemic marital instability became widely known. Increasing percentages of women were rearing children by themselves, generally with minimal economic contributions from former husbands and fathers.[9] Yet rising numbers of single mothers who worked full time, year-round, were not earning wages sufficient to lift their families above the official poverty line.[10]

Even as marriage bonds lost their adhesive, they came to serve as a major axis of economic and social stratification. Increasingly, families required two incomes to sustain a middle-class way of life. The married female "secondary" wage earner can lift a former working-class or middle-class family into relative affluence, while the loss or lack of access to a male income drove millions of women and children into poverty.[11] In short, the drastic increase in women's paid employment in the post-industrial period yielded lots more work for mother, but with very unevenly distributed economic benefits and only modest improvements in relative earnings between women and men.[12]

In the context of these developments, many women (and men) became susceptible to the profamily appeals of an antifeminist backlash. Because of our powerful and highly visible critique of the modern family, and because of the sensationalized way by which the media disseminated this critique, feminists received much of the blame for family and social crises that attended the transition from an industrial to a postindustrial order in the United States. "Feminist ideology told women how foolish and exploited they were to be wives and mothers," turning them into "a vicious cartoon," wrote Connaught Marshner, "chairman" of the National Pro-Family Coalition, in her manifesto for the profamily movement, *The New Traditional Woman*[13] [...]

Ronald Reagan was an undeserving beneficiary of the profamily reaction, as humorist Delia Ephron observes in a book review of Maureen Reagan's dutiful memoir: "It is funny and a bit pathetic that Ronald and Nancy Reagan keep finding out their family secrets by reading their children's books. It is also ironic that this couple who symbolized a return to hearth, home and 1950's innocence should, in reality, be candidates for a very 1980s study on the troubled family."[14] The former president's less dutiful daughter, Patti Davis, agrees: "Anyone who hasn't been living in a coma for the past eight years knows that we're not a close-knit family."[15] It seems an astonishing testimony to Reagan's acclaimed media magic, therefore, that despite his own divorce and his own far-from-happily blended family, he and his *second* lady managed to serve so effectively as the symbolic figureheads of a profamily agenda, which his economic and social policies helped to further undermine.

The demographic record demonstrates that postmodern gender and kinship changes proceeded unabated throughout the Reagan era. The proportion of American households headed by single mothers grew by 21 percent, while rates of employment by mothers of young children continued their decades of ascent. When "profamily" forces helped elect Reagan to his first term in 1980, 20 percent of American children lived with a single parent, and 41 percent of mothers with children under the age of three had joined the paid labor force. When Reagan completed his second term eight years later, these figures had climbed to 24 and 54 percent respectively.[16] The year of Reagan's landslide reelection, 1984, was the first year that more working mothers placed their children in public group child care than in family day care.[17] Reaganites too hastily applauded a modest decline in divorce rates during the 1980s – to a level at which more than half of first marriages still were expected to dissolve before death. But demographers who studied marital separations as well as divorce found the years from 1980 to 1985 to show "the highest level of marital disruption yet recorded for the U.S."[18] Likewise, birth rates remained low, marriage rates fell, and homeownership rates, which had been rising for decades, declined throughout the Reagan years.[19] [. . .]

Recombinant Family Life

[. . .] [W]omen and men have been creatively remaking American family life during the past three decades of postindustrial upheaval. Out of the ashes and residue of the modern family, they have drawn on a diverse, often incongruous array of cultural, political, economic, and ideological resources, fashioning these resources into new gender and kinship strategies to cope with postindustrial challenges, burdens, and opportunities. [. . .] [F]or example, we observe people turning divorce into a kinship resource rather than a rupture, creating complex, divorce-extended families like those gathered to celebrate Junior's not-so-futuristic birthday. [We have also found] religious "traditionalists" who draw on biblical and human potential movement precepts to form communal households that join married and single members of an evangelical ministry.

And as Americans have been remaking family life, the vast majority, even those seemingly hostile to feminism, have been selectively appropriating feminist principles and practices and fusing these, patchwork style, with old and new gender, kinship, and cultural patterns. [. . .] [I]n our society, married women struggle to involve reluctant spouses in housework and child care; unmarried white women choose to have children on their own; homosexual couples exchange marriage vows and share child-rearing commitments; evangelical ministers counsel Christian husbands to learn to communicate with their wives and advise battered women to leave their abusive mates.

I call the fruits of these diverse efforts to remake contemporary family life "the postmodern family." I do this, despite my reservations about employing such a fashionable and elusive cultural concept, to signal the contested, ambivalent, and undecided character of contemporary gender and kinship arrangements. "What is the post-modern?" art historian Clive Dilnot asks rhetorically in the title of a detailed discussion of literature on postmodern culture, and his answers apply readily to the domain of present family conditions in the United States.[20] The postmodern, he maintains, "is first, an uncertainty, an insecurity, a doubt." Most of the "post-" words provoke uneasiness, because they imply simultaneously "both the end, or at least the radical transformation of, a familiar pattern of activity or group of ideas" and the emergence of "new fields of cultural activity whose contours are still unclear and whose meanings and implications...cannot yet be fathomed." The postmodern, moreover, is "characterized by the process of the linking up of areas and the crossing of the boundaries of what are conventionally considered to be disparate realms of practice."[21]

Like postmodern culture, contemporary family arrangements are diverse, fluid, and unresolved. Postindustrial social transformations have opened up such a diverse range of gender and kinship relationships as to undermine the claim in the memorable opening line from Tolstoy's *Anna Karenina*: "All happy families are alike, but every unhappy family is unhappy after its own fashion."[22] Today even happy families no longer are all alike! No longer is there a single culturally dominant family pattern to which the majority of Americans conform and most of the rest aspire. Instead, Americans today have crafted a multiplicity of family and household arrangements that we inhabit uneasily and reconstitute frequently in response to changing personal and occupational circumstances. [...]

We are living, I believe, through a transitional and contested period of family history, a period *after* the modern family order, but before what we cannot foretell. Precisely because it is not possible to characterize with a single term the competing sets of family cultures that coexist at present, I identify this family regime as postmodern. *The* postmodern family is not a new model of family life, not the next stage in an orderly progression of family history, but the stage when the belief in a logical progression of stages breaks down.[23] Rupturing evolutionary models of family history and incorporating both experimental and nostalgic elements, "the" postmodern family lurches forward and backward into an uncertain future. [...]

Study Questions

1   Why do you think Stacey titled her book, *Brave New Families*? What is "new" and what is "brave" about the American families she discusses? What do you think are her most interesting examples? Why?

2   What are the differences between the traditional, modern, and postmodern families that Stacey describes? Which of these patterns best describe your family over the past three generations?

3   What does Stacey mean when she says that feminism shaped the postmodern family?

4   What other kinds of postmodern family formations can you think of besides the ones that Stacey discusses? If she were writing her book today, how would she have to update her "Introduction"?

Notes

1. "When 'Families' will have a New Definition." 9 May, 1983.
2. Writing the majority opinion in the New York ruling, Judge Vito Titone elaborated four judicial criteria for determining what constitutes a family: (1) "exclusivity and longevity of a relationship"; (2) the "level of emotional and financial commitment"; (3) how a couple has "conducted their everyday lives and held themselves out to society"; (4) the "reliance placed upon one another for daily family services." Philip Gutis, "Court Widens Family Definition to Gay Couples Living Together," *New York Times*, 7 July 1989, pp. A1, A13.
3. Kathy Bodovitz, "Referendum Petitions Block S.F. Domestic Partners Law," *San Francisco Chronicle*, 7 July 1989, pp. A1, A30; and Don Lattin, "How Religious Groups Stopped Partners Law," *San Francisco Chronicle*, 10 July 1989, A1, A20.
4. For pessimistic assessments of family decline, see Christopher Lasch, *Haven in a Heartless World* (New York: Basic Books, 1977); Kingsley Davis, "The Meaning and Significance of Marriage in Contemporary Society," *Contemporary Marriage: Comparative Perspectives on a Changing Institution*, ed. Kingsley Davis and Amyra Grossbard-Schectman (New York: Russell Sage Foundation, 1985); and Peter Berger and Bridgitte Berger, *The War Over the Family* (Garden City, NY: Anchor Press/Doubleday, 1983). For optimistic appraisals of "the family," see Mary Jo Bane, *Here to Stay: American Families in the Twentieth Century* (New York: Basic Books, 1976); Theodore Caplow et al., *Middletown Families: Fifty Years of Change and Continuity* (Toronto: Bantam Books, 1983) and Randall Collins, *Sociology of Marriage and the Family: Gender, Love, and Property* (Chicago: Nelson-Hall, 1985). More centrist but still somewhat anxious evaluations of the state of "the family" include Alan Wolfe, *Whose Keeper? Social Science and Moral Obligation* (Berkeley: University of California Press, 1989); Bellah et al., *Habits of the Heart* (Berkeley: University of California Press, 1985); and Andrew Cherlin, "Marriage, Divorce, Remarriage: From the 1950s to the 1980s" (paper presented at the annual meeting of the American Sociological Association, San Francisco, 11 August 1989).
5. Linda Gordon, *Heroes of Their Own Lives* (New York: Viking, 1988), p. 3.
6. Jessie Bernard, *The Future of Marriage* (New York: Bantam Books, 1973).
7. See Heidi Hartmann, "Changes in Women's Economic and Family Roles in Post-World War II United States," *Women, Households, and the Economy*, ed. Lourdes Beneria and Catharine R. Stimpson (New Brunswick, N.J.: Rutgers University Press, 1987).
8. A study that attempted to operationalize Marxist criteria for assigning class categories to workers in the United States (and which excluded housewives from its sample) found "that the majority of the working class in the United States consists of women (53.6%)." Erika Olin Wright et al, "The Transformation of the American Class Structure, 1960–1980," *American Sociological Review* vol. 47, no. 6 (1982): 22. Between 1979 and 1984 job growth in middle-income occupations dropped almost 20 percent while growth of low-income jobs soared. More than 20 percent of the year-round, fulltime jobs created paid less than $7,000 (1984 dollars). In the same period white men suffered a net loss of one million jobs in the above-$28,000 bracket, while 97 percent of net employment gain for white men was in the below $7,000 bracket. Katherine Newman, *Falling from Grace: The Experience of Downward Mobility in the American Middle Class* (New York: Free Press, 1988), p. 31. See also Bennett Harrison and Barry Bluestone, *The Great U-Turn* (New York: Basic Books, 1988).
9. The much-publicized findings from Lenore Weitzman's study of no-fault divorce in California underscore this fact. In the first year after divorce, women and their minor children suffered a 73 percent decline in their standard of living, while husbands enjoyed a 42 percent gain. Lenore Weitzman, *The Divorce Revolution: The Unexpected Social and Economic Consequences for Women and Children in America* (New York: Free Press, 1985).

See also Terry Arendell, *Mothers and Divorce: Social, Economic and Social Dilemmas* (Berkeley: University of California Press, 1986); and Newman, chap. 7.

10. In 1980 households headed by fully employed women had a poverty rate almost three times greater than husband-wife households and twice that of households headed by unmarried men. For the relationship between female employment and poverty, see Joan Smith, "The Paradox of Women's Poverty: Wage-Earning Women and Economic Transformation," *Signs* 10, no. 2 (1984): 291–310. The concept "feminization of poverty," however, misrepresents significant features of contemporary poverty, particularly the worsening conditions for minority men. See Pamela Sparr, "Reevaluating Feminist Economics: 'Feminization of Poverty' Ignores Key Issues," *For Crying Out Loud: Women and Poverty in the United States*, ed. Rochelle Lefkowitz and Ann Withorn (New York: Pilgrim Press, 1986), and Linda Burnham, "Has Poverty Been Feminized in Black America?," *For Crying Out Loud*.

11. In 1960 households with working wives had 25 percent more income than those with only husbands working. By 1983 the former had 47 percent more income than the latter. Susan Van Horn, *Women, Work, and Fertility* (New York University Press, 1988), p. 173. The lower a family's annual income, the higher the proportion contributed by women. Paradoxically, however, there is now an inverse relationship between family income and the percentage of wives in the labor force. See Barbara F. Reskin and Heidi I. Hartmann, eds., *Women's Work, Men's Work: Sex Segregation on the Job* (Washington, DC: National Academy Press, 1986), p. 4. Families with unemployed wives have been losing economic ground both in absolute terms and relative to two-earner families. Between 1975 and 1983, the median income of married-couple households with employed wives rose by 0.6 percent while that of married-couple households without employed wives fell by 7.3 percent. Newman, *Falling from Grace*, p. 38.

12. There are recent indications, however, of more substantial reductions in the persistent earnings gap between women and men. Although between 1960 and 1980 the average hourly wages of full-time women workers remained near 60 percent of male hourly wages, by 1986 the ratio based on weekly earnings of full-time workers had increased to 70 percent. Stephen D. McLaughlin et al., *The Changing Lives of American Women* (Chapel Hill: University of North Carolina Press, 1988), p. 113. However, a portion of this gain was caused by a decline in earnings for blue-collar men.

13. Connaught Marshner, *The New Traditional Woman* (Washington, DC. Free Congress Research and Education Foundation, 1982), p. 1; Faye Ginsburg, *Contested Lives: The Abortion Debate in an American Community* (Berkeley: University of California Press, 1989), an ethnographic study of activists on both sides of the abortion struggle in North Dakota, documents the widespread perception of feminists as antinurturant.

14. Delia Ephron, "The Teflon Daddy," *New York Times Book Review,* 26 March 1989.

15. "The Daughter Who Begs to Differ," *San Francisco Chronicle,* 22 September 1989, p. A10.

16. Congressional report, "U.S. Children and Their Families: Current Traditions and Recent Trends," quoted in Larry Liebert, "Gloomy Statistics and the Future of Poor Children," *San Francisco Chronicle,* 2 October 1989, p. A2. See also Sara A. Levitan et al, *What's Happening to the American Family? Tensions, Hopes, Realities*, rev. ed. (Baltimore: Johns Hopkins University Press, 1988).

17. Karen Skold, "The Interests of Feminists and Children in Child Care," *Feminism, Children, and the New Families*, eds. Sanford M. Dornbusch and Myra H. Strober (New York: Guilford Press, 1988), p. 119. Also note that a sharp increase in the use of formal childcare occurred during Reagan's first term, from 16 percent in 1982 to 25 percent in 1985. Sara A. Levitan, Richard S. Belous, and Frank Gallo, *What's Happening to the American Family?: Tensions, Hopes, Realities*, rev. ed. (Baltimore: Johns Hopkins University Press, 1988).

18. Larry Bumpass and Theresa Castro, "Recent Trends in Differentials in Marital Disruption," Working Paper 87-20 (University of Wisconsin-Madison: Center for Demography

and Ecology, September 1988). They project that two-thirds of recent marriages will dissolve before death. Levitan, Belous, and Gallo, writing earlier, projected that 54 percent will divorce. *What's Happening to the American Family?*, p. 102. The temporary decline in divorce rates was due to "cohort effects" – a decline in the proportion of the population currently in the age and marital status categories that place them "at risk" for divorce.

19. In 1987 there were 1.8 births per woman. Levitan, Belous, and Gallo, *What's Happening to the American Family?*, p. 42 [. . .] Marriage rates during peak marriage ages dropped by 50 percent between 1975 and 1985. Bumpass and Castro, "Recent Trends," p. 24. A study for the Joint Economic Committee of Congress found that home ownership, which had been rising throughout the post-World War II period, peaked at 65.6 percent of the population in 1980 and then began falling, hitting 63.9 percent in 1988. Reported in Jennifer Dixon, "Senator Bentsen Says Home Ownership Has Declined," *San Francisco Examiner*, 22 October 1989, p. F10. See also Barbara Ehrenreich, *Fear of Falling: The Inner Life of the Middle Class* (New York: Pantheon, 1989), p. 205.

20. Clive Dilnot, "What is the Post-Modern?" *Art History* 9, no. 2 (June 1986): 245–63.

21. Ibid., pp. 245, 249

22. Leo Tolstoy, *Anna Karenina* (1877); New York: New American Library, 1961), p. 17.

23. The postmodern condition emerges, Jean-François Lyotard argues in *The Postmodern Condition: A Report on Knowledge* (translated by Geoff Bennington and Brian Massumi, 1979, Reprint. Manchester: Manchester University Press, 1984), when legitimation through grand historical narratives has broken down. I sidestep here the debate over whether the postmodern represents a clear break with the modern, or as Nancy Scheper-Hughes argued during a conference on "Anthropology and Modernity" held at the University of California, Berkeley, in April 1989, is simply "capitalism on speed." Mascia-Lees et al. discuss feminist concerns that the rejection of grand narratives coincides with new attempts by women and other subordinated groups to write their own. (Frances E. Mascia-Lees, Patricia Sharpe, and Colleen Ballerino Cohen, "The Postmodernist Turn in Anthropology: Cautions From a Feminist Perspective," *Signs* 15, no. 1 (Autumn 1989): 7–33.) For additional useful discussions of feminism, modernism, and postmodernism, see Janet Wolff, *Feminine Sentences: Essays on Women and Culture* (Berkeley: University of California Press, 1990).

CHAPTER 41

From *Jasmine*

Bharati Mukherjee

Once described as "the foremost chronicler of the multicultural new America," Bharati Mukherjee (1940–) is a novelist, short-story writer, and teacher. Born to upper-class Brahmin parents in Calcutta, India, she was raised in a large household of relatives. Her mother, who was married at age 16, encouraged her to attend college and seek a professional career. Mukherjee moved to the US in 1959, received her MFA in Creative Writing in 1963, and her PhD in English at the University of Iowa in 1969. She lived for 12 years in Canada, and has taught at numerous universities. The most persistent themes in Mukherjee's fiction center on the conflicts of adapting to a new culture and the ways that immigrants influence contemporary American life. The excerpt that follows is from her best-known novel, Jasmine *(1989), whose heroine takes on numerous identities and families in order to meet the challenges of an increasingly globalized US society.*

Chapter 1

Lifetimes ago, under a banyan tree in the village of Hasnapur, an astrologer cupped his ears – his satellite dish to the stars – and foretold my widowhood and exile. I was only seven then, fast and venturesome, scabrous-armed from leaves and thorns.

"No!" I shouted. "You're a crazy old man. You don't know what my future holds!"

"Suit yourself," the astrologer cackled. "What is to happen will happen." Then he chucked me hard on the head.

I fell. My teeth cut into my tongue. A twig sticking out of the bundle of firewood I'd scavenged punched a star-shaped wound into my forehead. I lay still. The astrologer re-entered his trance. I was nothing, a speck in the solar system. Bad times were on their way. I was helpless, doomed. The star bled.

"I don't believe you," I whispered.

The astrologer folded up his tattered mat and pushed his feet into rubber sandals. "Fate is Fate. When Behula's bridegroom was fated to die of snakebite on their wedding night, did building a steel fortress prevent his death? A magic snake will penetrate solid walls when necessary."

I smelled the sweetness of winter wildflowers. Quails hopped, hiding and seeking me in the long grass. Squirrels as tiny as mice swished over my arms, dropping nuts. The trees were stooped and gnarled, as though the ghosts of old women had taken root. I always felt the she-ghosts were guarding me. I didn't feel I was nothing.

"Go join your sisters," the man with the capacious ears commanded. "A girl shouldn't be wandering here by herself." He pulled me to my feet and pointed to the trail that led out of the woods to the river bend.

I dragged my bundle to the river bend. I hated that river bend. The water pooled there, sludgy brown, and was choked with hyacinths and feces from the buffaloes that village boys washed upstream. Women were scouring brass pots with ashes. Dhobis were whomping clothes clean on stone slabs. Housewives squabbled while lowering their pails into a drying well. My older sisters, slow, happy girls with butter-smooth arms, were still bathing on the steps that led down to the river.

"What happened?" my sisters shrieked as they sponged the bleeding star on my forehead with the wetted ends of their veils. "Now your face is scarred for life! How will the family ever find you a husband?"

I broke away from their solicitous grip. "It's not a scar," I shouted, "it's my third eye." In the stories that our mother recited, the holiest sages developed an extra eye right in the middle of their foreheads. Through that eye they peered out into invisible worlds. "Now I'm a sage."

My sisters scampered up the slippery steps, grabbed their pitchers and my bundle of firewood, and ran to get help from the women at the well.

I swam to where the river was a sun-gold haze. I kicked and paddled in a rage. Suddenly my fingers scraped the soft waterlogged carcass of a small dog. The body was rotten, the eyes had been eaten. The moment I touched it, the body broke in two, as though the water had been its glue. A stench leaked out of the broken body, and then both pieces quickly sank.

That stench stays with me. I'm twenty-four now, I live in Baden, Elsa County, Iowa, but every time I lift a glass of water to my lips, fleetingly I smell it. I know what I don't want to become.

Chapter 2

Taylor didn't want me to run away to Iowa. How can anyone leave New York, he said, how can *you* leave New York, you belong here. Iowa's dull and it's flat, he said.

So is Punjab, I said.

You deserve better.

There are many things I deserve, not all of them better. Taylor thought dull was the absence of action, but dull is its own kind of action. Dullness is a kind of luxury.

Taylor was wrong. Iowa isn't flat, not Elsa County.

It's a late May afternoon in a dry season and sunlight crests the hillocks like sea foam, then angles across the rolling sea of Lutzes' ground before snagging on the maples and box elders at the far end of ours. The Lutzes and Ripplemeyers' fifteen hundred acres cut across a dozen ponds and glacial moraines, back to back in a six-mile swath. The Ripplemeyer land: Bud's and mine and Du's. Jane Ripplemeyer has a bank account. So does Jyoti Vijh, in a different city. Bud's father started the First Bank of Baden above the barber's; now Bud runs it out of a smart low building between Kwik Copy and the new Drug Town.

Bud wants me to marry him, "officially," he says, before the baby comes. People assume we're married. He's a small-town banker, he's not allowed to do impulsive things. I'm less than half his age, and very foreign. We're the kind who marry. Going for me is this: he wasn't in a wheelchair when we met. I didn't leave him after it happened.

From the kitchen I can see the only Lutz boy, Darrel, work the ground. Darrel looks lost these days, like a little boy, inside the double-wide, air-conditioned cab of a monster tractor. Gene Lutz weighed nearly three hundred pounds and needed every square inch.

This is Darrel's first planting alone. The wheels of his tractor are plumed with dust as fine as talcum. The contour-plowed fields are quilts in shades of pale green and dry brown. Closer in, where our ground slopes into the Lutzes', Shadow, Darrel's huge black dog, picks his way through ankle-high tufts of corn. A farm dog knows not to damage leaves, even when it races ahead after a weasel or a field mouse. The topsoil rising from Shadow's paws looks like pockets of smoke.

Last winter Gene and Carol Lutz went to California as they usually did in January, after the money was in and before the taxes were due, and Gene, who was fifty-four years old, choked to death on a piece of Mexican food. He was so heavy Carol couldn't lift him to do the Heimlich maneuver. The waiters were all illegals who went into hiding as soon as the police were called.

Gene looked after everything for me when Bud was in the hospital. Now Bud wants to do the same for Darrel and the Lutz farm, but he's not the man he once was. I can look out Mother Ripplemeyer's back window and not see to the end of our small empire of ownership. Gene used to say to Bud, "Put our farms smack in the middle of the Loop and we'd about reach from Wrigley to Comiskey."

In our three and a half years together, I have given Bud a new trilogy to contemplate: Brahma, Vishnu, and Shiva. And he has lent me his: Musial, Brock, and Gibson. Bud's father grew up in southern Iowa, and Gene's father came from Davenport. Ottumwa got Cardinal broadcasts, and Davenport got the Cubs. Baseball loyalties are passed from fathers to sons. Bud says he's a Cardinals banker in Cubbie land. He favors speed and execution: he'll lend to risk takers who'll plant new crops and try new methods. Gene Lutz went with proven power: corn, beans, and hogs. After a good year, he'd buy himself the latest gadget from the implement dealer: immense tractors with air-conditioned cabs, equipped with stereo tape deck. A typical Cubbie tractor, Bud would joke, all power and no mobility – but he approved the purchase anyhow. Gene even painted an official Cubs logo on its side. I thought it said *Ubs*. Darrel painted the Hawkeye logo over it.

Darrel has a sister out in San Diego, married to a naval officer. Carol moved to be near her. With all the old Iowans in Southern California, she does not think she'll be a widow for long. Darrel had a girl living with him last fall, but she left for Texas after the first Alberta Clipper.

Darrel talks of selling, and I don't blame him. A thousand acres is too much for someone who graduated from Northern Iowa just last summer. He'd like to go to New Mexico, he says, and open up a franchise, away from the hogs and cold and farmer's hours. Radio Shack, say. He's only a year younger than I, but I cannot guess his idea of reality. I treat him as an innocent.

Yesterday he came over for dinner. People are getting used to some of my concoctions, even if they make a show of fanning their mouths. They get disappointed if there's not *something* Indian on the table. Last summer Darrel sent away to California for "Oriental herb garden" cuttings and planted some things for me – coriander, mainly, and dill weed, fenugreek and about five kinds of chili peppers. I always make sure to use his herbs.

Last night he said that two fellows had come up from Dalton in Johnson County with plans for putting in a golf course on his father's farm. Bud told me later that the fellows from Dalton are big developers. With ground so cheap and farmers so desperate, they're snapping up huge packages for future non-ag use. Airfields and golf courses and water slides and softball parks. It breaks Bud's heart even to mention it.

Darrel's pretty worked up about it. They'd have night golf with illuminated fairways. Wednesday nights would be Ladies' Nights, Thursday nights Stags Only, Friday nights for Couples. They're copying some kind of golf-course franchise that works out West. The plan is to convert the barn into a clubhouse, with a restaurant and what he calls sports facilities. I'm not sure what they'll do with the pig house and its built-in reservoir of nightsoil.

"If you're so set on sticking with a golf course," Bud said, "why don't you buy the franchise yourself?"

"I couldn't stand watching folks tramping down my fields," he said.

"So, what'll you call the club?" I asked Darrel. It didn't seem such a bad idea. A water slide, a nighttime golf course, tennis courts inside the weathered, slanting barn.

"The Barn," Darrel said. "I was hoping you'd come up with a prettier name. Something in Indian." He started blushing. I want to say to Darrel, "You mean in Hindi, not Indian, there's no such thing as Indian," but he'll be crushed and won't say anything for the rest of the night. He comes from a place where the language you speak is what you are.

The farmers around here are like the farmers I grew up with. Modest people, never boastful, tactful and courtly in their way. A farmer is dependent on too many things outside his control; it makes for modesty. They're hemmed in by etiquette. When they break out of it, like Harlan Kroener did, you know how terrible things have gotten.

Baden is what they call a basic German community. Even the Danes and Swedes are thought to be genetically unpredictable at times. I've heard the word "inscrutable." The inscrutable Swedes. The sneaky Dutch. They aren't Amish, but they're very fond of old ways of doing things. They're conservative people with a worldly outlook.

At dinner, Bud snapped Darrel's head off. "What farmer is nuts enough to golf three or four nights a week around here?" he asked.

Darrel tried to joke about it. "Times change. Farmers change. Even Wrigley's getting lights, Bud."

Bud's probably right. Most times he's right. But being right, having to point out the cons when the borrower wants to hear only the pros, is eating him up. He pops his stomach pills, on top of everything else. Blood pressure, diuretics, all sorts of skin creams. Immobility has made him more excitable. Later that night I tried to calm him down. I said, "Darrel won't have to sell. You'll see, it'll rain." Then I took his big pink hand, speckled with golden age spots and silky with reddish blond hairs, and placed it on my stomach. His hair is bushy and mostly white, but once upon a time he was a strawberry blond with bright blue eyes. The eyes are less bright, but still a kind of blue I've never seen anywhere else. Purple flecks in a turquoise pond.

I am carrying Bud Ripplemeyer's baby. He wants me to marry him before the baby is born. He wants to be able to say, Bud and Jane Ripplemeyer proudly announce . . .

He hooks his free hand around my neck and kisses me on the mouth, hard. "Marry me?" he says. I always hear a question mark these days, after everything he says.

Bud's not like Taylor – he's never asked me about India; it scares him. He wouldn't be interested in the forecast of an old fakir under a banyan tree. Bud was wounded in the war between my fate and my will. I think sometimes I saved his life by not marrying him.

I feel so potent, a goddess.

In the kitchen, today as on all Sundays, Mother Ripplemeyer is in charge. We have gone over to Mother's for our Sunday roast. Bud and his eight brothers and sisters were born in this house. From Baden, it's the first livable house on the second dirt road after you pass Madame Cleo's. Madame Cleo cuts and styles hair in a fuchsia pink geodesic dome.

When Bud and Karin's divorce became final, Karin got their fancy three-story brick house with the columns in front, their home for twenty-eight years. The house he bought after the divorce is low and squat, a series of add-ons. It had been a hired man's house. Eventually we'll take over Mother Ripplemeyer's house. Until then, we wait out here on three hundred acres, which isn't bad. My father raised nine of us on thirty acres.

This was a three-room frame house. He rents out the three hundred acres for hay. We added a new living room with an atrium when we moved in, and a small

bedroom when we got word from the adoption agency in Des Moines that Du had
made it out to Hong Kong. The house looks small and ugly from the dirt road, but
every time I crunch into the driveway and park my old Rabbit between the rusting,
abandoned machinery and the empty silo, the add-ons cozy me into thinking that all
of us Ripplemeyers, even us new ones, belong.

Du is a Ripplemeyer. He was Du Thien. He was fourteen when we got him; now
he's seventeen, a junior in high school. He does well, though he's sometimes
contemptuous. He barely spoke English when he arrived; now he's fluent, but with
a permanent accent. "Like Kissinger," he says. They tell me I have no accent, but I
don't sound Iowan, either. I'm like those voices on the telephone, very clear and
soothing. Maybe Northern California, they say. Du says they're computer generated.

It was January when Du arrived at Des Moines from Honolulu with his agency
escort. He was wearing an ALOHA, Y'ALL T-shirt and a blue-jean jacket. We'd brought a
new duffel coat with us, as instructed. Next to Bud, he seemed so tiny, so unmarked,
for all he'd been through. The agency hadn't minded Bud's divorce. Karin could have
made trouble but didn't. The agency was charmed by the notion of Bud's "Asian"
wife, without inquiring too deeply. Du was one of the hard-to-place orphans.

He had never seen snow, never felt cold air, never worn a coat. We stopped at a
McDonald's on the way back to Baden. When we parked, Du jumped down from the
back, leaving the new coat on the seat. The wind chill was −35, and he waited for us
in the middle of the parking lot in his ALOHA, Y'ALL T-shirt while we bundled up and
locked the doors. He wasn't slapping his arms or blowing on his hands.

The day I came to Baden and walked into his bank with Mother Ripplemeyer,
looking for a job, Bud was a tall, fit, fifty-year-old banker, husband of Karin, father of
Buddy and Vern, both married farmers in nearby counties. Asia he'd thought of only
as a soy-bean market. He'd gone to Beijing on a bankers' delegation and walked the
Great Wall.

Six months later, Bud Ripplemeyer was a divorced man living with an Indian
woman in a hired man's house five miles out of town. Asia had transformed him,
made him reckless and emotional. He wanted to make up for fifty years of "selfishness," as he calls it. One night he saw a television special on boat people in Thai
prisons, and he called the agency the next day. Fates are so intertwined in the modern
world, how can a god keep them straight? A year after that, we had added Du to our
life, and Bud was confined to a wheelchair.

Mother likes to cook, but she's crotchety this afternoon. It's one of her medium-
bad days, which means she'll wink out on us entirely by the end. She is seventy-six,
and sprightly in a Younkers pantsuit, white hair squeezed into curls by Madame Cleo,
who trained in Ottumwa.

In Hasnapur a woman may be old at twenty-two.

I think of Vimla, a girl I envied because she lived in a two-story brick house with
real windows. Our hut was mud. Her marriage was the fanciest the village had ever
seen. Her father gave away a zippy red Maruti and a refrigerator in the dowry. When

he was twenty-one her husband died of typhoid, and at twenty-two she doused herself with kerosene and flung herself on a stove, shouting to the god of death, "Yama, bring me to you."

The villagers say when a clay pitcher breaks, you see that the air inside it is the same as outside. Vimla set herself on fire because she had broken her pitcher; she saw there were no insides and outsides. We are just shells of the same Absolute. In Hasnapur, Vimla's isn't a sad story. The sad story would be a woman Mother Ripplemeyer's age still working on her shell, bothering to get her hair and nails done at Madame Cleo's.

Mother Ripplemeyer tells me her Depression stories. In the beginning, I thought we could trade some world-class poverty stories, but mine make her uncomfortable. Not that she's hostile. It's like looking at the name in my passport and seeing "Jyo – " at the beginning and deciding that her mouth was not destined to make those sounds. She can't begin to picture a village in Punjab. She doesn't mind my stories about New York and Florida because she's been to Florida many times and seen enough pictures of New York. I have to be careful about those stories. I have to be careful about nearly everything I say. If I talk about India, I talk about my parents.

I could tell her about water famines in Hasnapur, how at the dried-out well docile women turned savage for the last muddy bucketful. Even here, I store water in orange-juice jars, plastic milk bottles, tumblers, mixing bowls, any container I can find. I've been through thirsty times, and not that long ago. Mother doesn't think that's crazy. The Depression turned her into a hoarder, too. She's shown me her stock of tinfoil. She stashes the foil, neatly wrapped in a flannel sheet, in a drawer built into the bed for blankets and extra pillows.

She wonders, I know, why I left. I tell her, Education, which is true enough. She knows there is something else. I say, I had a mission. I want to protect her from too much reality.

She says she likes me better than she did Karin, though Karin grew up right here in Baden and Karin's mother, who is eighty-two, still picks her up for their Lutheran Mission Relief Fund's quilting group. Last year the Relief Fund raised $18,000 for Ethiopia. Mother's group's quilt went for eleven hundred dollars to a bald, smiling man from Chicago who said it was for his granddaughter, but I read the commercial lettering on his panel truck.

Just before the divorce, according to Bud, Karin was agitating to stick Mother in the Lutheran Home. Mother senses I have different feelings about family.

The table is set and ready. Du's made a centerpiece out of some early flowers and I've polished the display rack of silver spoons. Bud has five brothers and three sisters, and they were all born or at least christened with silver spoons in their mouths. I, too, come from a family of nine. Figure the odds on that, Bud says. He has a brother in Minneapolis and a sister in Omaha and a brother named Vern Ripplemeyer, Jr., who died in Korea, the family's only other encounter with Asia. All the others are in Texas or California. After the divorce, Mother asked Karin to give the spoons back. "Call me an Indian giver," Mother likes to joke. "I mean *our* kind."

Du and Scott, whose father works down in the corn sweetener plant, are sprawled on the rug watching *Monster Truck Madness*. It's trucks versus tanks, and the tanks are creaming them. We bought ourselves a satellite dish the day after we first talked long distance to Du. There's no telling where this telecast is coming from.

Du's first question to Bud, in painful English over trans-Pacific cable, was "You have television? You get?" He talked of having watched television in his home in Saigon. We got the point. He'd had two lives, one in Saigon and another in the refugee camp. In Saigon he'd lived in a house with a large family, and he'd been happy. He doesn't talk much about the refugee camp, other than that his mother cut hair, his older brother raised fighting fish, his married sister brought back live crabs and worms for him to eat whenever she could sneak a visit from her own camp. From a chatty agency worker we know that Du's mother and brother were hacked to death in the fields by a jealous madman, after they'd gotten their visas.

"Look at that sucker fly!" Scott shouts, crawling closer to the screen. "All right!" Mud scuds behind the Scarlet Slugger.

"Whoa, Nellie!" Du can match Scott shout for shout now. "Hold on, mama!" The Slugger is the body of a Chevy Blazer welded onto a World War II tank.

Mother wanders over to the television but doesn't sit down. In an instant replay we watch the Scarlet Slugger tear up the center of a bog. I can't help thinking, It looks like a bomb crater. Does Du even think such things? I don't know what he thinks. He's called Yogi in school, mainly because his name in English sounds more like "Yo." But he is a real yogi, always in control. I've told him my stories of India, the years between India and Iowa, hoping he'd share something with me. When they're over he usually says, "That's wild. Can I go now?"

"Holy Toledo!" Mother is into it.

"Mom, it's okay, isn't it, if Scott stays for dinner?"

"If it's okay with his parents."

Scott grins at me with his perfect teeth. I envy him his teeth. We had no dentist in Hasnapur. For a long time we had no doctor either, except for Vaccinations-sahib, who rode in and out of the village in a WHO jeep. My teeth look as though they've been through slugfests. Du's seventeen and wears braces. Orthodontics was the Christmas present he asked for.

"And if the two of you wash the beans," I add.

"You aren't making the yellow stuff, Mrs. R.?" I detect disappointment.

"I will if you name it."

I see him whispering to Du, and Du's bony shoulder shrug. "Globey?" he says.

It's close enough. I took gobi aloo to the Lutheran Relief Fund craft fair last week. I am subverting the taste buds of Elsa County. I put some of last night's matar panir in the microwave. It goes well with pork, believe me.

Bud wheels himself in from his study. "I can't let the kid do it!" The kid is Darrel, whose financial forms he's been studying. "It's plain stupid. Gene would never forgive me."

I've sent away for the latest in wheelchairs, automated and really maneuverable. The doctor said, "I had a patient once who had his slugs pierced and hung on a chain around his neck." Bud said to throw them out. He didn't want to see how flattened they'd got, bouncing off his bones. The doctor is from Montana. I haven't been west of Lincoln, Nebraska. Every night the frontier creeps a little closer.

Think of banking as your business, I want to tell Bud. Don't make moral decisions for Darrel. It's his farm now. He can make half a million by selling, buy his franchise and a house, and I can look out on a golf course, which won't kill me. Bud gets too involved. It almost killed him two years ago.

"Watch him, Dad!" Du whoops. "Watch him take off!"

Bud puts away the Financial Statement and Supporting Schedules form he's been penciling. He skids and wheels closer to Du to watch the Python.

"Can you do a wheelie yet, Mr. R.?" Scott jokes.

"Boy!" He smiles. "That thing gives the guy great air!"

The Python's built himself a fancy floating suspension. Father and son watch the Snakeman win his class.

On the screen Cut Tire Class vehicles, frail as gnats, skim over churned-up mud. Helmeted men give me victory signs. They all plan on winning tonight. Nitro Express, Brawling Babe, Insane Expectations. Move over, I whisper.

Over the bleached grounds of Baden, Iowa, loose, lumpy rainclouds are massing. Good times, best times, are coming. Move over.

Mother paces between the windows. "Poor Vern." Her hands pick at lint balls I can't see. "It's blowing so hard he'll never find his way back from the barn. A man can die in a storm like this."

Bud flashes anxiety at me. His father was Vern. I calm him with a touch. He rests his head on my hip. "Kiss an old fool for love?" He grins. I bring my face down close to his big face. He kisses my chin, my cheeks, my eyelids, my temples. His lips scuttle across my forehead; they warm the cold pale star of my scar. My third eye glows, a spotlight trained on lives to come. This isn't a vision to share with Bud. He is happy. And I am happy enough.

The lemon-pale afternoon swirls indoors through torn window screens. The first lightning bugs of summer sparkle. I feel the tug of opposing forces. Hope and pain. Pain and hope.

Mother moves around the room, turning on lamps. "Seen the quilt?" she says. "How much do you think it'll bring? Thirty-five? Forty?"

In the white lamplight, ghosts float toward me. Jane, Jasmine, Jyoti.

"It'll depend on the Christian conscience of strangers," Bud jokes. "You might get more than thirty-five."

"Think how many people thirty-five dollars will feed out there."

Out there. I am not sure what Mother imagines. On the edge of the world, in flaming deserts, mangled jungles, squelchy swamps, missionaries save the needy. Out There, the darkness. But for me, for Du, In Here, safety. At least for now.

Oh, the wonder! the wonder!

Study Questions

1   What do you learn about Jasmine's identity in Chs. 1 and 2 of Mukherjee's novel? How has her family's situation in India during the 1960s shaped her ideas of religion, education, and marriage?
2   How do you know that Jasmine is telling her story during the 1980s? Find supporting evidence from Bluestone, Springsteen, or Stacey.
3   According to Jasmine, how is India reshaping American identities?
4   What does being American mean if Jasmine is a representative of the new American pioneers?

CHAPTER 42

Growing Up Biracial and Bicultural

Claudine Chiawei O'Hearn

Claudia Chiawei O'Hearn (1971–) was born in Hong Kong to a working-class Irish-American father and a Chinese mother. Raised as an American in Singapore, Belgium, and Taiwan, she moved to the United States to attend Oberlin College. After graduating in 1993, she moved to New York and worked as an editor at Pantheon books. The following excerpt comes from the "Introduction" to Half and Half: Writers on Growing Up Biracial and Bicultural *(1998), an anthology of essays by 18 writers who reflect on the complex social locations that have shaped their experiences and their identities.*

I was walking down the street the other day, on my way home from the gym, when a large woman with wiry hair run amok approached me, mumbling to herself and looking somewhat deranged, as only New Yorkers can look. As she neared me, she looked me in the eye and barked, "Half-breed bitch." I had already passed her by the time I figured out what she had said. Shocked, my first reaction was a mix of surprise and even pleasure: "How'd she know? What gave it away?" It wasn't until a block later that I became enraged and thought of a witty retort.

I stopped being American when I first came to the States to live eight years ago. Growing up in Asia, I knew being mixed set me apart, but I didn't have to name it until people began to ask, Where are you from? My father was raised in a working-class Irish American family in Fall River, Massachusetts. My mother was born near Shanghai, China, but when she was seven, on the eve of the communist revolution, she and her family fled to Taiwan. They met, romantically, and I think aptly, on an airplane (my mother was a flight attendant) and soon married – though not without first encountering resistance. My father's family were familiar with only stereotypes of Asian women, and so were not eager to invite China into the O'Hearn fold. My mother's family felt the same and took it a step further by hiring a private detective, who fortunately was unable to dig up anything incriminating about my father. Both sides eventually got over it, so we can laugh about it now, and frequently do. Following my mother's example, both of her sisters married Caucasians, creating a whole generation of hapas (Hawaiian for half) in our family.

My parents settled in Hong Kong, where I was born, and moved to Singapore, Belgium, and Ohio and finally settled in Taiwan. I consider these all to be home, with the exception of Akron, Ohio, where I experienced my first sting of racism when preschool classmates pushed me off playground slides, pulled tight their eyes, and idiotically chanted, "Ching, Chang, Chong, Chinese." Early learners. As coached by my mother, I retorted, "Chinese are better." But since these places are all home, they forfeit their definition as a single place I can come from. Suspended, I can go anywhere but home.

I don't look especially Chinese – my eyes are wide and lidded, and my hair has a Caucasian texture and color. When my mother and I walked together, people would stare, often rudely. I could see questions in their curious looks: "Is this your daughter?" We looked incongruous. It never occurred to me that my mother and I looked any more different than any other mother and daughter; and even if we did, that it would affect how we related to each other. I don't think I minded so much because I assumed that I would find a home in the States when I went there for college. To me, America was summer vacations; getting up at six in the morning to watch *Scooby Doo* and the rest of the Saturday morning cartoons; eating Pop Rocks and macaroni and cheese (which I would inhale in large amounts); and best of all, shopping at the mall. Coupled with what I saw in the movies, this was my small window into American life.

Because most people didn't know where to place me, I made up stories about myself. In bars, cabs, and restaurants I would try on identities with strangers I knew I would never meet again. I faked accents as I pretended to be a Hawaiian dancer, an Italian tourist, and even once a Russian student. It always amazed me what I could get away with. Being mixed inspired and gave me license to test new characters, but it also cast me as a foreigner in every setting I found myself in.

My brother looks Chinese – 70 percent to my 30 percent. And though he might dispute this, I have always felt that he was more readily accepted as being Chinese. I resented him for the ease with which he could slip into the culture, whereas I had to constantly prove and explain myself. I remember how during Chinese New Year, as tradition, we would go from house to house, eating large meals, playing mah jong, and collecting red envelopes containing untold amounts of cash that would later be gambled away. I dreaded these occasions because I felt excluded, whereas my brother, it seemed, was welcomed. Questions about what he planned to do with his life, when was he going to find a girlfriend, etc., were asked of him, while I was mostly treated with polite comments about the style of my dress and carted off to watch TV. I'd sit in the corner, grumbling as I snacked on M&Ms and watermelon seeds and watched badly dubbed American movies. My parents were exasperated by my long face and didn't understand why I was bothered even as they had me pegged as the American one. My mother accused me of not dating Chinese guys as proof of my being Americanized. Of course when I did eventually date one, she didn't approve of him because he wore an earring, dressed all in black, and was known to smoke cigarettes.

My decision to study in Ireland on a semester abroad rather than in China, a country I have yet to visit, seemed to further confirm my predilection. I defended my choice because it conveniently fit my English major and why wouldn't I want to explore my Irish heritage. Truthfully, I was afraid to go to China because it was foreign to me. This may seem absurd considering that I had been living in Taiwan for over ten years, but I knew it would require something of me that I was not prepared to give. I wasn't ready to take that journey yet. During the time I lived in Taiwan, China had seemed forbidding – I remember hearing stories about people we knew going and being detained for long periods of time. It wasn't until after I left for college that government restrictions preventing travel between the two countries were relaxed.

But then I would also benefit from the privileges of being an American. I remember how I would bypass long lines and the price of admission at nightclubs that welcomed foreigners, while my brother had to present a passport as proof of his citizenship. Even though I attended an international school, my friends fell into two groups – the Asians and the foreigners. The biracials blended in both directions, moving between the groups, though always somewhat outside each. Looking back, I think the distinctions came more into focus as we grew older. I remember once one of my American friends let slip a racial slur, something about irreputable, gold-digging Chinese women trying to trap Western men. Appalled, I pointed to my face – the product of such "unholy" joinings. She responded, "Oh, you're not *really* Chinese" – as though this were a plus.

When I came to the States for college, I became another sort of expatriate. Since I lacked the cultural tools necessary to roam undetected (knowledge of key television shows, important cultural references, even the subtle nuances of American English that you miss out on when you grow up abroad), I had to fake it and laugh at jokes I didn't get. Luckily I was familiar with *The Simpsons*, had seen almost every episode of *The Love Boat* on videotape, and vaguely knew who Howard Stern was. I got tired of hearing, "Oh, you wouldn't understand, you're not from here."

Toward the end of my first year, I went to hear Angela Davis speak. In making a point about the racism and inequality of the American educational system, she asked the white students to raise their hands if they had taken a course in black/Asian/etc. studies. A few proud students lifted their arms, and I was one of them. Then she asked the students of color to raise their hands if they had taken a course that focused on white/Western studies. Every one of them raised their hands, and the point was made. One was made for me as well, for I had hesitated, unsure whether to join them, although I wasn't sure why I assumed I belonged to the first group any more than the second. I ended up raising my hand for both, looking around to see if anyone noticed. I realized that although I had been making a point all year of letting people know that I was Chinese and enjoyed surprising them, I had learned to believe that I was American/white – I didn't differentiate. Could I be both, or did one trump the other?

It's easier to be white. To be Chinese, to be half Chinese, is work. I often find myself cataloguing my emotions, manners, and philosophies into Chinese and American, wary if the latter starts to outweigh the former. Three points Asia. How can I be Chinese if I prefer David Bowie to Chinese pop, if I can more easily pass as an

American, if I choose to live in New York and not return to Asia where my family still lives, if English is my first language and Chinese remains a distant second? How can I be Chinese when I struggle to communicate with my grandparents? I am unable to tell them about friends, boyfriends, life-altering experiences, beliefs, new jobs – to tell them about my life and who I have become – and the result is they don't really know me. I'm ashamed to admit that there have been times I dreaded visiting them because of the humiliation of having to resort to hand gestures and second-grade Chinese.

And yet I play the part of a foreigner here all the time. I insist on not being American and tell people about the various customs that are foreign to me – Thanksgiving Day turkey and football, milk shakes, *It's a Wonderful Life* at Christmas, and fireworks on the Fourth of July. I remember once I got carded when I was an underage summer school student at Tufts University trying to get a drink at a T.G.I. Fridays in Boston. Undaunted, I decided to try a different tactic and responded, in exchange-student-accented English, "Ah, we do not have IDs in China. I do not understand your strange customs." The waitress looked baffled, but I still didn't get any rum in my Coke. When I visit my American cousins, though they are welcoming, I can't help but notice that familial ties don't wash over cultural differences. Sometimes, when I would visit for more than a couple days, I would start speaking with a grossly exaggerated Boston accent, in an attempt to get whitified and bridge the gap. By sharing an accent, perhaps I could be more a part of the family and share their history. Very rarely do the two families come together, and when they do, it is a jarring family portrait.

I think back to what my mother replied when I asked her if it bothered her that I looked so Western, so *not*-Chinese. What did she think when she looked at me? With seemingly uncomplicated conviction, she told me that she didn't care because she didn't break me down into Chinese and American. "I see my daughter, finish your dinner." Ultimately, I think she is right, for racial and cultural identity becomes an inherent sum of who you are and what your experiences have been. But I question how much she really believes what she says. My parents' difficulty with my recent choices of partners has exposed their belief that I will marry a Caucasian and that my brother will marry a Chinese, an assumption based on some vague and undefinable notion of what we look like and how they see us. My brother, it happens, is dating a Chinese woman, whose parents, ironically, don't approve of him because he isn't Chinese enough. "Why make life harder for yourself than it has to be? Different cultures will make marriage difficult," is what my father says when he sees me getting angry. Exasperated, I point to his own marriage as a sign of his illogic. "Have you forgotten that you're married to a Chinese woman?" But more important, I wonder whose racial and cultural background will match my own. I get silence for an answer.

For those of us who fall between the cracks, being "black," being "white," being "Chinese," being "Latino," is complicated. [...] Skin color and place of birth aren't accurate signifiers of identity. One and one don't necessarily add up to two. Cultural and racial amalgams create a third, wholly indistinguishable category where origin and home are indeterminate. And yet, I am also reminded of a comment made by a notable mixed-race fiction writer in response to Tiger Woods's declaration of his

Asian and black heritage (and I paraphrase): "When the black truck comes around, they're gonna haul his ass on it."

What name do you give to someone who is a quarter, an eighth, a half? What kind of measuring stick might give an accurate estimation? If our understanding of race and culture can ripen and evolve, then new and immeasurable measurements about the uniqueness of our identities become possible.

Study Questions

1   How was O'Hearn viewed "from the outside" as a mixed race person growing up in Asia (Singapore and Taiwan)? How did she view herself "from the inside"?
2   How did the outside/inside views of O'Hearn shift when she came to live in the US?
3   Compare O'Hearn's ethnic American identity formation with Kesaya Noda's or with Jack Agüeros's. What additional factors come into play for a mixed race person living in the US at the turn of the twenty-first century?

CHAPTER 43

From *The Business of Fancydancing:*
Stories and Poems

Sherman Alexie

Born in 1966 on the Spokane Indian Reservation in Wellpinit, Washington, Native American poet and fiction writer Sherman Alexie is a vibrant contemporary literary voice. Alexie's father was a truck driver and logger who spent little time with his family; his mother, a quilter, sold her work to make ends meet. An American Studies graduate of Washington State University in 1991, Alexie's interest in writing was sparked during a college creative writing workshop, which led to his first major book, The Business of Fancydancing *(1992). He has published several highly praised works of fiction and poetry, and two screenplays, one of which,* Smoke Signals *(1998), became the first Hollywood film produced, directed, and acted entirely by Indians. Alexie writes with unflinching candor about the realities and conflicts of Indian life and identity on and off the Reservation. The following three poems give a hint of his poetic breadth, the first two written with biting irony; the third, with warm tenderness.*

13/16

1.

I cut myself into sixteen equal pieces
keep thirteen and feed the other three
to the dogs, who have also grown

tired of U.S. Commodities, white cans
black letters translated into Spanish.
"Does this mean I have to learn

the language to eat?" Lester FallsApart asks
but directions for preparation are simple:
a. WASH CAN; b. OPEN CAN; c. EXAMINE CONTENTS

OF CAN FOR SPOILAGE; d. EMPTY CONTENTS
OF CAN INTO SAUCE PAN; e. COOK CONTENTS
OVER HIGH HEAT; f. SERVE AND EAT.

2.

It is done by blood, reservation mathematics, fractions:
father (full-blood) + mother (5/8) = son (13/16).

It is done by enrollment number, last name first, first name last:
Spokane Tribal Enrollment Number 1569; Victor, Chief.

It is done by identification card, photograph, lamination:
IF FOUND, PLEASE RETURN TO SPOKANE TRIBE OF
INDIANS, WELLPINIT, WA.

3.

The compromise is always made
in increments. On this reservation
we play football on real grass
dream of deserts, three inches of rain

in a year. What we have lost:
uranium mine, Little Falls Dam
salmon. Our excuses are trapped
within museums, roadside attractions

totem poles in Riverfront Park.
I was there, watching the Spokane River
changing. A ten-year-old white boy asked
if I was a real Indian. He did not wait

for an answer, instead carving his initials
into the totem with a pocketknife: J.N.
We are what we take, carving my name
my enrollment number, thirteen hash marks

into the wood. A story is remembered
as evidence, the Indian man they found dead
shot in the alley behind the Mayfair.
Authorities reported a rumor he had relatives

in Minnesota. A member of some tribe or another
his photograph on the 11 o'clock news. Eyes, hair
all dark, his shovel-shaped incisor, each the same
ordinary identification of the anonymous.

4.

When my father disappeared, we found him
years later, in a strange kitchen searching
for footprints in the dust: still

untouched on the shelves all the commodity
cans without labels – my father opened them
one by one, finding a story in each.

Evolution

Buffalo Bill opens a pawn shop on the reservation
right across the border from the liquor store
and he stays open 24 hours a day, 7 days a week

and the Indians come running in with jewelry
television sets, a VCR, a full-length beaded buckskin outfit
it took Inez Muse 12 years to finish. Buffalo Bill

takes everything the Indians have to offer, keeps it
all catalogued and filed in a storage room. The Indians
pawn their hands, saving the thumbs for last, they pawn

their skeletons, falling endlessly from the skin
and when the last Indian has pawned everything
but his heart, Buffalo Bill takes that for twenty bucks

closes up the pawn shop, paints a new sign over the old
calls his venture THE MUSEUM OF NATIVE AMERICAN CULTURES
charges the Indians five bucks a head to enter.

At Navajo Monument Valley Tribal School

*from the photograph
by Skeet McAuley*

the football field rises
to meet the mesa. Indian boys
gallop across the grass, against

the beginning of their body.
On those Saturday afternoons,
unbroken horses gather to watch

their sons growing larger
in the small parts of the world.
Everyone is the quarterback.

There is no thin man in a big hat
writing down all the names
in two columns: winners and losers.

This is the eternal football game,
Indians versus Indians. All the Skins
in the wooden bleachers fancydancing,

stomping red dust straight down
into nothing. Before the game is over,
the eighth-grade girls' track team

comes running, circling the field,
their thin and brown legs echoing
wild horses, wild horses, wild horses.

Skeet McAuley, Navajo Monument Tribal School near Goulding, Utah, 1985.
Reproduced courtesy of Skeet McAuley. Original in color

Study Questions

1   How does Alexie use humor to tell painful truths about contemporary
    Indians' lives? Does the humor strengthen or weaken the points he is
    making? Explain, using an example from one of the three poems.
    "13/16"
    1   What issues about Indian identity is Alexie raising in this poem? Why
        does he have to cut himself up into pieces?
    2   How do the issues Alexie raises compare with those raised by Vine Deloria,
        Jr.?
    "Evolution"
    1   Who is Buffalo Bill? Why are the Indians pawning everything to him,
        including their skeletons?
    2   What do the pawn shop and "The Museum of Native American Cultures"
        tell us about Alexie's view of what has happened to Indians' cultural
        heritage?
    "At Navajo Monument Valley Tribal School"
    1   Explain how Skeet McAuley's photograph affects your reading of the
        poem, and how the poem affects your reading of the photograph.
    2   What makes the football games practiced by these high school students
        different from professional football?
    3   Why does Alexie compare the boys and girls to wild horses?

CHAPTER 44

Through a Glass Darkly:
Toward the Twenty-first Century

Ronald Takaki

Ronald Takaki (1939–) was born and raised in Honolulu, Hawaii, but he recalls that when he arrived in Ohio for college, "most people did not see me as an American." His mother, who was born on a sugar plantation, ran a restaurant with her husband during Takaki's high school years. Takaki received his PhD in history at the University of California Berkeley in 1967, during the height of the Civil Rights Movement. A professor of Ethnic Studies, he has published numerous books, including Strangers from a Different Shore: A History of Asian Americans *(1989) and* A Different Mirror: A History of Multicultural America *(1993). In this excerpt from the concluding chapter of* A Different Mirror, *Takaki examines the implications of the US's increasingly diverse immigrant and ethnic populations for the future of American society and culture.*

T he myth of the Asian-American "model minority" has been challenged, yet it continues to be widely believed. One reason for this is its instructional value. For whom are Asian Americans supposed to be a "model"? Shortly after the Civil War, southern planters recruited Chinese immigrants in order to pit them against the newly freed blacks as "examples" of laborers willing to work hard for low wages. Today, Asian Americans are again being used to discipline blacks. If the failure of blacks on welfare warns Americans in general how they should not behave, the triumph of Asian Americans affirms the deeply rooted values of the Protestant ethic and self-reliance. Our society needs an Asian-American "model minority" in an era anxious about a growing black underclass. Asian-American "success" has been used to explain the phenomenon of "losing ground" – why the situation of the poor has deteriorated during the last two decades while government social services have expanded. If Asian Americans can make it on their own, conservative pundits like Charles Murray are asking, why can't other groups? Many liberals have joined this chorus. In 1987, CBS's *60 Minutes* presented a glowing report on the stunning achievements of Asian Americans in the academy.

"Why are Asian Americans doing so exceptionally well in school?" Mike Wallace asked and quickly added, "They must be doing something right. Let's bottle it." Wallace then suggested that failing black students should try to pursue the Asian-American formula for academic success.[1]

Betraying a nervousness over the seeming end of the American Dream's boundlessness, praise for this "super minority" has become society's most recent jeremiad – a call for a renewed commitment to the traditional virtues of hard work, thrift, and industry. After all, it has been argued, the war on poverty and affirmative action were not really necessary. Look at the Asian Americans! They did it by pulling themselves up by their bootstraps. For blacks shut out of the labor market, the Asian-American model provides the standards of acceptable behavior: blacks should not depend on welfare or affirmative action. While congratulating Asian Americans for their family values, hard work, and high incomes, President Ronald Reagan chastised blacks for their dependency on the "spider's web of welfare" and their failure to recognize that the "only barrier" to success was "within" them.[2]

But comparisons of Asian-American "success" and black "dependency" have shrouded the impact of the Cold War economy on the problems of unemployment and poverty. The strategic nuclear weapons program under the Reagan presidency was financed by enormous deficits. Defense expenditures under the Reagan administration more than doubled from $134 billion in 1980 to $282 billion in 1987. In that year, defense spending amounted to 60 cents out of every dollar received by the federal government in income tax. Meanwhile, resources were diverted from our social needs: defense spending was $35 billion greater in 1985 than in 1981, while funds for entitlement programs such as food stamps and welfare were cut by $30 billion. Moreover, the focus of our research and development on strategic nuclear weapons has greatly harmed our general economy. Since 1955, the federal government has spent more than $1 trillion on nuclear arms and other weaponry for the Cold War – a sum representing 62 percent of all federal research expenditures. This concentration on the military needs of the US-Soviet rivalry drained our national resources and at the same time undermined our ability to produce competitive consumer goods, which in turn, generated trade imbalances and contributed to a decline in commercial manufacturing, especially for those sectors of the industrial economy where many blacks had been employed.[3]

These macrocosmic political and economic realities have even reached remote Indian reservations. During the nineteenth century, as white settlement expanded westward toward the "Stony mountains," policy-makers like Francis Amasa Walker had moved Indian tribes onto reservations. Many of these reservations later became valuable sites for resources vital to the Cold War's nuclear weapons program as well as our energy-consuming economy. Fifty-five percent of our uranium deposits are located on Indian-owned lands, and nearly 100 percent of current mining occurs in Indian territory. In the Southwest, this industry employs 20 percent of working Laguna Pueblo Indians. The United Mine Workers Union estimated that approximately 80 percent of the workers in the uranium shaft mines will die of lung cancer.

Native Americans living near the shafts are also in danger, for they have been exposed to air and drinking water contaminated by radiation from the tailings generated by the mining and milling of uranium. In Edgemount, South Dakota, three million pounds of tailings were dumped near the Cheyenne River, and cancer rates for people drinking that water have been 50 percent higher than in any other county in the state. In 1978, the Department of Energy released a report stating that the risk of lung cancer for persons living near the tailings piles was twice that of the general population. Involved in the extract of uranium have been powerful corporations – Kerr-McGee, Exxon, Atlantic Richfield, Mobil Oil, and United Nuclear.[4]

By 1980, 740,000 Indians – more than half of the total Native American population – no longer lived on reservations. Instead, they resided in cities such as New York, San Francisco, Oakland, Seattle, Tulsa, Minneapolis–St. Paul, Chicago, and Los Angeles. In 1940, only 24,000 Native Americans, or 13 percent of the group's national population, lived in urban areas. World War II had attracted thousands of them to work in urban war-related industries. The major migration, however, occurred between 1953 and 1972: under the Bureau of Indian Affairs relocation program, 100,000 Indians left the reservations for the cities. One of the movers and shakers behind this new policy was Dillon S. Meyer. Appointed Commissioner of Indian Affairs in 1950s, he had been the director of the War Relocation Authority, responsible for administering the Japanese-American internment camps during World War II. Meyer's goal had been to assimilate Japanese Americans by resettling them across the country. This idea of incorporation through dispersal became the basis of the Voluntary Relocation Program, which provided job training and transportation to cities where Indians would be given assistance in finding employment and housing. Like Commissioner Francis Amasa Walker, Meyer hoped to integrate Native Americans into modern urban society.[5] [. . .]

Recently, 40,000 Soviet Jews have been entering the United States annually, and altogether they total over 200,000. Like the Jewish immigrants of the late nineteenth century, they have been selling their houses and furniture, giving away almost everything, and leaving with only what they can carry wrapped in bedspreads or packed in suitcases. After their arrival, they have had to start all over again. Describing the plight of a Jewish refugee family, Barbara Budnitz of Berkeley, California, explained: "These people have nothing. I offered them an old desk. They said they wanted it, but what they really needed was a bed." Many of these refugees had been engineers in the old country, but here they have been suffering from unemployment. Lacking English language skills and possessing technical knowledge that has limited transferability, many have been forced to find jobs as apartment managers, janitors, or even as helpers at McDonald's. According to Barbara Nelson of the Jewish Family Services in Oakland, California, about 80 percent of the Jewish refugee families have been compelled to seek welfare support.[6]

Still the Jews are glad to be in America where there is religious freedom. "My five-year-old daughter is attending school at the synagogue – something she could not do in the Ukraine," explained Sofiya Shapiro, who came with her family in 1991. "I am glad she can get to know Jewish tradition." Indeed, many of the refugees are learning about Judaism for the first time in their lives. But like the Jewish immigrants of earlier times, the recent refugees are hopeful this country will offer them an opportunity to begin again. "That's what America is," commented Budnitz. "We need to keep it that way."[7]

America's continuing allure has also been as a place for a fresh economic start. This has been particularly true for the recent arrivals from Ireland. Like the nineteenth-century Irish immigrants fleeing hunger and the ravages of the potato famine, these recent newcomers have been pushed by grim economic conditions at home: in 1990, unemployment in Ireland was a staggering 18 percent. Seeking work in America, many have entered illegally in the past decade. Undocumented Irish workers have been estimated to total as many as 120,000. "It's an anonymous floating population," stated Lena Deevy, director of the Irish Immigration Reform Movement office in Boston. "It's like counting the homeless." These illegal aliens constitute what one of them described as "an underclass," forced to take "the crummiest jobs at the lowest wages." The 1987 Immigration Reform Act, which made it unlawful for employers to hire undocumented workers, has created economic and social borders for many Irish. "You can't apply for a job," explained an Irish waitress who came to Boston in 1986. "You can't answer a want ad [because of the 1987 law]. It's all word of mouth." Undocumented Irish workers have to keep a low profile, she added: "My social life is limited to the Irish sector. I can't talk to Americans – you just have to tell too many lies." Director Deevy described their nervousness: "It's like living on the edge. There's a lot of fear" that someone "will squeal to the INS [Immigration and Naturalization Service]." In 1990, a new immigration law provided for the distribution of 40,000 green cards to be awarded by lottery, with 16,000 of them reserved for Irish. "I plan to fill out at least a thousand applications," said Joanne O'Connell of Queens, New York, as she looked forward to this "Irish Sweepstakes."[8]

Most of today's immigrants, however, come from Asia and Latin America. Over 80 percent of all immigrants have been arriving from these two regions, adding to America's racial diversity – a reality charged with consequences for our nation's work force. By the year 2000, there will be more than 21 million new workers. They will be 44 percent white, 16 percent black, 11 percent Asian and other groups, and 29 percent Hispanic. A preview of the significance of this racial diversity in the twenty-first century can be seen in California. There, Hispanics, composed mostly of Mexican Americans, number 4.5 million, or approximately 20 percent of the state's popula-tion. Many of them are recent newcomers, pulled here again by dreams of El Norte. Compared to the Anglos, the Hispanics are young. In 1985, they represented 32 percent of the youth (aged birth to fifteen years) and only 8 percent of the elderly (sixty-five years and over), compared to 52 percent and 83 percent for Anglos. The number of Hispanics entering the work force will increase, while Anglos will continue to constitute a large majority of the elderly.[9] [...]

Together, we have created what Gloria Anzaldúa celebrated as a "borderland" – a place where "two or more cultures edge each other, where people of different races occupy the same territory." How can all of us meet on communal ground? "The struggle," Anzaldúa responded, "is inner: Chicano, *indio*, American Indian, *mojado*, *mexicano*, immigrant Latino, Anglo in power, working class Anglo, Black, Asian – our psyches resemble the bordertowns and are populated by the same people.... Awareness of our situation must come before inner changes, which in turn come before changes in society."[10]

Such awareness, in turn, must come from a "re-visioned" history. What Gloria Steinem termed "revolution from within" must ultimately be grounded in "unlearning" much of what we have been told about America's past and substituting a more inclusive and accurate history of all the peoples of America. "To finally recognize our own invisibility," declared Mitsuye Yamada, "is to finally be on the path toward visibility." To become visible is to see ourselves and each other in a different mirror of history. As Audre Lorde pointed out,

> It is a waste of time hating a mirror
> or its reflection
> instead of stopping the hand
> that makes glass with distortions.[11]

By viewing ourselves in a mirror which reflects reality, we can see our past as undistorted and no longer have to peer into our future as through a glass darkly. The face of our cultural future can be found on the western edge of the continent. "California, and especially Los Angeles, a gateway to both Asia and Latin America," Carlos Fuentes observed, "poses the universal question of the coming century: how do we deal with the Other?" Asked whether California, especially with its multiethnic society, represented the America of the twenty-first century, Alice Walker replied: "If that's not the future reality of the United States, there won't be any United States, because that's who we are." Walker's own ancestry is a combination of Native American, African American, and European American. Paula Gunn Allen also has diverse ethnic roots – American Indian, Scotch, Jewish, and Lebanese. "Just people from everywhere are related to me by blood," she explained, "and so that's why I say I'm a multicultural event. . . . It's beautiful, it's a rainbow. . . . It reflects light, and I think that's what a person like me can do." Imagine what "light" a "multicultural event" called America can reflect. America has been settled by "the people of all nations," Herman Melville observed over a century ago, "all nations may claim her for their own. You can not spill a drop of American blood, without spilling the blood of the whole world." Americans are not "a narrow tribe"; they are not a nation, "so much as a world." In this new society, Melville optimistically declared, the "prejudices of national dislikes" could be "forever extinguish[ed]."[12] [. . .]

America's dilemma has been our resistance to ourselves – our denial of our immensely varied selves. But we have nothing to fear but our fear of our own diversity. "We can get along," Rodney King reassured us during an agonizing moment of racial hate and violence. To get along with each other, however, requires self-recognition as well as self-acceptance. Asked whether she had a specific proposal for improving the current racial climate in America, Toni Morrison answered: "Everybody remembers the first time they were taught that part of the human race was Other. That's a trauma. It's as though I told you that your left hand is not part of your body." In his vision of the "whole hoop of the world," Black Elk of the Sioux saw "in a sacred manner the shapes of all things in the spirit, and the shape of all shapes as they must live together like one being." And he saw that the "sacred hoop" of his people was "one of many hoops that made one circle, wide as daylight and as starlight, and in the center grew one mighty flowering tree to shelter all the children of one mother and one father." Today, what we need to do is to stop denying our wholeness as members of humanity as well as one nation.[13]

As Americans, we originally came from many different shores, and our diversity has been at the center of the making of America. While our stories contain the memories of different communities, together they inscribe a larger narrative. Filled with what Walt Whitman celebrated as the "varied carols" of America, our history generously gives all of us our "mystic chords of memory." Throughout our past of oppressions and struggles for equality, Americans of different races and ethnicities have been "singing with open mouths their strong melodious songs" in the textile mills of Lowell, the cotton fields of Mississippi, on the Indian reservations of South Dakota, the railroad tracks high in the Sierras of California, in the garment factories of the Lower East Side, the canefields of Hawaii, and a thousand other places across the country. Our denied history "bursts with telling." As we hear America singing, we find ourselves invited to bring our rich cultural diversity on deck, to accept ourselves. "Of every hue and caste am I," sang Whitman. "I resist any thing better than my own diversity."[14]

Study Questions

1   What is the myth of the Asian-American "model minority"? Why, according to Takaki, does American society need this myth? How is it used against other minorities?

2   How did immigration patterns in the late twentieth century compare with earlier immigration patterns? What were the most important differences?

3   How helpful do you find Takaki's concept of the US as a "borderland"? How does it compare with the older notion of the US as a "melting pot"?

4   Takaki says that Americans will not be able to find "communal ground" until we have an accurate understanding of US history that includes "all the peoples of America." Discuss two examples of individuals or groups that you have learned about in this book which have increased your understanding of American history and culture.

Notes

1.   Charles A. Murray, *Losing Ground: American Social Policy, 1950–1980* (New York, 1994), p. 55; Ronald Takaki, "Asian Americans in the University," *San Francisco Examiner* April 16, 1984; William Raspberry, "Beyond Racism (Cont'd)," *Washington Post*, November 19, 1984; Barry Bluestone and Bennett Harrison, *The Deindustrialization of America: Plant Closings, Community Abandonment, and the Dismantling of Basic Industry* (New York: 1982); Barbara Ehrenreich, *Fear of Falling: The Inner Life of the Middle Class* (New York, 1989), p. 15.

2. Peter Schmeisser, "Is America in Decline?" *New York Times Magazine*, April 17, 1988; William Julius Wilson, *The Truly Disadvantaged: The Inner City, the Underclass., and Public Policy* (Chicago 1987) p. 65; President Ronald Reagan, speech to a group of Asian and Pacific Americans in the White House, February 23, 1984, reprinted in *Asian Week*, March 2, 1984; Ronald Takaki, "Poverty Is Thriving under Reagan," *New York Times*, March 3, 1986; Ronald Reagan, quoted in James Reston, "Reagan Is the Issue," *San Francisco Chronicle*, September 13, 1984. This disciplining also includes the middle class; see Chris Tilly, "U-Turn on Equality: The Puzzle of Middle Class Decline," *Dollars & Sense*, May 1986, p. 11 ("middle-class" income is defined as between 75 percent and 125 percent of median household income); Bob Kuttner, "The Declining Middle," *Atlantic Monthly*, July 1983, pp. 60–72; Barbara Ehrenreich, "Is the Middle Class Doomed?" *New York Times Magazine*, September 7, 1986, pp. 44, 50, 62; Tom Wicker, "Let 'Em Eat Swiss Cheese," *New York Times*, September 2, 1988; Don Wycliff, "Why the Underclass in Still Under," *New York Times*, November 16, 1987; Murray, *Losing Ground*, pp. 32, 55, 146, 220, 227.

3. William Broad, "Swords Have Been Sheathed But Plowshares Lack Design," *New York Times*, February 5, 1992, pp. A1, A8.

4. Bruce Johansen and Roberto Maestras, *Wasi'chu: The Continuing Indian Wars* (New York, 1979), pp. 154–166; Anthony Lewis, "The Cost of Reagan," *New York Times*, September 7, 1989.

5. James S. Olson and Raymond Wilson, *Native Americans in the Twentieth Century* (Urbana, Ill., 1986), pp. 144, 152, 153, 163–164.

6. Statistics from Natasha Kats of the Bay Area Council of Soviet Jews, San Francisco, interview, August 28, 1992; interview with Barbara Budnitz, August 22, 1992.

7. Interview with Sofiya Shapiro (pseudonym), August 30, 1992; interview with Barbara Budnitz, August 22, 1992.

8. Al Kamen, "Irish Will Win 'Green Card' Sweepstakes," *San Francisco Chronicle*, July 29, 1991; Richard Lacayo, "Give Me Your Rich, Your Lucky...," *Time*, October 14, 1991, p. 27.

9. Wilma Randle, "The Changing Face of the Work Force," *San Francisco Examiner*, January 7, 1990; David Hayes-Bautista, Werner Schink, and Jorge Chapa, *The Burden of Support: Young Latinos in an Aging Society* (Stanford, Calif., 1988), pp. 35–36.

10. Gloria Anzaldúa, *Borderlands, La Frontera: The New Mestiza* (San Francisco, 1987), first page of preface, p. 87.

11. Gloria. Steinem, *Revolution from Within: A Book of Self-esteem* (Boston, 1993), p. 107; Mitsuye Yamada, "Invisibility Is an Unnatural Disaster: Reflections of an Asian American Woman," in Cherrie Moraga and Gloria Anzaldúa (eds.), *This Bridge Called My Back: Writings by Radical Women of Color* (New York, 1983), p. 40; Audre Lorde, "Good Mirrors Are Not Cheap," in Lorde, *From a Land Where Other People Live* (Detroit, 1973), p. 15. My thanks to Henry Louis Gates, Jr., for bringing my attention to this poem in *Loose Canons: Notes on the Culture Wars* (New York, 1992), p. 192.

12. Carlos Fuentes, *The Buried Mirror: Reflections on Spain and the New World* (Boston, 1992), p. 348; Reese Erlich, "Alice's Wonderland," an interview with Alice Walker, *Image, San Francisco Examiner*, July 19, 1992, p. 12; Paula Gunn Allen, interview, in Laura Coltelli (ed.), *Winged Words: American Indian Writers Speak* (Lincoln, Nebr., 1990), p. 17; Herman Melville, *Redburn* (Chicago, 1969; originally published in 1849), p. 169, also quoted in, Gates, *Loose Canons* pp. 116–117, and Michael Paul Rogin, *Subversive Genealogy: The Politics and Art of Herman Melville* (New York, 1983), p. 69.

13. Rodney King's statement to the press, *New York Times*, May 2, 1992, p. 6; interview with Toni Morrison, *Time*, May 22, 1989, p. 121; Black Elk, *Black Elk Speaks: Being the Life Story of a Holy Man of the Oglala Sioux*, as told to John G. Neihardt (Lincoln, Nebr., 1988), p. 43.

14. Joy Kogawa, *Obasan* (Boston, 1982), opening page; Lincoln, "First Inaugural Address," *The Annals of America*, vol. 9, 1863–65: *The Crisis of the Union* (Chicago, 1968), p. 255; Walt Whitman, *Leaves of Grass* (New York, 1958), pp. 9, 10, 38.

CHAPTER 45

"To live in the Borderlands means you"

Gloria Anzaldúa

Feminist poet, fiction writer, activist, and cultural theorist, Gloria Anzaldúa (1942–2004) was one of the first openly lesbian Chicana writers to publish in the US. Born to Mexican-American farm owners in Jesus Maria of the Valley, Texas, she moved with her family to Arkansas where they worked as migrant field hands after the death of her father. The first person from her community to attend college, Anzaldúa earned her BA in English from Pan American University in 1969, and her MA in English from the University of Texas at Austin, in 1972. Her prize-winning first book, This Bridge Called My Back: Writings by Radical Women of Color *(edited with Cherrie Moraga, 1981), brought third-world women's writing to national prominence. Anzaldúa's most influential book,* Borderlands/La Frontera *(1987), from which the following poem comes, explores the challenges and possibilities that face multiracial women who live on the "borderlands" between cultures.*

> To live in the Borderlands means you
>   are neither *hispana india negra española*
>   *ni gabacha, eres mestiza, mulata*, half-breed
>   caught in the crossfire between camps
>   while carrying all five races on your back
>   not knowing which side to turn to, run from;
>
> To live in the Borderlands means knowing
>   that the *india* in you, betrayed for 500 years,
>   is no longer speaking to you,
>   that *mexicanas* call you *rajetas*,
>   that denying the Anglo inside you
>   is as bad as having denied the Indian or Black;
>
> *Cuando vives en la frontera*
>   people walk through you, the wind steals your voice,
>   you're a *burra, buey*, scapegoat,
>   forerunner of a new race,

half and half – both woman and man, neither –
a new gender;

To live in the Borderlands means to
    put *chile* in the borscht,
    eat whole wheat *tortillas*,
    speak Tex-Mex with a Brooklyn accent;
    be stopped by *la migra* at the border checkpoints;

Living in the Borderlands means you fight hard to
    resist the gold elixer beckoning from the bottle,
    the pull of the gun barrel,
    the rope crushing the hollow of your throat;

In the Borderlands
    you are the battleground
    where enemies are kin to each other;
    you are at home, a stranger,
    the border disputes have been settled
    the volley of shots have shattered the truce
    you are wounded, lost in action
    dead, fighting back;

To live in the Borderlands means
    the mill with the razor white teeth wants to shred off
    your olive-red skin, crush out the kernel, your heart
    pound you pinch you roll you out
    smelling like white bread but dead;

To survive the Borderlands
    you must live *sin fronteras*
    be a crossroads.

gabacha – a Chicano term for a white woman
rajetas – literally, "split," that is, having betrayed your word
burra – donkey
buey – oxen
sin fronteras – without borders

Study Questions

1   What are the costs and benefits of living in the "Borderlands," according to Anzaldúa?

2   How many identities does Anzaldúa "contain" and where do they come from? Which of these are identities are imposed from without and which determined from within?

3   How does Takaki's discussion of the US as a borderland provide a context for Anzaldúa's idea of borderlands? How does her idea of the US as a "*mestiza*" (mixed) culture compare with O'Hearn's?

4   Can Americans live "*sin fronteras*"? What would this mean for you personally? For the nation at large?

CHAPTER 46

From *No Logo:*
Taking Aim at Brand Bullies

Naomi Klein

An influential voice in the international anticorporate movement, Naomi Klein was born in Montreal in 1970 after her parents emigrated there to protest the Vietnam War. Klein says that she initially fought against her family's activism, embracing consumerism as a form of rebellion. While a student at the University of Toronto, Klein began writing for student publications and was shocked by the violent and negative responses to her feminist arguments. Facing rape threats, she dropped out of school (returning to graduate later) to pursue journalism. Klein's articles have appeared nationwide. Her first book, No Logo: Taking Aim at the Brand Bullies (2000), represents a new generation of activists who question the power that large international companies hold over global politics. In this excerpt, Klein focuses on the ways students have organized as consumers in response to corporate–campus partnerships.

[...] When corporations sponsor an event on a university campus or sign a deal with a municipal government, they cross an important line between private and public space – a line that is not part of a consumer's interaction with a corporation as an individual shopper. We don't expect morality at the mall but, to some extent, we do still expect it in our public spaces – in our schools, national parks and municipal playgrounds.

So while it may be cold comfort to some, there is a positive side effect of the fact that, increasingly, private corporations are staking a claim to these public spaces. Over the past four years, there has been a collective realization among many public, civic and religious institutions that having a multinational corporation as a guest in your house – whether as a supplier or a sponsor – presents an important political opportunity. With their huge buying power, public and non-profit institutions can exert real public-interest pressure on otherwise freewheeling private corporations. This is nowhere more true than in the schools and universities.

Students Teach the Brands a Lesson

[...] [S]oft-drink, sneaker and fast-food companies have been forging a flurry of exclusive logo allegiances with high schools, colleges and universities. [...]

However, these same corporations have at times discovered that there can be an unanticipated downside to these "partnerships": that the sense of ownership that goes along with sponsoring is not always the kind of passive consumer allegiance that the companies had bargained for. In a climate of mounting concern about corporate ethics, students are finding that a great way to grab the attention of aloof multi-nationals is to kick up a fuss about the extracurricular activities of their university's official brand – whether Coke, Pepsi, Nike, McDonald's, Starbucks or Northern Telecom. Rather than simply complaining about amorphous "corporatization," young activists have begun to use their status as sought-after sponsorees to retaliate against forces they considered invasive on their campuses to begin with. In this volatile context, a particularly aggressive sponsorship deal can act as a political catalyst, instigating wide-ranging debate on everything from unfair labor conditions to trading with dictators. Just ask Pepsi.

Pepsi [...] has been at the forefront of the drive to purchase students as a captive market. Its exclusive vending arrangements have paved the way for copycat deals, and fast-food outlets owned by PepsiCo were among the first to establish a presence in high schools and on university campuses in North America. One of Pepsi's first campus vending deals was with Ottawa's Carleton University in 1993. Since market-ing on campus was still somewhat jarring back then, many students were immedi-ately resentful at being forced into this tacit product endorsement, and were determined not to give their official drink a warm welcome. Members of the university's chapter of the Public Interest and Research Group – a network of campus social-justice organizations stretching across North America known as PIRGs – discovered that PepsiCo was producing and selling its soft drinks in Burma, the brutal dictatorship now called Myanmar. The Carleton students weren't sure how to deal with the information, so they posted a notice about Pepsi's involvement in Burma on a few on-line bulletin boards that covered student issues. Gradually, other universities where Pepsi was the official drink started requesting more information. Pretty soon, the Ottawa group had developed and distributed hundreds of "campus action kits," with pamphlets, petitions, and "Gotta Boycott" and "Pepsi, Stuff It" stickers. "How can you help free Burma?" one pamphlet asks. "Pressure schools to terminate food or beverage contracts selling PepsiCo products until it leaves Burma."

Many students did just that. As a result, in April 1996 Harvard rejected a proposed $1 million vending deal with Pepsi, citing the company's Burma holdings. Stanford University cost Pepsi an estimated $800,000 when a petition signed by two thousand students blocked the construction of a PepsiCo-owned Taco Bell restaurant. The stakes were even higher in Britain where campus soft-drink contracts are coordinated centrally through the National Union of Students' services wing. "Pepsi had just beat out Coke for the contract," recalls Guy Hughes, a campaigner with the London-based group Third World First. "Pepsi was being sold in eight hundred student unions across the UK, so we used the consortium as a lever to pressure Pepsi. When [the student union] met with the company, one factor for Pepsi was that the boycott had become international."[1]

Aung San Suu Kyi, the leader of Burma's opposition party that was elected to power in 1990, only to be prevented from taking office by the military, has offered encouragement to this nascent movement. In 1997, in a speech read by her husband (who has since died) at the American University in Washington, DC, she singled out students in the call to put pressure on multinational corporations that are invested in Burma. "Please use your liberty to promote ours," she said. "Take a principled stand against companies which are doing business with the military regime of Burma."[2]

After the campus boycotts made it into *The New York Times*, Pepsi sold its shares in a controversial Burmese bottling plant whose owner, Thien Tun, had publicly called for Suu Kyi's democracy movement to be "ostracized and crushed." Student activists, however, dismissed the move as a "paper shuffle" because Pepsi products were still being sold and produced in Burma. Finally, facing continued pressure, Pepsi announced its "total disengagement" from Burma on January 24, 1997. When Zar Ni, the coordinator of the American student movement, heard the news, he sent an E-mail out on the Free Burma Coalition listserve: "We finally tied the Pepsi Animal down! We did it!! We all did it!!! . . . We now KNOW we have the grassroots power to yank one of the most powerful corporations in the world."

If there is a moral to this story, it is that Pepsi's drive to capture the campus market landed the company at the center of a debate in which it had no desire to participate. It wanted university students to be its poster children – its real live Generation Next – but instead, the students turned the tables and made Pepsi the poster corporation for their campus Free Burma movement. Sein Win, a leader in exile of Burma's elected National League for Democracy, observed that "PepsiCo very much takes care of its image. It wanted to press the drink's image as 'the taste of a young generation,' so when the young generation participates in boycotts, it hurts the effort."[3] Simon Billenness, an ethical investment specialist who spearheaded the Burma campaign, is more blunt: "Pepsi," he says, "was under siege from its own target market."[4] And Reid Cooper, coordinator of the Carleton University campaign, notes that without Pepsi's thirst for campus branding, Burma's plight might never have become an issue on campuses. "Pepsi tried to go into the schools," he tells me in an interview, "and from there it was spontaneous combustion."

Not surprisingly, the Pepsi victory has emboldened the Free Burma campaign on the campuses. The students have adopted the slogan "Burma: South Africa of the Nineties" and claim to be "The largest human rights campaign in cyberspace."[5] Today, more than one hundred colleges and twenty high schools around the world are part of the Free Burma Coalition. The extent to which the country's liberty has become a student cause célèbre became apparent when, in August 1998, eighteen foreign activists – most of them university students – were arrested in Rangoon for handing out leaflets expressing support for Burma's democracy movement. Not surprisingly, the event caught the attention of the international media. The court sentenced the activists to five years of hard labor, but at the last minute deported them instead of imprisoning them.

Other student campaigns have focused on different corporations and different dictators. With Pepsi out of Burma, attention began to shift on campuses to Coca-Cola's investments in Nigeria. At Kent State University and other schools where Coke won the campus cola war, students argued that Coke's high-profile presence in Nigeria offered an air of legitimacy to the country's illegitimate military regime (which, at the time, was still in power). Once again, the issue of Nigerian human rights might never have reached much beyond KSU's Amnesty International Club, but because Coke and the school had entered into a sponsorship-style arrangement, the campaign took off and students began shouting that their university had blood on its hands.

There have also been a number of food fights, most of them related to McDonald's expanding presence on college campuses. In 1997, the British National Union of Students entered into an agreement with McDonald's to distribute "privilege cards" to all undergraduates in the UK. When students showed the card, they got a free cheeseburger every time they ordered a Big Mac, fries and drink. But campus environmentalists opposed the deal, forcing the student association to bow out of the marketing alliance in March 1998. In providing its reasons for the change of heart, the association cited the company's "anti-union practices, exploitation of employees, its contribution to the destruction of the environment, animal cruelty and the promotion of unhealthy food products" [...].[6]

As the brand backlash spreads, students are beginning to question not only sponsorship arrangements with the likes of McDonald's and Pepsi, but also the less flashy partnerships that their universities have with the private sector. Whether it's bankers on the board of governors, corporate-endowed professorships or the naming of campus buildings after benefactors, all are facing scrutiny from a more economically politicized student body. British students have stepped up a campaign to pressure their universities to stop accepting grant money from the oil industry, and in British Columbia, the University of Victoria Senate voted in November 1998 to refuse scholarship money from Shell. This agenda of corporate resistance is gradually becoming more structured, as students from across North America come together at annual conferences such as the 1997 "Democracy Teach-In: Campus Democracy vs. Corporate Control" at the University of Chicago, where they attend seminars like "Research: For People or Profit?" "Investigating Your Campus" and "What Is a Corporation and Why Is There a Problem?" In June 1999, student activists again came together, this time in Toledo, Ohio, in the newly formed Student Alliance to Reform Corporations. The purpose of the gathering was to launch a national campaign to force universities to invest their money only with companies that respect human rights and do not degrade the environment.

It should come as no surprise that by far the most controversial campus-corporate partnerships have been ones involving that most controversial of companies: Nike. Since the shoe industry's use of sweatshop labor became common knowledge, the deals that Nike had signed with hundreds of athletic departments in universities have become among the most contentious issues on campuses today, with "Ban the Swoosh" buttons rivaling women's symbols as the undergraduate accessory of choice. And in what Nike must see as the ultimate slap in the face, college campuses where the company has paid out millions of dollars to sponsor sports teams (University of North Carolina, Duke University, Stanford, Penn State and Arizona State, to name just a few) have become the hottest spots of the international anti-Nike campaign. According to the Campaign for Labor Rights, "These contracts, which are a centerpiece of Nike marketing, have now turned into a public relations nightmare for the company. Nike's aggressive campus marketing has now been forced into a defensive posture."[7] [...]

The Real Brand U

While many campuses are busily taking on the brand-name interlopers, others are realizing that their universities are themselves brand names. Ivy League universities, and colleges with all-star sports teams, have extensive clothing lines, several of which rival the market share of many commercial designers. They also share many of the same labor problems. In 1998, the UNITE garment workers union published a report on the BJ&B factory in an export processing zone in the Dominican Republic. Workers at BJ&B, one of the world's largest manufacturers of baseball hats, embroider the school logos and crests of at least nine large American universities, including Cornell, Duke, Georgetown, Harvard and University of Michigan. The conditions at BJ&B were signature free-trade-zone ones: long hours of forced overtime, fierce union busting (including layoffs of organizers), short-term contracts, paychecks insufficient to feed a family, pregnancy tests, sexual harassment, abusive management, unsafe drinking water and huge markups (while the hats sold, on average, for $19.95, workers saw only 8 cents of that).[8] And of course, most of the workers were young women, a fact that was brought home when the union sponsored a trip to the US for two former employees of the factory: nineteen-year-old Kenia Rodriguez and twenty-year-old Roselio Reyes. The two workers visited many of the universities whose logos they used to stitch on caps, speaking to gatherings of students who were exactly their age. "In the name of the 2,050 workers in this factory, and the people in this town, we ask for your support," Reyes said to an audience of students at the University of Illinois.[9]

These revelations about factory conditions were hardly surprising. College licensing is big business, and the players – Fruit of the Loom, Champion, Russell – have all shifted to contract factories with the rest of the garment industry, and make liberal use of free-trade zones around the world. In the US, the licensing of college names is a $2.5 billion annual industry, much of it brokered through the Collegiate Licensing Company. Duke University alone sells around $25 million worth of clothing associated with its winning basketball team every year. To meet the demand, it has seven hundred licensees who contract to hundreds of plants in the US and in ten other countries.[10] [. . .]

This fast-growing movement has a somewhat unlikely rallying cry: "Corporate disclosure." The central demand is for the companies that produce college-affiliated clothing to hand over the names and addresses of all their factories around the world and open themselves up to monitoring. Who makes your school clothing, the students say, should not be a mystery. They argue that with the garment industry being the global, contracted-out maze that it is, the onus must be on companies to prove their goods *aren't* made in sweatshops – not on investigative activists to prove that they are. The students are also pushing for their schools to demand that contractors pay a "living wage," as opposed to the legal minimum wage. By May 1999, at least four administrations had agreed in principle to push their suppliers on the living-wage issue. [. . .] However, there is no agreement about how to turn those well-meaning commitments into real changes in the export factories. Everyone involved in the anti-sweatshop movement does agree, however, that even getting issues like disclosure and a living wage on the negotiating table with manufacturers represents a major victory, one that has eluded campaigners for many years.

In a smaller but equally precedent-setting initiative, Archbishop Theodore McCarrick announced in October 1997 that his Newark, New Jersey, archdiocese would become a "no sweat" zone. The initiative includes introducing an anti-sweatshop curriculum into all 185 Catholic schools in the area, identifying the manufacturers of all their school uniforms and monitoring them to make sure the clothes are being produced under fair labor conditions – just as the students at St. Mary's in Pickering, Ontario, decided to do.

All in all, students have picked up the gauntlet on the sweatshop issue with an enthusiasm that has taken the aging labor movement by storm. United Students Against Sweatshops, after only one year in existence, claimed chapters on a hundred US campuses and a sister network in Canada. Free the Children, young Craig Kielburger's Toronto-based anti-child-labor organization (he was the thirteen-year-old who challenged the Canadian prime minister to review child-labor practices in India) has meanwhile gained strength in high schools and grade schools around the world. Charles Kernaghan, with his "outing" of Kathie Lee Gifford and Mickey Mouse, may have started this wave of labor organizing, but by the end of the 1998–99 academic year, he knew he was no longer driving it. In a letter to the United Students Against Sweatshops, he wrote: "Right now it is your student movement which is leading the way and carrying the heaviest weight in the struggle to end sweatshop abuses and child labor. Your effectiveness is forcing the companies to respond."[11]

Times have changed. As William Cahn writes in his history of the Lawrence Mill sweatshop strike of 1912, "Nearby Harvard University allowed students credit for their midterm examinations if they agreed to serve in the militia against the strikers. 'Insolent, well-fed Harvard men,' the *New York Call* reported, 'parade up and down, their rifles loaded . . . their bayonets glittering.'"[12] Today, students are squarely on the other side of sweatshop labor disputes: as the target market for everything from

Guess jeans to Nike soccer balls and Duke-embossed baseball hats, young people are taking the sweatshop issue personally. [. . .]

Study Questions

1　According to Klein, how is "brand backlash" manifesting itself on college campuses?
2　Why is disclosure such a focus of the antisweatshop movement?
3　What relationship can you see between the working conditions abroad deplored by Klein and her generation of activists, and the economic problems that concern Bruce Springsteen?
4　How has the growth of the Internet affected the student organizing Klein describes?

Notes

1.　Personal interview.
2.　G. Kramer, "Suu Kyi Urges U.S. Boycott," Associated Press, 27 January 1997.
3.　Farhan Haq, "Burma-Finance: Oil company digs in heels despite Rangoon's record," Inter Press Service, 4 February 1997.
4.　"Pepsi, Burma, Take 2: Pepsi Responds to Aims of Target Audience," Dow Jones News Service, 27 January 1997.
5.　Free Burma Coalition Web site.
6.　"NUS Withdraws from McDonald's 'Privilege Card' Scheme," McLibel Support Campaign press release, 14 April 1998.
7.　"Nike Campaign Strategy, Part 1," Labor Alerts, 14 January 1998.
8.　"Was Your School's Cap Made in This Sweatshop? A UNITE Report on Campus Caps Made by BJ&B in the Dominican Republic," released 13 April 1998.
9.　"Dominican Republic Workers Urge University of Illinois to Demand Humane Factory Conditions," Daily Illini, 24 April 1998.
10.　Steven Greenhouse, "Duke to Adopt a Code to Prevent Apparel from Being Made in Sweatshops," New York Times, 8 March 1998.
11.　"An Open Letter to the Students," by Charles Kernaghan, undated.
12.　William Cahn, Lawrence 1912: The Bread & Roses Strike (New York: The Pilgrim Press, 1977), 174.

PART V

The Future of Us All?

I n the last section of this book, we invite you to consider and to imagine some present and future possibilities for the United States as a nation, and for yourselves as individuals, citizens and residents, workers, parents, sons and daughters. The first two essays in this section offer examples of richly diverse communities in which people from all over the world, from different social backgrounds and racial groups, have found ways to work and play together in small American communities (a Los Angeles high school, a borough of New York City) that model both a real and possible America. The final essay provides an outline for a utopian, or ideal, American society, in which the norm for each citizen is based on what is the common good for all. We hope these concluding essays will lead to a lively discussion in your class that will encourage you to share your own American dreams for the future of us all.

CHAPTER 47

Brave New World:
Gray Boys, Funky Aztecs, and Honorary Homegirls

Lynell George

Born and raised in Los Angeles, award-winning journalist Lynell George (1962–) loves her city. "As a native," she writes, "I constantly box with the city and its issues and I'm proud of how it belligerently redefines itself... [There is] no better place/moment to be a journalist where race and culture and language and crisis constantly converge before they converse." Specializing in culture, art, and race, she has published articles in numerous magazines, such as Vibe, Newsday, Essence, *and* African American Review. *George has been a staff writer for the* Los Angeles Times *and cohost of StoryLines California, a talk-radio program that features discussions of literature. In the following article, published in 1993, she shows the astonishing ways that high school students in Los Angeles cross racial, immigrant, and ethnic borders as they create hybrid forms of American popular culture.*

Let's call him "Perry."

If you grew up in Los Angeles (back when it was still hip to dub the mix "melting pot") and sat through a homeroom roll call sandwiching you somewhere between a Martinez, Masjedi, Matsuda and Meizel, you knew one – but more than likely two. This Culver City "Perry," a classmate of mine, had Farrah Fawcett-feathered blond hair, moist blue-gray eyes and a Tiger Beat dimple in his chin. Tall and gregarious, at first glimpse he seemed destined for the surfers' corner in the cafeteria – that tight tangle of dreamy adolescents who, in wet suits under their hooded Bajas, made their way down to Zuma Beach on slate-gray February mornings. Blaring Led Zeppelin, Boston or Aerosmith, they trailed westward, away from the sun.

In broad-lapel Qianna shirts and denim flares, Perry, who looked less like Peter Frampton than Barry Gibb, embraced the electronic trickery of Parliament-Funkadelic, the East Coast soul of the Isley Brothers, or some Ohio Players midnight jam swelling from the boombox. He certainly never surfed. He shadowed the intricate steps of the Soul Train dancers, sat with the black basketball players in the back of the bus and attempted to chat up their little sisters in a sonorous baritone carefully fashioned after (who else but) Barry White.

"Oh, man, he's like KC, you know, in the Sunshine Band," those who knew him would tease. But new faces would take a second look, then bristle and inevitably inquire: "Hasn't anybody told him he ain't black?"

"Chill out," Perry's best partner, the tallest, most imposing BMOC would always defend. "He's OK. He's gray. . . ."

After a while, most everyone forgot what Perry wasn't – even forgot that he was "gray": the hard-won badge worn by those white kids who seemed much more comfortable hovering in the space between.

It often worked other ways, too. White kids, honorary homeboys and homegirls who dressed like *cholos* and talked the grand talk about *mi vida loca*. Blue-blood black kids who surfed and played mean, tireless sets of country club tennis. Japanese kids who saved their lunch money to buy Forum floor seats for Earth, Wind and Fire spectaculars and were slipping everyone hallway high-fives during passing period long before it became pro-ball decorum.

Over the years, LA's mix has only evolved into a much more complex jumble as immigration patterns shift and swell, as blurred neighborhood boundaries subdivide or change hands. However, Los Angeles [. . .] is still a segregated city, despite such "border towns" as Culver City, Echo Park, or Carson and the disparate bodies that inhabit them, blending and sharing their cultural trappings and identifiers. These contiguous neighborhoods inspire intercultural dialogue. And those living at the fringes have (not without incident) found it necessary to learn something about adaptation. Dealing not in dualities but in pluralities, survival in this city requires a cultural dexterity heretofore unimagined.

LA has metamorphosed into a crazy incubator, and the children who live on these streets and submit to their rhythm rise up as exquisite hothouse flowers. They beget their own language, style, codes – a shorthand mode of communication and identification. It's more than learning a handy salutation in Tagalog, being conversant in street slang or sporting hip-hop-inspired styles. This sort of cultural exchange requires active participation and demands that one press past the superficial toward a more meaningful discourse and understanding.

By no means a full-blown movement, these young people, a small coterie, exhibit large-scale possibilities. Unaware and without fanfare, they are compelling examples of how effortless and yet edifying reaching out can be.

Their free-form amalgamation billows up in street style (like the "Gangsta"/*cholo*-style baggy chinos and Pendletons that hit the mainstream fashion pages a few months back) as well as in street music. Latino rapper Kid Frost shook it up with his icy, tough-as-nails Public Enemy delivery, then sharpened the edges with staccato snatches in Spanish. For raw power, post-punk badboys the Red Hot Chili Peppers don't have a thing on their counterparts, the Badbrains.

Recently, the Funky Aztecs have taken the baton. Their new recording, "Chicano Blues," offers samples from soul crooner Bill Withers while vamping on traditional 12-bar delta blues. When not dipping into reggae dub-style or funk, Merciless, Indio and Loco pay homage to the rich California melange with the raucous single, "Salsa *con* Soul Food."

For Merciless, who's 19, the mixing was almost inevitable. His family moved to an all-black neighborhood in Vallejo when he was 9, and before he shaved his head a year ago, "I had real curly hair," he says. "Just, I guess, by the way I dress, a lot of people mix me up with either being black or mixed with black." And the rhythms of hip-hop were a break from the street. "My Chicano partners they were all into their little gangs, you know, their little Notre XIV. Everyone was talking about gangster stuff: 'I'ma kill you,' 'I gotta gun,' 'this bitch is my "ho." ' But I wasn't into that, I was more like expressing myself politically. It was mainly my black friends who were into rapping and deejaying and stuff like that.

"It's a trip because my own race trips off me. I even got chased out of my own barrio. But the brothers are real cool with me. It's not that I side on them or whatever because my race always puts me down. It's not like that, but if you're cool to me, I don't care what color you are – I'm going to give you that love right back."

Lives and attitudes like that wreak havoc with stubborn stereotypes and archaic notions about what it is to be African-American, Latino, Asian-American or Anglo in a quickly transfiguring metropolitan center. In a recent Village Voice Literary Supplement, LA expatriate Paul Beatty eloquently shared a vision of home: "Growing up in Los Angeles," writes Beatty, "I couldn't help noticing that language was closely tied to skin color" but not exclusively. "Black folks was either 'fittin' ' or 'fixin' ' to go to Taco Bell. . . . The four Asian kids I knew talked black. . . . When I started writing, I realized that me and my friends had difficulty processing the language. We felt like foreigners because no one understood us. We were a gang of verbal mulattoes. Black kids with black brains but white mouths – inbred with some cognitively dissonant Mexicans who didn't speak Spanish and looked crazy at anyone who thought they did."

Some argue that this sort of mixing dilutes culture and creates innumerable lost souls; but many of those who live it see this sharing as realistically inclusive and ultimately enriching – so long as one holds on to integral bits and pieces of one's own. Those more optimistic hear rumblings in and of this New Age patois as harbingers; these young people are well-equipped bellwethers of the new cultural hybrids of Los Angeles.

The mixing starts earlier and earlier, as Jai Lee Wong of the LA County Human Relations Commission points out: "My child is $4\frac{1}{2}$ and is fluent in Spanish because his baby-sitter teaches it to him." He tends, she explains, to identify people by the language they speak, not by their racial or ethnic designations. "If they speak English they are English or American. If they speak Korean, they're Korean," Wong says. "And even though his father is Chinese and speaks only English, my son thinks he's American. For him it's not based on race or ethnicity. He hears me and his father sitting around identifying people by race and it confuses him. Then one day he started talking about that 'green kid over there.' Turns out that he was talking about a white kid wearing a green shirt." Race is a concept not beyond, but perhaps already behind him, Wong realizes; a clumsy piece of baggage that already weighs him down.

The new world view? "It's a people thing," Merciless says. "It's not a black or brown or white or red or orange thing. It's a people thing. We all just need to grow up." [. . .]

The mere fact of LA's diversity makes the contentious concept of assimilation far less cut-and-dried than it was in the past, when widespread use of the term *melting pot* suggested that a soul branded with "minority" status in the United States had to "melt down" his or her cultural trappings – language, dress, religious ritual or even body type – to aspire to the American ideal.

Here, where Central and South America meet the Pacific Rim and West Indies, the definitions of what it means to be black, white, brown or yellow blur, and fitting in requires an entirely different set of tools and techniques. Paule Cruz Takash, a UC San Diego anthropologist and ethnic studies professor, notes that "assimilation is not a one-way street," with everyone striving to adopt Anglo culture. As the phrase "Ellis Island West" spices news reports about the growing lines winding around the city's Immigration and Naturalization Service office, the question of assimilation becomes broader, takes on new definitions.

Ironically enough, in the past two decades, the media and other information arteries, traditional tools for stratifying cultures with the uncomplicated, and erroneous, shorthand of stereotypes, have been invaluable tools for breaking down stereotypes and reworking prevailing theories about cultural identity. New mixes take shape at monster movie-plexes, super-bookstores and the alternative glitz of underground clubs (and the easy access to them). The ears and eyes take it all in – and the brain then reassembles it, gives it new form.

And an increasing number of LA newcomers embody and advance the recombinant culture. Nahom Tassew, a 17-year-old Ethiopian who's a junior at Belmont High, came to the United States knowing "just what I saw on movies and TV" about African-Americans. "I thought if I came here, I'd have to become a thief," he says, "or that was what people would think I was." After $2\frac{1}{2}$ years, he has a new attitude ("I saw that [African-Americans at Belmont] were people . . . that there were good people and bad people, that every race has good people") as well as friends from Mexico, Guatemala, El Salvador, Japan and China. And he's studying Spanish. "I need some Spanish words," he says. Just what will emerge from these admixtures is difficult to say. Tassew, at least, will acquire an early-age sophistication, learning classroom English along with the street Spanish of his neighborhood, finding astonishing cultural parallels (from salutation rituals to food) with his Chinese friends. In that environment, he and others have found, there is no room for xenophobia. [. . .]

The students have unfurled a cloth banner and hung it high above the stage of Belmont High School's cavernous auditorium. In electric, wild-style lettering it proclaims: La Raza Unida (The United Race). As the SRO crowd mills around her, principal Martha Bin stands on the sidelines, blond hair folded into an elegant updo, her walkie-talkie poised in a freshly manicured hand. This year, voting to pass on the usual Columbus Day assembly, the student body, Bin explains, chose instead to pay homage to the campus's Latin cultural mix – spanning several countries and continents.

In what looks like an elaborate show-and-tell, students bring bits and pieces of their culture to Belmont's stage. Since the auditorium won't accommodate the 4,000-plus student body at one seating, there are two assemblies – one morning, another in the afternoon. The second performance begins with several girls in frothy turquoise dresses, their partners in dark, pressed suits, displaying *rancheras*. Later come the *cumbias*, a mambo and an elaborate dance performed with lit candles that originated in Peru. Capping the show is a trio in below-the-knee, extra-large baggy shorts, who rap and joke in English, Spanish, and French.

"We are a school of immigrants," says Bin, sitting down for a moment in a quiet classroom next to the auditorium, her walkie-talkie close by. "Many of the black kids are Hispanic. We have Chinese-Cubans. We have Koreans who speak Portuguese." Belmont, one of the largest high schools in the nation, with 4,500 students on campus, buses out another 3,000 to accommodate the crush of the Temple/Beaudry/Echo Park district youth population from which it draws. Bin says 78% of the student body is Latino; the rest is a mix that includes citizens of Romania, Colombia, Armenia, Ethiopia and Biafra. "You sit them together," Bin says, "they just have to get along – *conjunto* – together."

William Han, an 18-year-old Belmont senior, thinks he knows why. "Students who attend Belmont," he says, "are first-generation American students, whereas at other schools they are second or third. We are immigrants. This is our first experience." Han knows the struggle to adjust. It was just four years ago that he and his Korean parents moved here from their home in Brazil. A bright and talkative "American" teen, he wears an oversized jersey with "William" embroidered in green, green/gray pressed slacks and black sneakers. His black hair is close-cropped and sticks up like the bristles of a stiff brush. Like many of the kids around him, he's something of a citizen of the world – he speaks Portuguese, Spanish, English and Korean. "Things at Belmont are honest," he says. In the common fight to cope with a new culture, "people accept you for who you are."

Because of the intricate cultural mix surrounding the school, there are concerns and needs that are unique to Belmont. "Our ESL students tend to be Spanish speaking, but a lot of Asians speak Spanish before English on our campus because they hear it in their neighborhood," says assistant principal Rosa Morley, herself an embodiment of ethnic and cultural blending. (She has Chinese parents but grew up in Cuba. Fluent in Spanish, she feels most connected to Cuban culture.)

"The kids feel that the whole world is like this," Bin says, and that can be a problem later on. "They have some difficulty when they move out of this environment and are no longer the majority."

"We don't tell them this isn't the real world," Morley says. "They will find out sooner or later. We are sheltering them in a sense but cannot control what life will bring for them."

By college, one doesn't see as many "Culver City Perrys." The university, for those who make it, is often the startling baptism, a reawakening or first-awakening of self. Students moving out of ethnically/racially diverse environments and into the austere university setting come face to face with cultural stratification. It is, for many, the first time that they are called upon to choose sides or feel a need to become politically active.

The Institute for the Study of Social Change, based at UC Berkeley, reported on diversity at the university level a year ago in a study called the Diversity Project. The study's goal was to address "a vital and constantly unfolding development emerging in American social life," focusing primarily on demographic changes in the country and how they affect interpersonal communication on college campuses. There would be no solution to the problems of diversity, the report stressed, as long as we think in polar terms. The extremes of "assimilation to a single dominant culture where differences merge and disappear vs. a situation where isolated and self-segregated groups (retreat) into ... enclaves" don't work, researchers concluded. The report was based on 69 focus-group interviews with 291 UC Berkeley students.

The report advises a "third and more viable" option: "the simultaneous possibility of strong ethnic and racial identities (including ethnically homogeneous affiliations and friendships) *alongside* a public participation of multiracial and multiethnic contacts that enriches the public and social sphere of life."

In testimonials in the Diversity Project, students spoke frankly about the problems of bridging two worlds and the inexorable pressure to fit in. An Asian-American male was traumatized when presented with a completely alien environment: "I was totally unaccustomed to being in (a) social situation where only Asians were there. So I was completely lost.... I got so frustrated, I rejected ... my Asian-American identity and had a lot of Hispanic friends."

In this period of self-searching, what will help these students realize this "third experience" – recognizing diversity while maintaining their own distinctive cultural identity – is to develop the cultural equivalent of achieving bilingual or multilingual proficiency, to be sensitive enough to adapt to one's surroundings without losing sight of self.

This concept of cultural pluralism – where each group makes an influential and duly recognized contribution to American society – may seem naive or merely whimsical, but in light of the tremendous cultural shift, it is tenable.

"Racial and ethnic identities are always formed in dialogue with one another," says George Lipsitz, professor of ethnic studies at UC San Diego and author of "Time Passages," a collection of essays on diversity and contemporary pop culture. "So to be Chicano in LA means to have a long engagement with black culture. What kind of Anglo you are depends on what group of color you're in dialogue with."

Lipsitz has noted that this mixing once was a more class-based phenomenon, but that drift has altered dramatically in recent years. "When I see desegregated groups of graffiti writers, one of the things that strikes me is that they're also mixed by class," he says. "Style leaders are working-class kids who present themselves as poorer than they are but they have a suburban following. One writer told me: 'Y'know, I go down to the Belmont Tunnel, I go out to the motor yard in Santa Monica, I meet a guy who lives in Beverly Hills, I meet someone who went to Europe last summer.' It's the way they expand what's open to them."

Lipsitz doesn't see this mixing as a grievous threat or as diluting culture, as some nationalists do. People find allies wherever they find them, he believes. "For example, there is a group of graffiti writers who call themselves 'ALZA' – which stands for African, Latino, Zulu and Anglo. ALZA, Lipsitz says, is Chicano slang for *rise up*. They found each other. Nobody set this up. Nobody put an ad in the paper. They look for spaces that are what we call 'multicultural.' I don't think that they ever think to look at it in those ways. But there's a sense of interest and excitement and delight in difference that makes them look for more complexity."

But painting this phenomena as some sort of "we are the world" harmonious culture fest would be erroneous. Like those in the Diversity Project, Lipsitz has witnessed some of the more painful outcomes of "fitting nowhere," what isolation and alienation can do to a young person's spirit and soul. "I've talked to many students who are either from racially mixed backgrounds or who have what they consider to be an odd history – maybe they were the only black student in a white high school or something like that," he explains. "Then at the university it seems that there is an inside that they are not part of, and there is no obvious subgroup that they can join.

"They don't feel comfortable maybe with African-American culture. Or there are Chicanos who come in but they don't speak Spanish well enough for MEChA (a college-level Latino political organization); or there are Asian-Americans who are Korean or Vietnamese, and the campus is dominated by Japanese- or Chinese-Americans. It is their love of difference, danger and heterogeneity that brings them together. When a singer like George Clinton comes along – who's too black for the whites, too white for the blacks – "in a way he's talking to people whose lives are like that." [. . .]

Those who might be viewed by some as having "odd histories" because they've spent their lives juggling codes or responding to the various influences within them are breaking down walls and erecting sturdy bridges through the mere act of living their lives. Granted, this vision appears mere chimera, almost utopian. But it is, for them, proving to be an integral component of psychic survival. In this period of uneasy transition, complicated by overwhelmingly rapid change, young people ride the periphery, and their lives do impressive battle with notions of a now-archaic "norm." But their quiet revolution is fueled by much more than simply the adolescent ache to belong. It is a more honest, eyes-wide-open way to reach out and greet a world as confounding as they are.

Study Questions

1   What is the meaning of "Gray Boys, Funky Aztecs, and Honorary Home-girls"? What has brought this "brave new world" into being, according to George?

2   What roles have the mass media, popular music, dance, and fashion played in constructing the hybrid identities of the LA high school students profiled in this article? How would she have to update these if she were publishing her article today?

3   How would Judith Stacey's "brave new families," Bharati Mukherjee's heroine Jasmine, or Claudine O'Hearn fit into the picture George presents?

4   Why does George find all this cultural and social "mixing" exhilarating and hopeful? Do you think she provides an accurate description of contemporary US culture? Why or why not?

CHAPTER 48

From *The Future of Us All*

Roger Sanjek

Roger Sanjek (1944–) is a professor of anthropology who has written frequently on the topic of community activism. He is the author of At Work in Home: Household Workers in World Perspective *(1990), and coauthor, with Anthony Leeds, of* Cities, Classes, and the Social Order *(1994). Sanjek's* The Future of Us All: Race and Neighborhood Politics in New York City *(1998) is based on a 13-year study conducted by a multiethnic team of researchers. The book examines the dramatic changes that took place in the Elmhurst-Corona neighborhood of New York City as it became one of the most ethnically mixed urban communities in the US. The following excerpt from his "Conclusion" outlines the most important strategies Sanjek learned from the community he studied for affecting positive political and social change.*

At no one's request and by no one's design, Elmhurst-Corona was transformed from a solidly white neighborhood in 1960 to "perhaps the most ethnically mixed community in the world" by the 1990s. The United States is still at the early stages of a similar transition. The arrival of a "majority-minority" population on a national scale in the next century will not repeat the story told in this book, nor will the many local transitions from now to then follow any single script. Still, the elements and forces of change that transformed Community District 4 are already at work elsewhere and will recur in varying combinations and patterns in the coming decades. If our goal as citizens and neighbors is indeed, in Lani Guinier's definition, "an integrated body politic in which all perspectives are represented, and in which all people work together to find common ground," we need to ask what lessons may be drawn from the Elmhurst-Corona story.

Government Matters

In contemporary America, government is involved at every step in the movement toward common ground. It is not simply by individual choice that people of so many diverse orgins live together in CD4. Individual whites, blacks, and immigrants indeed chose to move to, stay in, or leave Elmhurst-Corona, but they did so in response to shifting job opportunities, federal highway and housing programs, suburban zoning restrictions, inconsistent fair-housing law enforcement, and changing immigration policies – all the results of government actions.

Neighborhood New Yorkers endured assaults on quality of life resulting from the 1975 fiscal crisis and continuing budget cuts, clearly the product of permanent-government and mayoral decisions. Zoning regulations and diminished housing-code enforcement defined neighborhood realities for all residents of Elmhurst-Corona and set the stage for their struggles to change them. Individuals innovated new alliances and forms of organization but did so within a political field shaped by decentralized community boards, district cabinets, and school boards – structures created by city policies that dated to the very years in which Elmhurst-Corona's majority-minority transition began.

All this occurred within a field of power relationships. The power of resources in New York City faced a major threat as the speculative-electronic economy dispersed nationally and globally, and the office buildings that had housed it began to empty. The power of numbers, divided by race, ethnicity, language, religion, and cultural background, faced new organizational challenges. Lubricatory power, either serving to contain the coalescing power of numbers in neighborhood New York or used on its behalf by wardens, renegade professionals, and citywide advocates, was more important than ever. [. . .]

What Brings People Together?

Politics is about more than attitudes. It is also about interpersonal connections and group action. Too much social science research defines only attitude surveys as "real," and brands real-life, real-time ethnographic observation as "anecdotal" or "unrepresentative." The struggles, defeats, and victories that constitute neighborhood politics occur not because attitudes somehow change but because wardens act, leaders innovate, people meet, and numbers coalesce. Those who watch and listen systematically in places where this happens can observe politics unfold. Those who limit themselves to interviews and opinion polls miss all this and are left to design after-the-fact explanations of why political change occurs.

Community District 4's extreme racial and ethnic diversity is unique, but more neighborhoods and cities will "look like Elmhurst-Corona" as America's great transition proceeds. Some whites will resist or move away, but others will increasingly interact with new neighbors across ethnic and racial lines. As this occurs, people first sort one another according to their own sets of racial and ethnic categories; then, over time, they begin to add to their networks actual persons with names, occupations, families, and individual characteristics.[1] Where and how in Elmhurst-Corona does this second step start to happen?

First, self-introductions, exchanges of pleasantries, and sometimes friendships arise between neighbors on blocks and in apartment buildings. New residents frequently next encounter a local warden who offers advice on garbage collection or other immediate street and building matters. Sometimes they are also approached by members of block, tenant, co-op, and civic associations, or they see a newsletter or flyer and find their way to an organization meeting. Only a few will become active members of such groups, but along with neighborly ties these are the residential frontlines in bridging ethnic and racial borders. Categorical and personal relations with others, of course, also emerge in workplaces, and ties there affect the way people view and relate to neighbors.

For many whites, houses of worship are another site of cross-ethnic and crossracial contact.[2] Immigrants also establish their own houses of worship where languages other than English are spoken and little contact occurs with established white or black Americans – yet even here one often finds diverse congregations sharing space, and second-generation English-speaking youth groups beginning to appear. Just as Dutch, German, Polish, Italian, and other European-language congregations in Elmhurst-Corona's past became English-speaking and multiethnic over time, today's new houses of worship may face similar futures; already non-Chinese worship at Elmhurst's Ch'an Buddhist temple. In both predictable and no doubt unexpected ways, houses of worship will be important locations for solidifying and expanding interethnic and interracial ties.

Neighbor-to-neighbor relationships and houses of worship are "private," but wardens and civic groups involve residents with government policies and with efforts to influence and change them. Wardens ask neighbors to "obey the law" about the placement of garbage for collection and other matters; block watchers and "feelers in the community" form connections to police precincts, district-level city agency personnel, and local government bodies such as community boards and their district managers. Block and civic associations do the same, and tenant and co-op associations, though formed for "private" purposes, make use of public laws and courts and frequently take on civic-association-like activities.[3]

This field of local political action brings participants together across racial and ethnic lines and can be expected to do so even more in coming decades. It is what these wardens and associations actually do, however, not any "joiner" impulse, that motivates them and their supporters. Most important, they struggle against assaults on the quality of life resulting from government shrinkage and budget cuts. In Elmhurst-Corona people of all races want effective policing to control drug trafficking, prostitution, gambling, and illegal dumping; and they want livable neighborhoods where parking, public transportation, schools, recreation facilities, access to hospitals, and a safe, decent housing supply are in balance.

The most universally supported quality-of-life concerns in CD4 focus on children: the two-decades-long struggle, still not over, *against* school overcrowding and *for* more youth programs. White wardens fought for expanded hours at the Elmhurst Branch Library and organized afterschool and summer youth programs and the Teen Center; black wardens ran summer cleanup and sports programs and tutored at the Lefrak City Branch Library; Latin Americans organized afterschool and summer programs; Latin American, Asian, and African American candidates ran for seats on School Board 24, and a Chinese woman from Elmhurst was its first member of color.

Some youth programs drew on CD4's annual two-dollar-per-child city youth services allocation and supplemented this money with volunteer adult effort. The need for sites, programs, and adult involvement, however, is far greater than what exists, and schools and youth programs remain underfunded. In 1989 two thirds of New York City voters favored tax increases over cuts in programs, and six years later 61 percent of New York City parents were ready to pay higher taxes to improve public education. In 1997 two-thirds of New Yorkers remained dissatisfied with their city's schools.[4] Parents of all races well understand the importance of education to their children's future. Joint efforts to secure more resources for schools and youth programs will promote racial and ethnic comity and accord.

Expect More Rituals

Rituals, ceremonies, commemorations, and demonstrations are "transmitters of culture" in human societies and are "generated in social relations." As culture becomes more variegated and complex and social relations more categorical and unpredictable, new rituals emerge to affirm old beliefs and routines, to integrate new ensembles of cultural elements, and to "bring order into experience" for changing groups of neighborhood co-residents.[5]

Rituals of ethnic celebration are created to mark the presence of new ethnic groups and to affirm the persistence of established ones, and more of these rituals will appear as American communities become more diverse. Their ethnic particularity, however, rubs against the multiethnicity of street neighborhoods and city districts; hence, they migrate to central locations where they draw upon areawide populations; Israeli and St. Patrick's Day parades in Manhattan, the Dominican parade in the Bronx, the West Indian – American Day Carnival in Brooklyn, and ethnic festivals in Flushing Meadows – Corona Park provide examples. Their audiences, however, become more diverse over time; public officials of all races appear as marchers and guests; and their formal properties grow increasingly alike.[6]

Civic rituals such as Christmas tree lightings and Memorial Day observances are organized by established whites and celebrate values of continuity. They are revived when newcomers increase in number and these values are under question, but those that remain inwardly focused are unstable and may not survive. When they do, it is because they begin to incorporate newcomers, not only as audience members but as participants, and the parochial assertion of local priority yields to the communal value of place. When this happens, civic rituals no longer belong exclusively to their creators, and like Corona's tree lighting they continue because they now help "neighborhoods...retain their identities and boundaries despite...shifts in ethnic composition."[7]

Whereas civic rituals deemphasize ethnicity and race, rituals of inclusion openly celebrate diversity. Cultural Sharing Days, International Nights, and Parades of Nations symbolize multiethnic and multiracial communities and seek to promote tolerance, respect, and harmony. In these quintessentially American rituals the distilled, vestigial form in which European ethnicities survive becomes the model for assimilating new foreign cultures. The living cultures of adult immigrants evident in rituals of ethnic celebration risk trivialization as they are reduced to a song, a sharable food, a dance, a costume, a greeting, and a holiday. Perhaps rituals of inclusion work best when enacted by children, because assemblages of children are in themselves a positive symbol to adults of all races and ethnicities.[8]

If participation matters more than content in rituals of inclusion, content is paramount in quality-of-life rituals. These submerge ethnic and racial diversity to stress common neighborhood identity in celebrating new parks and clean streets, or in protesting drugs, prostitution, subway crowding, and other assaults on quality of life. Neighborhood residents who "share a common fate at the hands of city planners, realtors, [and] politicians" are reminded by these rituals that they "simply cannot ignore each other."[9] The power of numbers is valorized symbolically in quality-of-life rituals, and they bolster the work of wardens and local associations.

Listen to Women (They Listen to Each Other)

[...] In the mid-1970s women began moving into Elmhurst-Corona's district-level political field and unblocking the channels between whites, immigrants, and blacks. As the sociologist Herbert Gans observes, "In communities where similarity of backgrounds...is scarce, collective action requires a sizeable amount of interpersonal negotiation and compromise – and leaders who can apply personal skills that persuade people to ignore their differences."[10] It was women more than men who supplied this leadership, and one should be prepared for more female leadership everywhere as America's majority-minority transition unfolds.[11] Male wardens continued to be active in Elmhurst-Corona civic politics, but by the mid-1980s women held key leadership positions, and racial and ethnic relations began to change. [...]

Why was it women more than men who formed this network of cross-racial ties in Elmhurst-Corona? Sociologist Nancy Chodorow would trace these patterns to maternal socialization, which incorporates daughters into a world of women characterized by "relational" identification and "connection to other people," whereas sons exit this world to adopt male roles emphasizing "positional" identification and individual achievement. Consequently, as linguist Deborah Tannen observes, women's ways of talking are more likely to stress "a community of connection," whereas men's talk operates "to preserve their independence in a hierarchical world." Furthermore, as historian Temma Kaplan posits, "the gender system of their society... assigns women the responsibility of... guarding their neighbors, children and mates against danger"; under conditions of change "a sense of community that emerges from shared routines binds women to one another" and "politicizes the networks of daily life." Political scientist Carol Hardy-Fanta concludes that women more than men "focus on... connecting people to other people to achieve change" but that such "participatory qualities are [not] the unique realm of women [and] these skills and values are within the abilities of men."[12]

In Elmhurst-Corona women certainly acted to "guard their children." When one district cabinet meeting turned to Parks Department capital projects, Rose Rothschild remarked, "I always suggest preschool buildings [in park reconstruction plans] because I'm a mother. Men never look at that." Nonetheless, men such as Bob Tilitz, Al Fernicola, Richard Italiano, Tom Rodriguez, and Al Blake did champion library, afterschool, and recreation programs for school-age youth. Male wardens, particularly men who grew up or had long resided in the neighborhood, could also possess "a sense of community that emerges from shared routines."[13]

As for race, women moved sooner from categorical to personal ties, relating more readily to women of another race as women than men did to other men. The "positional" and "hierarchial" values that continue to mark race relations in the United States are not only more characteristic of male socialization and gender roles but reinforced by the structural relationships of workplaces and hierarchical organizations. Many of Elmhurst-Corona's women leaders were housewives or worked from their homes; men were more likely to be employed in formal settings. Women who entered civic politics, moreover, had frequently had experience in school, religious, or block association groups where improvisation and abilities to involve others were more important than tables of organization and titled positions.

Strengthen Local Democracy

As the quality of life in neighborhood New York worsened after 1975, local "parapolitical" activity expanded, and the city's 3,500 civic, block, tenant, ethnic, and other associations in 1977 grew to 8,000 by 1995. Community boards, where many of these groups voiced their views on municipal services, land-use issues, and budget recommendations, provided new arenas for local politics at a time when political party clubs were becoming less powerful. Whatever their short-comings, community boards strengthened local democracy. "Resolution of the grievances experienced at the level of communities," organizer Prudence Posner points out, "requires the exercise of power that can enforce policies, regulations, and restrictions on very powerful economic entities." This power of numbers working through community boards was exemplified in the 1989 downzoning of Elmhurst-Corona and in the 1996 defeat of Mayor Giuliani's megastore plan.[14]

Neighborhood New Yorkers of all races – in 1988, 78 percent of Roman Catholic "white ethnics," 79 percent of Asians, 84 percent of African Americans, and 88 percent of Latin Americans – favored *more* government decentralization.[15] City charters affirming the power of community boards were approved by voters in 1975 and 1989. Eight-year limits for city council members, approved twice by voter referendum, will take effect in 2001, potentially devolving more power to the district-level political field. Still, community boards by the mid-1990s were less inclusive than they could have been. Their members were appointed, not elected, and particularly in racially and ethnically diverse community districts they did not fully "look like New York City." [. . .]

Welcome a Multiethnic, Multilingual City

Coalescing the power of numbers among whites, immigrants, and blacks, whether in Elmhurst-Corona, in New York City, or nationwide, will require reciprocal recognition of one another's concerns as well as common goals. Angelo Falcón, founder of the Institute for Puerto Rican Policy, raised this matter at a 1990 forum:

> [We] need to . . . understand that our strength is in our community and in our identification as Latinos in terms of our numbers. . . . The fact that we're 25 percent of the city's population is something we've got to find ways of leveraging [to] create some sort of counterforce. . . . The question of language policy – for years our people can't get services. . . . You'd think by this time that New York would already have a mechanism for incorporating new populations who don't speak the language. . . . If we're successful in getting New York to adopt a language policy . . . we're leaving a legacy . . . for future generations, . . . for the Asian community, [and] for other communities. . . . We need to frame our own issues in that broader context.[16]

Many white Americans today believe that immigrants resist learning English and that bilingual education perpetuates "linguistic separatism." In fact, of the 41 percent of New Yorkers who spoke another language at home in 1990, three-quarters *also* spoke English. The quarter who did not turned to adult English classes and the public schools to learn, but by 1993 only 30,000 English-class seats were available for 600,000 non-English-speaking adults; government support for these classes amounted to only $20 million per year, and waiting lists ranged from four months to three years. Federal bilingual education funds for the 150,000 "limited English proficiency" students in New York City's public schools had been cut by half during the 1980s, even while the number of children availing themselves of such programs continued to rise.

Children of primary school age acquire English rapidly: in New York City most of them "mainstream" from bilingual to regular classes in three years or less; many do so more quickly in Elmhurst-Corona, where the large number of different languages facilitates English learning among children themselves in both school and neighborhood play groups. Older youth have a harder time, and many immigrant high school students take longer to graduate (although their drop-out rate is lower) than US-born students. Long Island Congress member and "English Only" advocate Peter King distorts the issue by emphasizing that sixth- to ninth-grade immigrant teenagers take longer than three years to "mainstream" in the crowded, underfunded city schools of the 1990s. The alternative – English-language "immersion" – works well when trained instructors, full-day programs, and small teacher-pupil ratios are provided. Even immersion proponent Diane Ravitch admits, "It is not a new [English-only] law that is needed, but better education in the English language for children and adults."[17]

Notwithstanding the meager assistance government provides, in fact today's "immigrants and their children may be acquiring English faster than in the past," Philip Martin and Elizabeth Midgley point out. Although the immigrant parents or grandparents of Elmhurst-Corona whites "rarely learned English well during their lifetimes," their children were fully or partly bilingual, and the third generation was monolingual in English. Most third-generation Latin Americans also speak English exclusively. Today, however, "the handicaps of not knowing English" are increasing, and much evidence suggests that "the three-generation shift to English may shrink to two generations by 2000."[18] Still, as the linguist Ana Celia Zentella advocates, steps to preserve the linguistic resources of America's 40 million bilingual residents could prove advantageous in the global economy of the twenty-first century. By the 1980s less than one-fifth of US students studied a second language as compared with four-fifths earlier in this century.[19]

Large numbers of white Americans also believe that the country is "saturated" with foreign-born newcomers, even though today's 8 percent immigrant population is less than the 14 percent of 1910 and is not likely to reach that level before the 2040s. (New York City's higher 33 percent foreign-born population in 1995 is also below its 41 percent foreign-born peak in 1910.) Further, many mistakenly believe that the majority of newcomers are "illegal aliens." In 1995 the Census Bureau estimated that 4 million of the nation's 23 million immigrants were undocumented, or only 1 in 6. In New York City the ratio was also 1 in 6, but here 90 percent of undocumented immigrants were "overstayers" who had entered the country legally with nonresident visas, versus just 40 percent nationally. Two of New York's three largest undocumented groups, moreover, were white – Italians and Poles – and together they accounted for 1 in 9 of the city's "illegal alien" population.[20]

In Elmhurst-Corona three-quarters of the population by 1990 consisted of immigrants and their children.[21] The cries against "illegal aliens" that stirred numbers of whites in the mid-1970s continued to be raised occasionally at public meetings, by both whites and Latin Americans, but with little effect. At a 1988 school-site hearing one man asked, "How many who will go here are children of illegal aliens? . . . If they did a survey, how many would be deported along with their parents, and free up space for other children?" Only one audience member applauded, and the meeting's business resumed. CB4 did pass a resolution in 1994 calling on Mayor Giuliani to end

Mayor Koch's 1985 executive order that prevented city agencies from reporting undocumented immigrants to federal authorities in cases not involving criminal activity. But later that year, when an audience member introduced "illegal aliens" as a quality-of-life problem, CB4 members Luz Leguizamo and Clara Salas objected, and the discussion ended.

Support for decreasing immigrant admissions rose from 42 to 61 percent nationally between 1977 and 1993 but has fallen since.[22] Leadership makes a difference in fanning or dampening anti-immigrant sentiments, and they run lower in New York City, where Mayor Dinkins continued the Koch executive order; so did Mayor Giuliani, who objected publicly both to its nullification by a federal court in 1997 and to the anti-immigrant positions of several national Republican leaders:[23] In Elmhurst-Corona, Carmela George and Lucy Schilero both depended on bilingual members of their block associations, and Schilero invited immigration-rights speakers to her coalition meetings. White civic associations using only English saw their numbers contract.

The 1990 and 1996 federal immigration laws raised yearly admission ceilings but restricted opportunities for family reunification. The 1990 act increased the annual number of occupational visas from 54,000 to 140,000, and by the mid-1990s US technical and professional workers found their employers sponsoring lower-paid immigrants to replace them. An attempt in the 1996 bill to reduce this number and increase funds for scientific and technical US education was killed by business lobbyists and supply-side conservatives who wanted even more such "quality" immigrants. The impact of this policy, curtailing "market" demands to invest in education, is enormous and affects both the US-born and immigrants already here. "The question is, should immigration be encouraged or should national policy encourage training to allow those here, including blacks, to take those jobs?" asked the African American economist Arthur Brimmer. "My own view is that we should do both." Whether both are done will depend upon coalescing the power of numbers against the power of resources.[24]

In 1994, 69 percent of whites and 61 percent of blacks nationwide were registered to vote, as were only 53 percent of Latin Americans and Asians. California's Proposition 187 limiting immigrant rights, which passed in 1994, and similar national legislation proposed by Republicans and passed in 1996 have frightened legal immigrants and increased naturalization rates. The number of immigrants becoming citizens jumped nationally from 270,000 in 1990 to 1.1 million in 1996; in the New York metropolitan area the numbers rose from 30,000 in 1991 to 141,000 in 1995, and a million more immigrants were eligible for citizenship.[25]

The power of numbers in the coming century will need to cross language borders and welcome ethnic alliance. As the journalist Ellis Cose advises, "If we are wise ... we will realize that the problems of blacks, or Latinos, or whites, or Asian-Americans, inevitably, in an inextricably interrelated society, affect us all."[26] [...]

Study Questions

1 How, according to Sanjek, can Elmhurst-Corona serve as a model for the future of the US?

2 What strategies helped bring the diverse peoples of Elmhurst-Corona together to improve the community for all the groups living there? Which of these strategies would work in your community and why? Why was the government's role crucial to their success?

3 What are Sanjek's recommendations for strengthening local democracy? Why does he argue that new immigrants can help in this endeavor? Would his recommendations work in suburban as well as urban communities? Why or why not?

4 How is what happened in Elmhurst-Corona an example of what Tom Hayden and Richard Flacks (authors of "The Port Huron Statement") mean by "participatory democracy"?

Notes

1. On categorical and personal relations, see J. Clyde Mitchell, "Theoretical Orientations in African Urban Studies," *The Social Anthropology of Complex Societies*, ed. Michael Banton (New York: Praeger, 1966), 51–56. In workplaces and other organizational settings, people also locate themselves and others according to what Mitchell terms structural relationships. On racial and ethnic categories used by Queens Koreans, see Kyeyoung Park, *The Korean American Dream: Immigrants and Small Business in New York City* (Ithaca: Cornell University Press, 1997).

2. In 1997 one-third of all Americans reported that they worshiped with immigrants (*New York Daily News [DN]*, 6/16/97).

3. I refrain from referring to these forms of organizations collectively as "civil society" or, in this book, engaging political debate concerning civil society, "mediating institutions," or "the private sector." Much of that debate is framed in abstract terms contrasting "the state" and "civil society" and focusing on national-level organizations and "movements," whereas I deal with local political action and the specific levels and policies of government which affect Elmhurst-Corona. As many argue concerning "civil society," however, this sphere of activity certainly "exists...against the state, in partial independence from it [and] includes those dimensions of social life which cannot be confounded with, or swallowed up in the state"; the purpose of these activities, moreover, is to "determine or inflect the course of state policy (Charles Taylor, "Modes of Civil Society," *Public Culture* 3 [1990]: 95, 100).

4. Asher Arian et al., *Changing New York City Politics* (New York: Routledge, 1990), 104–5; *DN*, 9/15/95; *New York Times [NYT]*, 4/1/97.

5. Mary Douglas, *Natural Symbols* (New York: Vintage, 1973), 42, 73; see also, 179–80.

6. See Rosa Estades, "Symbolic Unity: The Puerto Rican Day Parade," *The Puerto Rican Struggle: Essays on Survival in the U.S.*, eds. Clara Rodriguez, Virginia Sanchez Korrol, and Jose Oscar Alers, eds. (Maplewood, NJ: Waterfront Press, 1980), 82–89; Philip Kasinitz, *Caribbean New York: Immigrants and the Politics of Race* (Ithaca: Cornell University Press,

1992), 140–59; Kasinitiz and Freidenberg-Herbstein, "The Puerto Parade and West Indian Carnival: Public Celebrations in New York City 1987," *Caribbean Life in New York City: Sociocultural Dimensions*, ed. Constance R. Sutton and Elsa M. Chaney (New York: Center for Migration Studies, 1992). As Barth notes, "When political groups articulate their opposition in terms of ethnic criteria, the direction of cultural change is also affected . . . [Ethnic groups] tend to become structurally similar and differentiated only by a few clear diacritica" (Frederick Barth, ed., "Introduction," *Ethnic Groups and Boundaries* [Boston: Little, Brown, 1969], 35).

7. Gerald Suttles, *The Social Construction of Communities* (Chicago: University of Chicago Press, 1972), 27.

8. Douglas's approach to ritual suggests that rituals of inclusion will become less common as "informality . . . familiarity, [and] intimacy" develop among newcomers and established residents, and categorical relationships give way to personal ones; see Douglas 1973: 99–100, 103.

9. Suttles 1972:35, 50.

10. Herbert Gans, *Middle American Individualism: Political Participation and Liberal Democracy* (New York: Oxford University Press, 1988), 111; Gans also notes the price such leaders may pay: "At times the viability of collective action may ride on the ability or charisma of the leadership [and the] heavy burdens placed on leaders can also breed suspicions of their motives and thus impair attempts to work togather." Several attempts to limit or "monitor" district manager Rose Rothschild were waged by male CB4 members; Haydee Zambrana was ousted from her leadership position at CCQ. They and other female leaders were subjects of controversy and rumor. On the difference leadership makes in diverse neighborhoods, see Jonathan Reider, *Canarsie: The Jews and Italians of Brooklyn Against Liberalism* (Cambridge: Harvard University Press, 1985), 263.

11. The 1970s witnessed a large-scale movement of working and lower-middle-class women into grassroots politics. It included what Perlman terms both bottom-up "neighborhood organizing," like that in Elmhurst-Corona, and top-down "community organizing" by staff and local chapters of such groups as ACORN, National People's Action, and the Gray Panthers, many of which drew on 1960s civil rights movement and Office of Economic Opportunity experiences and participation. See Janice Perlman, "Grassrooting the System," *Social Policy*, September–October, 4–20, 1976; Janice Perlman, "Grassroots Empowerment and Government Response," *Social Policy*, September–October, 16–21, 1979; Nancy Seifer, *Absent from the Majority: Working-Class Women in America* (New York: American Jewish Committee, 1973). Joseph Kling and Prudence Posner's *Dilemmas of Activism Class, Community and the Politics of Local Mobilization* (Philadelphia: Temple University Press, 1990), a volume of essays on "class, community, and the politics of local mobilization" focuses on community organizing from the top-down perspective, and not the elementary forms of civic political action that I studied. Conceptualizing and actualizing connections between these two political worlds – between local wardens and associations and their "inherent ideologies" on one hand, and organizers and advocates and their "derived ideologies" on the other – remains an overarching "dilemma of activism": how do working and lower-middle-class formations of the power of numbers become linked to each other, and harnessed to effective lubricatory power?

12. Nancy Chodorow, "Family Structure and Feminine Personality," *Woman, Culture, and Society* ed. Michelle Rosaldo and Louise Lamphere (Stanford: Stanford University Press, 1974), 43–66; Carol Hardy-Fanta, *Latina Politics, Latino Politics: Gender, Culture, and Political Participation in Boston* (Philadelphia: Temple University Press, 1993), 13, 191; Temma Kaplan, "Female Consciousness and Collective Action: The Case of Barcelona, 1910–1918," *Signs* 7 (1982): 545–47; Deborah Tannen, *You Just Don't Understand: Women and Men in Conversation* (New York: Ballantine, 1990), 277.

13. Cf. Suttles 1972: 37–41.

14. Kling and Posner 1990: 15; *NYT* 25/2/96.

15. Roger Waldinger, "Race and Ethnicity," *Setting Municipal Priorities, 1990*, ed. Charles Breecher and Raymond Horton (New York: New York University Press, 1989), 70–71.

16. Institute for Puerto Rican Policy, *The Dinkins Administration and the Puerto Rican Community: Lessons from the Puerto Rican Experiences with African American Mayors in Chicago and Philadelphia* (New York: Institute for Puerto Rican Policy, 1990), 25–28; see also *NYT* 5/8/97.

17. Suzanne DeCamp, *The Linguistic Minorities of New York City* (New York: Community Service Society, 1991); Michael Fix and Wendy Zimmerman, *After Arrival: An Overview of Federal Immigration Policy in the United States* (Washington, DC: Urban Institute, 1993); Department of City Planning, *Language Spoken at Home for Persons 5 Years of Age and Over* (New York: City of New York, 1993); Department of City Planning [DCP], *Socioeconomic Profiles: A Portrait of New York City's Community Districts from the 1980 and 1990 Censuses of Population and Housing* (New York: New York City, 1993); *Business Week*, 7/1/92; *DN*, 4/28/93, 2/23/95; *New York Newsday* [ND] 3/12/95; *New York Times Magazine* [NYTM] 3/1/81, 5/6/83, 8/29/93, 12/5/95.

18. Philip Martin and Elizabeth Midgley, *Immigration to the United States: Journey to an Uncertain Destination* (Washington, D.C.: Population Reference Bureau, 1994), 37–38.

19. John Crewsdon, *The Tarnished Door: The New Immigrants and the Transformation of America* (New York: Times Books, 1983), 289; *Chronicle of Higher Education*, 11/23/88.

20. Jeffrey Passel and Barry Edmonston, *Immigration and Race in the United States* (Washington, DC: Urban Institute, 1992); Joseph Salvo, Ronald Ortiz, and Francis Vardy, *The Newest New Yorkers: Analysis of Immigration into New York City During the 1980s* (New York: Department of City Planning, 1992); *ND*, 7/21/97; *NYT*, 7/1/86, 6/27/93, 8/2/93, 8/30/95, 2/8/97; *NYTM*, 10/27/96 Evidence relating to the widely subscribed-to beliefs that immigrants take jobs from Americans and are a net tax "burden" is less clear-cut. A 1997 National Academy of Sciences study found that "immigration added perhaps $10 billion a year to the nation's output. . . . Job prospects of low-skilled native-born workers were sometimes hurt by competition with immigrants and . . . the incomes of native-born workers tended to fall as a result. . . . The vast majority of Americans are enjoying a healthier economy as a result of the increased supply of labor and lower prices that result from immigration [but] some black workers have lost their jobs to immigrants, especially in . . . New York City . . . where they compete for the same jobs" (*NYT* 5/18/97). The immigration scholar Wayne Cornelius concludes, "The proportion of immigrants using some form of public assistance has been estimated . . . at 5.1 percent by . . . Michael Fix and Jeffrey Passel and at 26.1 percent by George Borjas. . . . These and others disagree about the proper unit of analysis (should it be individuals or households?), which kinds of immigrants to include . . . (should political refugees, who have disproportionately high rates of welfare use, be excluded?), and even about which government programs should be classified as 'welfare'" (*CHE*, 11/15/96). Undocumented immigrants are ineligible for welfare benefits other than Medicaid for emergency treatment. Legal immigrants do not qualify for most welfare benefits during their first three years, and they lose opportunities to sponsor relatives when they do; the majority never do qualify. See Fix and Zimmerman 1993; Martin and Midgley 1994:28–34; *Business Week*, 7/13/92; *NYT*, 9/22/80, 8/2/84.

21. DCP 1992a, 1993b.

22. *DN*, 6/16/97; *ND*, 5/20/92; *NYT*, 7/1/86, 6/27/93.

23. *ND*, 2/27/94; *NYT*, 3/10/96, 7/5/97, 7/19/97.

24. Salvo, Ortiz, and Vardy, 17–20, 67; Nadia Youssef, *The Demographics of Immigration: A Socio-Demographic Profile of the Foreign-Born Population in New York State* (Staten Island, NY: Center for Migration Studies, 1992), 1–2, 161–62; *DN*, 8/25/95; *ND*, 8/22/94; *NYT*, 12/21/86, 3/16/88, 10/14/90, 8/28/95, 9/13/95, 1/26/96, 3/29/96, 3/16/97; *Wall Street Journal*, 10/9/95, 12/18/95, 1/3/96

25. Leadership Education for Asian Pacifics, "Reframing the Immigration Debate," 1996; *DN*, 12/29/95; *ND*, 11/27/93, 2/21/96; *NYT*, 9/25/95, 3/10/96, 9/13/96, 10/26/96; *NYTM*, 10/27/96; *Washington Post*, 2/24/94.
26. *DN*, 3/1/92.

CHAPTER 49

The Society That Unions Can Build

David Reynolds

David Reynolds (1963–) grew up outside Philadelphia. His father, a civil engineer, was the first in his family to go to college; his mother began college at age 50 and went on to earn an MA in Communication. Reynolds is a specialist in labor studies and an activist in labor–community coalitions, living wage issues, union political action, and economic development. His publications include Taking the High Road: Communities Organize for Economic Change *(2002) and* Partnering for Change: Unions and Community Groups Build Coalition for Economic Justice *(2004). The following essay is adapted from his chapter in Art Shostak's* Viable Utopian Ideas: Shaping a Better World *(2003).*

Today, fewer than one out of six American workers, or only 13 percent, are union members. Yet, according to the latest polls, 50 percent of the 110 million Americans who work in non-union workplaces would form a union if given a chance.[1] Were these 55 million people to join the ranks of the existing 16 million union members, the labor movement would encompass the majority of working Americans. How might this transform America?

In the workplace the answers are readily apparent. Union workers average $146 more per week than non-union workers. They enjoy better access to health, pension, vacation, and other benefits. Their workplaces are cleaner, healthier, and safer. Most important, people form unions to win basic respect. Without a union the boss can fire you at any time. That means a fundamental imbalance of power. If you are mistreated there is no binding grievance procedure. Experience, loyalty, years of service may not mean much if a company's unilateral cost cutting demands replacing you with a cheaper worker.

Through unions workers can sit across the bargaining table and negotiate what goes on in their workplace. They can win seniority systems, grievance procedures, and basic job protections. And they also gain far greater access to opportunities to better themselves through training, higher education, and leadership experiences. The result is a more committed and motivated workforce. One recent study, published in *Scientific American*, found union workplaces 16 percent more productive than non-union workplaces.

But what about the union impact outside the workplace? Since their beginning, labor unions have always been agents of broader social change. Indeed, at various times in the history of the labor movement building a more just and democratic society has been a greater focus than collective bargaining in the workplace. Reforms that at the time seemed like starry-eyed "utopian" dreams today we take for granted – such as the eight-hour workday and the two-day weekend. By looking at the kinds of social changes that unions have fought for in the past and today we can imagine what our society would look like if all who wanted to form unions got their wish. Let's think of a different America . . .

Higher Public Standards

While workers can gain much at the bargaining table with specific companies so long as other employers do not play by these same rules, business competition always threatens union gains. This is why unions have fought for broad public standards that all business must follow.

A unionized America would have far stronger laws to promote the union principle of a fair day's wage for a fair day's work. For one, the current $5.15 an hour federal minimum wage would increase to reflect the half-century increases in the cost of living. At least nine dollars an hour reflects a minimal wage above poverty by 2002 standards.[2] Second, there would also be a maximum wage cap on executive compensation. In the 1950s through 1970s, CEO pay at Fortune 500 companies averaged 40 times what an average worker made. Today, the ratio has skyrocketed to nearly 500 to one.[3]

Third, workers in female-dominated occupations would have tough new regulations assuring that they receive wages fully equal to those in comparable male-dominated professions. Fourth, similar laws would require employers to provide part-time, temporary, and other contingent workers – many of whom are younger workers – the same wages and pro-rated benefits as their full-time employees. Today, with nearly one-third of Americans working under contingent arrangements, many companies use such work to undercut basic wage, benefit, and employment standards.

As unions were the main lobbying force behind the establishment of the federal Occupational Safety and Health Administration in the 1970s, they would strengthen the existing system to reduce the grim reality that every year 10,000 workers are killed on the job and 100,000 die prematurely due to work-related health problems. Legal penalties would increase to eliminate the practice whereby management weighs the costs of health and safety improvements against the possible weak fines for breaking the law.

Although employer cries of "job losses" can get individual unions to oppose specific environmental regulations, overall the labor movement has fought for environmental protections. More people in unions would mean far higher pollution standards, better land use regulations, higher fuel economy standards, etc. Unions would be key players in helping our communities and nation develop more comprehensive plans for environmental recovery.

One of the biggest battles animating union organizing in the nineteenth century was control over work hours. Labor's great victory in winning the eight-hour workday and two-day weekend came after decades of struggle to first win twelve-and ten-hour days. The 40-hour workweek is now seventy years old. Worker productivity has more than doubled and tripled over this time, yet companies have used such gains to shed workers and to get people to buy more "stuff" rather than work less.[4] Rethinking the workweek down to 35 or 32 hours is long overdue. With a union majority all workers would enjoy legally mandated paid vacations of at least four to five weeks each year. And workers would enjoy far more options for negotiating with their employer over work time flexibility.

A strong labor movement would also establish completely new public standards. All workers would enjoy protections from job loss, as the boss would have to document valid reasons for firing an individual. Furthermore, companies could not simply close and leave a community. They would have to give notice and explain the economic rationale for their proposed decision before a public body. Such an authority would block the decision if the company's action would undermine public standards.

Greater Public Wealth for All

While unionized workers bargain for health care, pensions, education, and other benefits, such standards are undercut by non-union companies. Furthermore, when the quality of people's health, retirement, and other opportunities depends upon their job, then their lives have fewer options. How many people stay in a job they hate simply because they need family health care? By contrast, in a more unionized society a rich array of public resources would open to everyone.

The first obvious change would be some form of national healthcare system. The only industrial country without such a system, the United States has the single most expensive healthcare industry in the world. Yet, at least 40 million Americans have no health coverage. In our private-run healthcare system, an estimated one out of every six dollars is consumed in insurance paperwork. With prescriptions averaging $65 a shot, the pharmaceutical industry is the most profitable in the nation. With insurance rates exploding, many unions see demands for healthcare concessions as the number one item on management's bargaining agenda. Under a fully public healthcare system anyone could walk into a medical facility and have their needs met at no or little cost to themselves. Public policy could then address our nation's shortage of primary care family doctors and registered nurses by redirecting resources toward these needs. And the single public system, which would cover prescriptions, would have the power to bargain down the inflated costs of drugs. It would also place far greater resources into less drug-driven, more holistic health practices.[5]

Union political action would push a wide range of universal social programs. Just like high school, higher education would be free with the government providing stipends for room and board. Each person would have a wide range of opportunities for life-long learning. A fully comprehensive public training systems overseen by government authorities and run in close cooperation with businesses and unions would offer ongoing education outside of college. People would also gain sufficient time off from work to pursue learning. Indeed, in organized labor's "social democratic" America people would routinely get together in small study circles after work in which they discuss issues of common interest and public concern.

Greater public wealth would transform family life. Instead of the current law's 12 weeks of unpaid leave, parents would have the right to a year or more of paid leave from work to care for a newborn infant or elderly parent. All parents would receive a per-child money allowance from the government to help offset the cost of raising that child – poorer parents would receive an additional amount. All local childcare centers would be subsidized and, by law, fees would be based upon the parents' ability to pay. Parents would have the legal right to stay home from work to care for a sick child. They would also have the right to take a certain amount of time to participate in their child's school.

Routine family expenses such as rent, mortgage, and car insurance would be far less expensive from public-run, non-profit programs. Unemployment compensation would pick up most of a person's former salary until they get a job – not the current 26 weeks at a fraction of pay. Indeed, a constitutional amendment would guarantee all adults the right to a job – thus committing the government to providing whatever resources a person needs to train for and find work. Social security would not only continue to provide a retirement income and disability insurance, but the system would also likely be expanded so that the public pension would provide most of a generous retirement living. And the unpaid work spent on education and child rearing would count toward a pension.

In short, from cradle to grave a person would have the freedom of knowing that their basic needs are met irrespective of who they work for or even if they work for pay. The funds for such public wealth would come out of fair tax system based upon an individual's and company's ability to pay. Historically unions fought for and won the graduated income tax as a fairer system than the many flat taxes that hit rich and poor equally. Unfortunately, over the past fifty years the corporate portion of federal taxes has fallen by half, while the burden on the individual income tax has grown by over 50 percent. Meanwhile the marginal tax rate on the richest individuals has fallen from a peak of 80 percent to only 38 percent today – and these top rates continue to fall. A more unionized American would reverse this pattern.[6]

Democracy Everywhere

People organize unions under the belief that they should be able to participate in the economic decisions that affect them. This democratic value has broad application. For example, currently corporations are governed by representatives of those who own shares in the company. Workers who make a huge personal investment of their time and energy have no say. Yet, since corporations exist only at the creation of the law, government could require that at least half a company's board of directors be elected by the employees. These worker "stakeholders" would be voices for long-term planning. Under the current system, shareholder representatives all too often push short-term, 90-day returns. Studies have found that unionized workplaces can be up to 38 percent more productive than non-union workplaces.[7]

Just as the law today requires that employers formally recognize the existence of labor organizations once they have won an official government-monitored election, the law could also mandate that management consult with their employees on a range of daily issues. Under a codetermination system, management would have to secure the formal approval of workers (through elected works councils) for policy changes around health and safety, transfers, hiring, overtime, layoffs, training, and shift scheduling. While such mandatory power sharing would complicate the decision-making process, it would foster more thought-out decisions and quick implementation.

In large part thanks to unions, Americans own a good share of the financial wealth of the country through more than $4 trillion in pension assets. Laws could allow workers to set criteria for how their funds are invested. Wealth would not go to companies that pursue strategies that are anti-union, environmentally destructive, killers of small businesses, and creators of weapons. Pension wealth could support such alternative strategies as cooperative management, environmentally friendly products, worker ownership, and commitment to the community. Unions have also been a voice for employee buy-outs and ownership. In a more unionized America, government policy would actively support worker-owned firms – providing financial resources, technical support, and regulations supporting democratic management.

In a more unionized America public institutions at all levels would play a more extensive and more democratic role in planning the economy. Through new regional development boards people could create long-term visions for their area. Regional rules on land use, business investment, and public expenditures would replace the current fragmented anarchy of uncoordinated city and suburban practices. Communities would no longer compete with each other for who will offer a footloose company the most lucrative public gifts.

To provide a greater public role in steering economic decisions, many of our nation's major banks and financial institutions would become public-owned. A significant portion of basic infrastructure, such as electricity, oil, phone, cable, trains, and airlines would also become public-owned driven by democratically-set needs rather than profits maximization. The public broadcasting system, which today relies upon corporate contributions and influence, would also become more extensive and paid for entirely by public funds.

A more unionized America would change the way government functions. Today various groups, with corporations the most powerful, lobby behind the scenes to influence law making. Yet, a more formalized and balanced practice of social partnership would be far more democratic. By law, government bodies would be required to include representatives from various citizen groups and movements (unions, business, environmentalist, women's groups, civil rights organizations, etc.) formally in the decision-making process. Major policy decisions would also make much greater use of public referenda. The public could be asked, for example, whether it wants to continue to have half of all federal discretionary spending go to the military.[8]

Strong unions would transform our nations political parties. Historically, political parties began as elite clubs. Indeed, initially only people who possessed a certain level of property were allowed to vote. Such restrictions fell away and elections became a more mass affair (at least among white men) because the early labor movement organized local labor parties and political clubs. A stronger labor movement would either produce a new political party or completely transform the Democratic Party.

In either case, electoral politics would focus on issues rather than candidates. People would get together in neighborhood meetings to develop an agenda for their local, state, and national party platforms. Unlike today, these platforms would act as actual guides for government policy. Grassroots party members would have the power to recall elected candidates who did not uphold their promises. In short, more unions mean a more animated democracy as people in their workplaces, neighborhoods, and public press debate the crucial issues of the day.

It's Already Happening

The above vision is not an abstraction. Most of the public standards I have cited have been commonplace in different parts of Europe for years. Europeans, for example, enjoy four to six weeks of minimal paid vacation. France today has a 35-hour workweek. Denmark's minimum wage worked out to $14 an hour by 1994. The ratio of CEO pay to workers is closer to 50 times rather than 500 times. Today government policy in the Netherlands is guided by a comprehensive twenty-five-year plan for environmental recovery and restoration. Under German law companies must give up to six months notice and seek approval of a public labor board for mass layoffs or closures.[9]

Public wealth is also far greater in Europe and Canada than it is in the United States. All of the examples mentioned above are taken for granted in the Scandinavian countries of Sweden, Denmark, and Norway. Recent cutbacks of unemployment, sick pay, and parental leave in Sweden reduced the rates from ninety to eighty percent of original pay – an amount still staggeringly above our nation's unemployment system and non-existent paid illness and parental leave. In the 1990s, Denmark and Norway extended the idea of sabbatical leave – common among college faculty – to grant every citizen the right, once in their life, to take a year of paid leave from work for whatever they wanted!

While overall tax rates are high in Scandinavia, the tax rates for low- and middle-income families compare well with our country. Indeed, even traffic tickets are based on a sliding scale – with speeders having to pay a certain percentage of their income. Free health care and higher education, family allowances, and subsidized child-care are simply taken for granted throughout Europe.

Worker elections for a company's supervisory board and work councils have been part of the German system of codetermination laws since the 1950s. Public-owned companies, especially utilities and banks, have been features in Europe for over half a century. Until the 1990s, two-thirds of Austria's fifty-largest companies were public-owned, nationalized firms. Europeans routinely speak of social partnership in which labor and management participate in major social and economic policies. Austrian law requires that representatives from mandated "Chambers" of business, labor, and agriculture have a formal role in developing government policy. Worker study circles are a common way for people in Scandinavia to learn about and discuss the important issues of the day.

The strength of unions is a big part of the difference between the United States and Europe. In Scandinavia, at least 80 percent of the adult population are union members. Managers have their own unions. Clergy collectively bargain with their congregations. Prisoners have labor organizations to bargain over the job training funds for life after prison. German rates reveal 40 percent of German workers in unions and 75 percent covered by union contracts. In Italy union density is over 60 percent; in Britain and Canada it is over one-third. Furthermore, in all but Canada, the labor movement created the nation's largest or second largest political party.

This is not to say that Europe is problem free. Over the past twenty years social and economic strains have caused sharp debates. Some corporate and political voices call for becoming more like the United States. Others seek to build on the union/social democratic legacy by increasing public controls over corporate actions and establishing European-wide public standards and public wealth. A strong Green movement has also highlighted many weaknesses and limitations in the old labor/social democratic agenda. What is clear, however, is that for the past fifty years Western Europe has been able to combine a far greater degree of public standards, public wealth, and democratic values with comparable (or even superior) long-term economic success and a measurably higher standard of living.

Organizing at Home Today

The lesson for the United States is not to copy Europe, but to realize that today's reform efforts have great potential. Indeed, the above vision can also be seen in the grassroots reawakening developing today.[10]

For example, several states have raised the minimum wage above federal standards, thanks to such efforts as the Vermont Livable Wage Campaign and labor-community coalitions in Washington, Massachusetts, California, and Oregon. In over one hundred and seventy communities across the country, grassroots living wage campaigns have won or are organizing for laws requiring companies that receive public contracts or financial assistance to pay wages above poverty. Reforms in states such as Minnesota and Maine lead a growing corporate accountability movement that requires firms to live up to binding community standards when they receive public money. The National Alliance for Fair Employment provides a clearinghouse for labor-community efforts across the country to bring fairness to contingent employment. A bill drafted in Massachusetts would require equal pay for equal work. Labor-community coalitions in several parts of the country are pressuring temp agencies to sign onto a basic code of conduct.

The new AFL-CIO-affiliated Working for America Institute aids grassroots partnerships between unions, the community, and management to promote the high road business practices of worker training, product quality, worker empowerment, and environmental responsibility. For example, following decades of layoffs in manufacturing, Milwaukee added 6,000 new manufacturing jobs in the late 1990s thanks, in part, to an alliance of one hundred employers and thirteen unions that promotes worker training and worker participation in plant modernization and work reorganization decisions. In several parts of the country, healthcare unions have built partnerships with hospital management to improve patient care and train workers trapped in dead-end, bottom-rung healthcare jobs for career opportunities in such much-needed fields such as registered nursing.

As the healthcare crisis deepens, unions, such as the United Autoworkers, have called for a national healthcare system. In many states new labor-community alliance is pushing for a wide variety of healthcare reforms. In California, unions helped push for funds to provide twelve weeks of paid parental leave for families who need the time off, but can not afford to go without a pay check. A national union capital strategies taskforce has looked into ways to democratize our nations financial system. Recently, the AFL-CIO was instrumental in getting the federal Security and Exchange to require mutual fund companies to disclose to their investors how they cast proxy votes in shareholder meetings on behalf of those same investors.

Coalitions are also being formed between unions and environmentalists. The National Alliance for Sustainable Jobs and the Environment grew out of battles over timber cutting in the Pacific Northwest. Labor has also begun to join the mushrooming smart growth movement. Across the country citizen groups, environmentalists, government officials, and forward-looking developers are organizing to reorient our nation's development practices away from community- and environment-destroying sprawl and towards the kinds of integrated, compact communities that were once the norm in this country. Reformers visit places such as Portland, Oregon, and Chattanooga, Tennessee, to see how communities have combined environmental recovery with community redevelopment and economic health.

Unions and community groups across the country have fought to keep the anti-worker, small-business destroying Wal Mart and other big box chains out of their communities. Unions have also been central players in establishing new non-profits like the Los Angeles Alliance for New Economy and Working Partnerships USA (in Silicon Valley). These institutions help bring diverse groups together around building and implementing grassroots agendas for economic change.

A backdrop to all this activity is the rethinking that the labor movement began in the mid-1990s. In 1995, the new leadership of the AFL-CIO – the national umbrella organization to which most American unions belong – looked at a future of potential death for the American labor movement. Over the past half century, the labor movement had declined from representing one-third to less than one out of six workers. Employers had clearly become increasingly aggressive at opposing unions. Meanwhile, government protections over the right to organize had become so weak as to become meaningless.

Yet, the AFL-CIO concluded that much of the decline was also self-inflicted. Having fought the organizing battles in the 1930s–1950s, many unions transferred their energies into bargaining and enforcing ever-better contracts, not organizing new workers. Yet today, with huge non-union sectors even in traditional union strongholds, the American labor movement today can ill afford not to make organizing a top priority.

The AFL-CIO has called on unions to place as much as 30 percent of their resources into organizing. It has promoted new ways to use collective bargaining, political action, and member volunteers to support organizing. Institutional change is never easy, however. The labor movement is only at the beginning of a very long and bumpy road.

What has already emerged, however, are labor leaders who see the need to organize and also realize that unions can not go it alone. The great periods of labor resurgence – when unions have grown in this country – have always seen coalitions with the community. Union organizing has always been not just a matter of economic gains but also social vision – of moral standards, civil rights, community health, and basic democracy. As labor rebuilds itself it can not help but be part of the next great social movement to transform America.

Study Questions

1 What is a "utopia"?
2 Why does Reynolds argue that unions can bring the US closer to a "utopian society"? Which of his arguments do you find most/least convincing and why?
3 Which of the following would you be willing to work for/vote for? How could they be paid for?
   - National healthcare system
   - Shorter work week
   - Free higher education
   - Yearlong parental leave to care for newborns/elderly
   - Expanded unemployment compensation
   - Publicly owned banks, financial institutions, and infrastructure (electricity, phones, transportation)
4 How would the realization of Reynolds's neo-utopia affect our understanding of what it means to be a citizen or resident of the US?

For Further Reading

Collins, Chuck and Yeskel, Felice. *Economic Apartheid in America*. New York: The New Press, 2000.

Michel, Lawrence and Voos, Paul, Eds. *Unions and Economic Competitiveness*. Armonek, NY: M. E. Sharpe, 1992.

Ness, Immanuel and Eimer, Stuart, Eds. *Central Labor Councils and the Revival of American Unionism: Organizing for Justice in Our Communities*. Armonk, NY: M. E. Sharpe, 2001.

Nissen, Bruce, Ed. *Which Direction for Organized Labor?* Detroit: Wayne State University Press, 1999.

Reynolds, David. *Taking the High Road Communities Organize for Economic Change*. Armonk, NY: M. E. Sharpe, 2002.

Reynolds, David, Ed. *Partnering for Change: How Unions and Community Groups are Building Coalitions for Economic Justice*. Armonk, NY: M. E. Sharpe, 2004.

Schor, Juliet. *The Overworked American*. New York: Basic Books, 1991.

Working USA (www.workingusa.org) and *New Labor Forum* (www.qc.edu/newlaborforum) are two journals dedicated to covering and debating the ongoing transformation of the American labor movement.

Web Sites

www.aflcio.org – the national umbrella federation.
www.goodjobsfirst.org – corporate accountability; unions and sprawl.
www.workingforamerica.org – union-business partnerships
www.fairjobs.org – contingent work
www.acorn.org – living wage campaigns
www.walmartwatch.com
www.asje.org – the Alliance for Sustainable Jobs and the Environment
www.atwork.org – model labor-community action in Silicon Valley
www.laane.org – model labor-community action in Los Angeles
Readers can get up-to-date information on union activity that pursues the ideas laid out in the article at www.powerbuilding.wayne.edu

Notes

1. Peter D. Hart poll, 2002
2. $9.03 is the hourly wage needed for full-time work to produce an annual income at the 2002 federal poverty guideline for a family of four. Many researchers criticize today's federal guidelines for underestimating the minimal financial needs to support a family.
3. See *Common Sense Economics* presentation from the AFL-CIO. See also Chuck Collins and Felice Yeskel, *Economic Apartheid in America*, Ch. 2.
4. See Juliet Schor *The Overworked American*.
5. A good start for information concerning healthcare reform can be found at the www.uhcan.org. Blue Cross/Blue Shield of Michigan provided the prescription drug cost.
6. The tax information comes from the newsletters of Citizens for Tax Justice. See www.ctj.org.
7. See Dale Belman, "Unions, the Quality of Labor Relations, and Firm Performance, *Unions and Economic Competitiveness*, eds. Lawrence Mishel and Paula B. Voos (Armonk, NY: M. E. Sharpe, Inc., 1992) pp. 41–107.

8. This pattern is clear from the multi-decade yearly budget summaries found in the official publication of the 2003 Federal Budget. Once Social Security and Medicare, which are legally separate from the general budget, are removed and all the military related expenditures added together, the military becomes half of all discretionary spending.

9. For information on the standards, public wealth, and democracy found in Europe see Part One of David Reynolds *Taking the High Road*.

10. For more on these examples see *Taking the High Road*, Part Two.

Text and Illustration Credits

The editor and publisher gratefully acknowledge the permission granted to reproduce the copyright material in this book:

Texts

1. Gwyn Kirk and Margo Okazawa-Rey, "Identities and Social Locations: Who Am I? Who Are My People," pp. 59–69 from Gwyn Kirk and Margo Okazawa-Rey (eds.) (2004), *Women's Lives: Multicultural Perspectives*, 3rd edn. Mountain View, CA: Mayfield Publishing.

2. Stephanie Coontz, "What We Really Miss About the 1950s," pp. 33–45 and 186–9 (notes) from *The Way We Really Are: Coming to Terms With America's Changing Families*. New York: Basic Books, 1997.

3. John Bodnar, "Generational Memory in an American Town," pp. 619–23, 625–30 and 633–7 from *Journal of Interdisciplinary History* 26, no. 4 (Spring 1996). © 1996. Reprinted with the permission of the editors of the *Journal of Interdisciplinary History* and MIT Press.

4. Kesaya E. Noda, "Growing Up Asian in America," pp. 243–50 from Diane Yen-Mei Wong (ed.) (1989), *Making Waves: An Anthology of Writings By and About Asian American Women*. Boston: Beacon Press. Reprinted by permission of author

5. Maria Fleming Tymoczko, "War Babies," pp. 87–99 from Maria Tymoczko and Nancy Blackmun (eds.) (2000), *Born Into a World at War*. Manchester, UK: St. Jerome Publishing. Reprinted by permission of author.

6. Miné Okubo, pp. viii–ix, xi–xii; 7–10, 12, 22–3, 50, 136, 143, and 187 from *Citizen 13660*. Seattle: University of Washington Press, 1983.

7. Elaine Tyler May, "Containment at Home: Cold War, Warm Hearth," pp. 16–20, 22–4, 26–7, and 250–2 (notes) from *Homeward Bound: American Families in the Cold War Era*. New York: Basic Books, 1988.

8. Betty Friedan, "The Problem That Has No Name," pp. 11–18, 20–2, and 26–7 from *The Feminine Mystique*. New York: Dell, 1963. Used by permission of W.W. Norton & Company Inc.

9. William H. Chafe, "The Civil Rights Revolution, 1945–1960: The Gods Bring Threads to Webs Begun," pp. 67–72 and 98 (notes) from Robert Bremner and Gary W. Reichard (eds.) (1982), *Reshaping America: Society and Institutions, 1945–1960*. Columbus: Ohio University Press.

10. Alice Childress, pp. 1–3; 42–3; 53–5; 140–1 from *Like One of the Family: Conversations from a Domestic's Life*. Originally published in 1956; reprinted by Beacon Press, Boston, 1986. © 1956 renewed by Alice Childress in 1984. Used by permission of Flora Roberts, Inc.

11. Songs of the Chicago Blues, recorded by Chess Records: Bo Diddley, "I'm a Man"(1955), © by Jewel Music Publishing/Music Sales; Muddy Waters, "Just Make Love to Me" (1954), © by Independent Music Group; Jimmy Reed, "Bright Lights, Big City" (1961), © by Tristan Music Limited/Music Sales.

12. Jack Agüeros, "Halfway to Dick and Jane: A Puerto Rican Pilgrimage," pp. 85–8, 90–8, and 101–5 from Thomas Wheeler (ed.) (1971), *The Immigrant Experience: The Anguish of Becoming American*. New York: Dial Press.

13. Philip Roth, pp. 3–14 from *Goodbye, Columbus and Other Stories*. Boston: Houghton Mifflin, 1959.

14. Martin Luther King, Jr., "Letter from Birmingham City Jail," April 16, 1963, pp. 153–8 from Clayborne Carson et al. (eds.) (1991), *Eyes on the Prize: Documents, Speeches and First Hand Accounts from the Black Freedom Struggle, 1954–1990*. New York: Penguin Books. Reprinted by arrangement with the Estate of Martin Luther King, Jr., c/o Writers House as agent for the proprietor, New York, NY. © 1963 by Martin Luther King Jr., copyright renewed 1991 by Coretta Scott King.

15. Malcolm X, "Message to the Grass Roots," pp. 248–58 from Clayborne Carson et al. (eds.) (1991), *Eyes on the Prize: Documents, Speeches and First Hand Accounts from the Black Freedom Struggle, 1954–1990*. New York: Penguin Books.

16. Songs of the Civil Rights Movement: "Oh Freedom", "Keep Your Eyes on The Prize", "Ain't Gonna Let Nobody Turn Me Round"; "We Shall Overcome."

17. Port Huron Statement of Students for a Democratic Society (1963), excerpted. This document represented the results of several months of writing, discussion, and revision by the membership of Students for a Democratic Society (SDS) in preparation for their national convention meeting in Port Huron, Michigan, June 11–15, 1962. Originally published and distributed by SDS, 112 East 19 Street, New York.

18. Tom Hayden and Richard Flacks, "The Port Huron Statement at 40," pp. 18–21 from *The Nation*, August 5/12, 2002.

19. Christian G. Appy, pp. 11–15, 17–18 and 324–5 (notes) from *Working Class War: American Combat Soldiers and Vietnam*. Chapel Hill: University of North Carolina Press, 1993.

20. Ron Kovic, pp. 1–14 from *Born on the Fourth of July*. New York: McGraw-Hill, 1976.

21. Richard J. Ford III, pp. 33–41, 44–6, 50–1, and 52–5 from Wallace Terry (ed.) (1984), *Bloods: An Oral History of the Vietnam War by Black Veterans*. New York: Ballantine.

22. Stokely Carmichael and Charles V. Hamilton, "Black Power: Its Need and Substance," pp. 34–5, 37–53 and 55–6 from *Black Power: The Politics of Liberation in America*. New York: Vintage Press, 1967.

23. Aretha Franklin, "Respect" (written by Otis Reading), recorded by Atlantic Records, 1967. © Warner Chappell.

24. James Brown, "Say It Loud (I'm Black and I'm Proud)," recorded by Polygram Records, 1968. © Intersong/Independent Music Group.

25. Young Lords Party, "13-Point Program and Platform," pp. 235–8 from Philip Foner (ed.) (1970), *The Black Panthers Speak*. Philadelphia: J. P. Lippincott.

26. Sara M. Evans, "Sources of the Second Wave: The Rebirth of Feminism," pp. 190–2, 194–8, 200–2, 204–6, and 206–8 (notes) from Alexander Bloom (ed.) (2001), *Long Time Gone: Sixties America Then and Now*. Oxford: Oxford University Press.

27. National Organization for Women, "NOW Bill of Rights," pp. 512–14 from Robin Morgan (ed.) (1970), *Sisterhood is Powerful: An Anthology of Writing from the Women's Liberation Movement*. New York: Random House. © Robin Morgan

28. Pauli Murray, "The Liberation of Black Women," pp. 88–9, 91–2, 93, 95–6, 99, and 100–2 from Mary Lou Thompson (ed.) (1970), *Voices of the New Feminism*. Boston: Beacon Press. Reprinted by permission of the Estate of Pauli Murray.

29. Ellen Cantarow, "Jessie Lopez De La Cruz: The Battle for Farmworkers' Rights," pp. 102–7, 109–11, 114, 116, 117–18, 119–21, 129, 134–7, 142–5 from Ellen Cantarow (ed.) (1980), *Moving the Mountain: Women Working for Social Change*. New York: Feminist Press.

30. Vine Deloria, Jr., "This Country Was a Lot Better Off When the Indians Were Running It," originally published March 1970, and Indians of All Tribes, "The Occupation of Alcatraz Island," originally published November 1969, pp. 28–38 and pp. 40–3 from Alvin M. Josephy, Jr., Joanne Nagel, and Troy Johnson (eds.) (1999), *Red Power: The American Indians' Fight for Freedom*, 2nd edn. Lincoln: University of Nebraska Press.

31. John D'Emilio and Estelle B. Freedman, "Gay Liberation," pp. 318–24 and 398 (notes) from *Intimate Matters: A History of Sexuality in America*. New York: Harper & Row, 1988. © University of Chicago Press, 1988

32. A. Damien Martin, "The Fighting Irishman," pp. 332–41, and 342–4 from Eric Marcus (ed.) (1992), *Making History: The Struggle for Gay and Lesbian Equal Rights, 1945–1990: An Oral History*. New York: Harper. Reproduced by permission of Eric Marcus.

33. Rey "Sylvia Lee" Rivera, "The Drag Queen," pp. 187–96 from Eric Marcus (ed.) (1992), *Making History: The Struggle for Gay and Lesbian Equal Rights, 1945–1990: An Oral History* New York: Harper. Reproduced by permission of Eric Marcus.

34. Lisa McGirr, "New Social Issues and Resurgent Evangelicalism" pp. 217, 225–6, 240–1, 241–3, 257–8, 259–61, 340, 342, 343, 346, 347, from *Suburban Warriors, The Origins of the New American Right*. Copyright © 2001 by Princeton University Press. Reprinted by permission of Princeton University Press.

35. Bennett Harrison and Barry Bluestone, pp. 3–18 and 205–7 (notes) from *The Great U-Turn: Corporate Restructuring and the Polarizing of America*. New York: Basic Books, 1988.

36. Eric Alterman, pp. 129–38 from *"It Ain't No Sin To Be Glad You're Alive": The Promise of Bruce Springsteen*. Boston: Little Brown, 1999. © 2001 by Eric Alterman. Reproduced by permission of Little Brown & Company Inc.

37. A Musical Representation of Work in Postindustrial America: Bruce Springsteen, "Johnny 99," "Highway Patrolman," and "Atlantic City" from the album *Nebraska*, recorded by Columbia Records, 1982. © by Bruce Springsteen. All rights reserved. Reprinted by permission. Shelley Thunder, "Working Girl" from the album *Fresh Out the Pack*, recorded by Island Records, 1989. © Universal/Island Music/Music Sales. Canibus & Biz Markie, "Shove This Jay-Oh-Bee" from the album *Office Space: The Motion Picture Soundtrack*, recorded by Interscope Records, 1999. © Independent Music Press.

38. Gregory Mantsios, "Class in America: Myths and Realities (2000)," from Paula Rothenberg (ed.) (2004), *Race, Class, and Gender in the United States*, 6th edn. New York: Worth Publishers. Reproduced by permission of the author.

39. Kristin Luker, pp. 193–200, 202, 205, 206–7, 214–15 and 285 (note) from *Abortion and the Politics of Motherhood*. Berkeley: University of California Press, 1984.

40. Judith Stacey, "The Making and Unmaking of Modern Families," pp. 3–5, 12–18, 279 (notes), and 282–6 (notes) from *Brave New Families: Stories of Domestic Upheaval in Late Twentieth Century America*. New York: Basic Books, 1991.

41. Bharati Mukherjee, pp. 3–21 from *Jasmine*. New York: Grove Weidenfeld, 1999. © 1989 by Bharati Mukherjee. By permission of Grove/Atlantic, Inc.

42. Claudine Chiawei O'Hearn, "Growing Up Biracial and Bicultural," pp. vii–xiv from Claudine Chiawei O'Hearn (ed.) (1998), *Half and Half: Writers on Growing Up Biracial and Bicultural*. New York, Pantheon.

43. Sherman Alexie, "13/16," "Evolution," and "At Navajo Monument Valley Tribal School," pp. 16–17, 48, and 49 from *The Business of Fancydancing: Stories and Poems*. Brooklyn: Hanging Loose Press, 1992. The photograph of the Navajo Monument Valley Tribal School is reproduced by permission of Skeet McAuley.

44. Ronald Takaki, "Through a Glass Darkly: Toward the Twenty-first Century," pp. 416–21, 426–8 and 491–3 from *A Different Mirror: A History of Multicultural America*. Boston: Little Brown, 1993.

45. Gloria Anzuldúa, "To live in the Borderlands means you," pp. 194–5 from *Borderlands/La Frontera*. San Francisco: Aunt Lute Books, 1987.

46. Naomi Klein, pp. 400–7, 409–10, and 468–9 (notes) from *No Logo: Taking Aim at the Brand Bullies*. New York: Picador, 2000.

47. Lynell George, "Brave New World: Gray Boys, Funky Aztecs, and Honorary Homegirls," from *Los Angeles Times Magazine*, January 17, 1993.

48. Roger Sanjek, pp. 367–72, 374–5, 386–9, 421–2 (notes), and 425 (notes) from *The Future of Us All: Race and Neighborhood Politics in New York City*. Ithaca, NY: Cornell University Press, 1998.

49. David B. Reynolds, "The Society That Unions Can Build." This essay is a revised version of "The Society That Unions Can Build: Organized Labor's Neo-Utopian America" which appears in Art Shostak (ed.), *Viable Utopian Ideas: Shaping a Better World*. Armonk, NY: M. E. Sharpe, 2003.

Illustrations

Page 6 (clockwise from top right):
Gordon Parks, "Photograph of Ella Watson," 1942 (Library of Congress, Prints and Photographs Division); Danny Lion, "Photograph of two Latin girls," c. 1972 (National Archives and Records Administration); Lyntha Scott Eiler, "Community memorabilia on the walls of Frazier Gills' barbershop in Coal City," 1995 (Coal River Folklife Project, 1992–9 at the American Folklife Center, Library of Congress); "Freedom from Want," poster by Norman Rockwell, 1943 (reprinted by permission of the Norman Rockwell Family Agency, copyright © 1943 by the Norman Rockwell Family Entities).

Page 46 (clockwise from top right):
John Vachon, "Negro carrying sign in front of milk company," 1941 (Library of Congress, Prints and Photographs Division); Unknown photographer, "Fallout Shelter," c. 1960 (National Archives and Records Administration); Evert F. Baumgardner, "Family watching television,"

c. 1958 (National Archives and Records Administration); Dorothea Lange, "Hayward, California, two children of the Mochida family," 1942 (National Archives and Record Administration).

Page 112 (clockwise from top):
Marion S. Trikosko, "Martin Luther King and Malcolm X," 1964 (Library of Congress, Prints and Photographs Division); Lt. Cpl. A. C. Prentis, "Vietnam ... Corporal M. R. Carter guards an NVA soldier he captured during a ground movement ten miles northeast of An Hoa," 20 November 1968 (National Archives and Administration); Unknown photographer, "American Indians playing basketball," 1969 (© by Associated Press); Unknown photographer, "Florence Luscombe at International Women's Day," 1970s (from the collection of Catherine Russo).

Page 240 (clockwise from top):
Flip Schulke, "Family enjoys a Fourth of July holiday," 1974 (National Archives and Records Administration); Unknown photographer, "Unemployed protest plant closings, Traverse City, Michigan," 1987 (© by Bettmann / CORBIS); Mark Lipman, "Dudley Street Neighborhood Initiative" (photo still from the documentary film *Holding Ground: The Rebirth of Dudley Street* reprinted courtesy of Holding Ground Productions); David Turnley, "Father with child in their kitchen in the Poletown neighborhood of Detroit, later razed to make room for a General Motors plant," c. 1982 (© by David Turnley / CORBIS).

Every effort has been made to trace copyright holders and to obtain their permission for the use of copyright material. The publisher apologizes for any errors or omissions in the above list and would be grateful if notified of any corrections that should be incorporated in future reprints or editions of this book.

Index